WE ARE CONGO

RANKIN / OXFAM

Oxfam

Cover Image; Jasmine. Photographer

CONTENTS

This book is split into 4 sections. The opening segment, With Love from Congo, is a collection of remarkable love stories that we discovered on our most recent trip to Sange, DRC, in October 2009.

Whilst in Sange, we held a series of photographic workshops for the local community. The aim was to teach the people we met about photography, and give them the chance to visually document their lives. The photographs shot by the villagers and the displaced families they had taken into their homes, make up the second section of the book: The Congo Family Album. Here, the people of Sange take on the role of both the photographer and the subject. Their images create an intimate illustration of lives lived with love, in spite of adversity.

The third section, Cheka Kidogo (meaning "laugh a little" in Swahili),celebrates the vibrancy and resilience of the Congolese people living in the Mugunga refugee camp. We photographed them during our first visit to DRC's Goma region in 2008. These portraits attempt to capture the spirit of the camp's inhabitants - not as victims, but as people - highlighting their essential humanity and strength.

The final section is a 32-page panoramic portrait taken spontaneously in the heart of the Mugunga camp on the last day of the 2008 trip. At that time, the camp was home to 17,000 people displaced by violence. Everyone desperately wanted to take part in the project, and the enthusiasm was overwhelming. This epic group portrait is a snapshot of the faces of people whose lives have been changed forever by the violence in Eastern DRC.

We hope that this book goes some way in telling their stories.

Oxfam/Rankin 2010

Congo has been at war for over a decade. In that time, homes have been burned to the ground and families have been torn apart. But there are things that even war cannot seize from you, despite its best attempts, and those are humanity and hope.

Rankin's remarkable portraits remind us of that. His subjects – the everyday people of eastern Congo – shine out with warmth and vitality. Jasmine, a young girl, mimics Rankin with her own camera made from a tin can; and a young woman Sikito hugs her husband close. These people are caught in one of the worst wars that history has ever seen, but they are still living and still surviving. They get up each day, they work, they play, they struggle, and they carry on, despite their bitter circumstances.

The people of Congo have not lost hope for a better future and we owe it to them to keep that hope alive. With a spark of hope much can be done. I know this. Hope ended slavery, hope overturned apartheid, and hope can end war in the Congo. We need to tell our politicians that Congo matters to us, because humanity matters to us, and call on them to use their influence to end this war. I hope this new decade could be the decade when the guns fall silent in the Congo.

Emeritus Archbishop Desmond Tutu
Oxfam Global Ambassador

A BRIEF BACKGROUND
To The Conflict In The DRC

The humanitarian situation in the Democratic Republic of Congo (DRC) is one of the worst in the world. In eastern Congo alone, over 5.4 million people – equivalent to the population of Denmark – have died since 1998, the majority from lack of access to food, clean water or health care. That makes it the world's deadliest conflict since World War Two.

Since its independence in 1960, the history of the Congo has been one of civil war and corruption. Immediately after its independence it faced an army mutiny; a year later its Prime Minister, Patrice Lumumba, was killed. Soon after, in 1965, the army chief Joseph Mobutu seized power and renamed the country Zaire.

It was only when President Laurent Kabila came into power in 1997 that the country was renamed the Congo, with the Democratic Republic tag added to differentiate it from its northern neighbour Congo Brazzaville. Laurent Kabila's rule was short lived. He was assassinated in 2001 and his son Joseph Kabila took over the running of the country at the tender age of 29.

The origins of the current conflict date back to the early 1990s, in particular the aftermath of the Rwandan genocide, when both perpetrators and victims fled into eastern Congo. In 1997, Rwandan armies invaded Congo to root out genocidaires taking refuge in eastern Congo's forests, but the fight was taken right to the capital city of Kinshasa, over 1,500 miles from the east. The dictator Mobutu was overthrown and Laurent Kabila installed in his place.

But in 1998, just one year later, tensions mounted again. This stage of the conflict – often dubbed Africa's World War – drew in the surrounding countries of Rwanda, Uganda, Angola, Namibia and Zimbabwe. There was fighting right across Congo, a colossal country the size of Europe.

Congo's war officially ended in 2003 and the country's first democratic elections were held in 2006. Joseph Kabila became Congo's first democratically elected president, a job he had been doing for almost six years. Despite this, fighting has continued in the country's eastern provinces. Today over two million people in this region are displaced.

The conflict is fuelled in part by the illegal exploitation of mineral wealth; the weak state authority across large parts of the east; and armed groups taking advantage of this vacuum. With porous borders, weapons flow into the country with ease. This has fed cycles of violence, with civilians both caught in the crossfire and directly targeted by a range of armed groups. Long – term instability and insecurity has stripped much of eastern DRC of almost all modern infrastructure, leaving it with virtually no industry and limited opportunities for education and employment. The resulting poverty further fuels the violence by giving many young men an economic incentive to take up arms.

Three main belligerents have taken centre stage in recent years: the Congolese Army, often known by its acronym FARDC; the National Conference for the Defence of the People (CNDP), which mounted attacks that catalysed global media attention in late 2008; and the Democratic Forces for the Liberation of Rwanda (FDLR), an armed group formed by some of those responsible for the Rwandan genocide. But they are not the only armed factions. Others include self – styled community protection militias known as Mai Mai, and the Lord's Resistance Army (LRA), a Ugandan rebel group that is creating havoc in the far north corner of eastern Congo. The UN estimates that the LRA killed 1,200 people, half of them children, and abducted 1,400 civilians in the course of just 10 months in 2008 and 2009.

In early 2009, the dynamics of the conflict shifted suddenly. The head of the CNDP, Laurent Nkunda, was arrested in Rwanda, and CNDP fighters and other former rebels were hastily integrated into the Congolese army, with no vetting to screen out human rights abusers. The newly integrated army mounted an offensive to disarm the FDLR.

On the face of it, action to disarm an illegal armed group seems like a good idea, but the suffering unleashed on civilians far outweighed any positive impact. In 2009, a staggering 900,000 people were forced to flee their homes and at least 1,400 civilians were killed. Thousands of women and girls – some as young as four – were raped and over 6,000 homes were burned to the ground.

Violence meted out in the 2009 offensive was carried out by both sides. Sections of the army burned, looted and raped wherever they were posted, with newly integrated units responsible for much of the violence. The FDLR and other militias linked to it wreaked havoc and deliberately responded to the offensive with brutal attacks on civilians. Not only did Oxfam and other humanitarian and human rights groups condemn widespread attacks on the population, but a report by the UN's own Special Rapporteur on Extrajudicial Killings said that the offensive had been a disaster for civilians. Controversially, the offensive was backed by the UN Security Council, both politically and through its peacekeeping force. A new phase of joint UN – Congolese operations launched in 2010. The UN is attempting to put in place better safeguards for civilian protection this time around, and the peacekeeping force's 2010 mandate specifically stated that peacekeepers would withdraw support from Congolese army units found to be carrying out atrocities. The Congolese government has meanwhile declared a policy of zero tolerance for human rights abuses by its armed forces. The people of Congo will be waiting to see whether these measures will succeed in keeping civilians safe this time.

What is sure is that less risky means of disarming militia groups in eastern Congo are far from exhausted, including voluntary resettlement programmes and legal action against militia leaders and financial backers living in Europe and elsewhere. The international community also needs to renew efforts to curb the illicit trade in minerals and arms, which is fuelling this deadly war.

Just over one hundred years ago, on 19 November 1909, a crowd gathered at the Royal Albert Hall in London to speak out against atrocities in the Congo. Clearly, a century later, atrocities continue. But that should not make us despair. The gathering was part of the campaign against slavery in the Congo. It shows what ordinary compassionate people can do to put pressure on disengaged politicians and change events thousands of miles away. As we start 2010, we should take heed of the actions of those people 100 years ago and raise our voices for peace in the Congo. This conflict should not be forgotten.

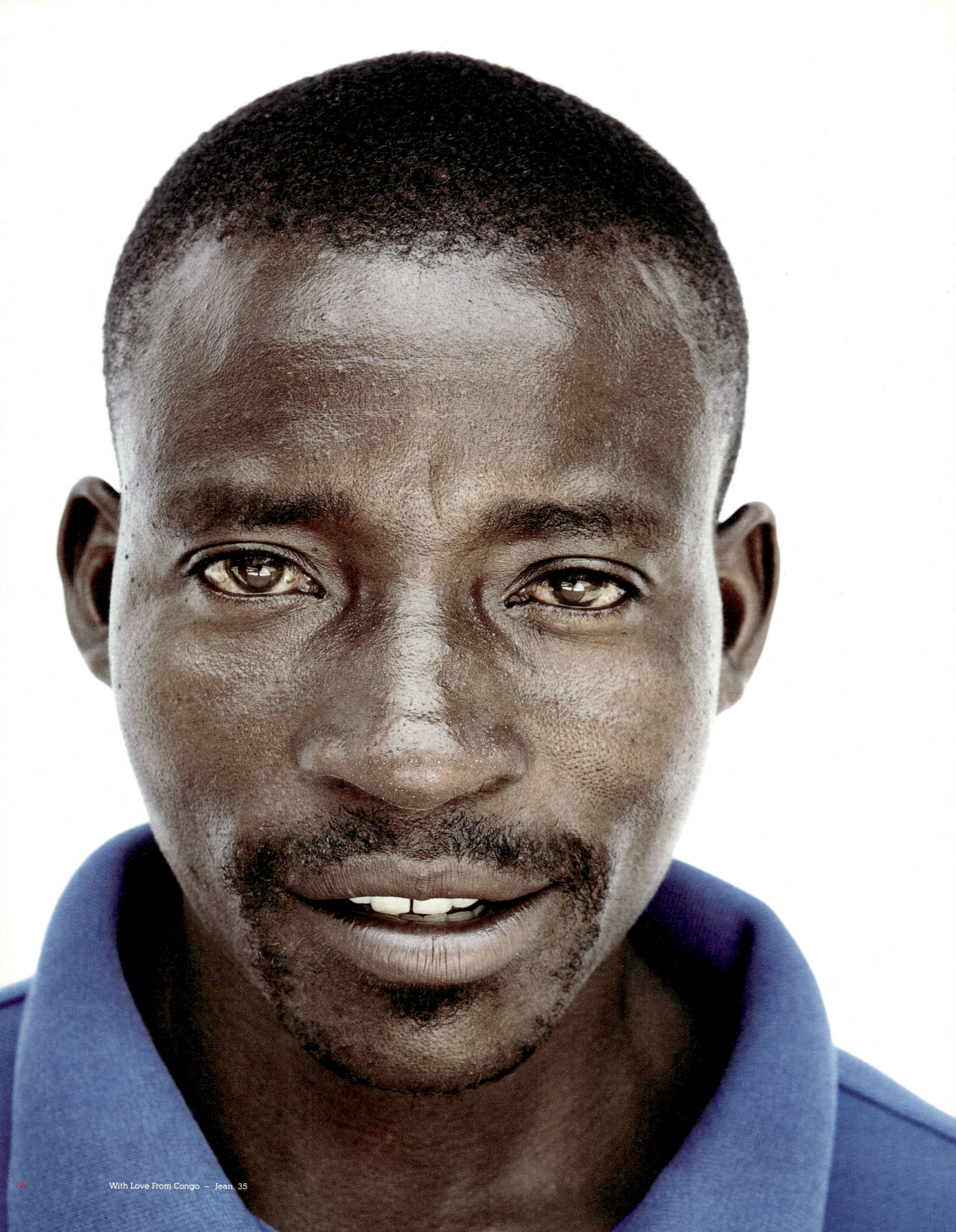

With Love From Congo — Jean, 35

The Democratic Republic of Congo (DRC) is one of the toughest places on earth to call home. Since 1998, five million people have died as a result of conflict here – and war continues to devastate the east of this vast country. Most people have been killed not by the fighting, however, but by the malnutrition and disease it has caused. The scale of suffering here is immense. Hundreds of thousands of homes have been destroyed. Rape is widespread.

And yet beyond the horror, hope remains. Amid the unspeakable violence, there is true kindness. Two million people have been forced from their homes across eastern DRC. But the majority don't live in makeshift camps. Instead, they live with families who have opened their homes to those who have lost everything – in many cases complete strangers. Most people here live in extreme poverty, and yet it is extreme generosity that shines through.

What Oxfam loves about Rankin's portraits is their ability to communicate the humanity of the people caught up in this brutal war. The personalities of people like Jasmine, Sikito and Charles shine out from their portraits with verve and warmth. These are not war victims. They are simply people, just like us. People who are living in the most difficult of times, but who are laughing, who are in love, who are working, carrying on with life, and hoping for a better future.

Our staff in DRC see this hope every day. It inspires our work. By buying this book, you've already shown that you share it. Because of you, more communities in the DRC will have clean water and decent sanitation.

So thank you for your support. As is clear from the photos in this book, a better world is possible.

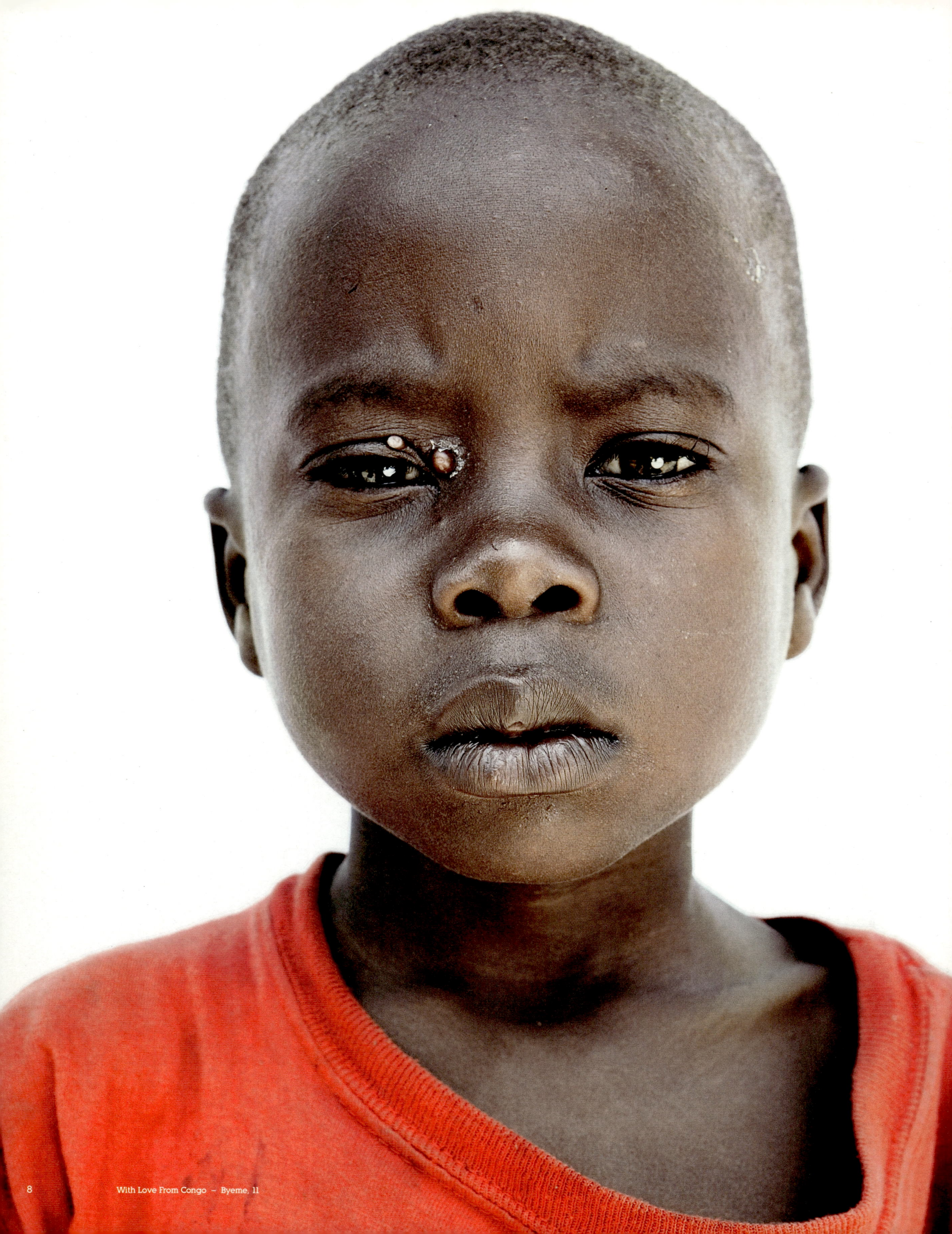

With Love From Congo — Byeme, 11

WE ARE CONGO

Foreword – By **Rankin**

I first visited the DRC with Oxfam in June 2008. I expected to be depressed. I had done my homework; the statistics were horrific. I could only imagine what the human face of those statistics would look like.

The people I met confounded my expectations. I met fathers, mothers, children... all getting on with life, making it through, even having a laugh and a joke. These people didn't see themselves as victims, despite the bad hand that fate had dealt them. They were human beings, exactly the same as you and me.

I wanted my portraits to do something different. The West has been anaesthetised to traditional pictures of disaster zones. My style of portraiture is always about bringing people out of themselves, getting them to share something. I chose to photograph the people against a stark white background instead of in their physical environment. The expressions in their eyes and on their faces - their humanity - was what I wanted people to notice and relate to.

It didn't seem morally or politically right to just go and take pictures. So I decided to put on a show in the refugee camp, and give the people prints of their portraits. Give them something back. It was incredible. One guy said to me, 'This photograph is amazing. I wanted to let you know that I will use it on my coffin when I die.' No-one has ever said anything so moving to me.

The overriding feeling I had while I was out in the DRC was one of anger and powerlessness. That taking a few snaps was inconsequential in the face of the insurmountable problems that were being faced there. But when I got back, we put on an exhibition. I pushed the images, did press interviews, raised awareness. I believe that it made a difference to the people I met.

I was inspired to return to the DRC in October 2009. I didn't want to do the same thing as I had done the year before and, as on my first trip, I felt that it was important and right to give something back. So this time I held photographic workshops. I gave out cameras so that the people could have authorship over their own images. - show us what was important in their lives. The collection of shots from my second trip builds on those from the first one, but focuses on the relationships that bind people to each other - a mother's love for her child, a husband's love for his wife, two friends. The basic, beautiful business of life.

I hope that these photographs can aid understanding. They are neither ugly images of brutality, nor sentimental images of suffering. The world needs a more sustainable form of imagery that, instead of encouraging pity and powerlessness, promotes understanding, connection, and ultimately action. It's about making people accessible to each other.

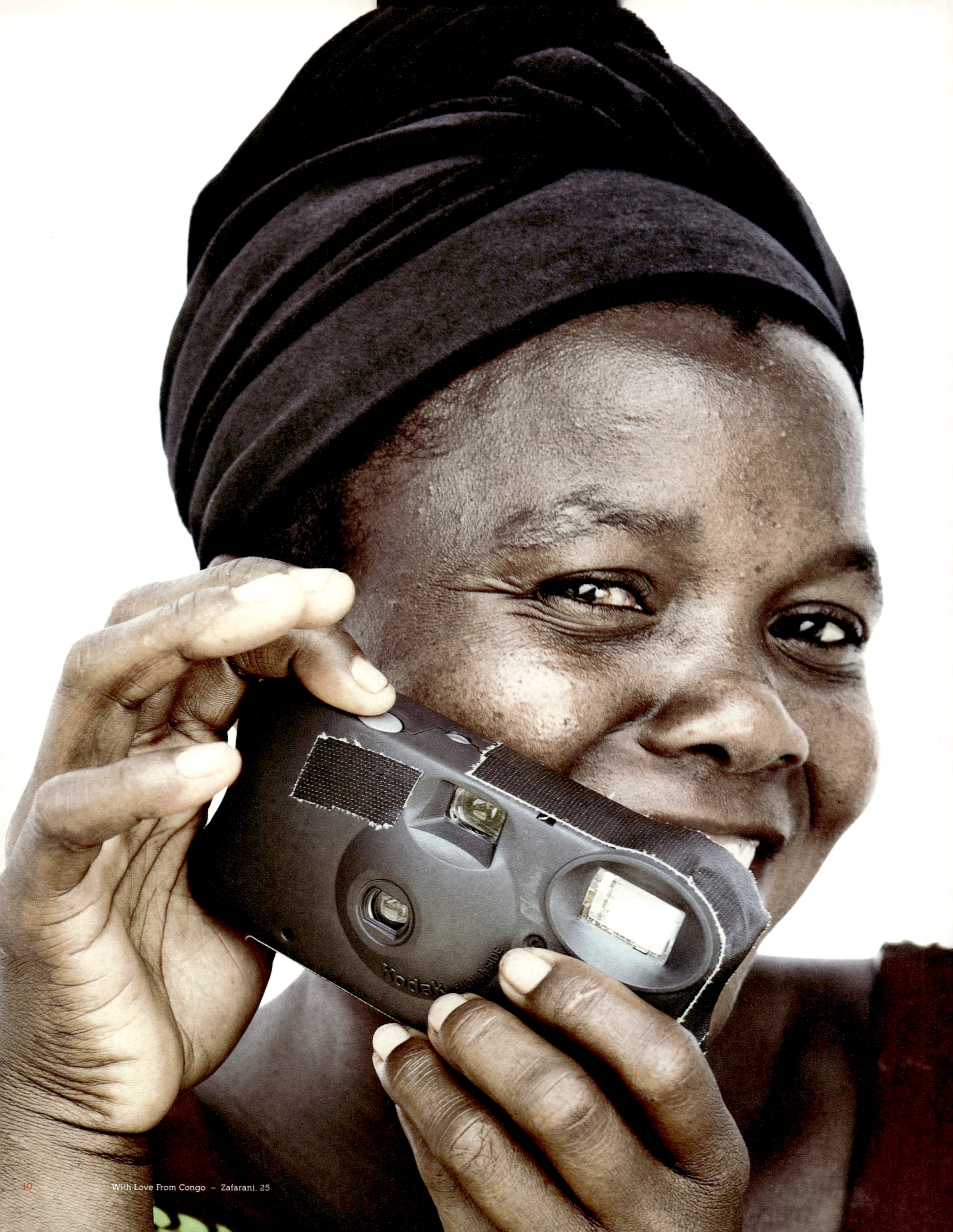

 With Love From Congo – Zafarani, 25

WITH LOVE FROM CONGO 2009

In 2009 Rankin returned to the DRC. On his second visit he travelled to Sange, where tens of thousands of people had recently arrived after being made homeless by renewed fighting. The population of the town had doubled in size, with families opening their homes, in many cases to six, seven or eight people. Their generosity inspired Rankin, and this collection focuses on the remarkable love stories he discovered in the DRC: the love of a mother, who coos and quietens her baby, keeping him safe from armed men nearby; the love of a young couple, unfailingly together as the horror unfolds around them.

An exhibition of these images will be displayed outside the National Theatre from; 12 February to the 11 April 2010

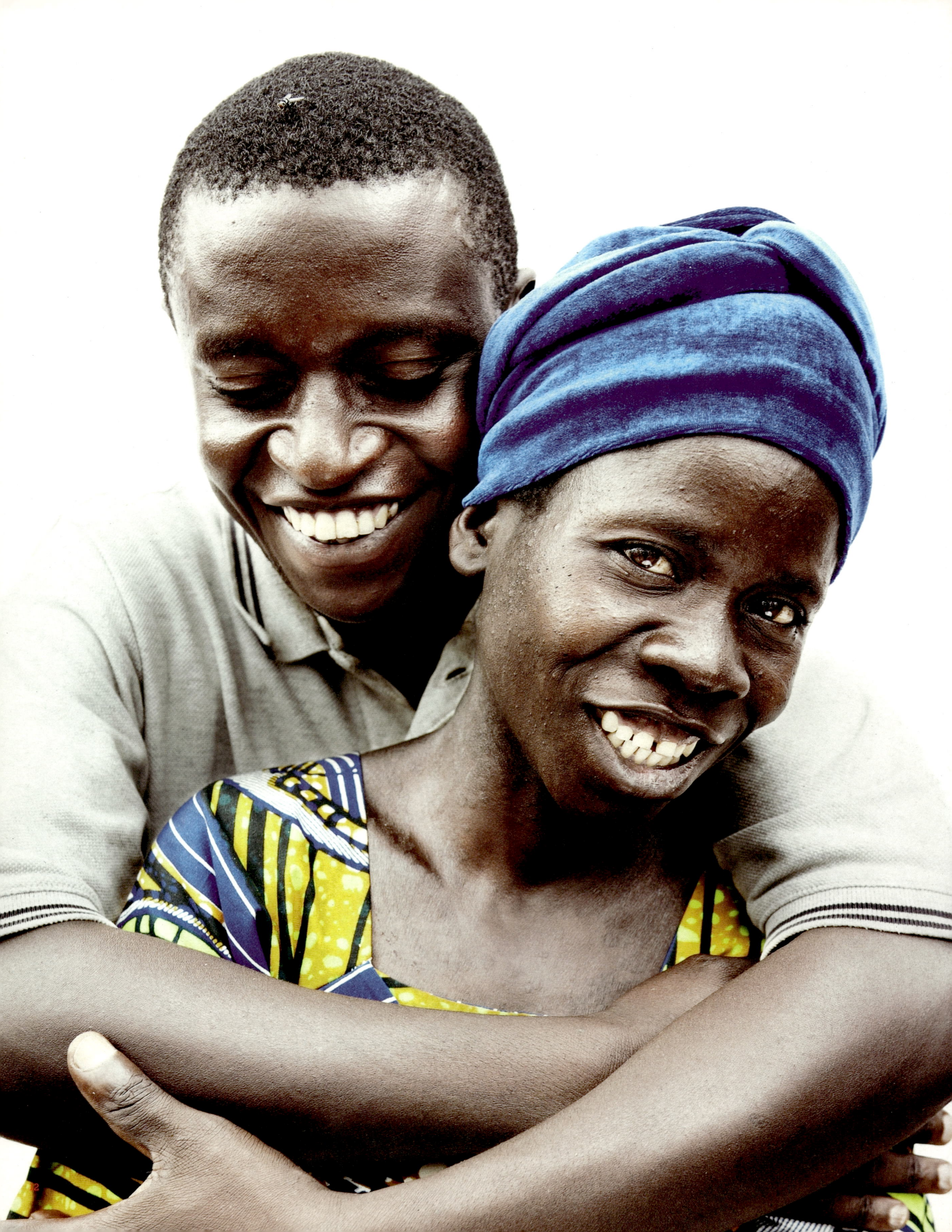

"I fell in love with my wife the first time I saw her. There was just something about her – the way she was talking, the way she was walking, her nose, her ears. When I saw her I thought she was very beautiful. I can't explain it. Some people may not think she is beautiful, but to me she is perfect. The first time I asked her to marry me she refused. It's a cultural thing in Congo: a woman always refuses the first time. But I kept asking. I wrote her a letter to tell her that I loved her. She wrote back to tell me that she needs a man who will never beat her, a man to treat her well. She said that if I could be that man her answer would be 'Yes'. Those words are something I will never forget. It's difficult for us to keep our love letters because of the war. I still have some photos but not letters. When we had to run I took the pictures and put them in my pocket. I can't go a day without looking at her."

"I was selling banana juice in the market the first time I saw my husband. I can't forget it because it was such a good day for me. I was 18. He was wearing black trousers and a red shirt. It was the kind of shirt you only wear for special occasions. I remember it wasn't tucked in! At first I was shy. I wasn't sure what his intentions were – some men just run after women for fun. They are not serious. He came back again the next day and we talked and talked. I think that's when we fell in love. He came back again the day after, with gifts. He brought soap and some talc. He wrote a letter to say that he wanted to marry me. My parents agreed but he was poor so it took two years for him to save enough for the dowry. In January 2000 we were finally married. And I love him even more today."

   With Love From Congo – Zafarani, 25, and her husband Nbyde

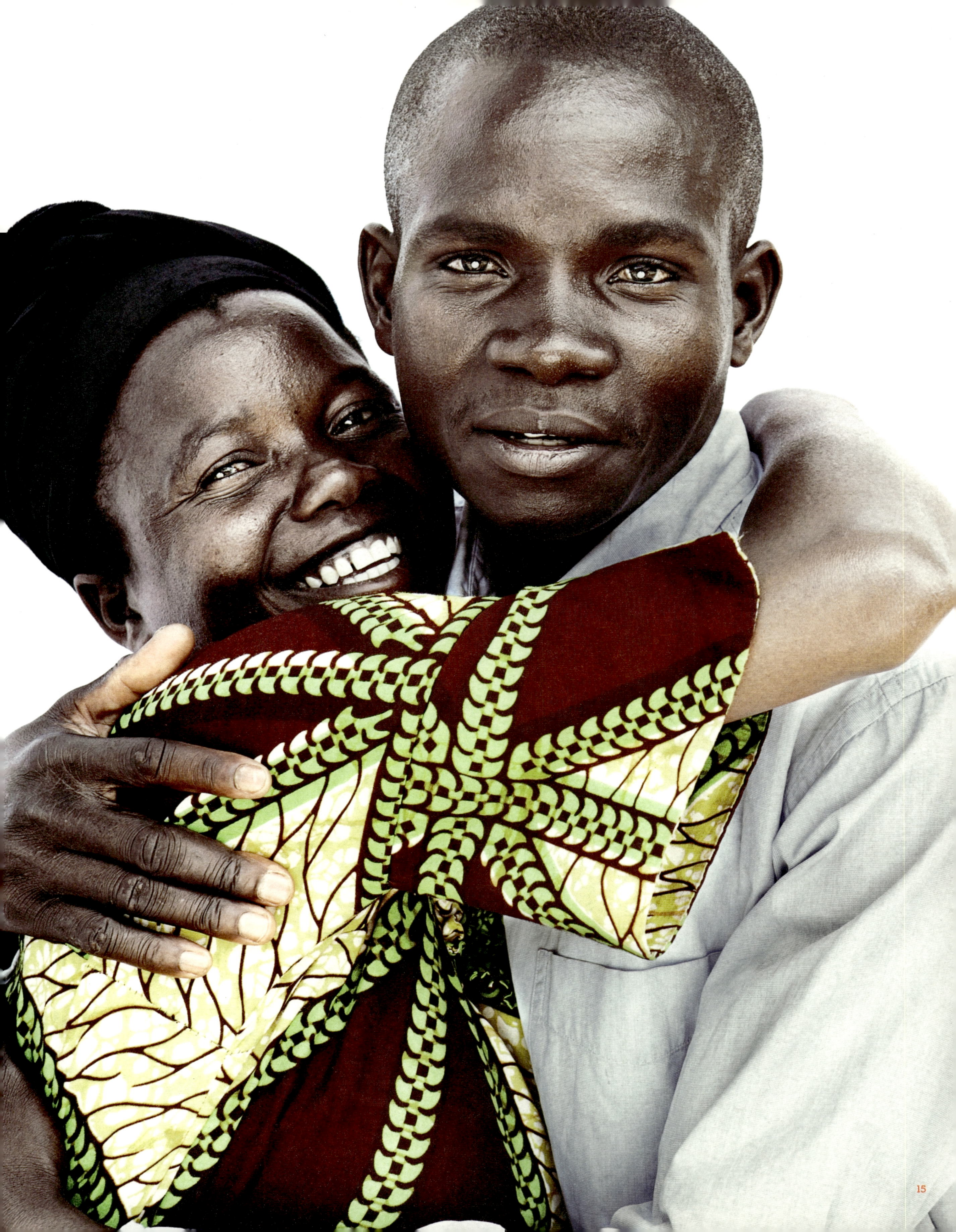

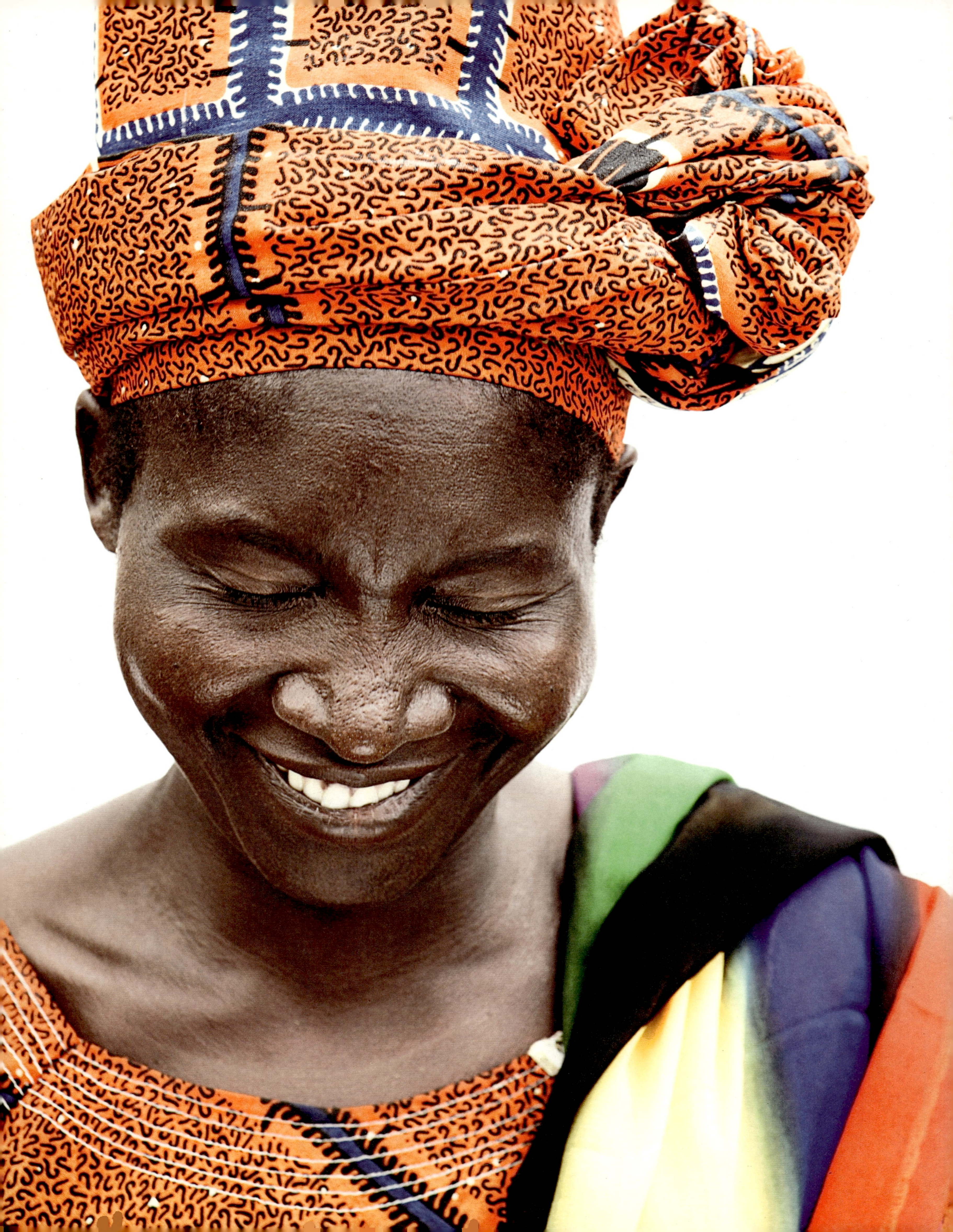

"I accepted them because I think it is good to help other people. In Congo anyone can be in need of help at any time. Today it is our friends; tomorrow it could be us. In the past when we have been displaced others helped us. Now I want to do the same for them. We had a second house that was old. Our children slept in one room in that house and the goats stayed in the other. I moved our children back into the big house with us and moved the goats outside so that our friends can have two rooms. We have become great friends. We eat together – we share our food. We are farming together. We go to different churches – my family are Protestants and our friends are Jehovah's Witnesses – but people are more important than their religions and it's our duty to look after each other."

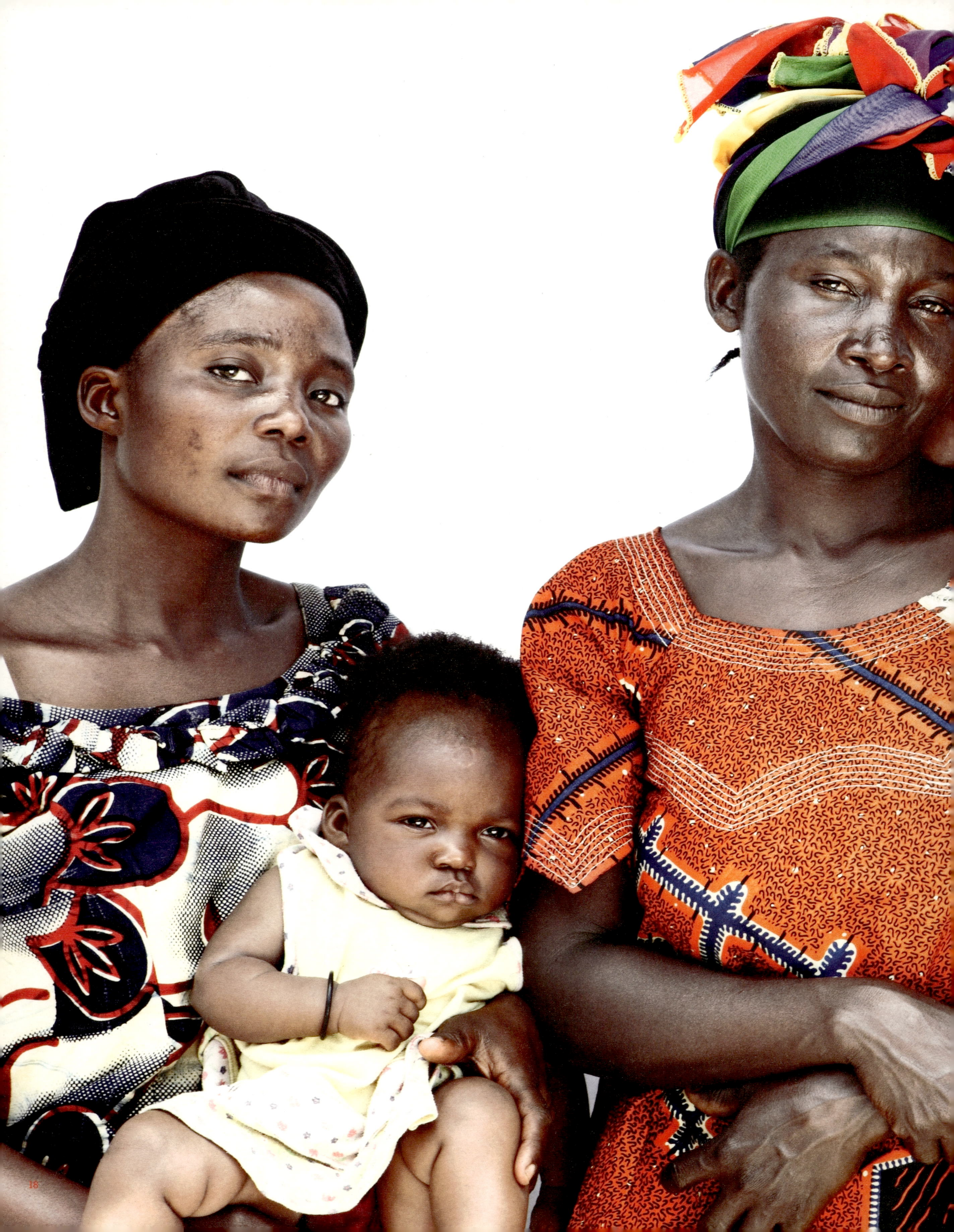

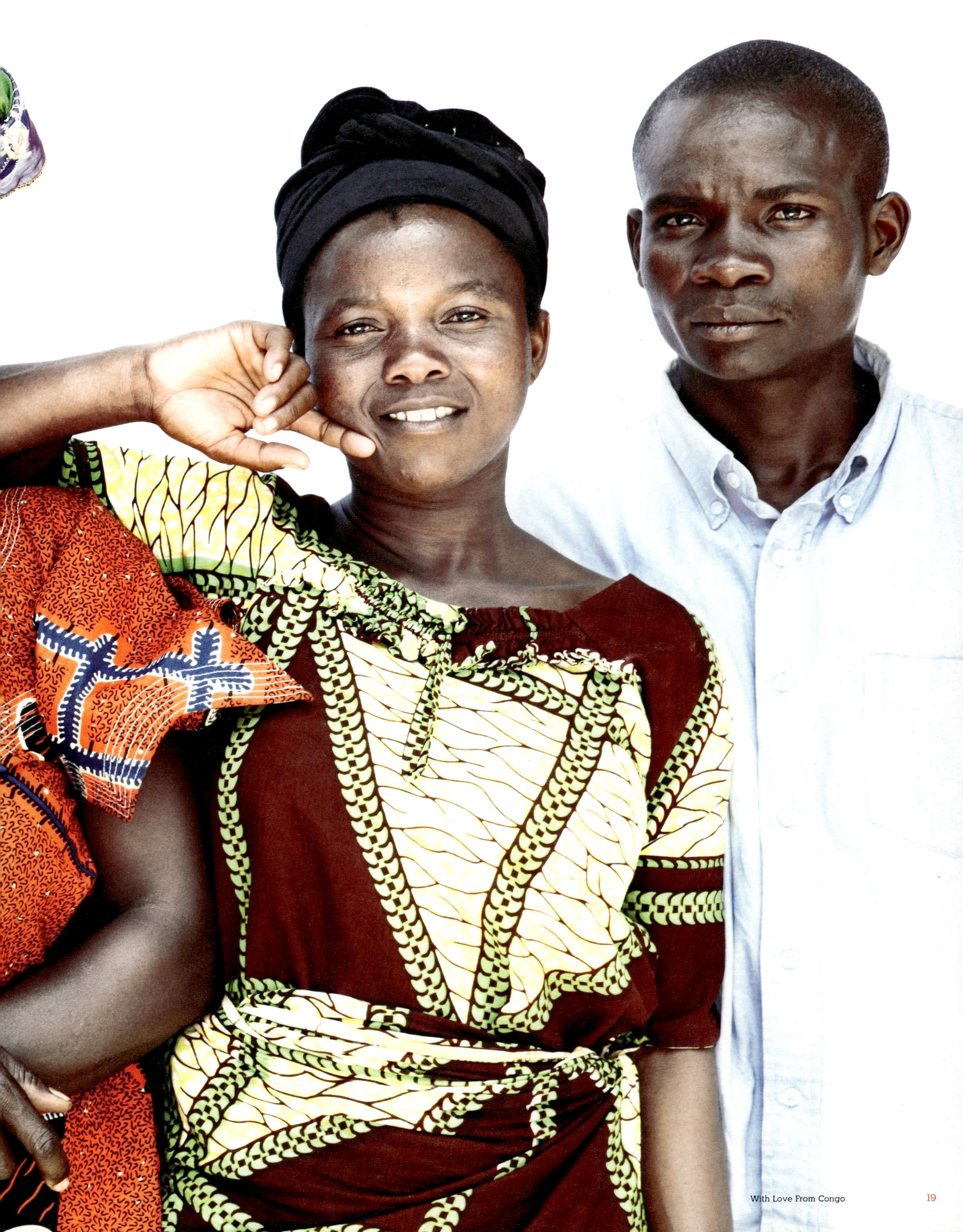

"When the fighting flared up thousands of people were arriving every day. They didn't know where to go – some were seeking shelter in schools, others were just sleeping under trees or in a broken house with no roof. How can you not feel compassion for people in need? We managed to take in one family of seven and a teenage orphan called Alfio. We are no longer a family of seven: now we are a family of 15. Before we were eating two meals a day, now we only eat one. We have all become good friends. Our daughter Marie and Chantelle, the daughter of the family we are helping, have become like sisters. They are the same age. They are inseparable. They even sleep together.

They are welcome to stay for as long as they need."

     With Love From Congo – Magdalene, 45

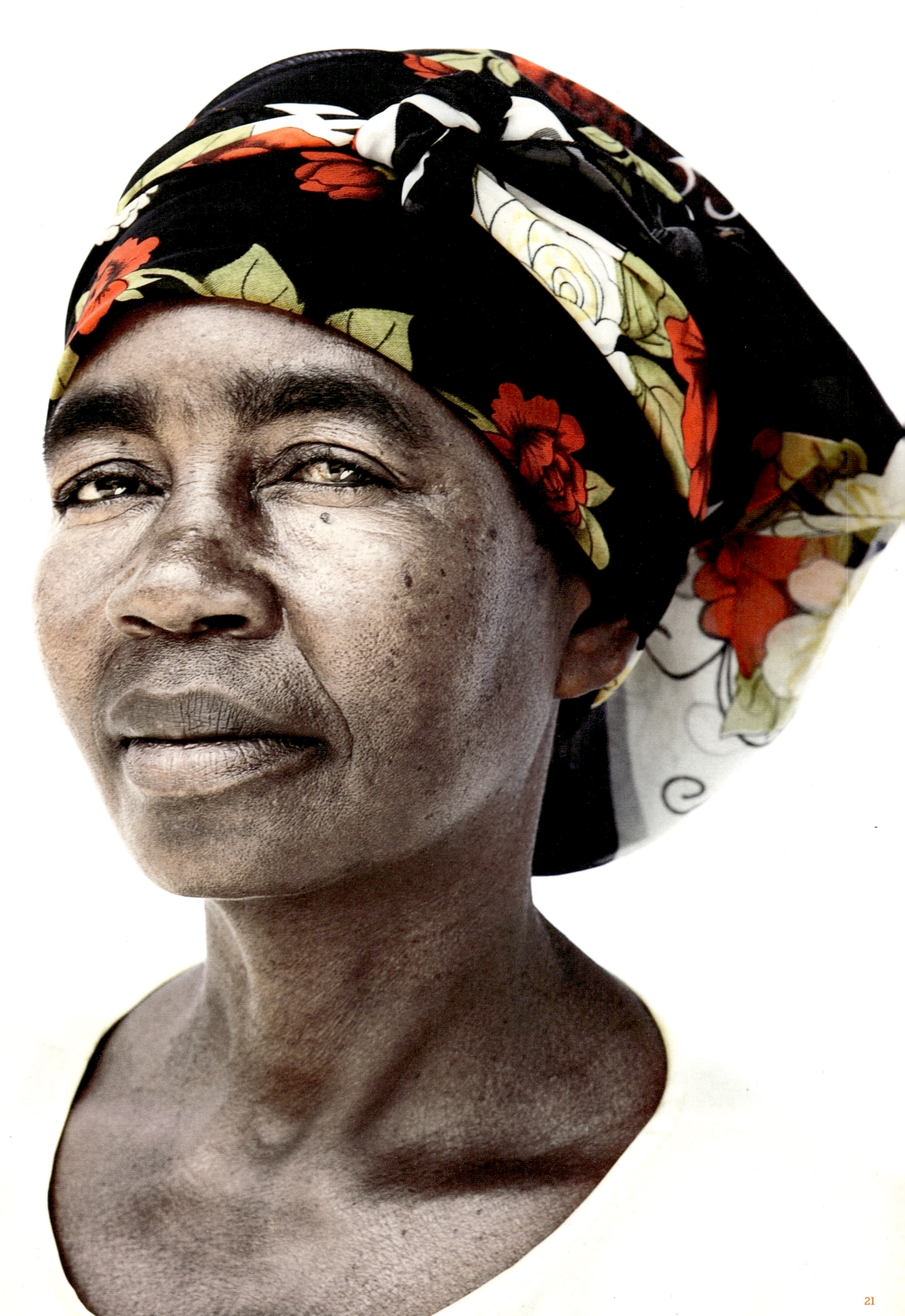

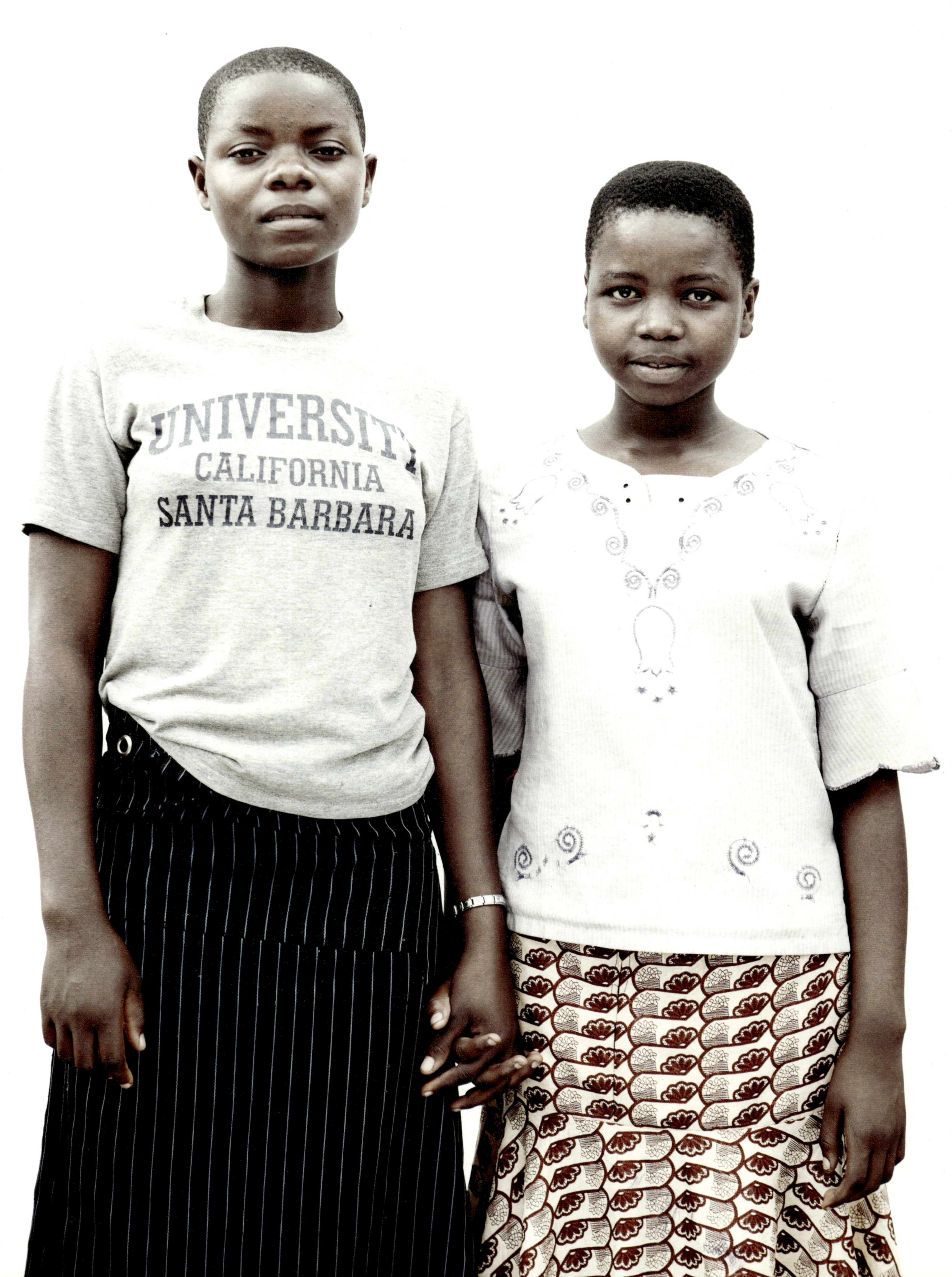
UNIVERSITY
CALIFORNIA
SANTA BARBARA

Chantelle:"I like Marie because she is generous. She always waits for me to eat. Sometimes she lets me wear her clothes. Even when I leave and go back to my village I will not forget Marie. She is my best friend."

Marie: "Sometimes I share what I learnt from school with Chantelle. I like her company. We do everything together. It's nice to have someone to chat to."

"I have my family but I have lost my love. My wife had been sick for a while; we knew she had a bad heart. But that terrible night was too much for her. The gunfire was so close and so loud that she just collapsed. My neighbours helped me carry her on a stretcher; we kept running, carrying her on our shoulders, and all the time the fighting was building – the sound of gunfire getting louder and louder. I kept looking at her to see if she was still alive. After a while we had to stop for a rest and I saw that she was already gone. We dug a shallow grave and buried her there. I cried all the way here.

I miss my wife very much. I remember the day we met: it was at a ceremony to celebrate the birth of twins. I was a dancer and I saw her through the crowd. She had such beautiful eyes and beautiful hair. Every time I looked at her my heart was pounding. After the ceremony I went up to her straight away and told her that I had to marry her.

From the day we were married we had a great time together. Now my life is very difficult. I used to love to dance but we cannot enjoy ourselves when times are hard. We can't sing. We can't dance. I have no time to think about pleasure now that my love has gone."

   With Love From Congo – Charles, 51. Grandfather, Widower and Retired Dancer

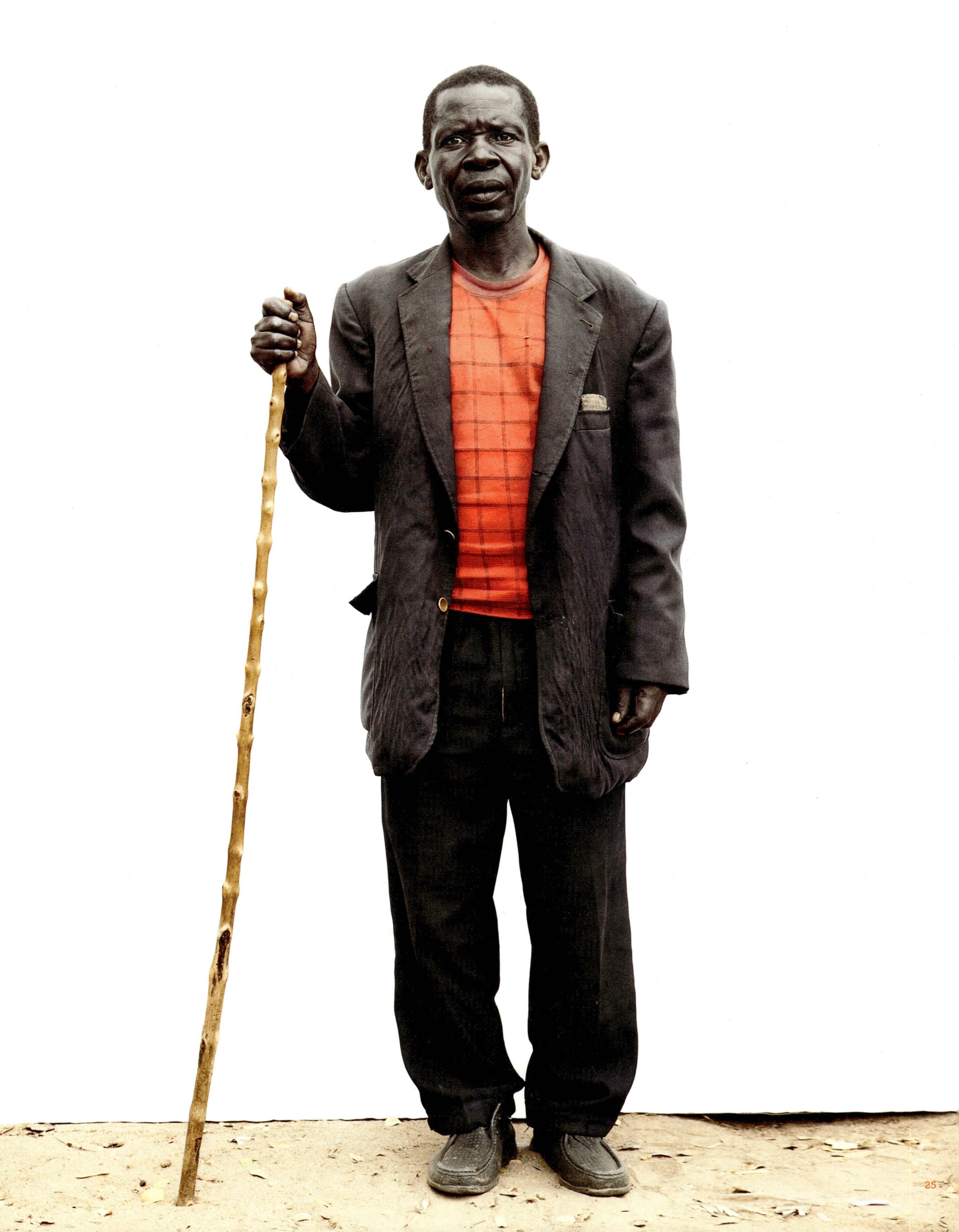

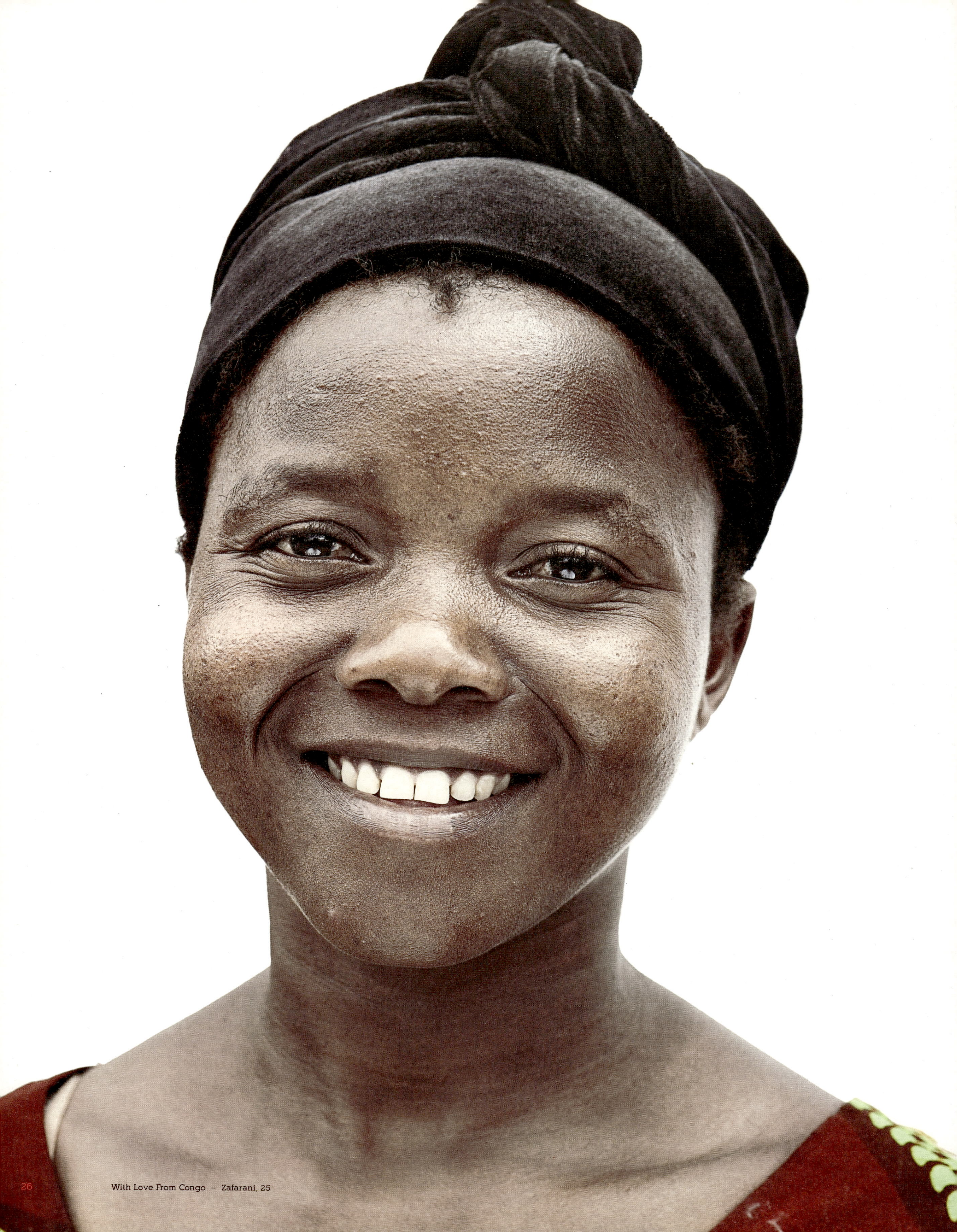

With Love From Congo – Zafarani, 25

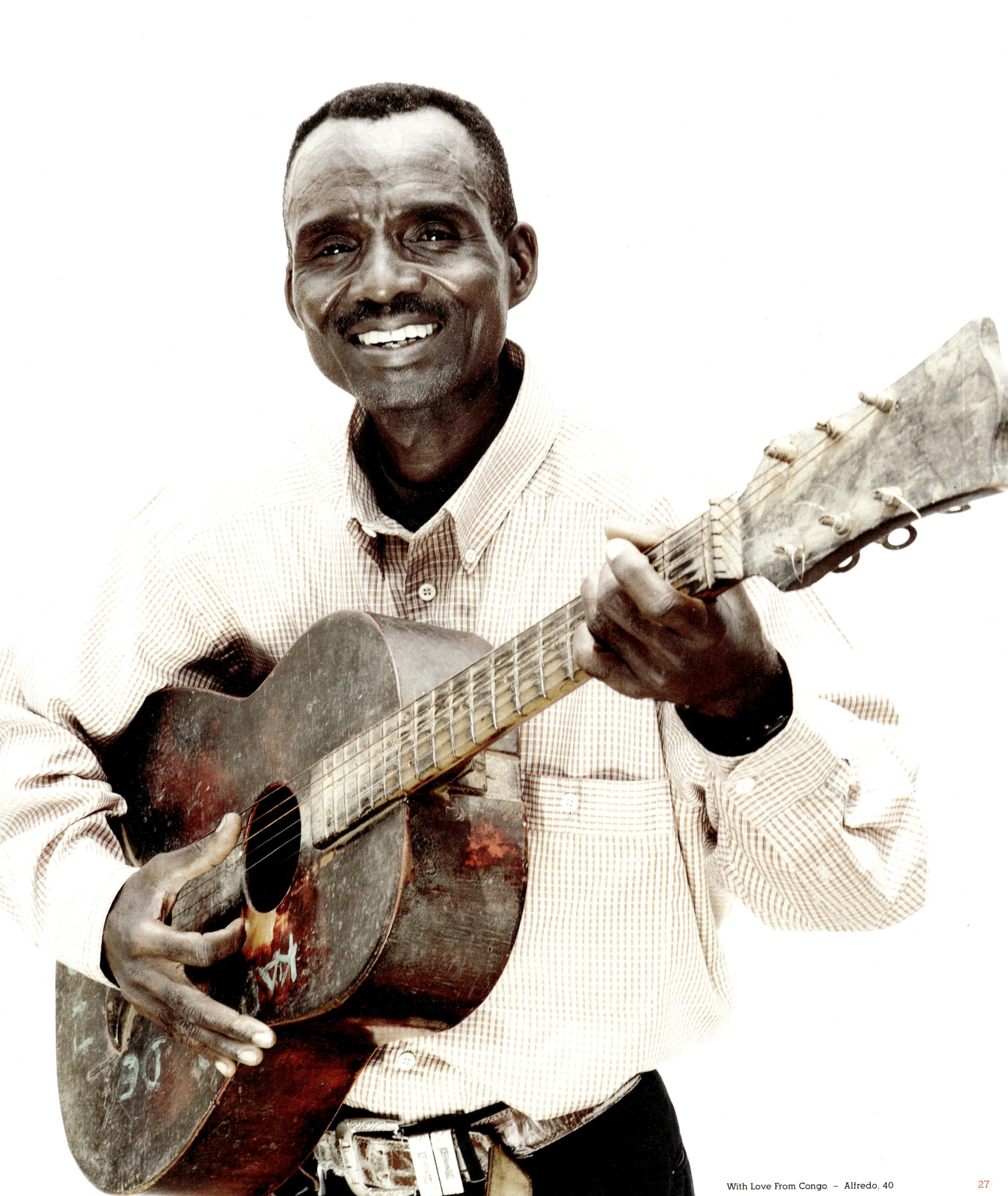

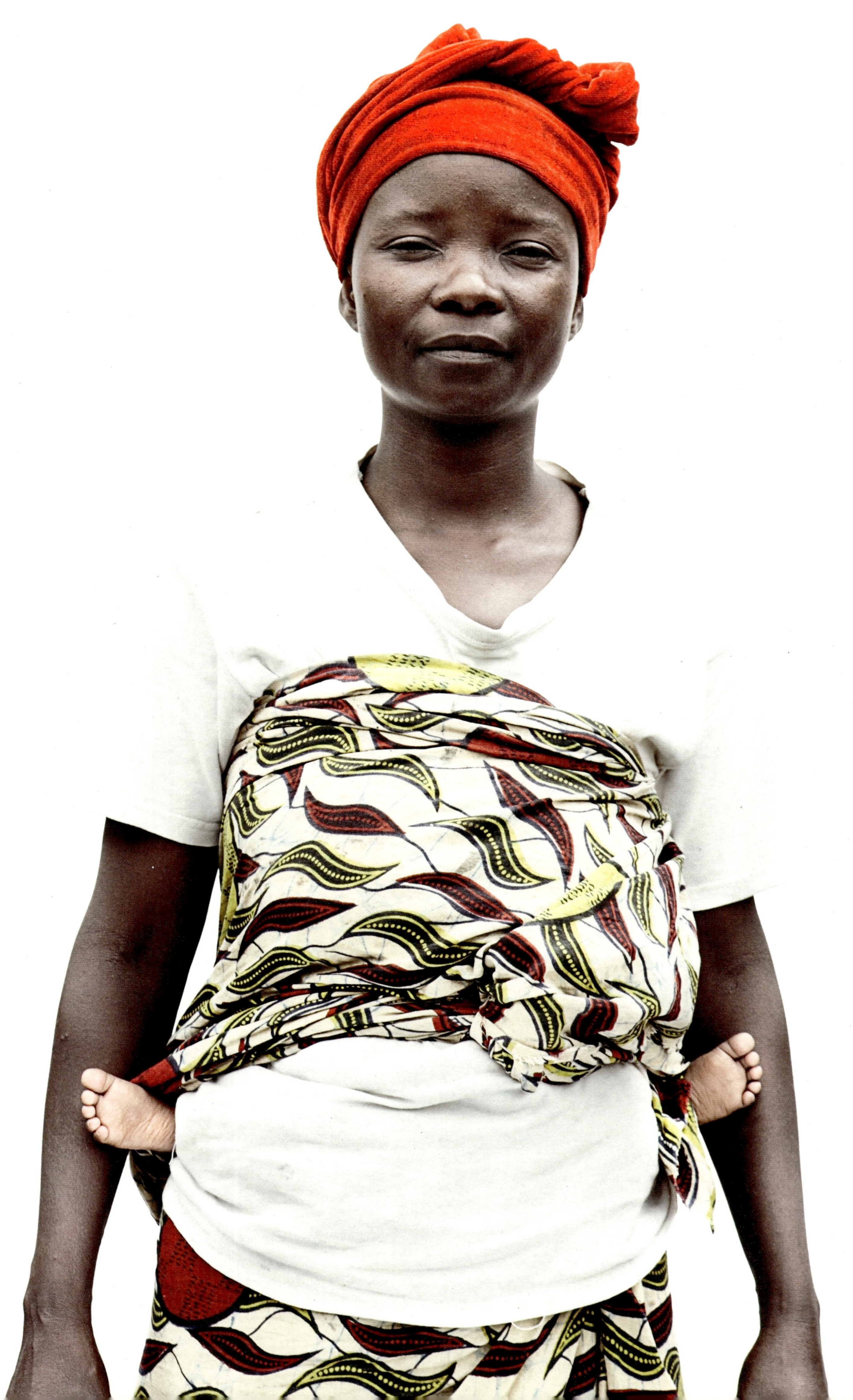

"We had to hide in the bush for four days before we found our way here. At times, when the gunfire was close, the children got scared. We were all scared. It's a very harsh environment to be in with children. We had to sleep outside without any food. The children got sick because of the mosquitoes and everyone was hungry. It's important not to make any noise when you are hiding in the bush. If they find you, they will kill you.

We know places to hide where the children can cry without anyone finding us. There are some caves in between two mountains. It's safer there because no one can hear them cry. We always search for places to hide where there is some water or a river. When the children are upset we can soothe them by washing them and giving them some water to drink. We also try to keep the children quiet by breast-feeding them when we can, but sometimes when they cry we have to put our hands over their mouths.

As a mother I am full of love for my children. When my children are happy, I am happy. When the children cry, I want to cry too. If something happens to any of my children – if they are sick or hungry – I do everything I can to find them something to eat. I want more than anything for my children to grow up in peaceful times."

"My daughter Byamungu died last week; she was 27. She died in childbirth. She had to have a caesarean. She died as soon as the baby was born; she didn't even get a chance to see her child. My heart broke that day when I saw that my daughter had died.

I was the first to hold the baby. I called her Chance. She is beautiful, just like her mother. I will love this baby as my own. I will love her and care for her as much as I loved and cared for my daughter. The baby makes me feel a little better because when my daughter died I didn't lose everything. I still have this beautiful baby to remind me of her."

    With Love From Congo – Muvida, 50 and week – old baby Chance

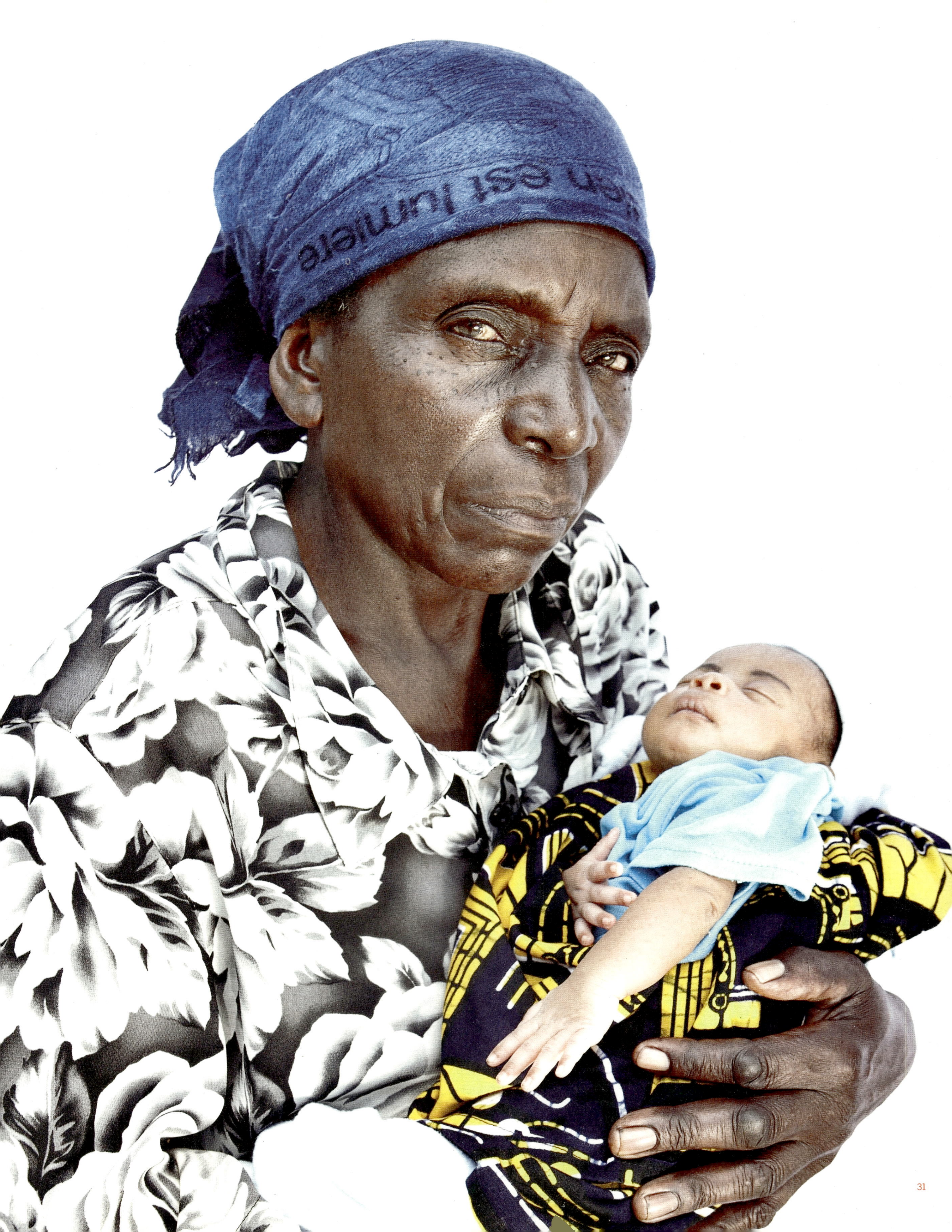

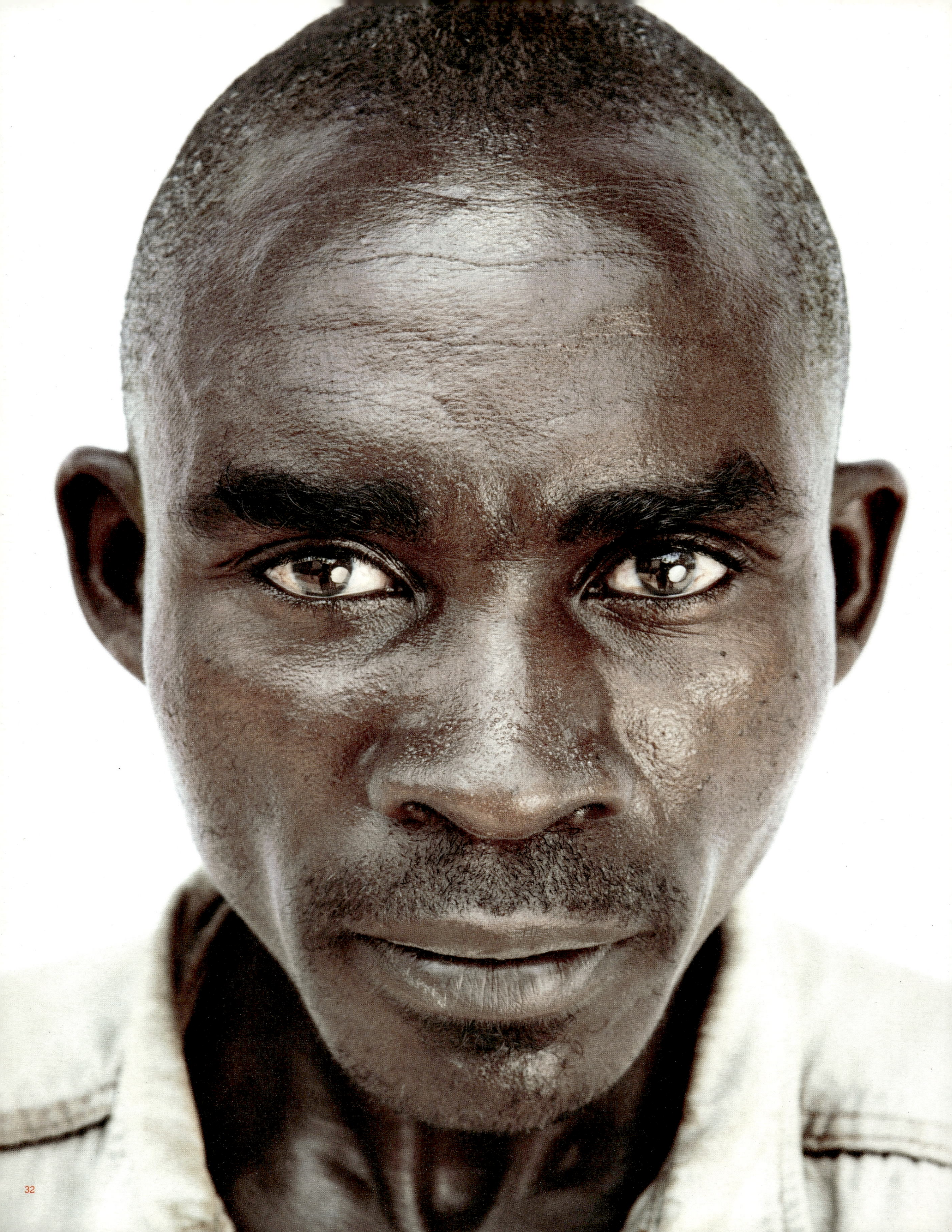

"One night we were woken by gunfire; we all jumped up, grabbed a few clothes and ran. We all ran together – my wife, our four children, my mother and father, my younger brother and his family, and all of our friends and neighbours. We all escaped unharmed.

When we arrived here we soon discovered that there was not enough food. A group of us decided to go to the bush (about 14km away – a two hour walk) to look for food. I went with my brother and my friend. We were returning when we met some rebels. They just took two people – my brother and my friend. They took them into the bush and stabbed them in the neck with a knife. None of us moved. We couldn't. If any of us had made the smallest movement they would have killed us too. It was the 3rd of August. That was the day I lost everything."

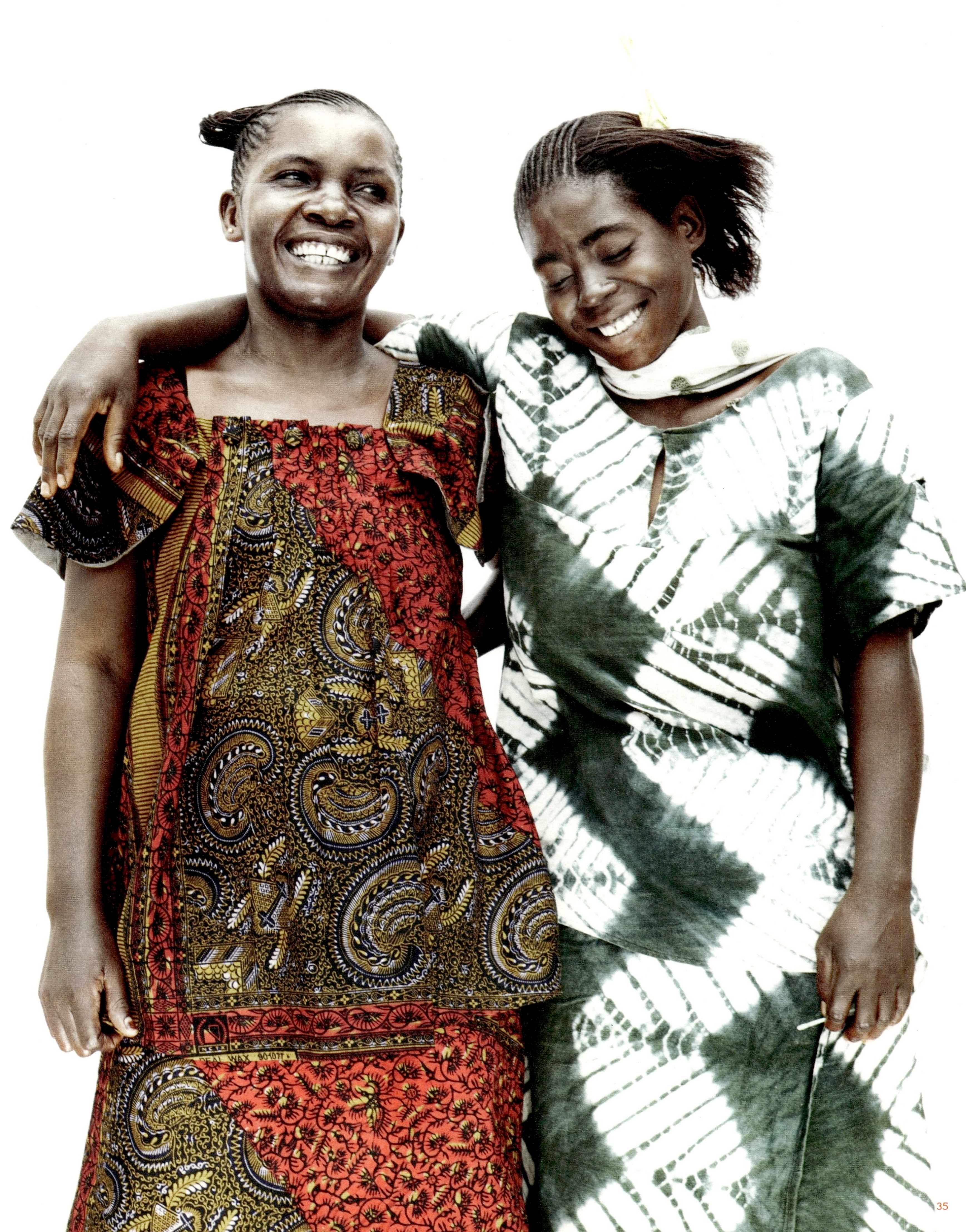

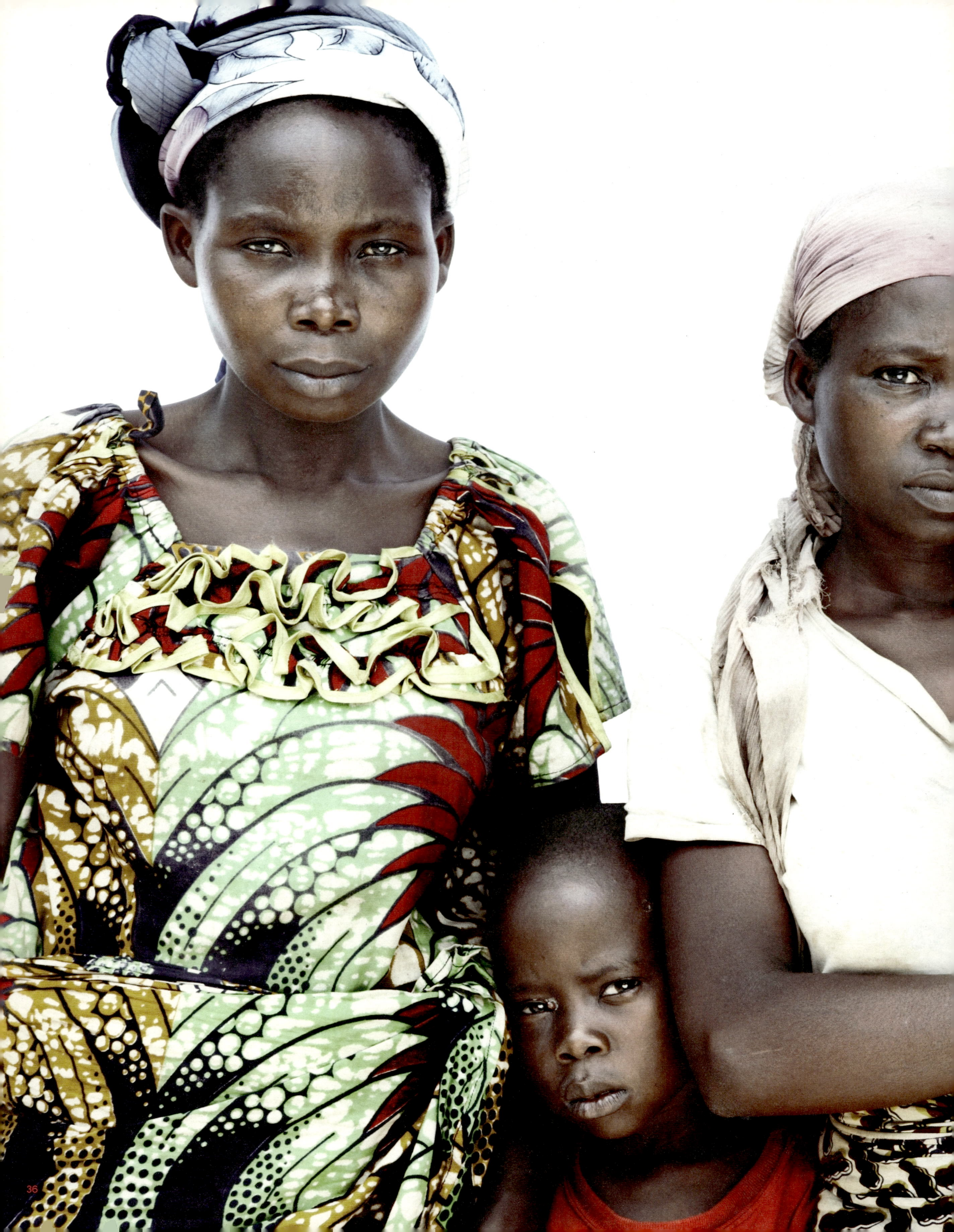

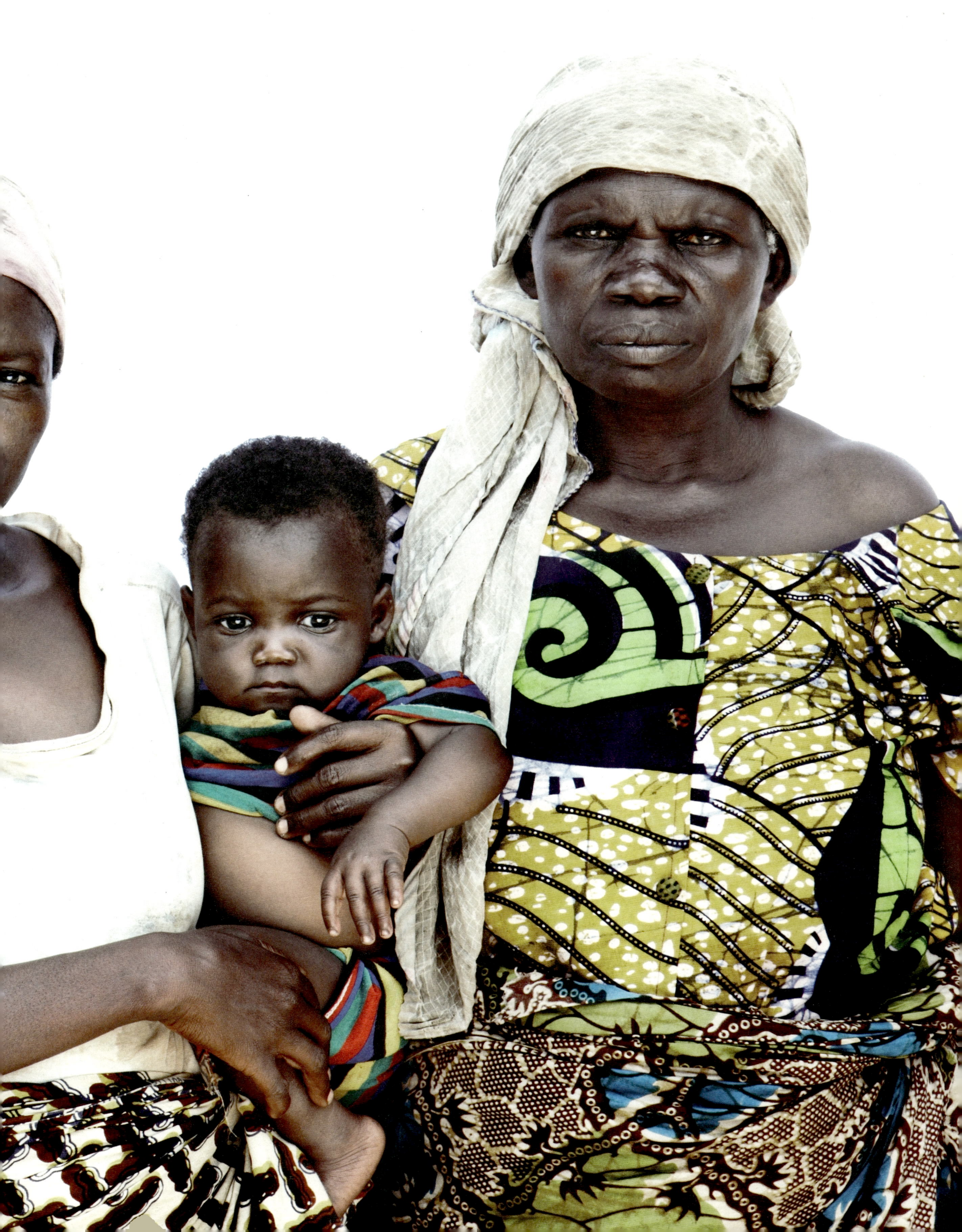

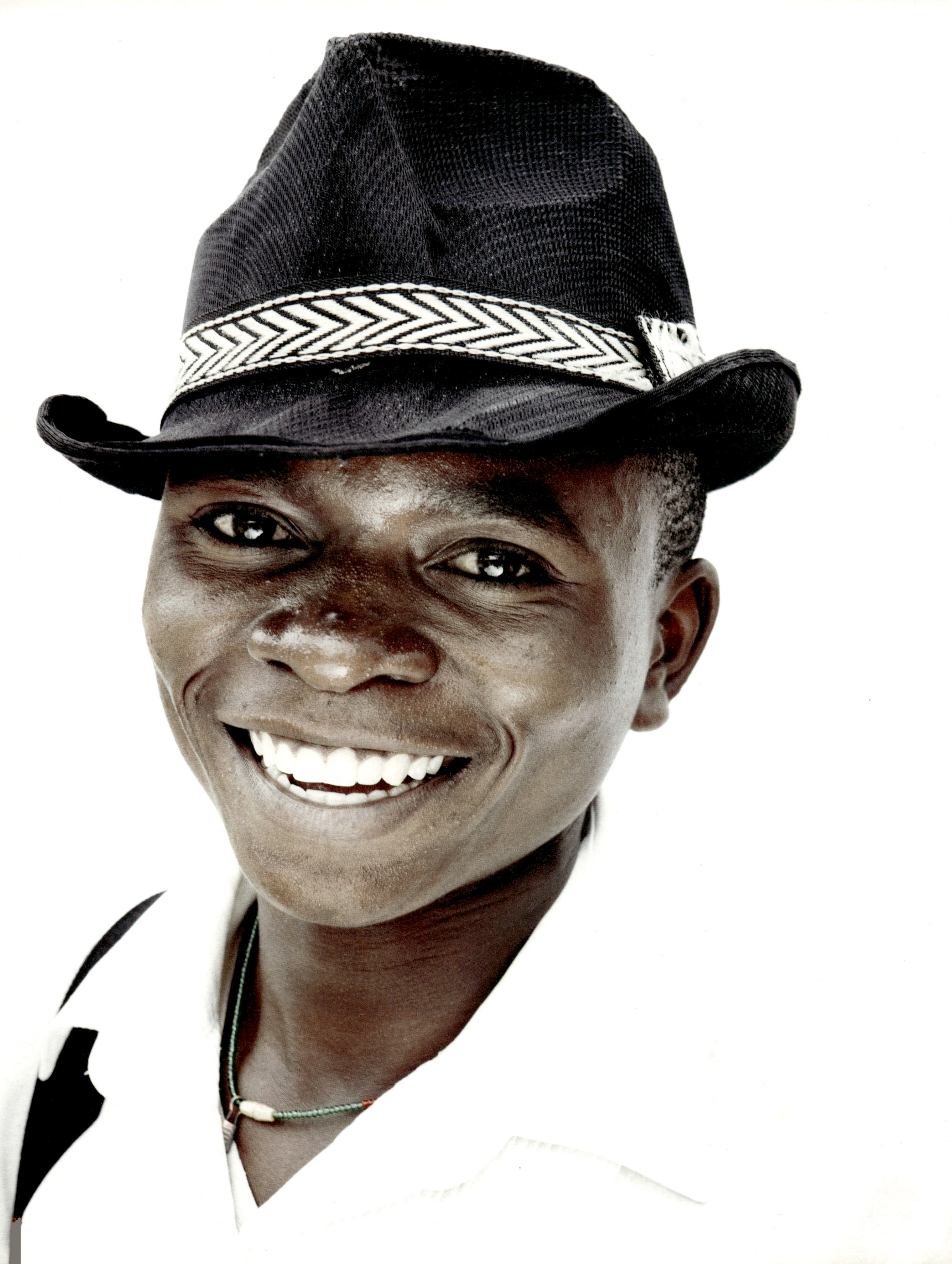

"I love my hat. I bought it in the market last year. I love my hat because it protects me from the sun. It's black so it doesn't get dirty and it looks good. I wear it every day after school."

"I love to have knowledge."

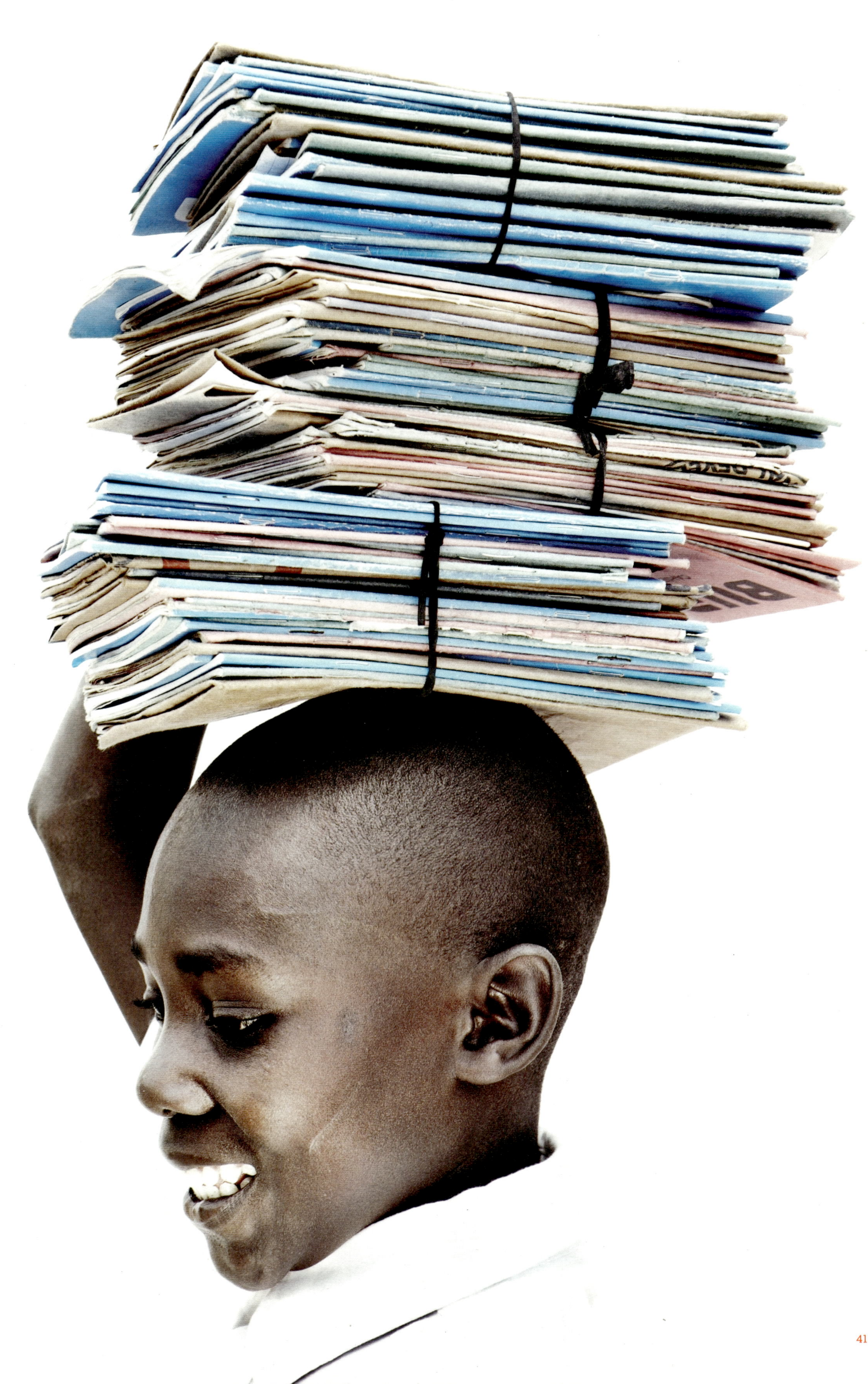

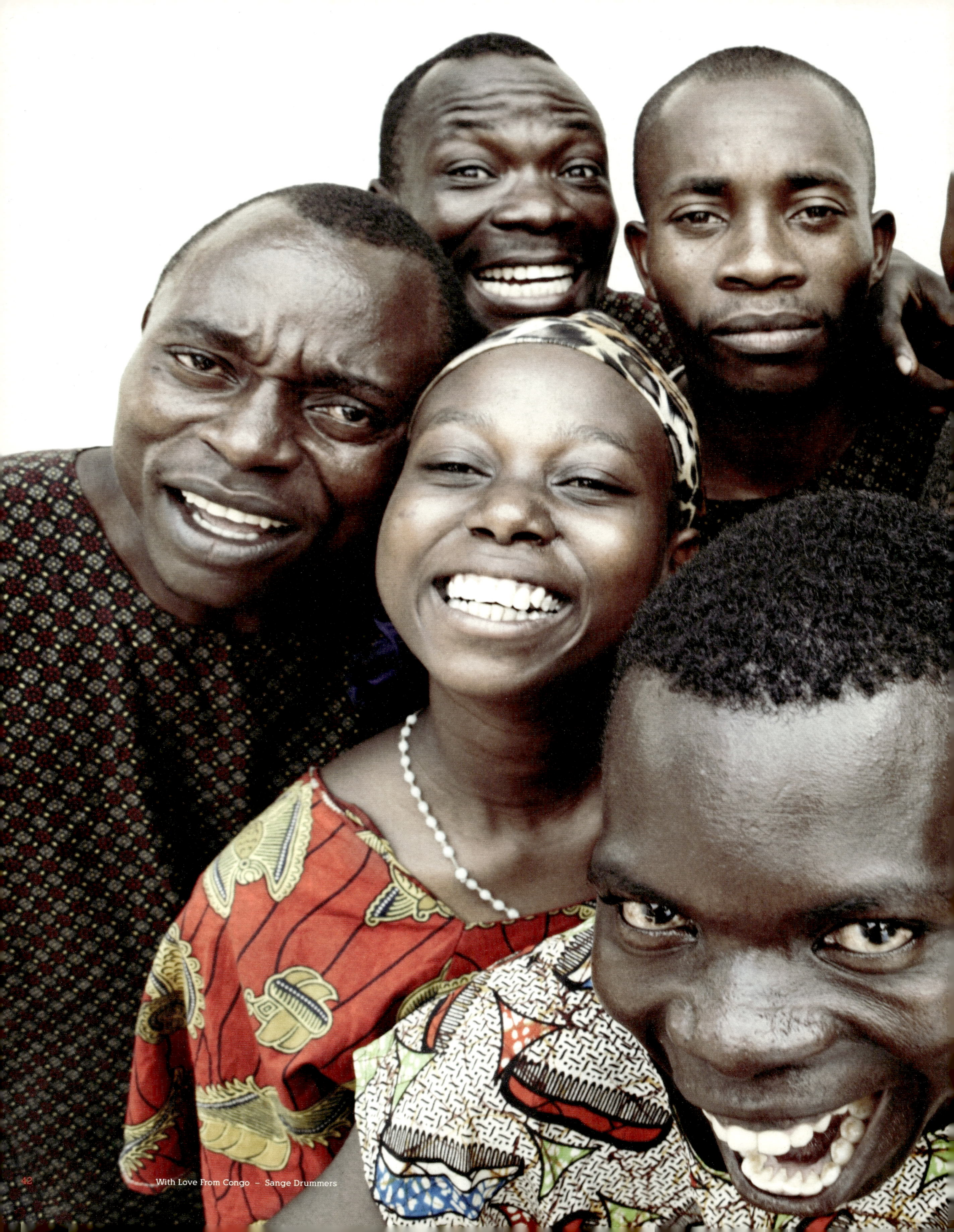

With Love From Congo – Sange Drummers

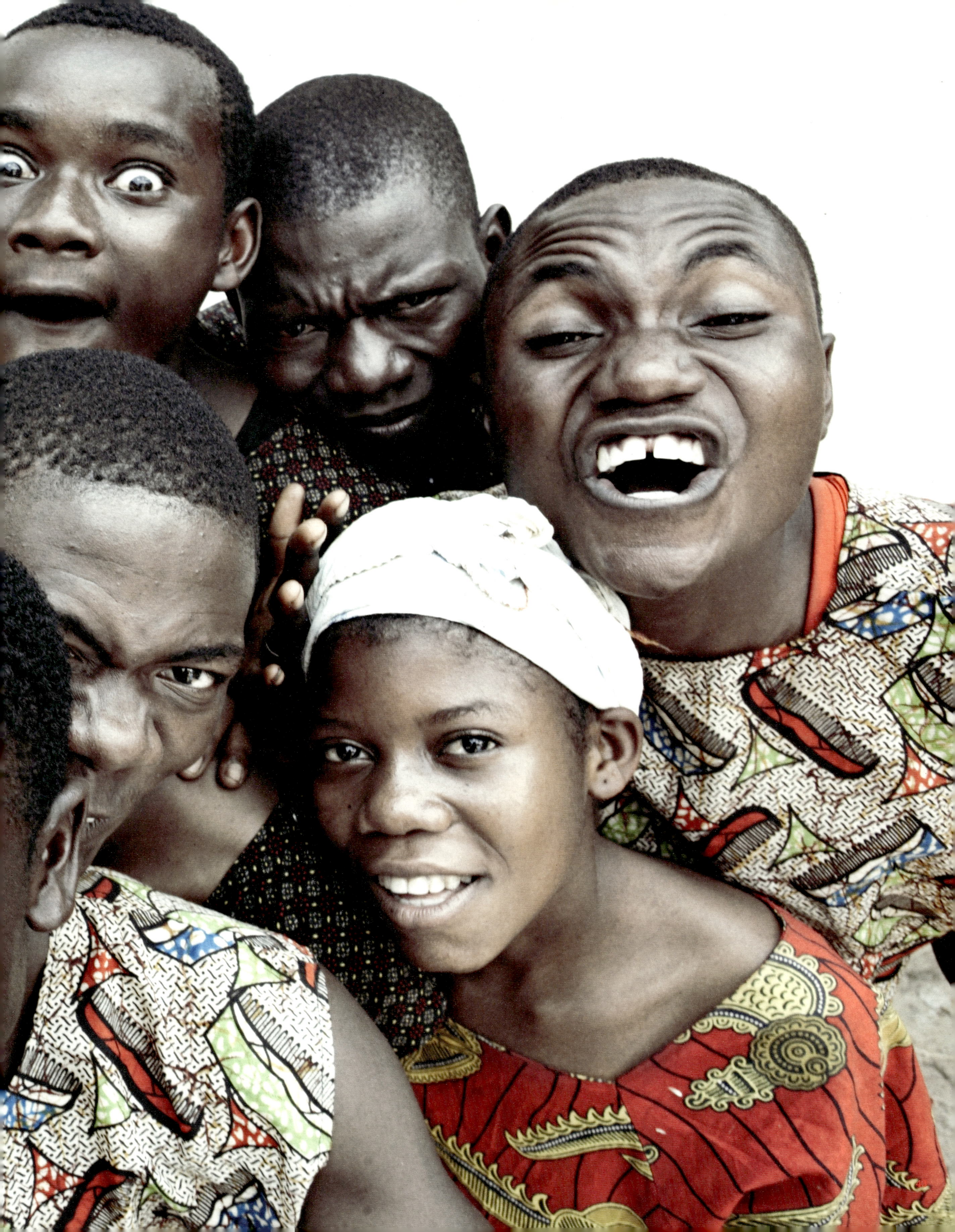

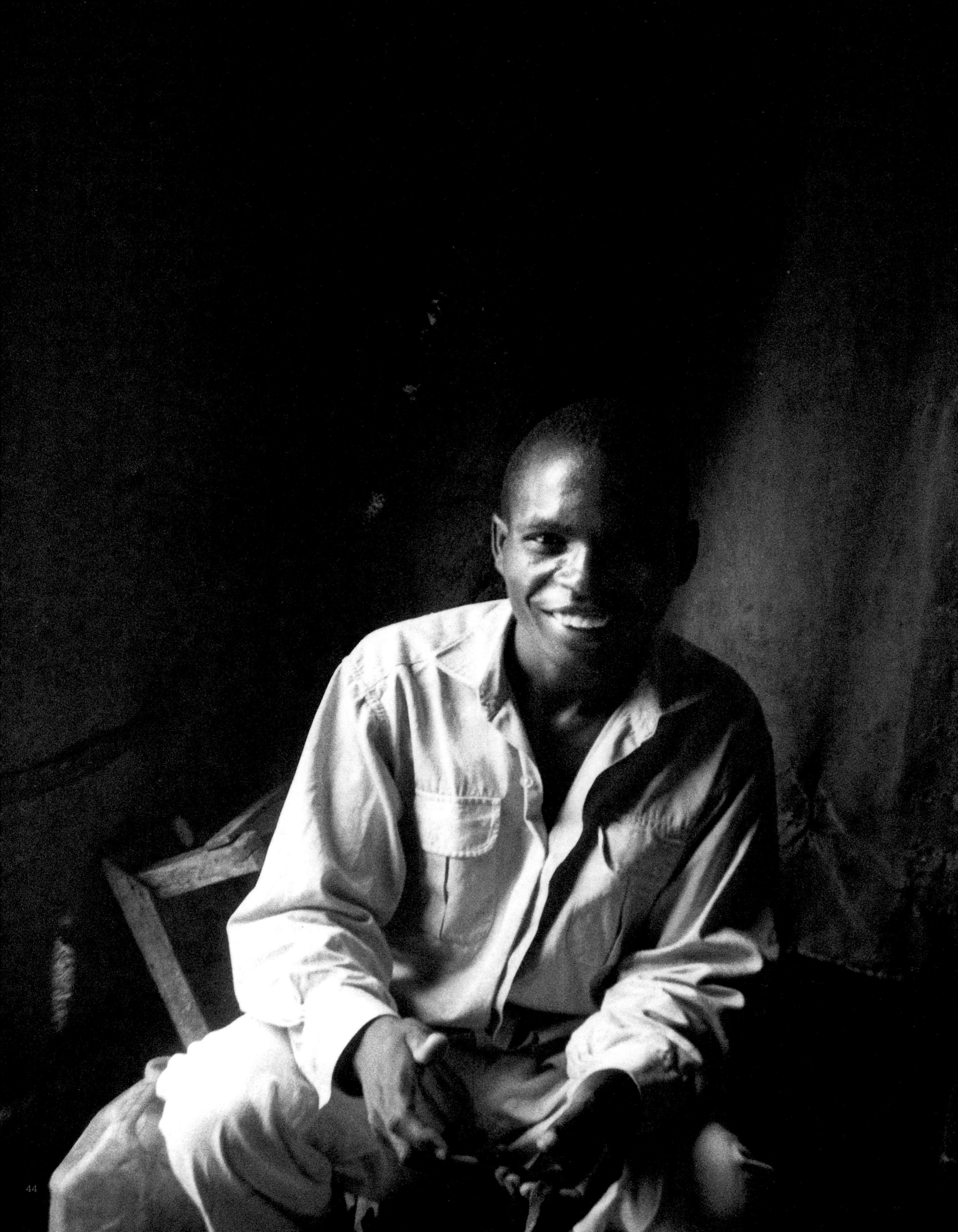

THE CONGO FAMILY ALBUM

PHOTOGRAPHS BY THE PEOPLE OF SANGE VILLAGE

As part of his 2009 visit to the DRC, Rankin ran a series of workshops, teaching around 200 people how to take their own images. Prior to the workshops, most had never seen a camera. Following the workshops, their brief was simple – take photos of the people and things you love.

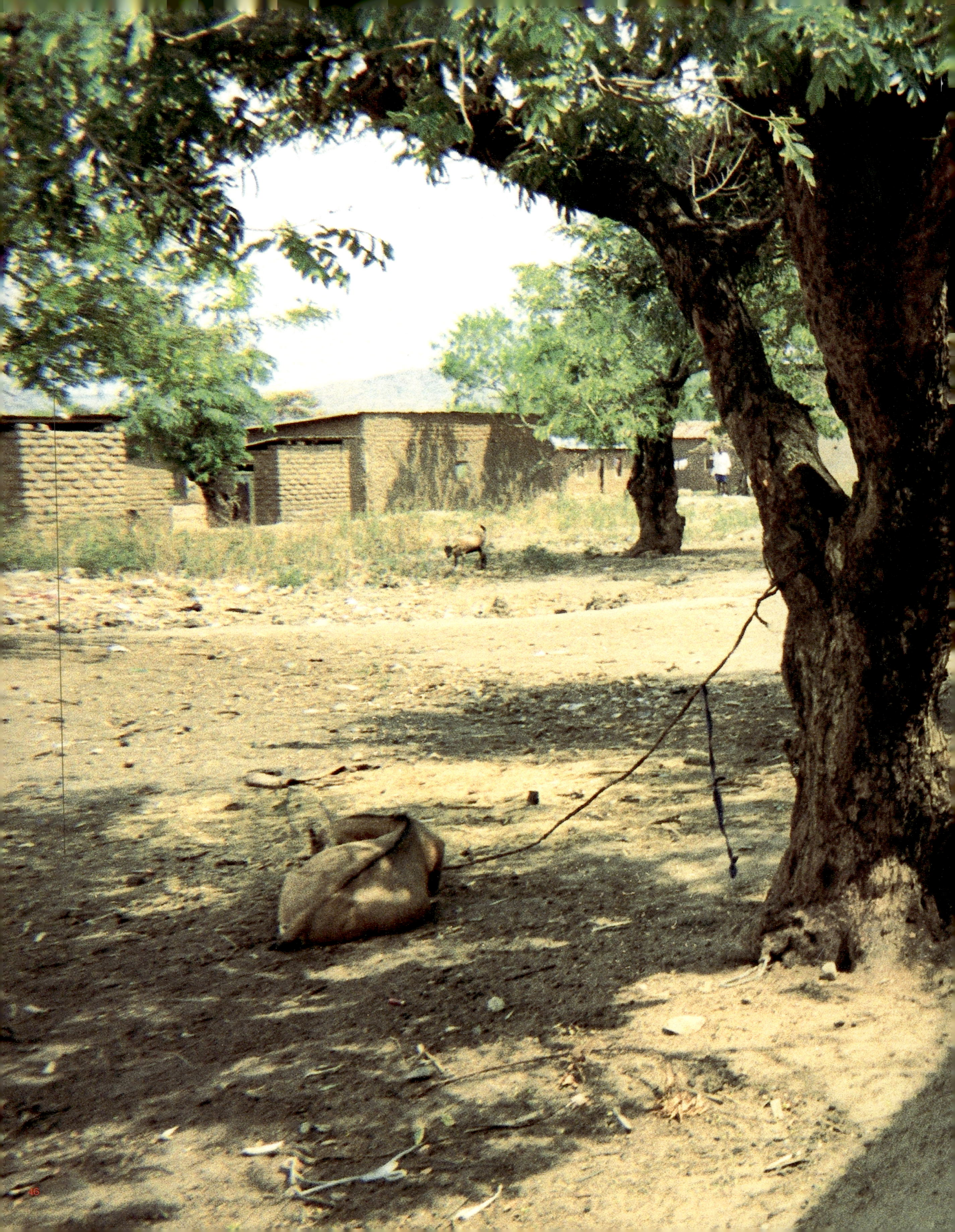

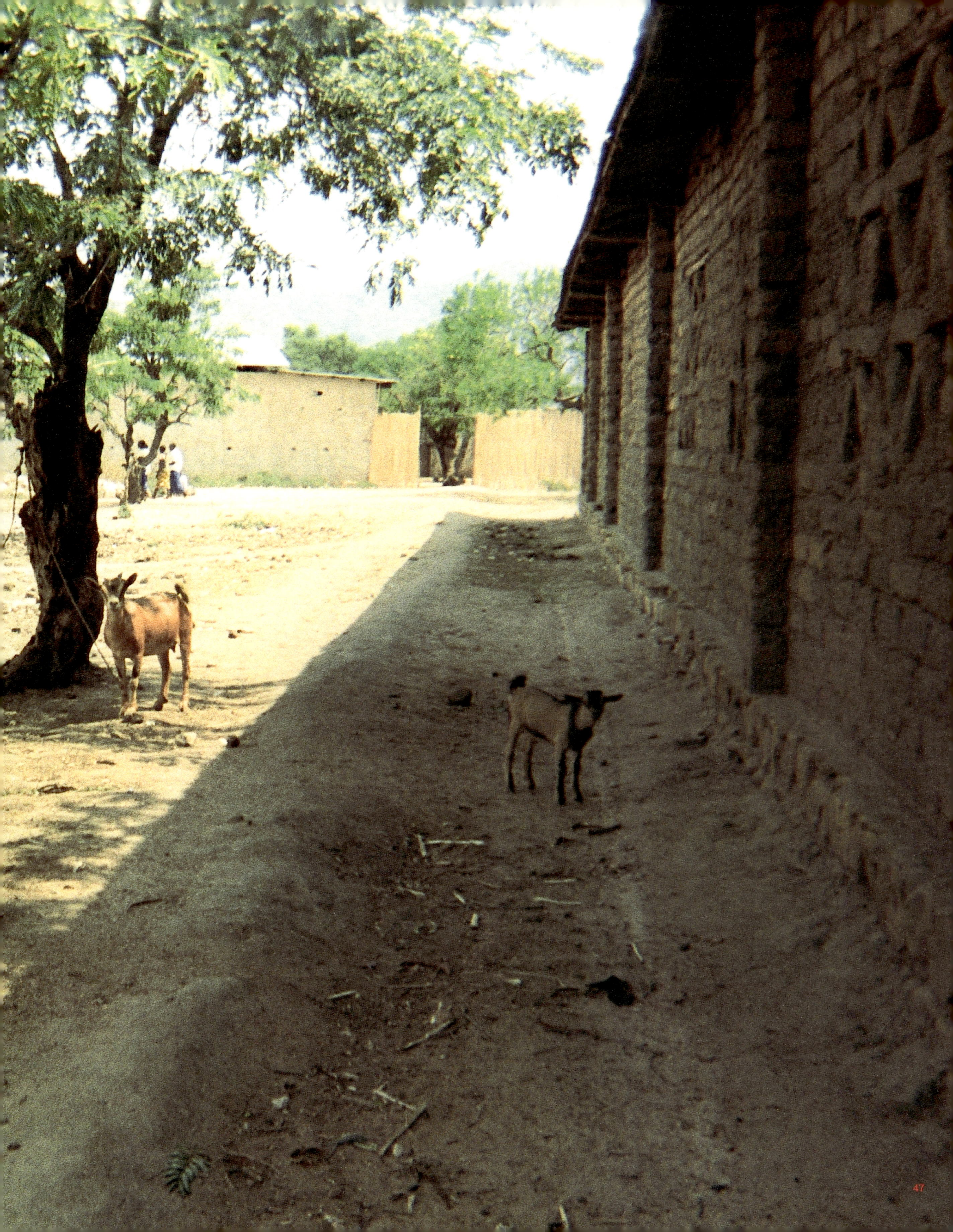

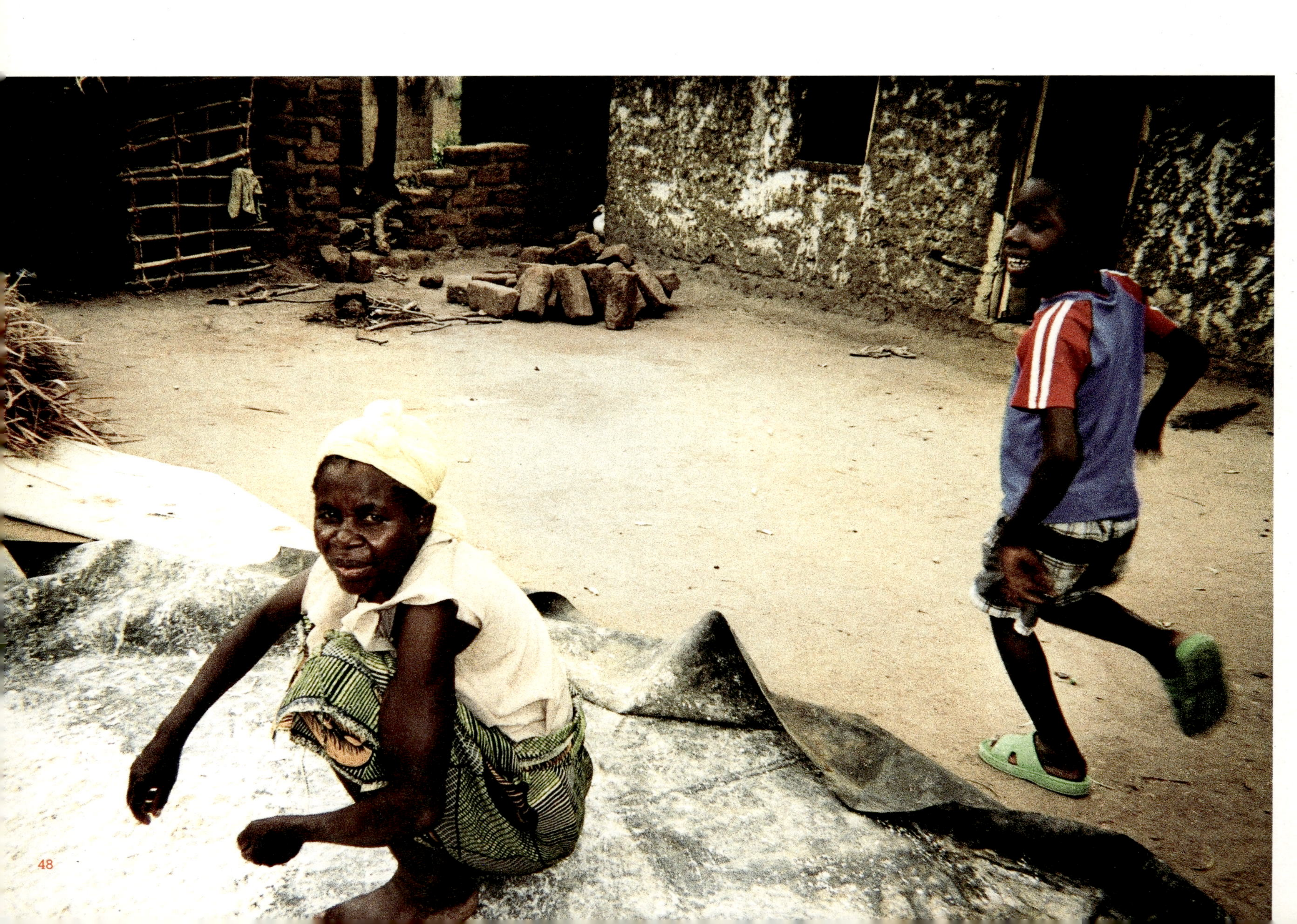

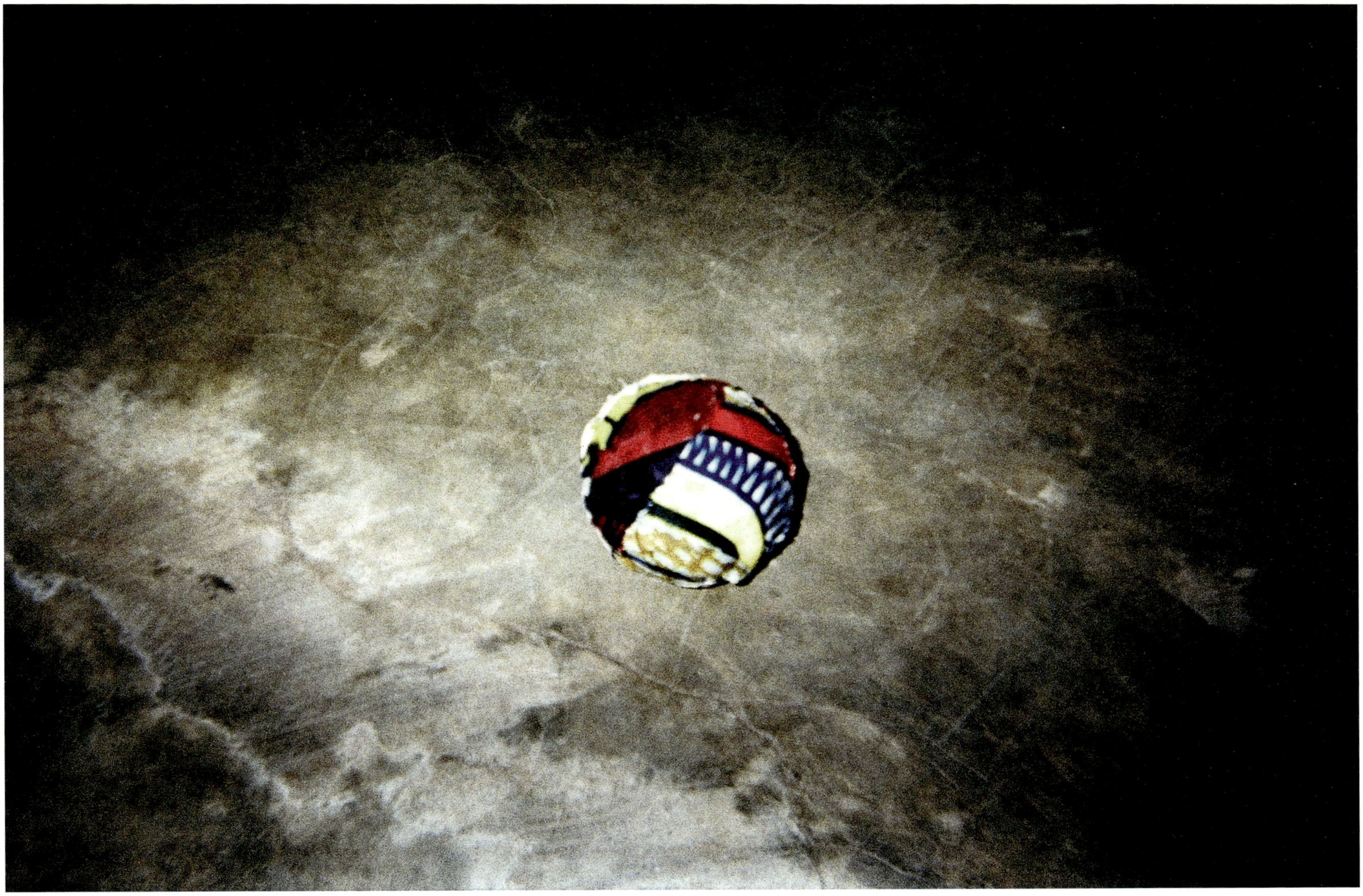

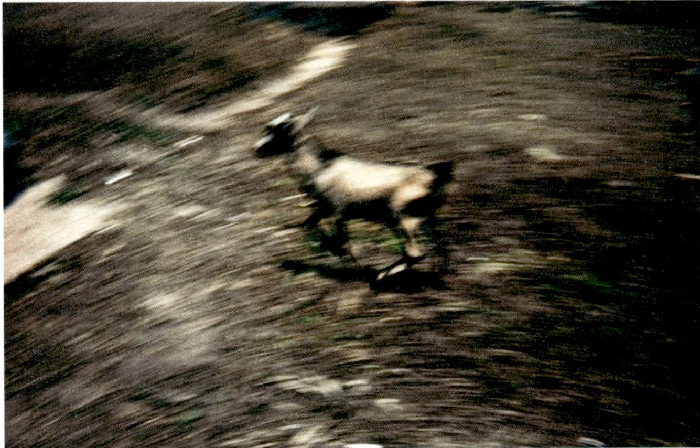

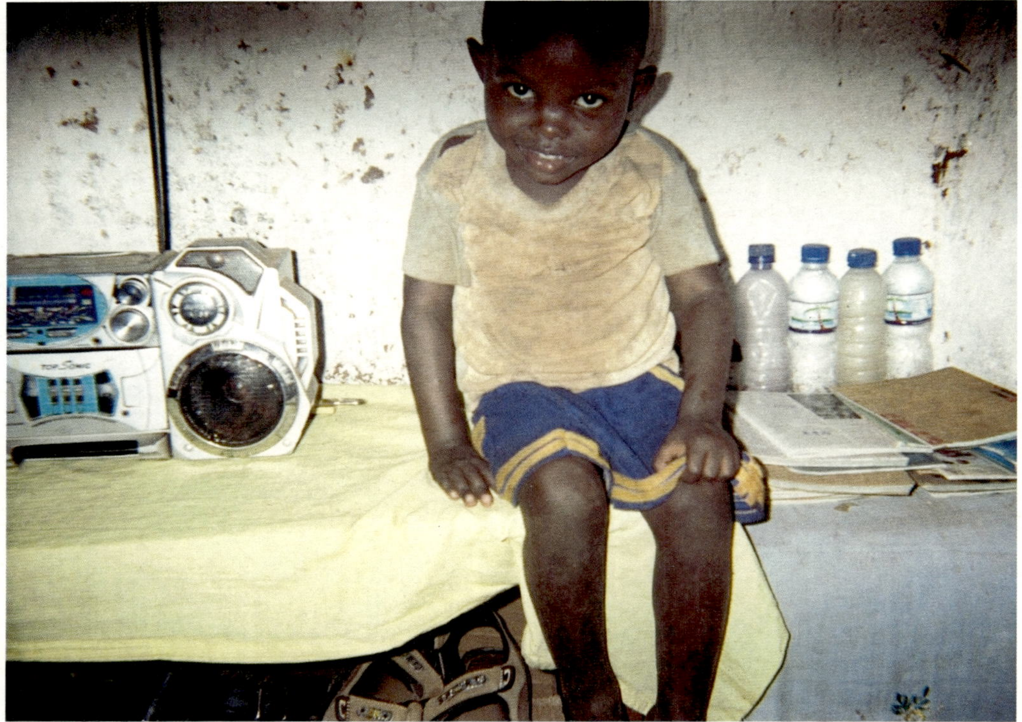

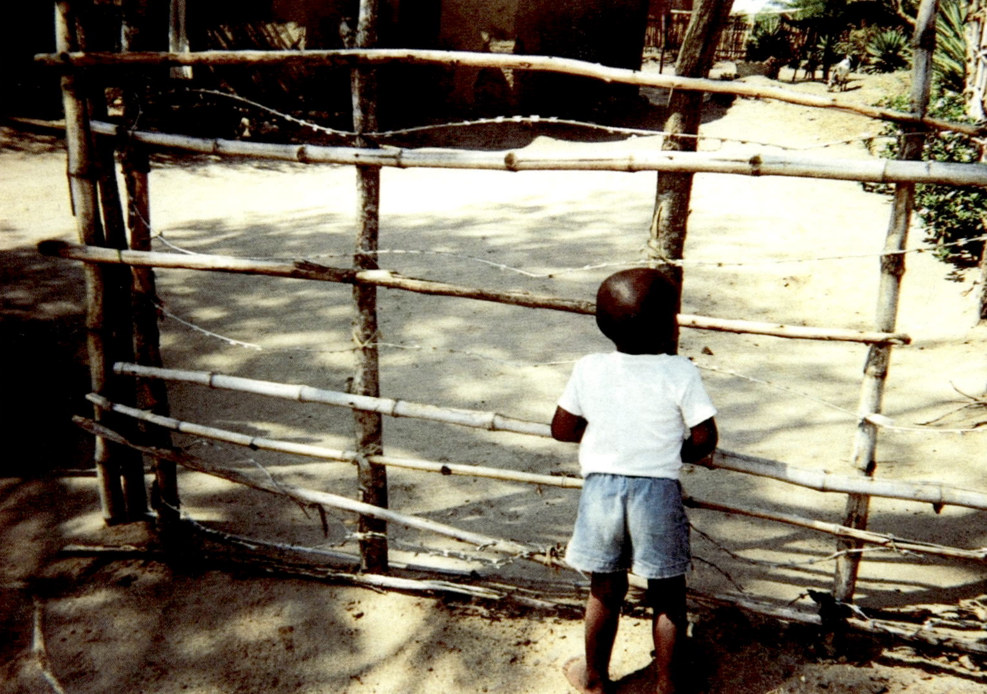

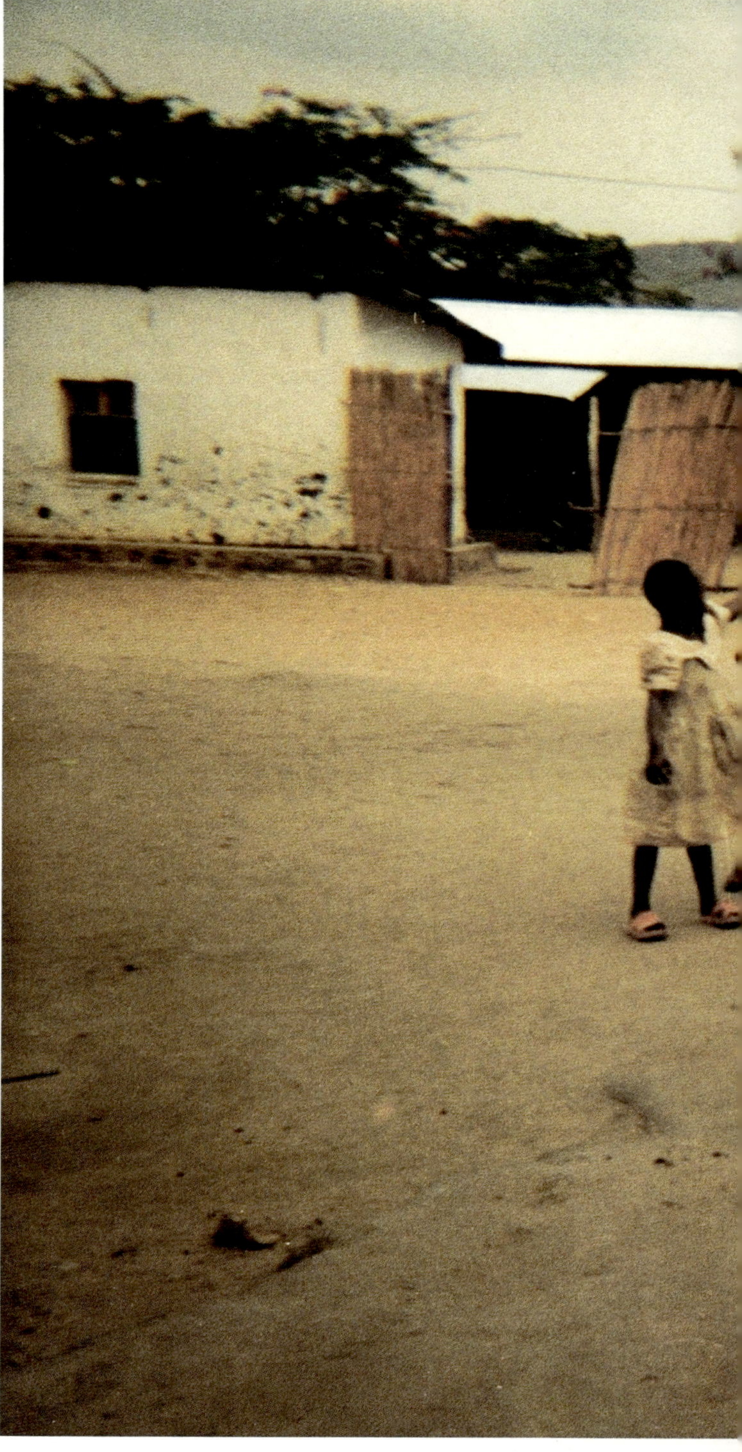

(Above)
– Photograph by Marie

"This is a picture of Saphari
(the neighbour's son). I love him."

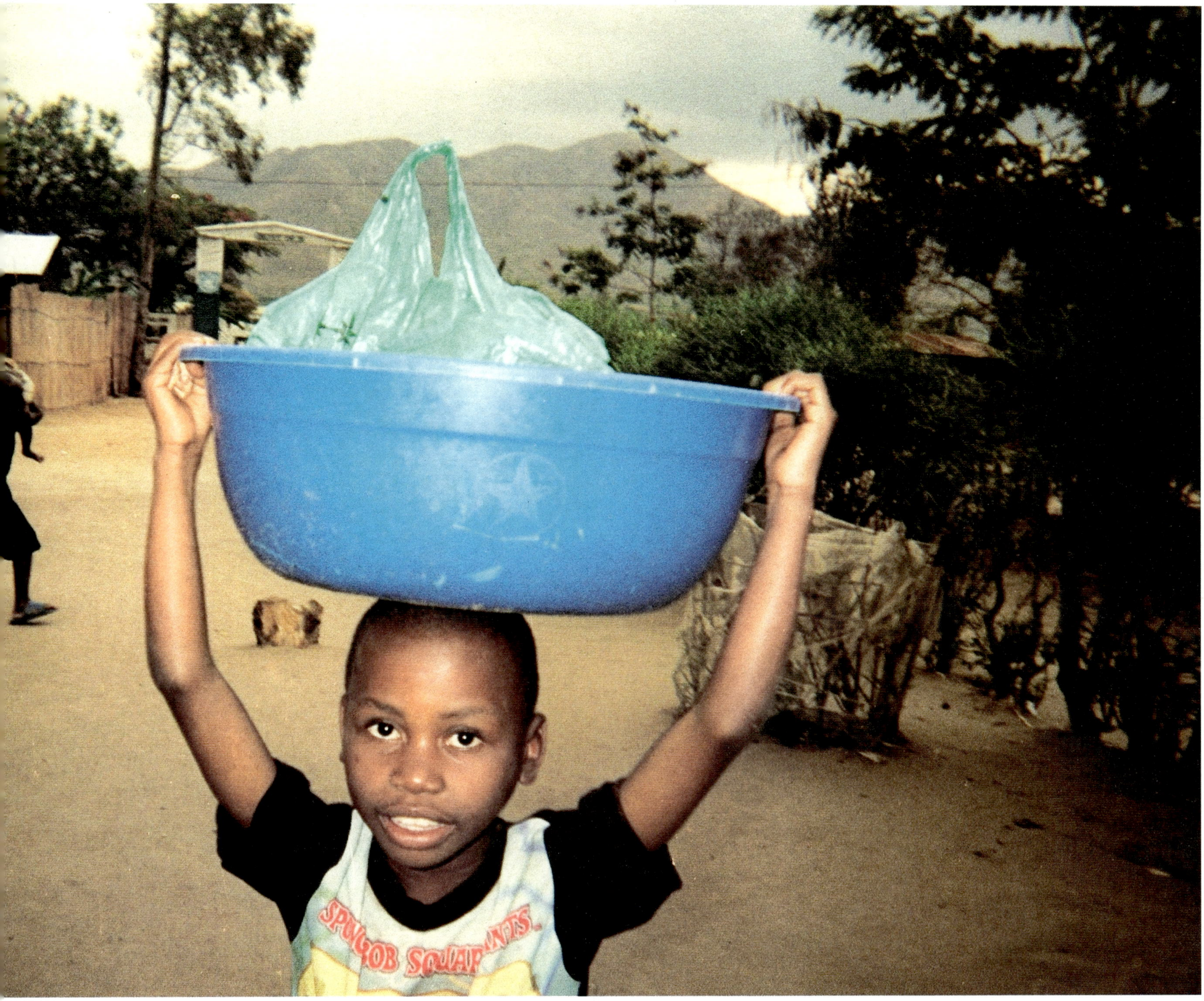

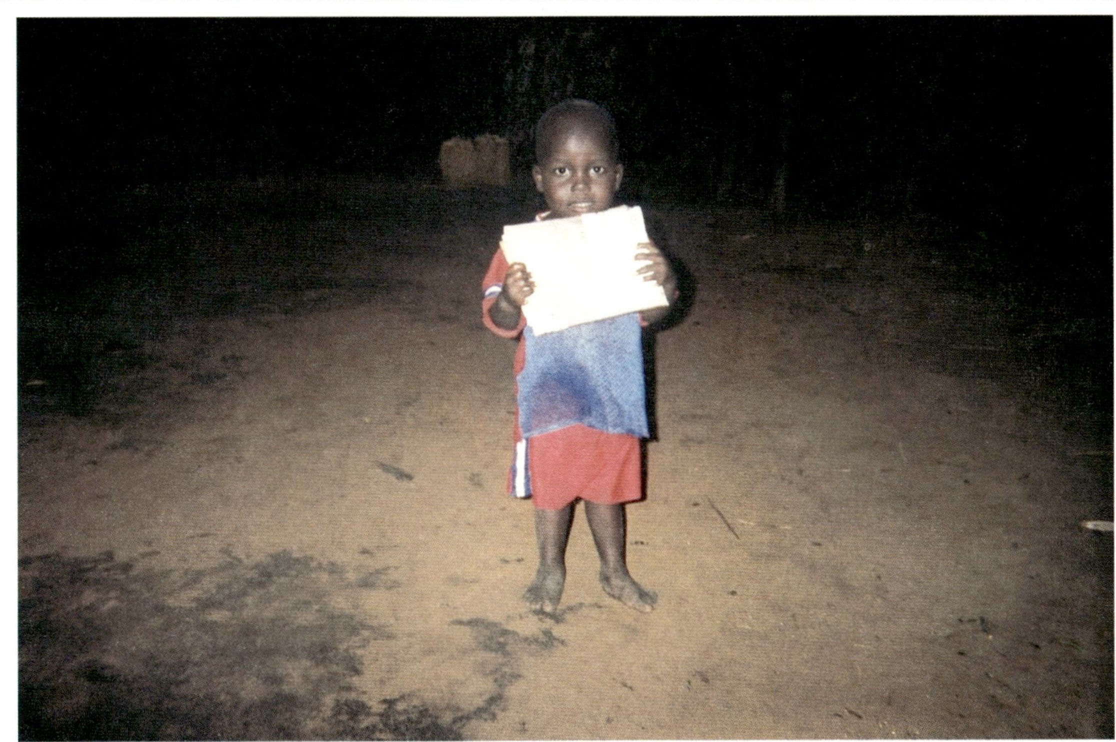

(Below)
 – Photograph by
Masumbuko Mugunyuro

"My brother was a mason; he was
murdered by the rebels last week
when he went to the fields to look
for food. When I see someone
building it reminds me of him.
I took this photograph so that every time I look at it I will think of
my brother Ndende."

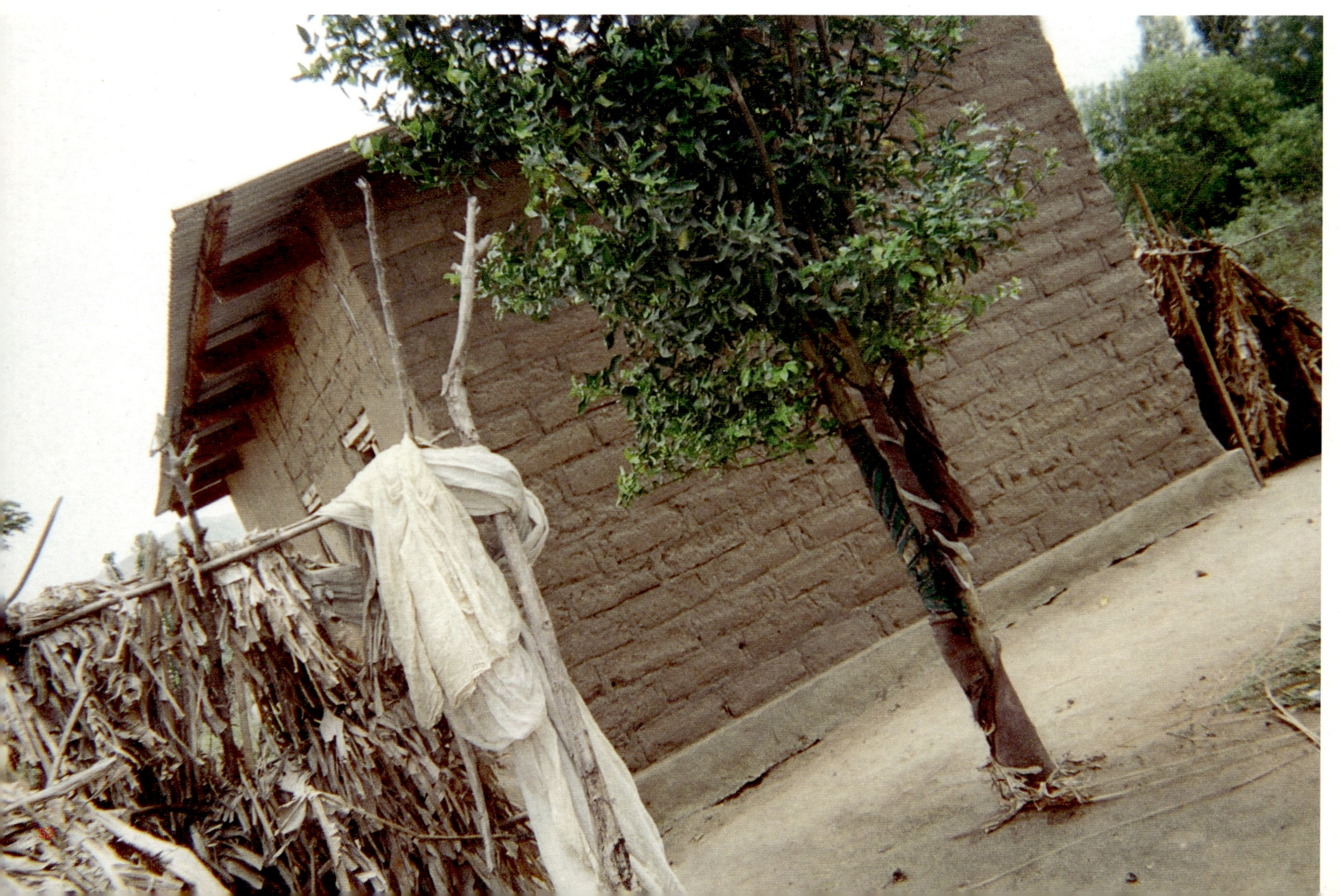

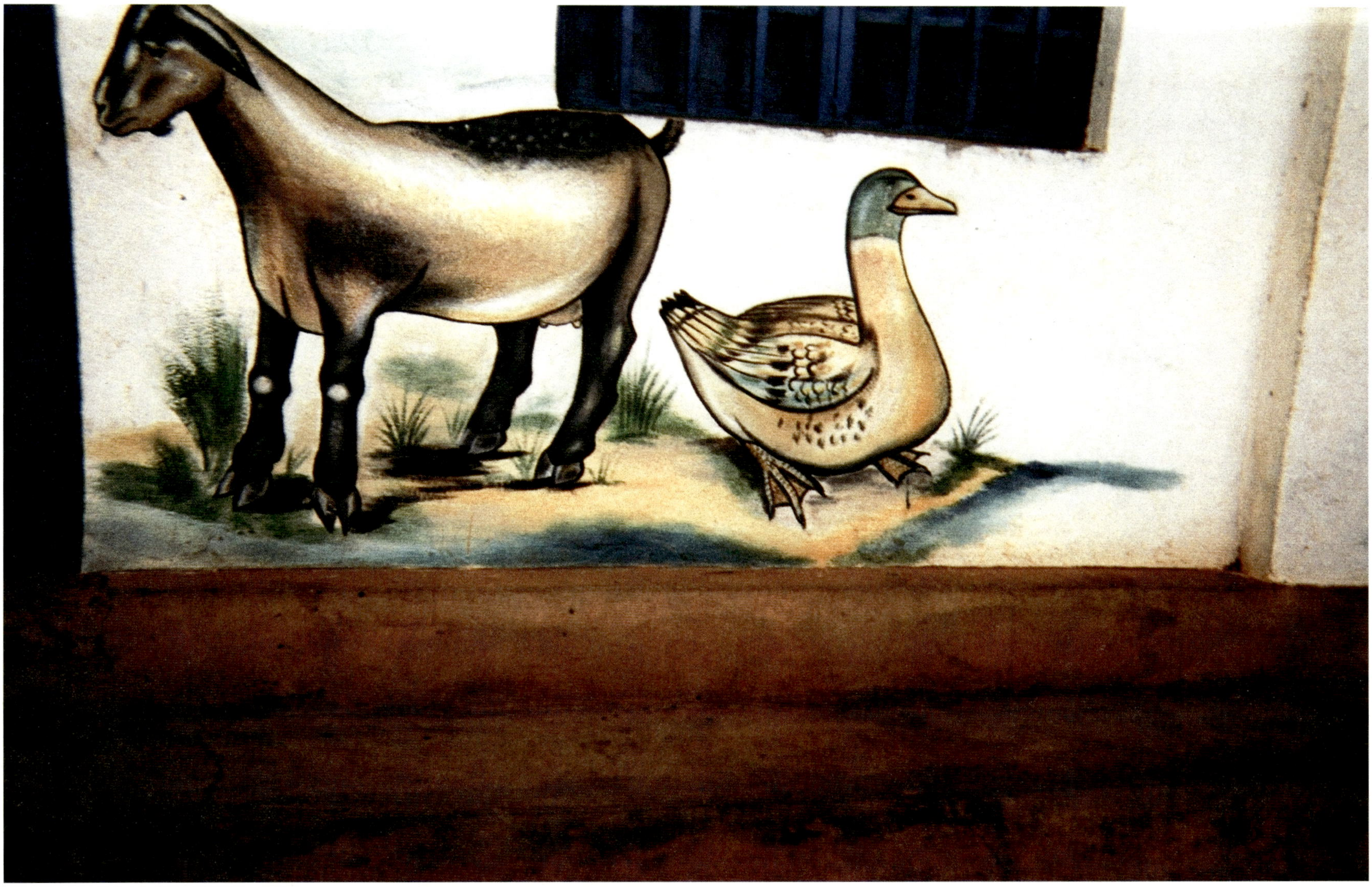

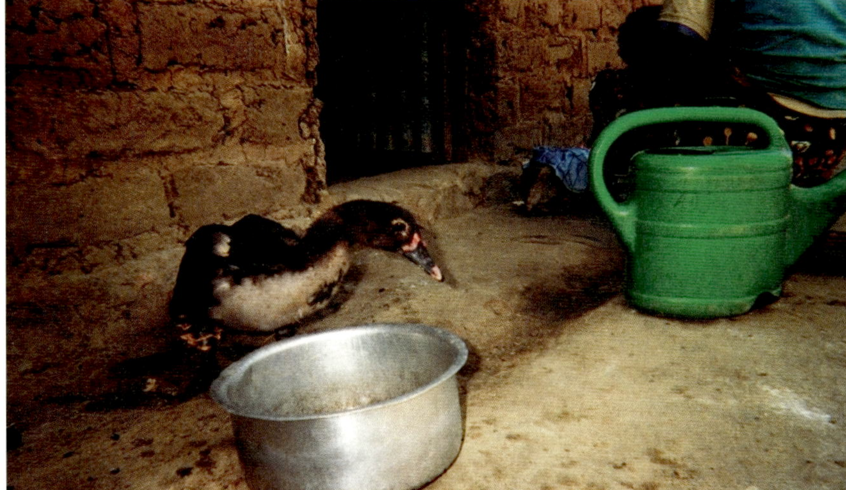

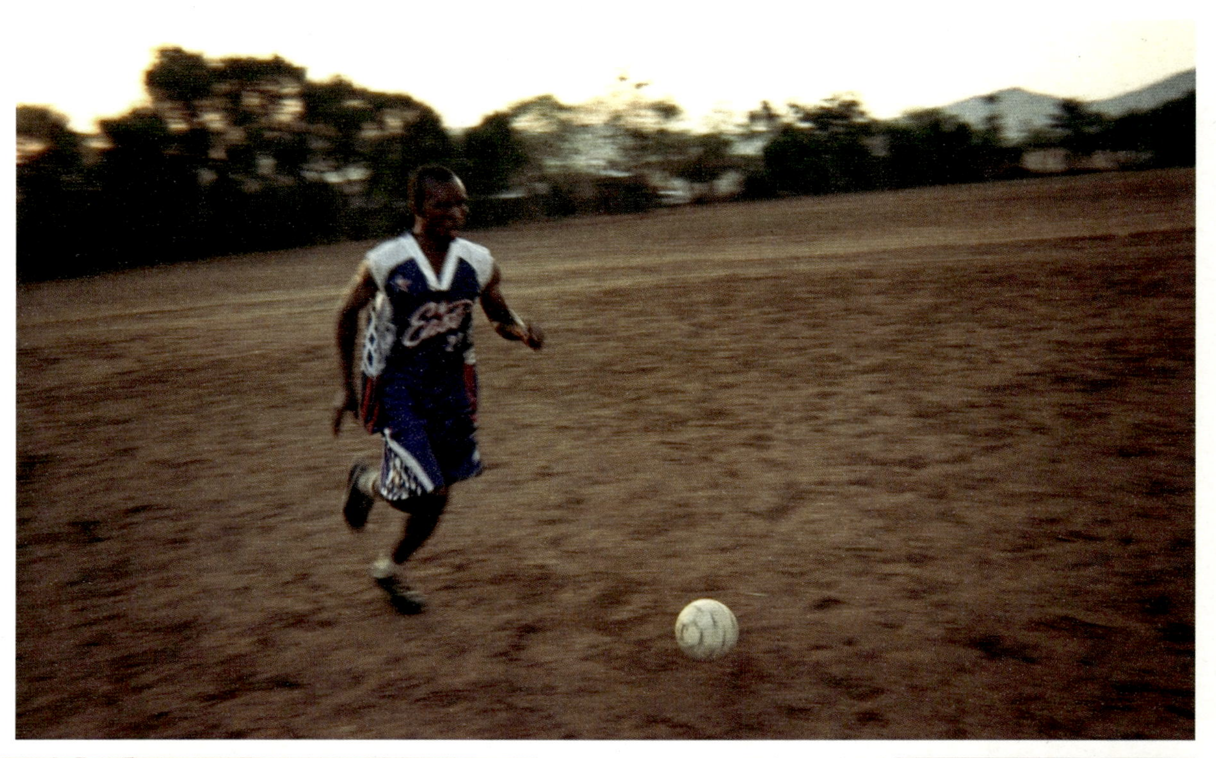

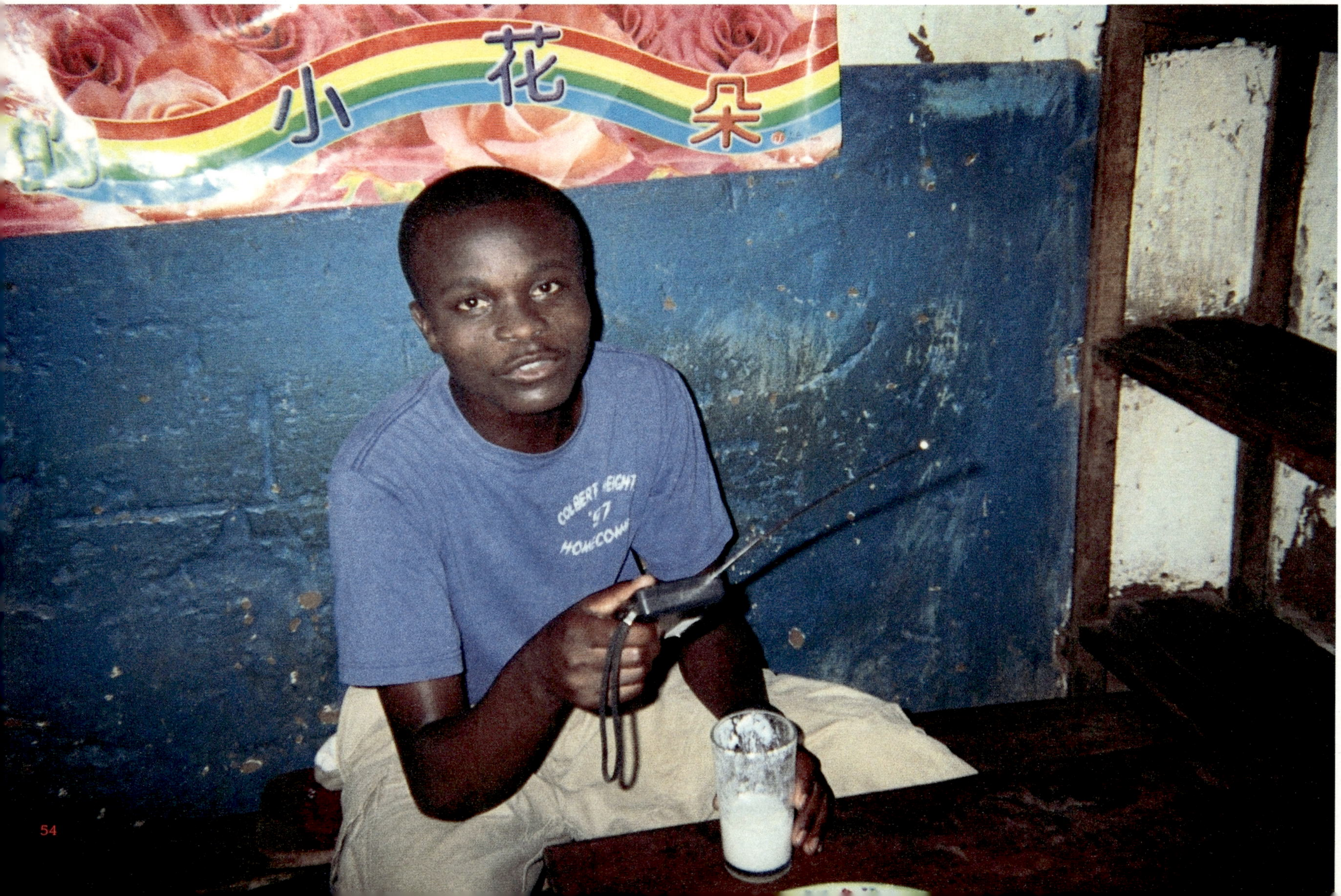

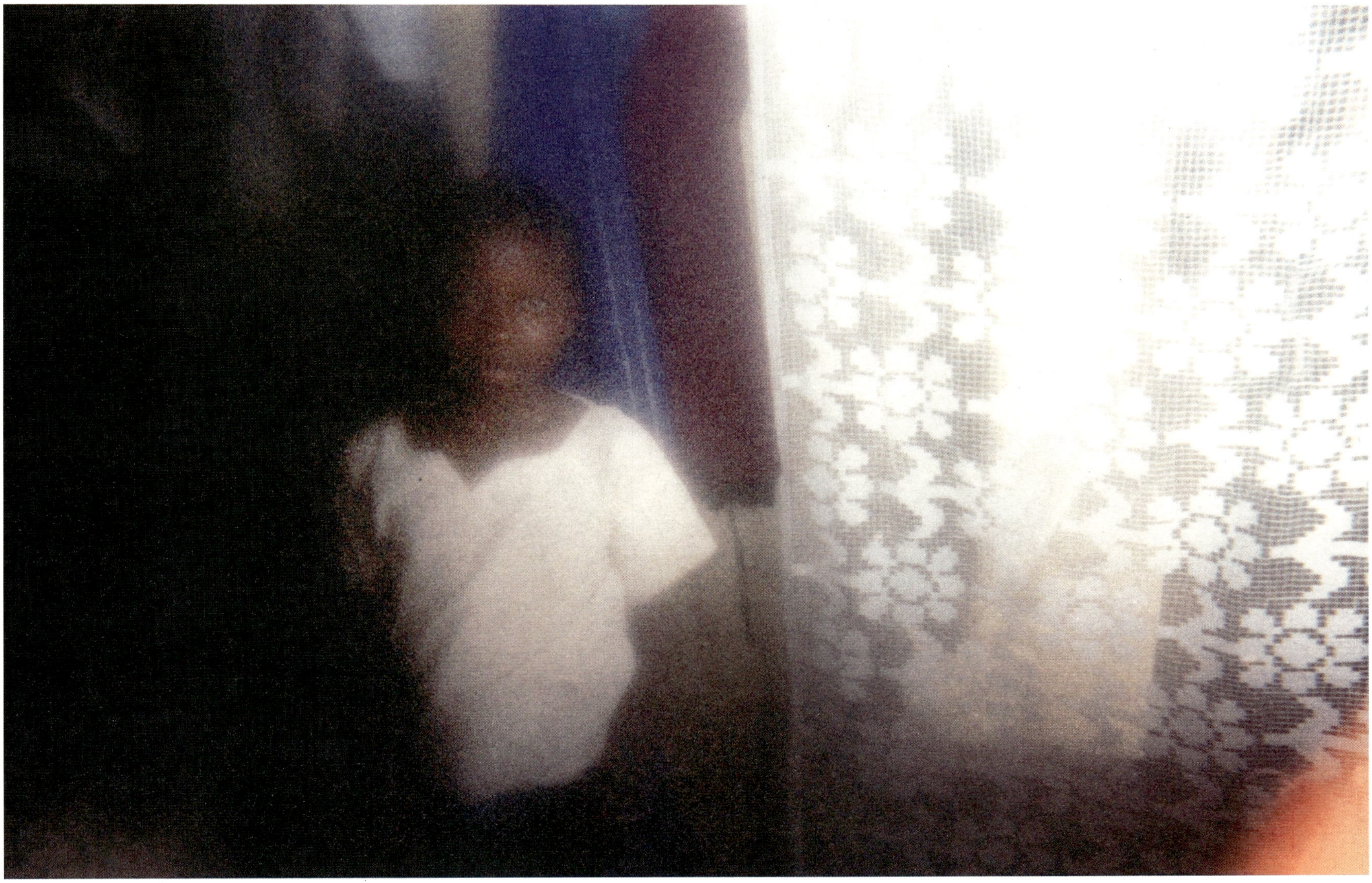

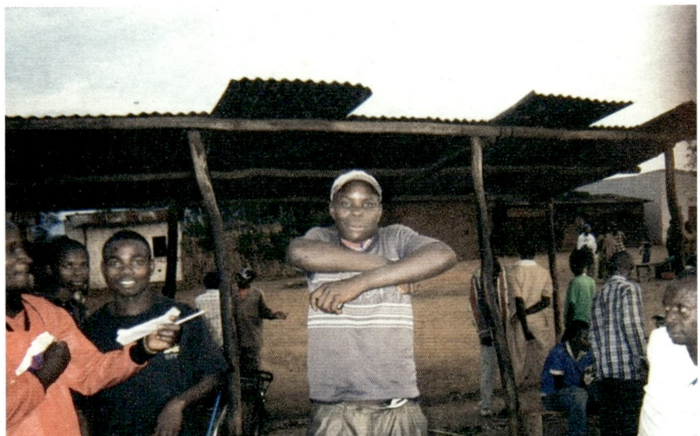

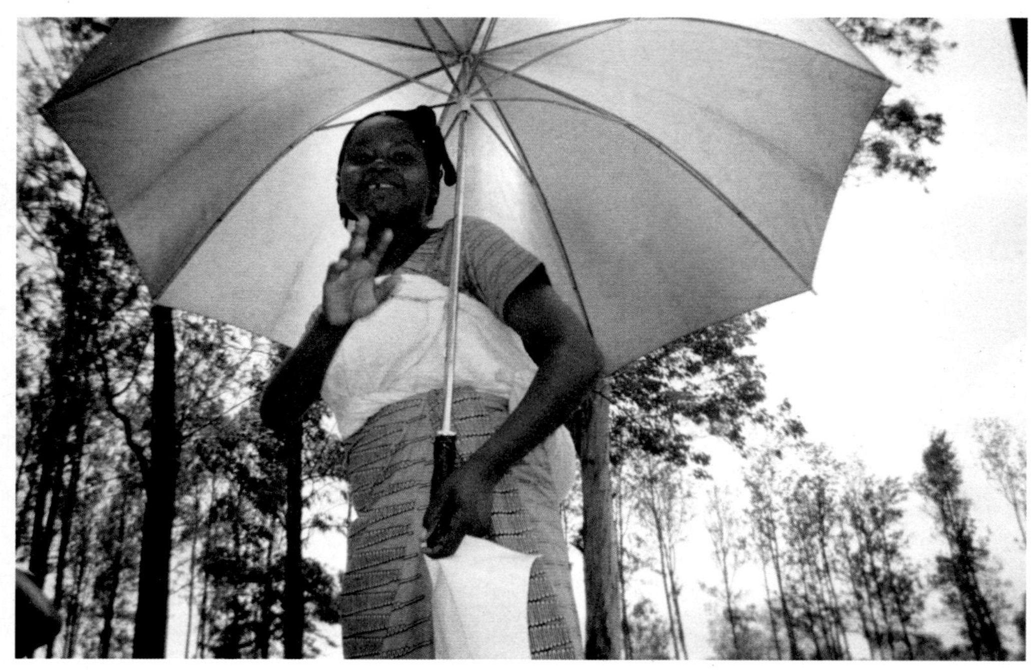

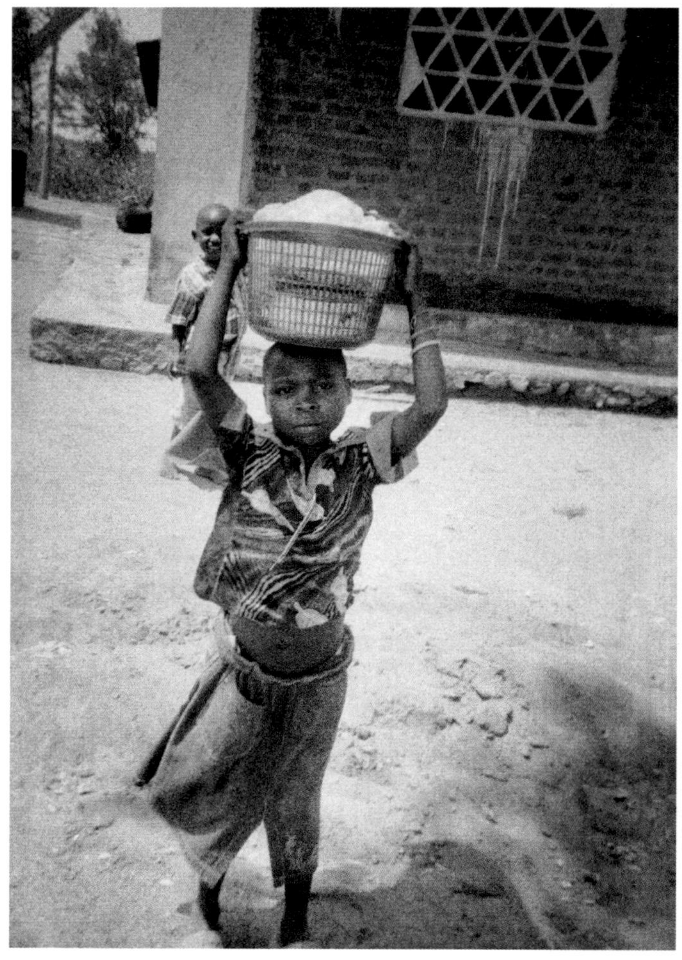

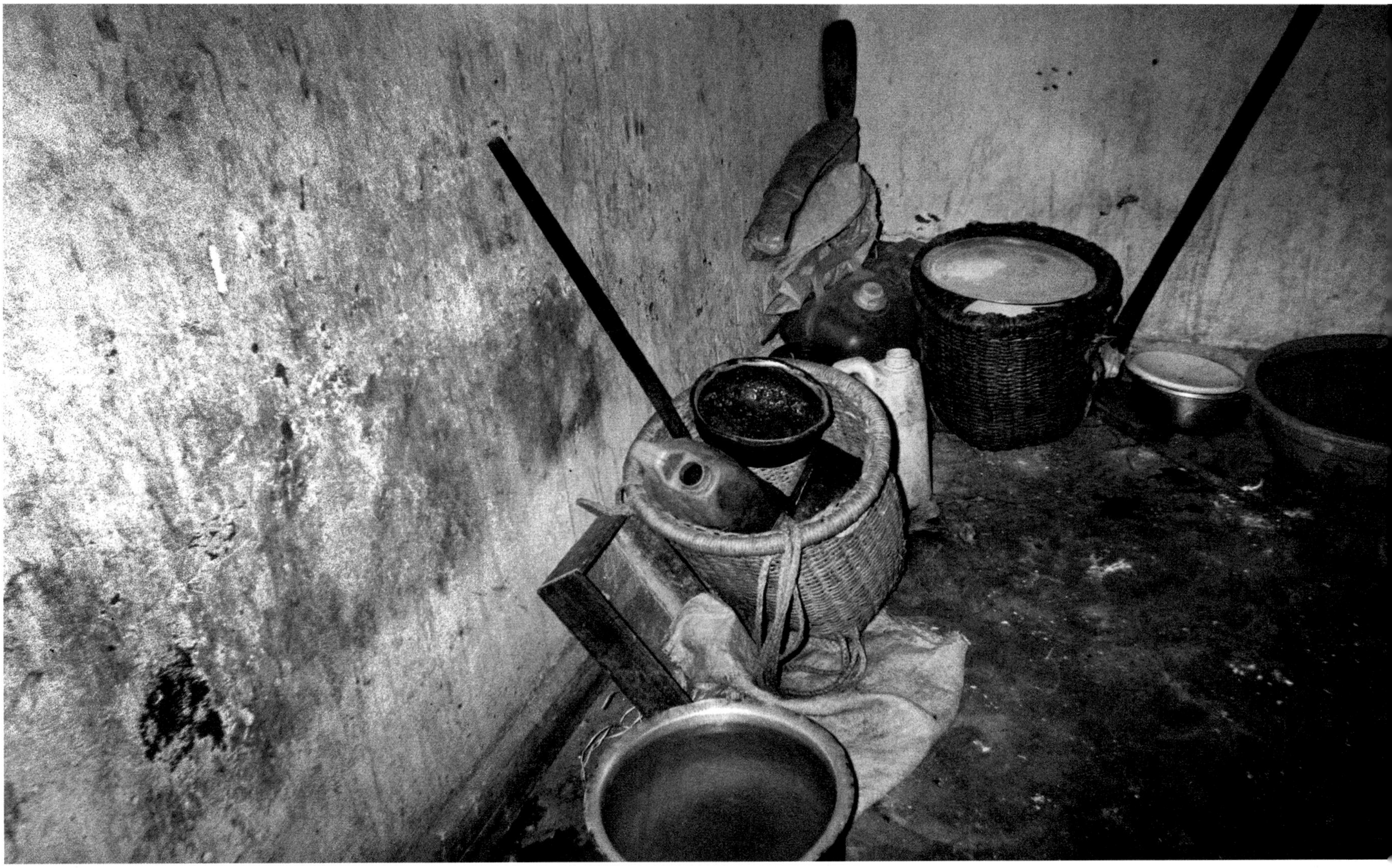

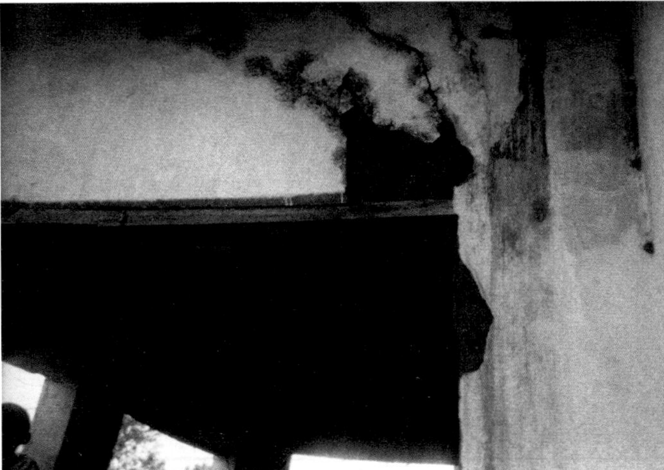

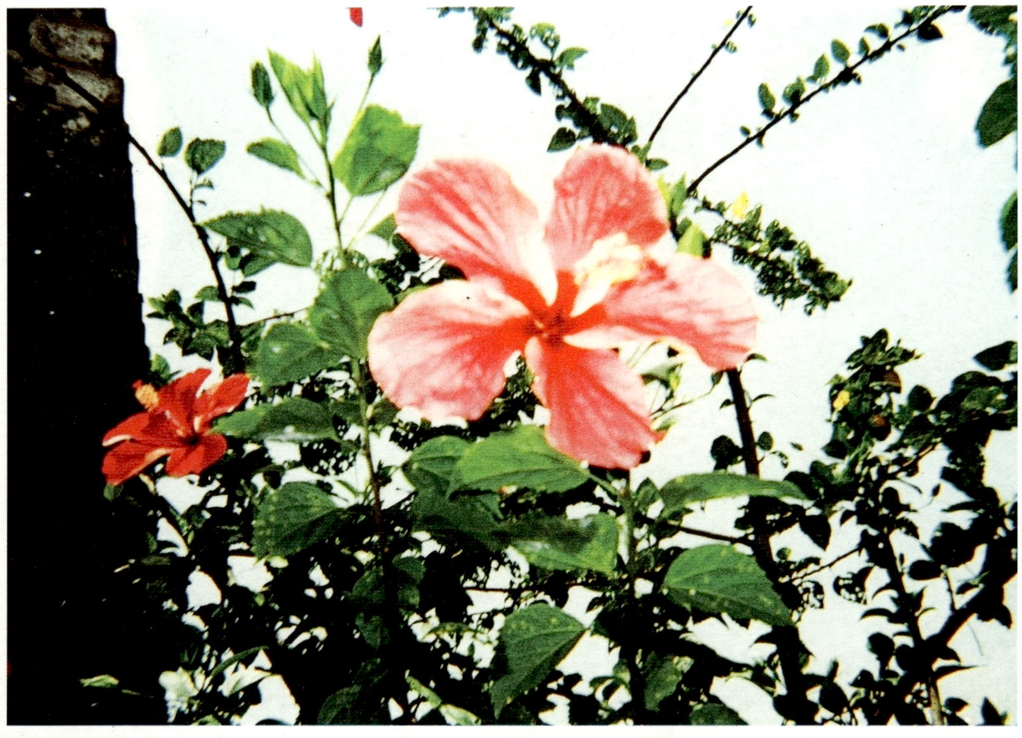

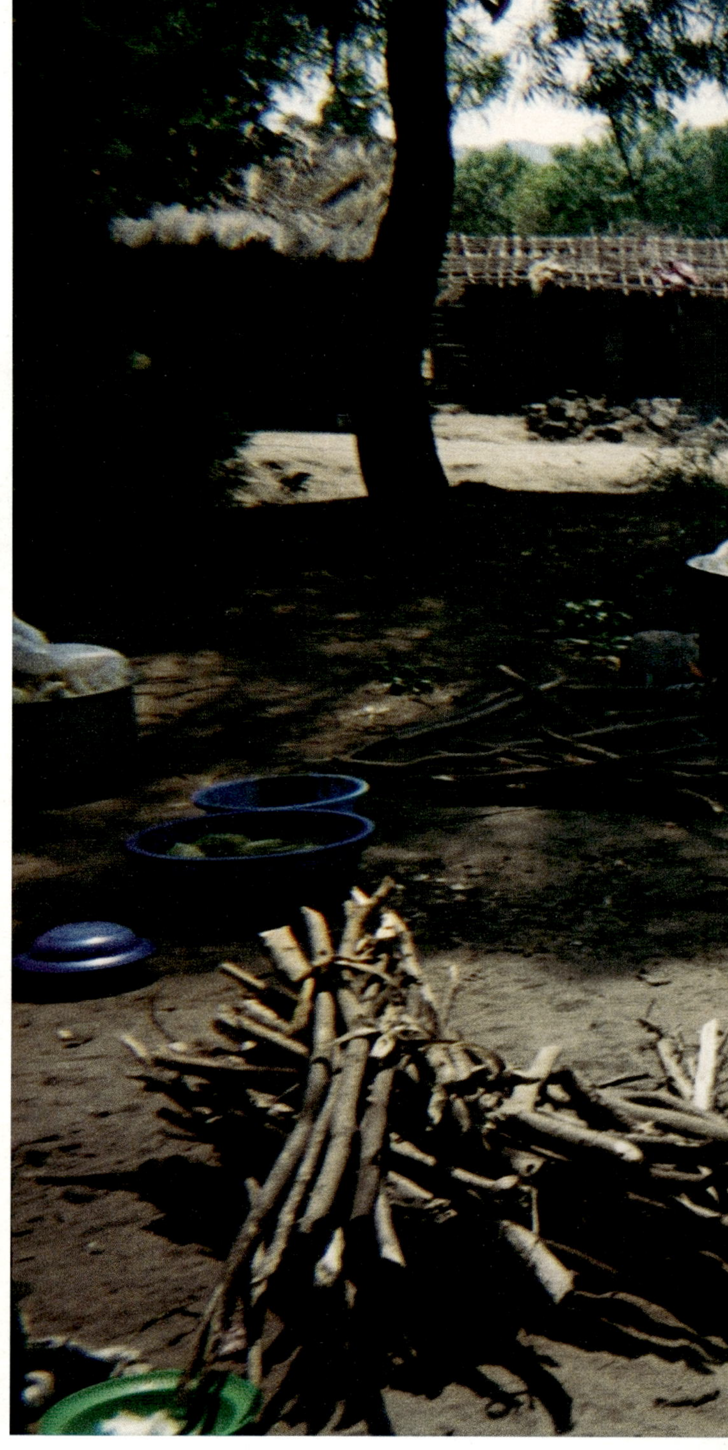

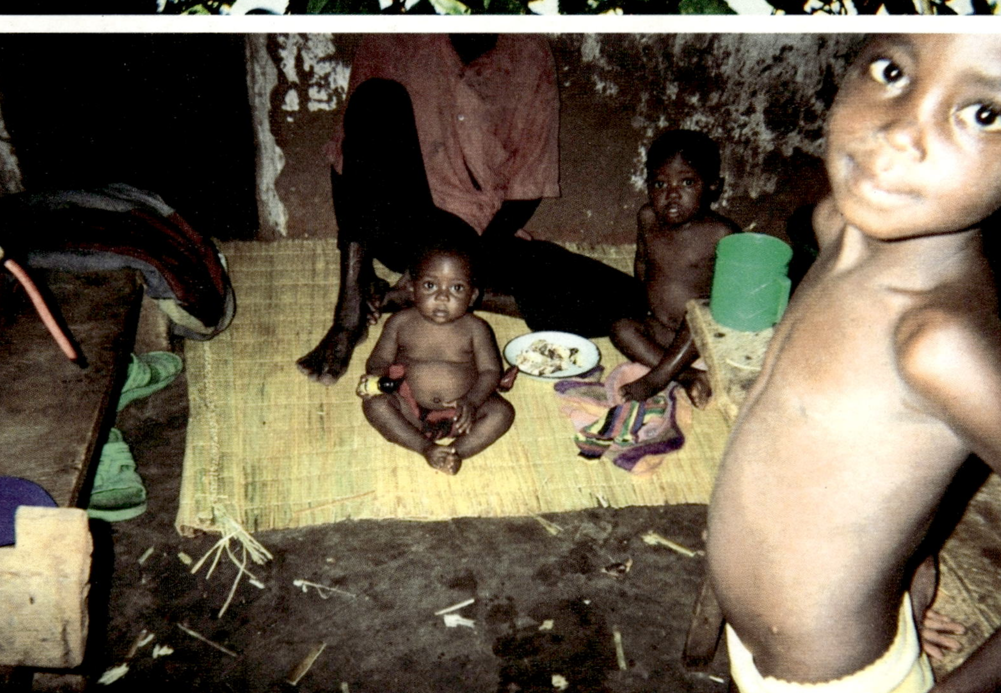

(Top Left)
– Photograph by Mwangaza

"I love nature. We had lots of flow-
ers and trees in our garden at
home in the hills."

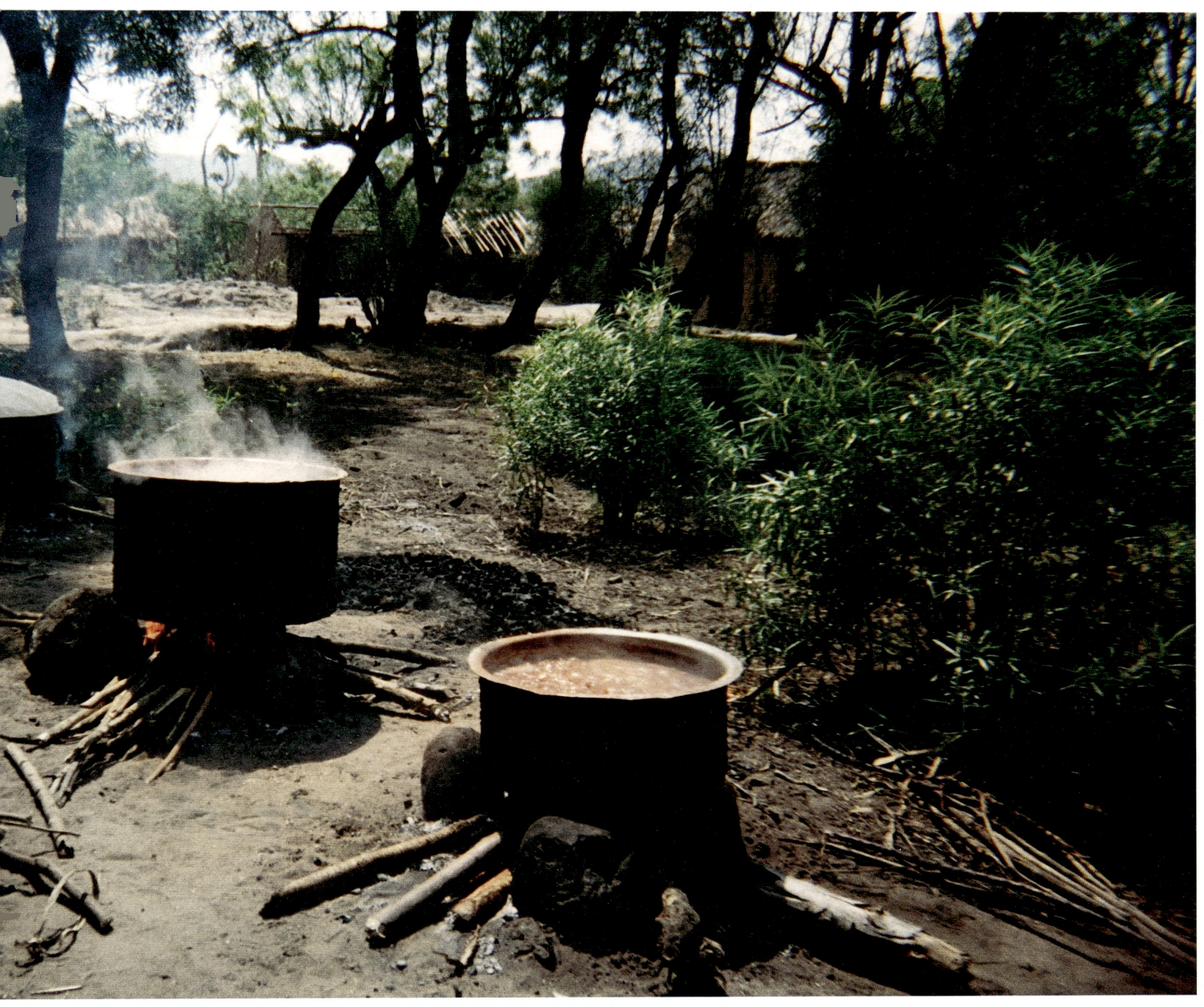

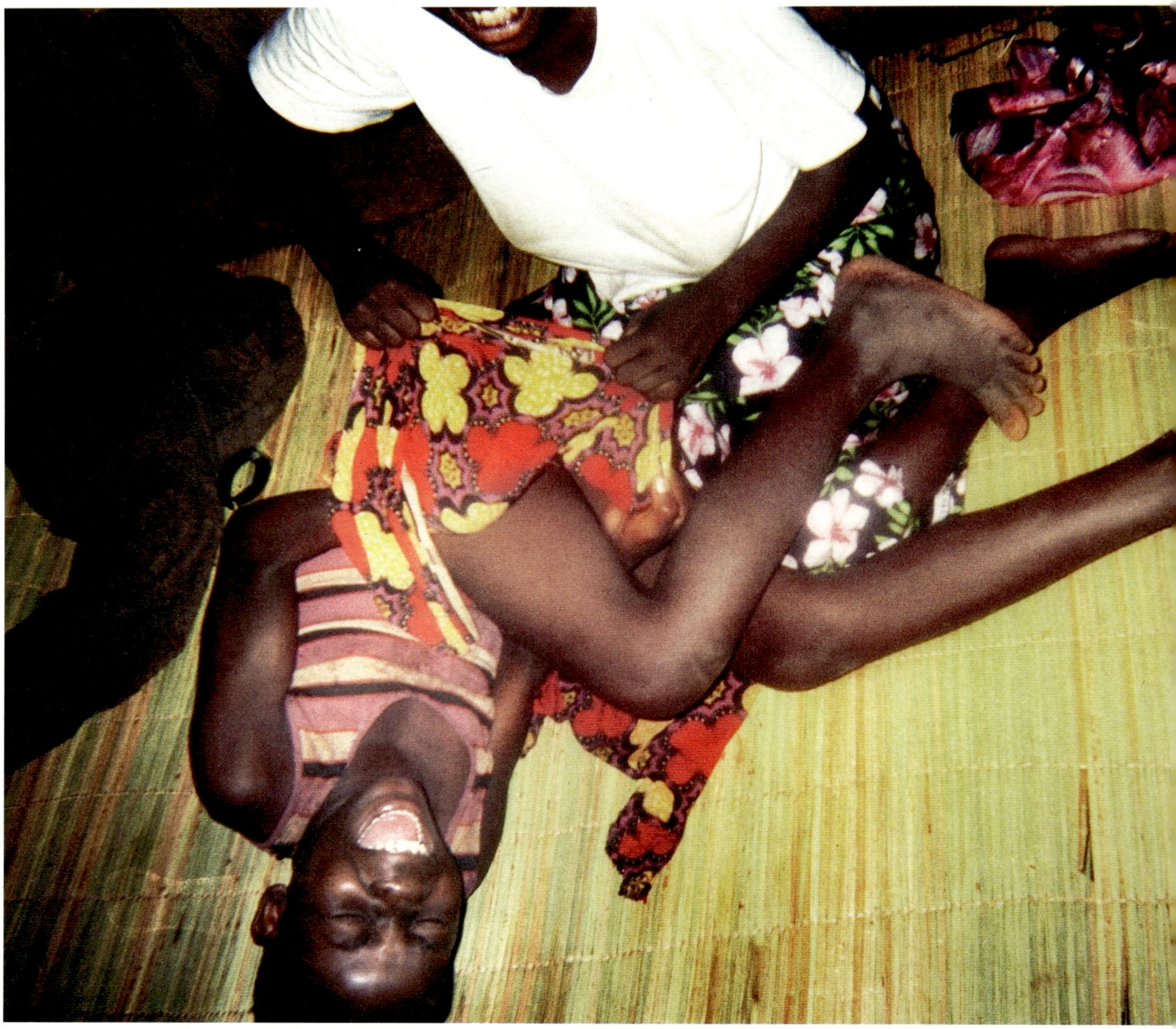

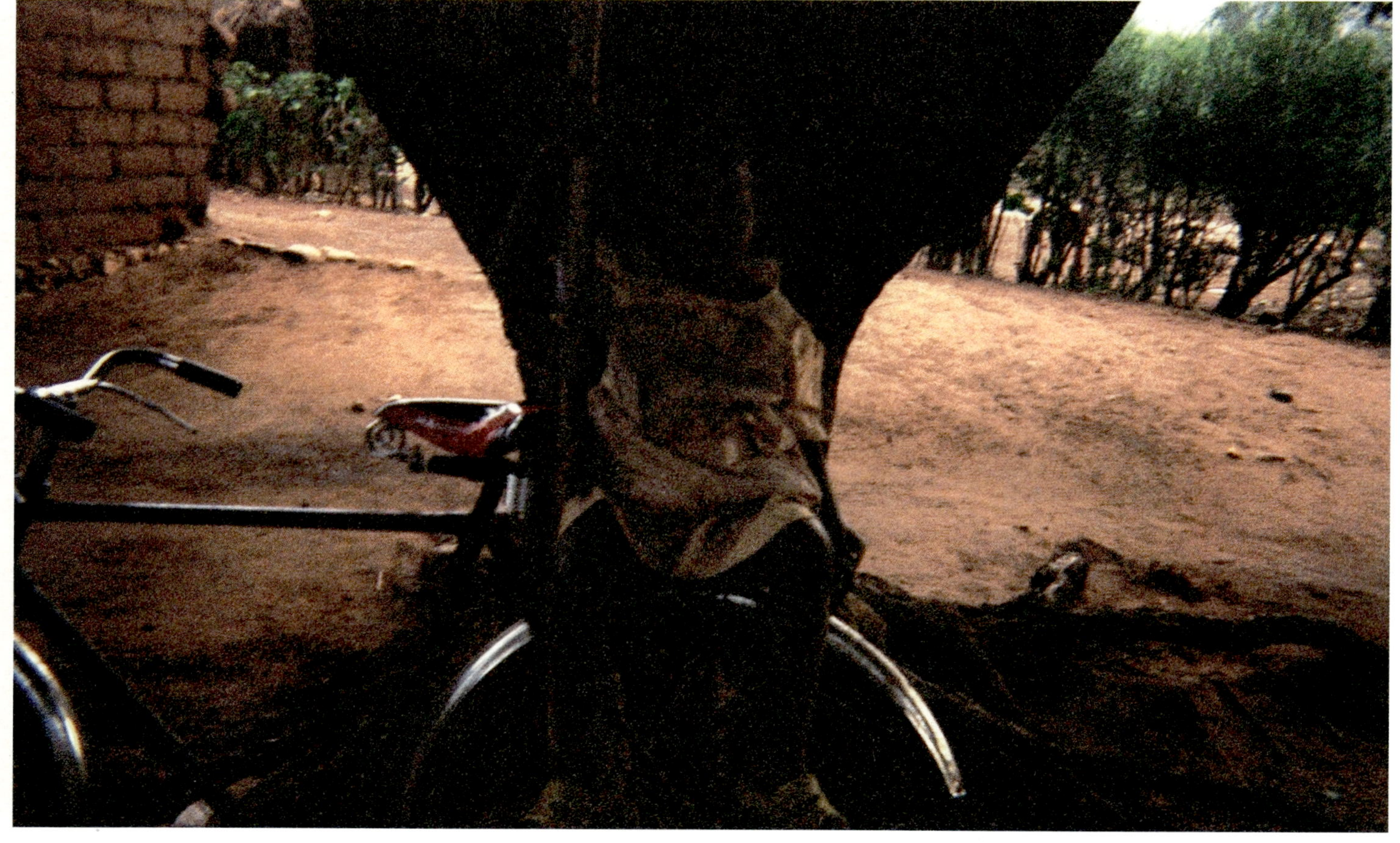

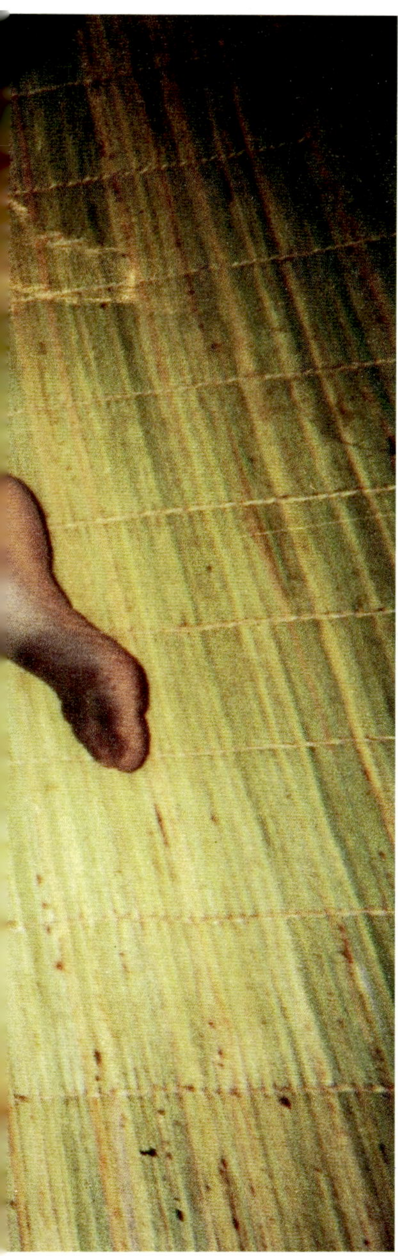

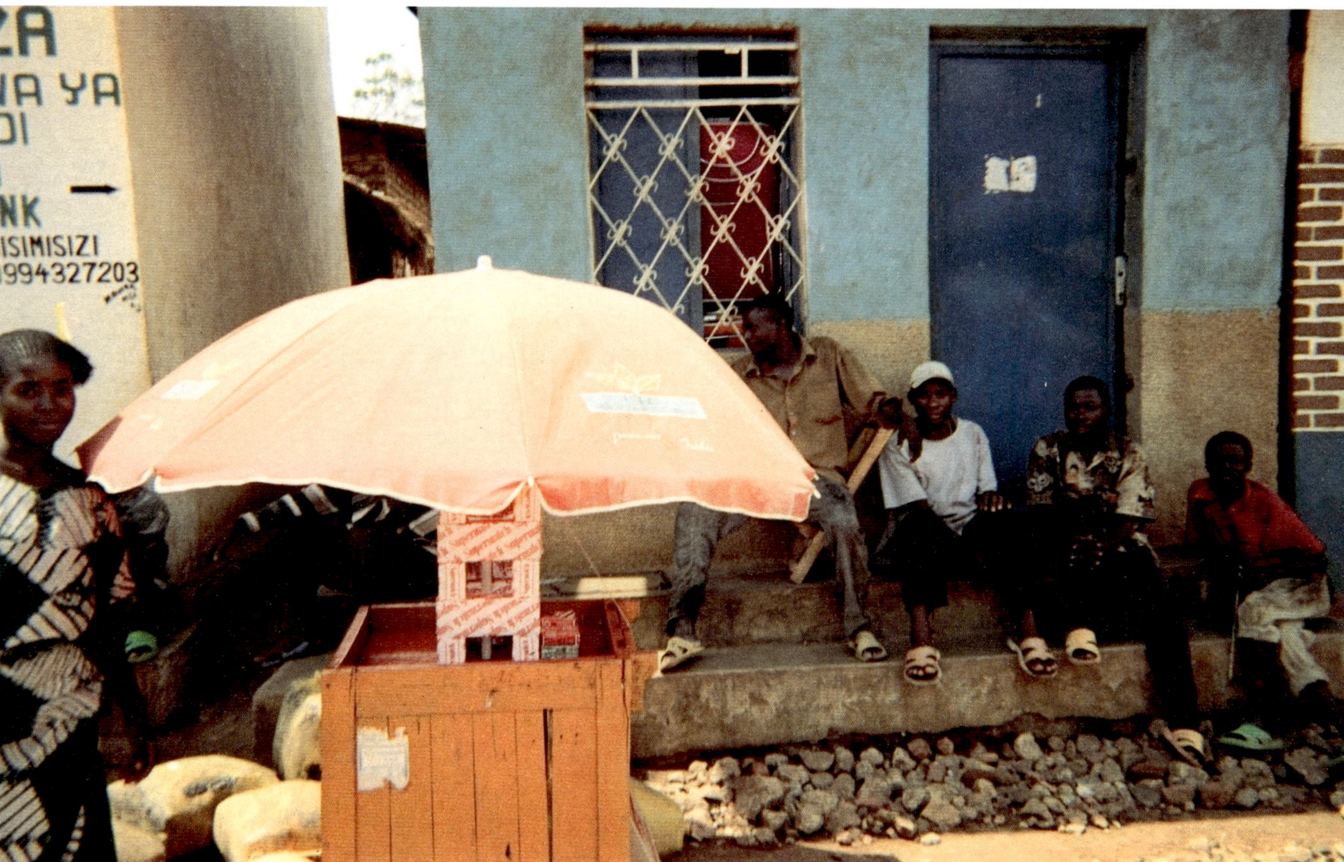

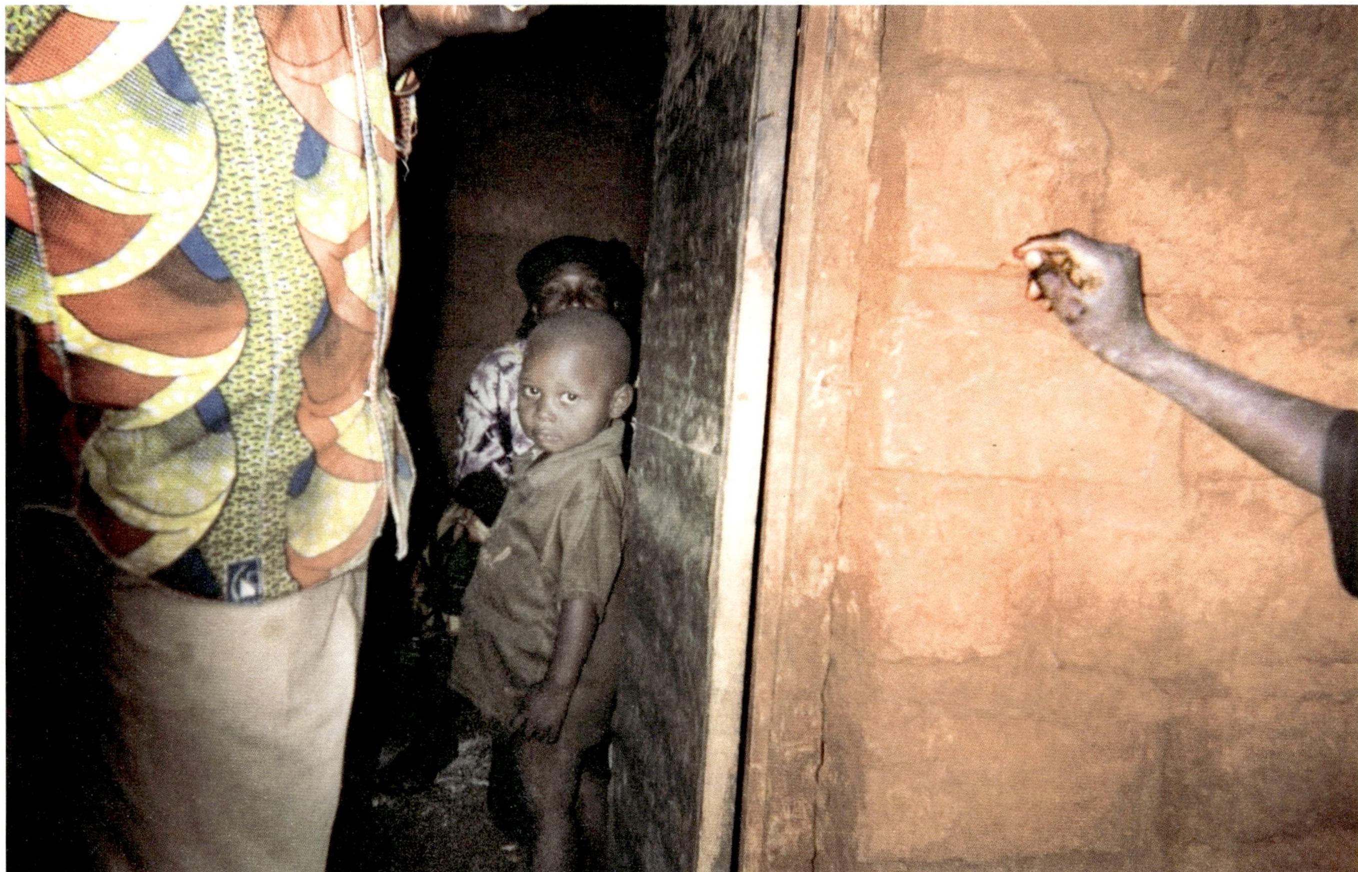

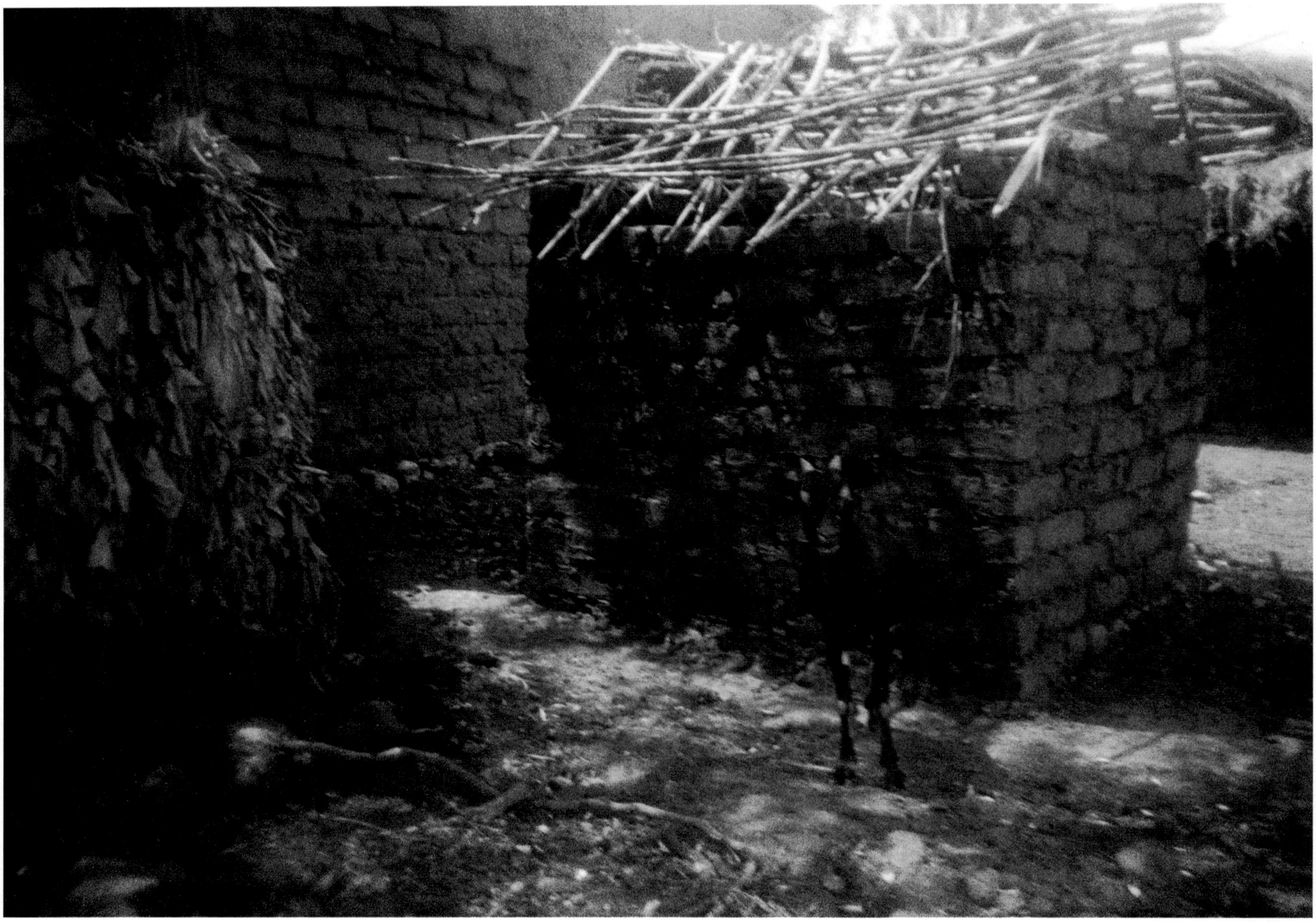

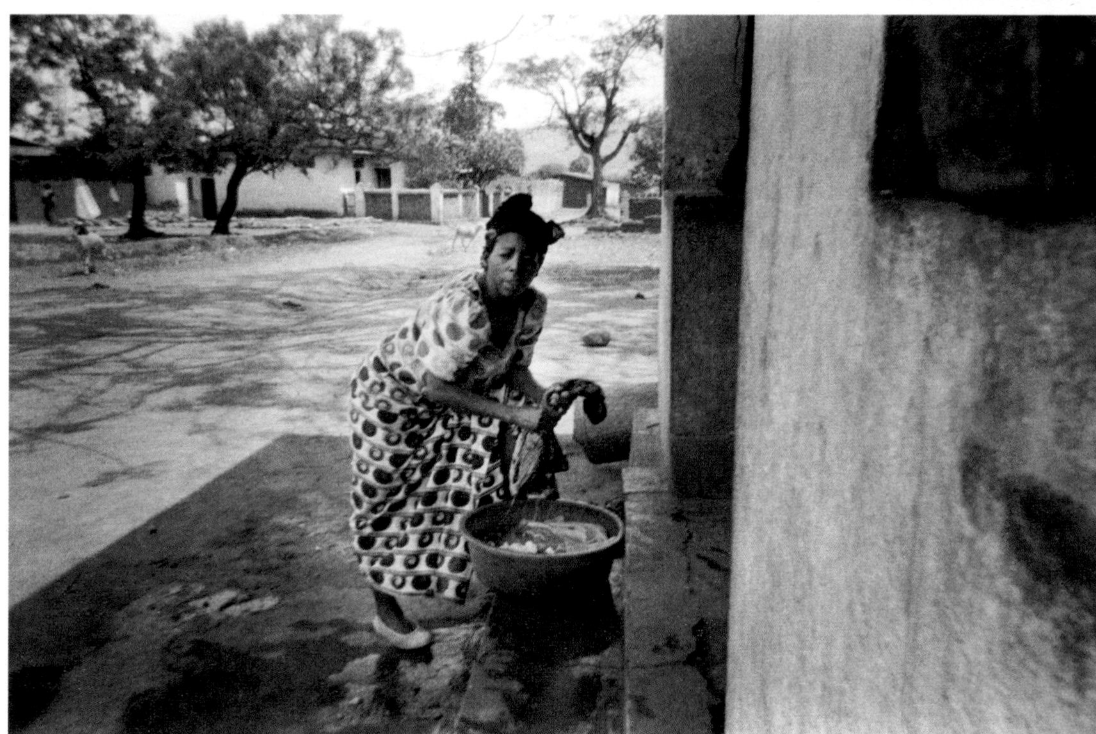

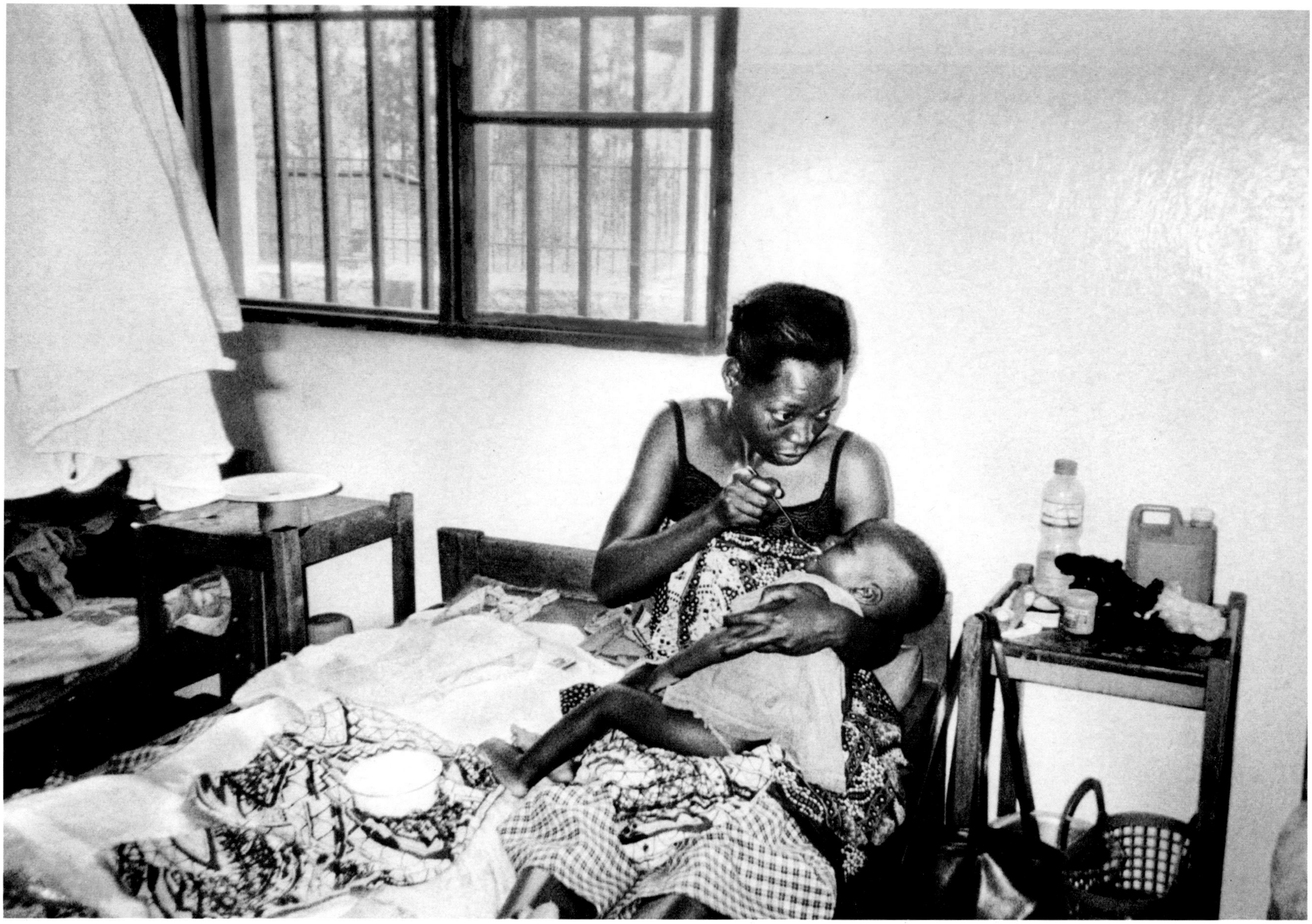

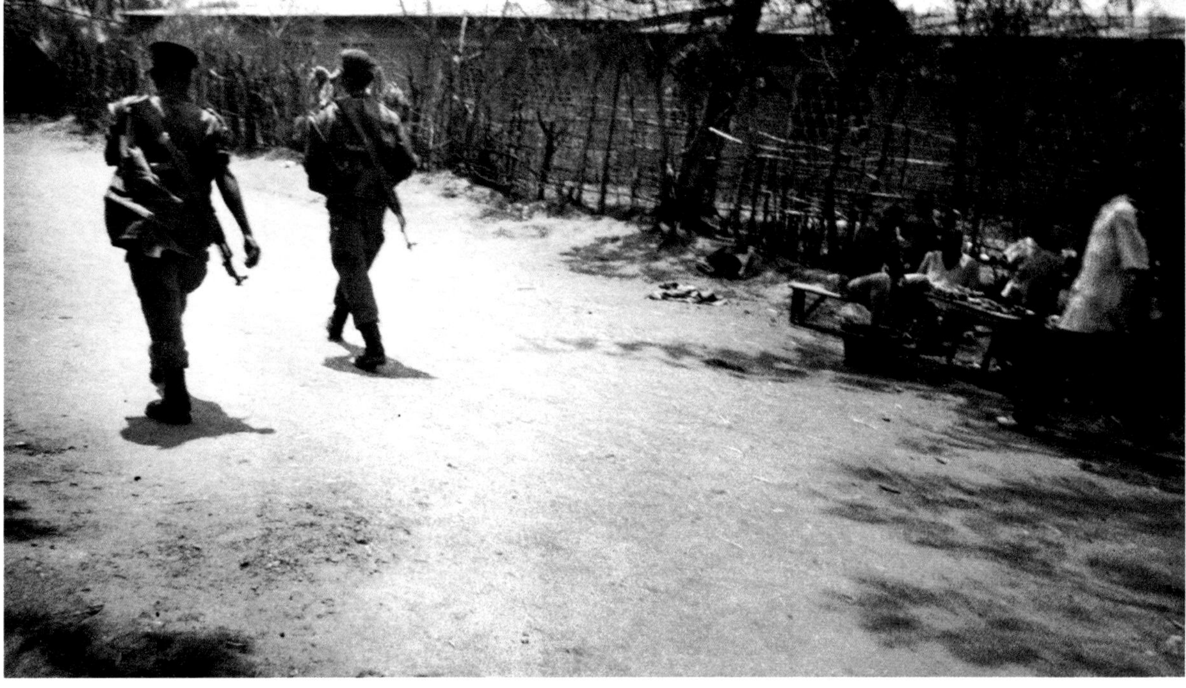

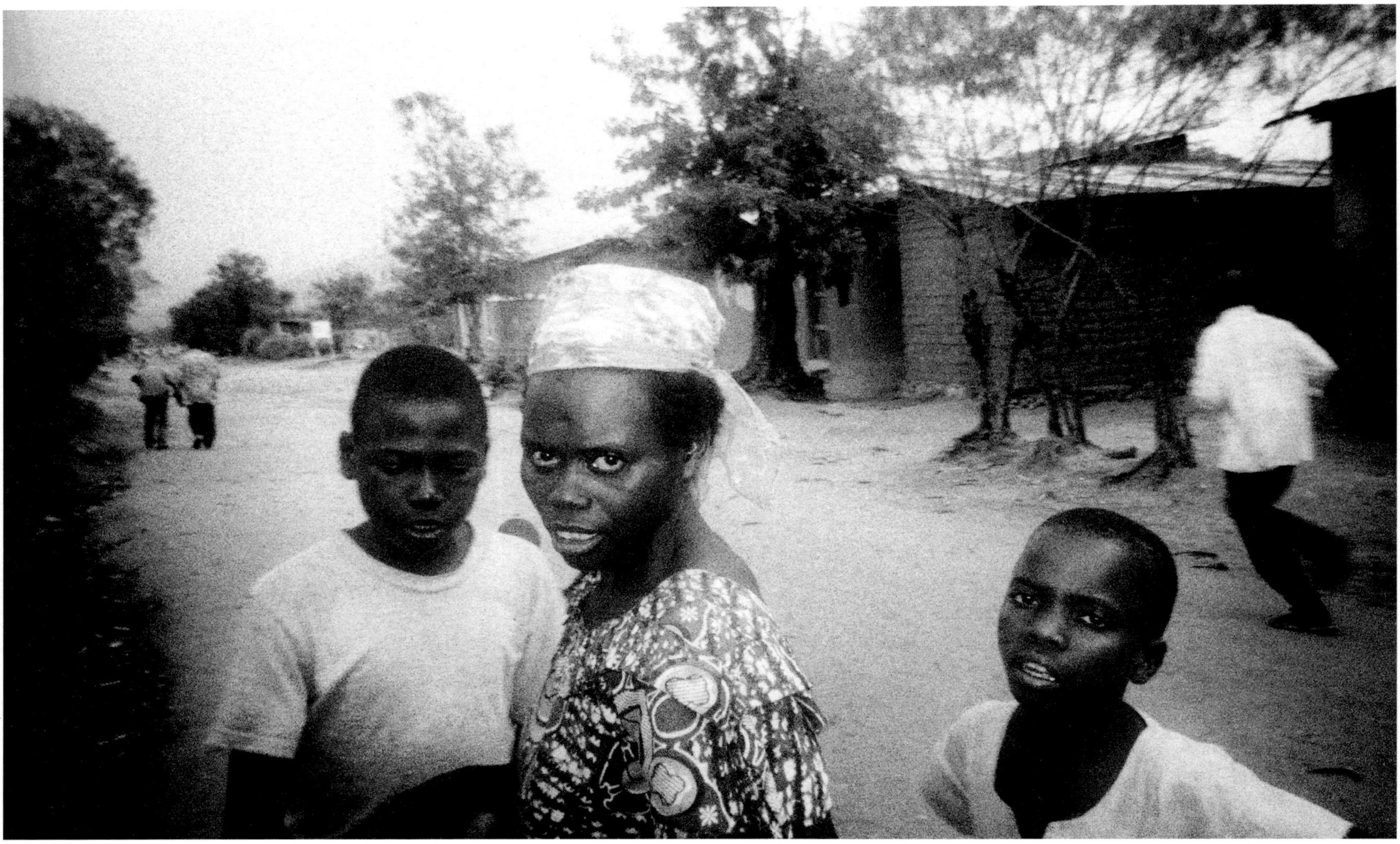

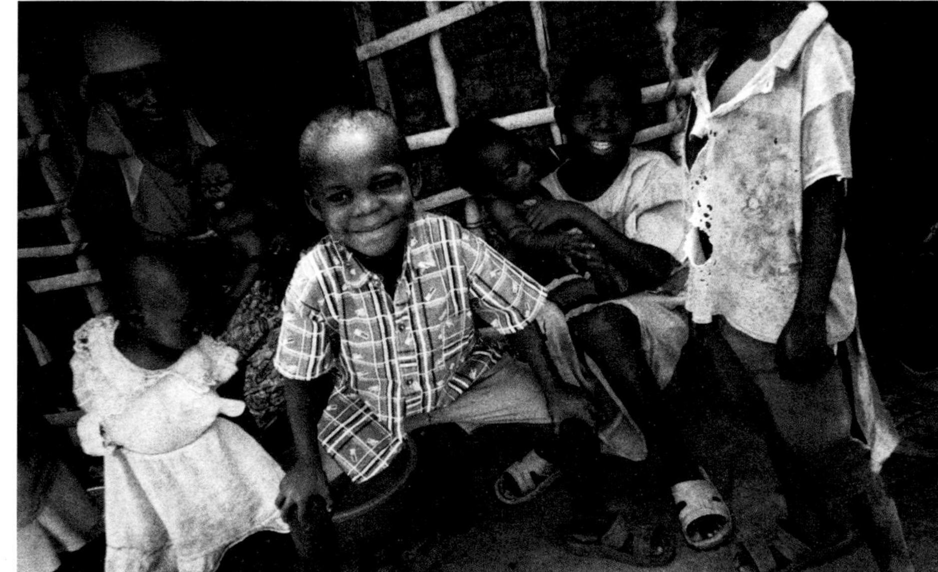

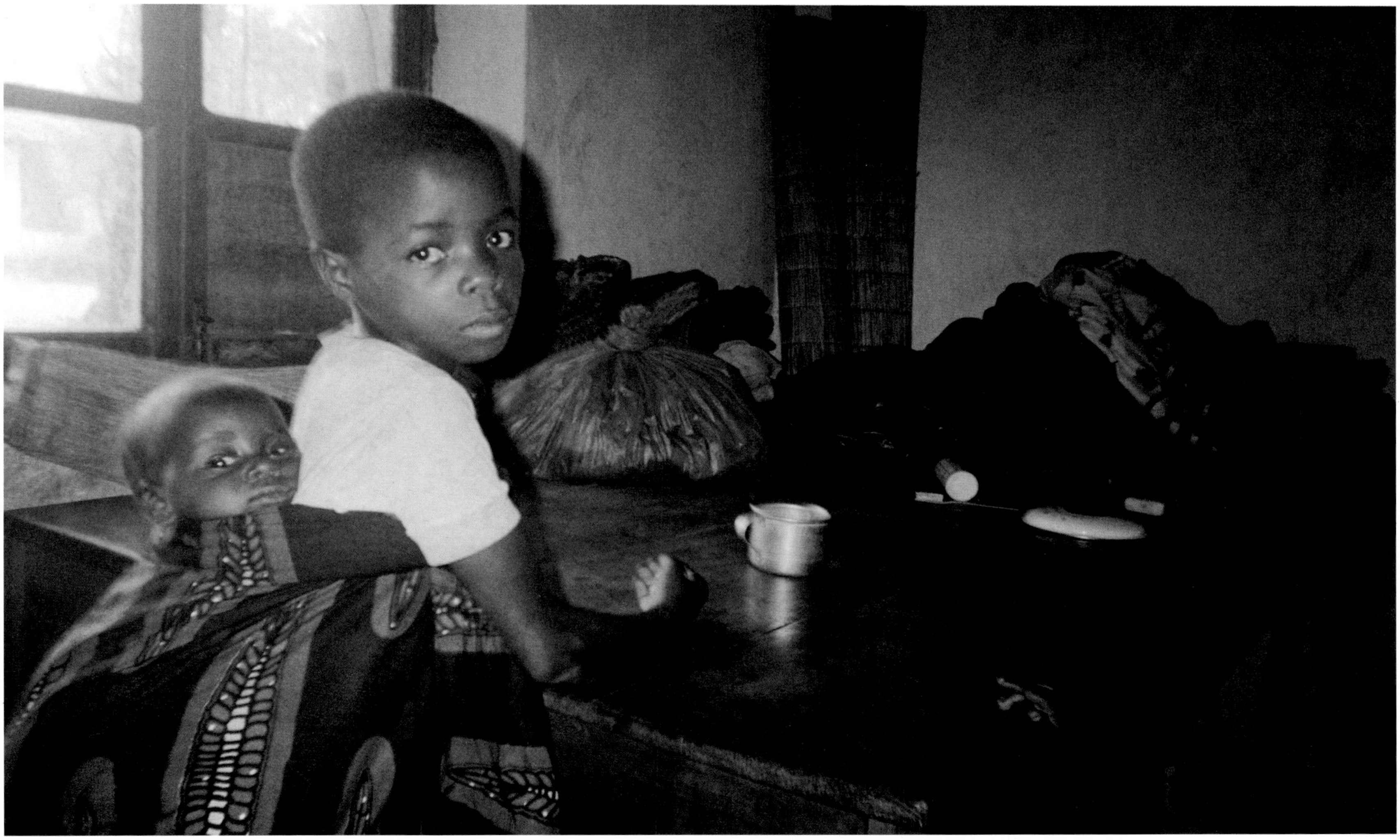

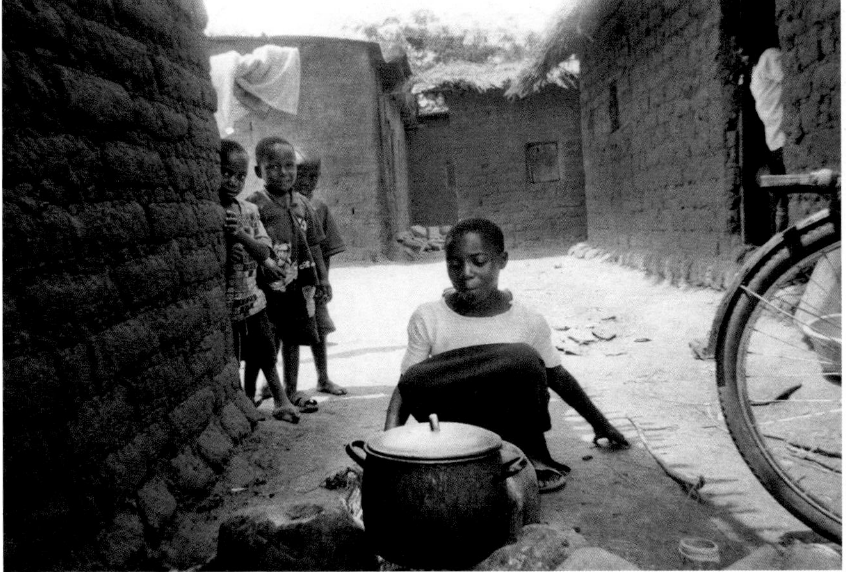
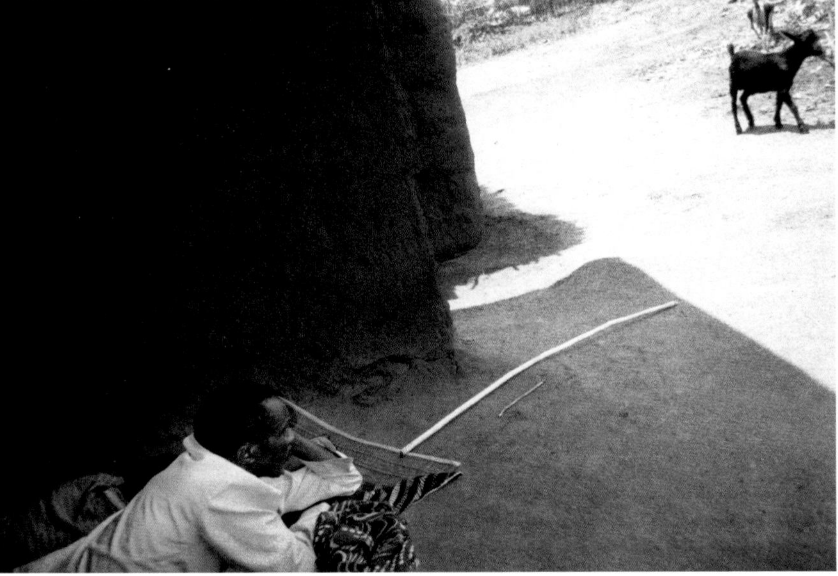

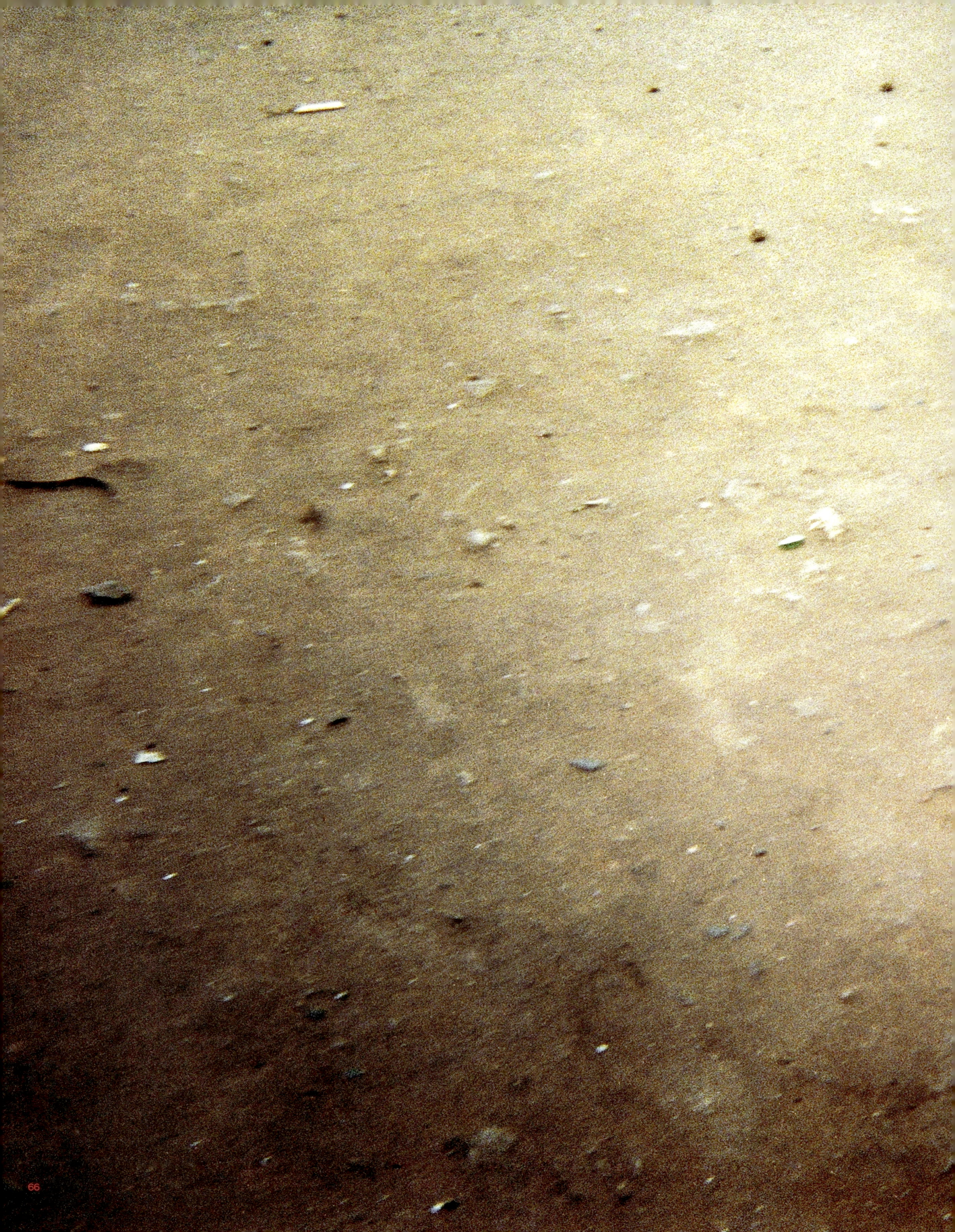

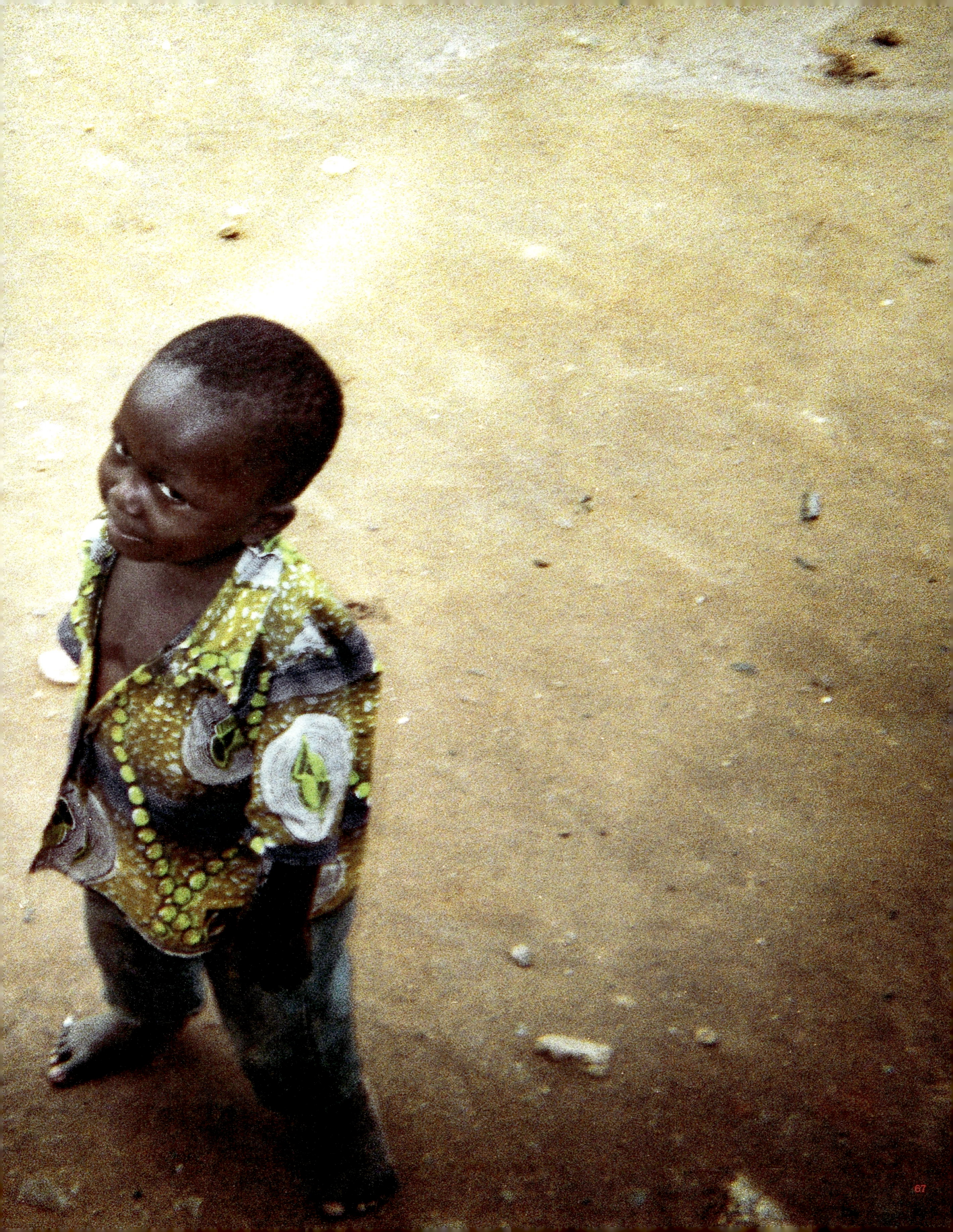

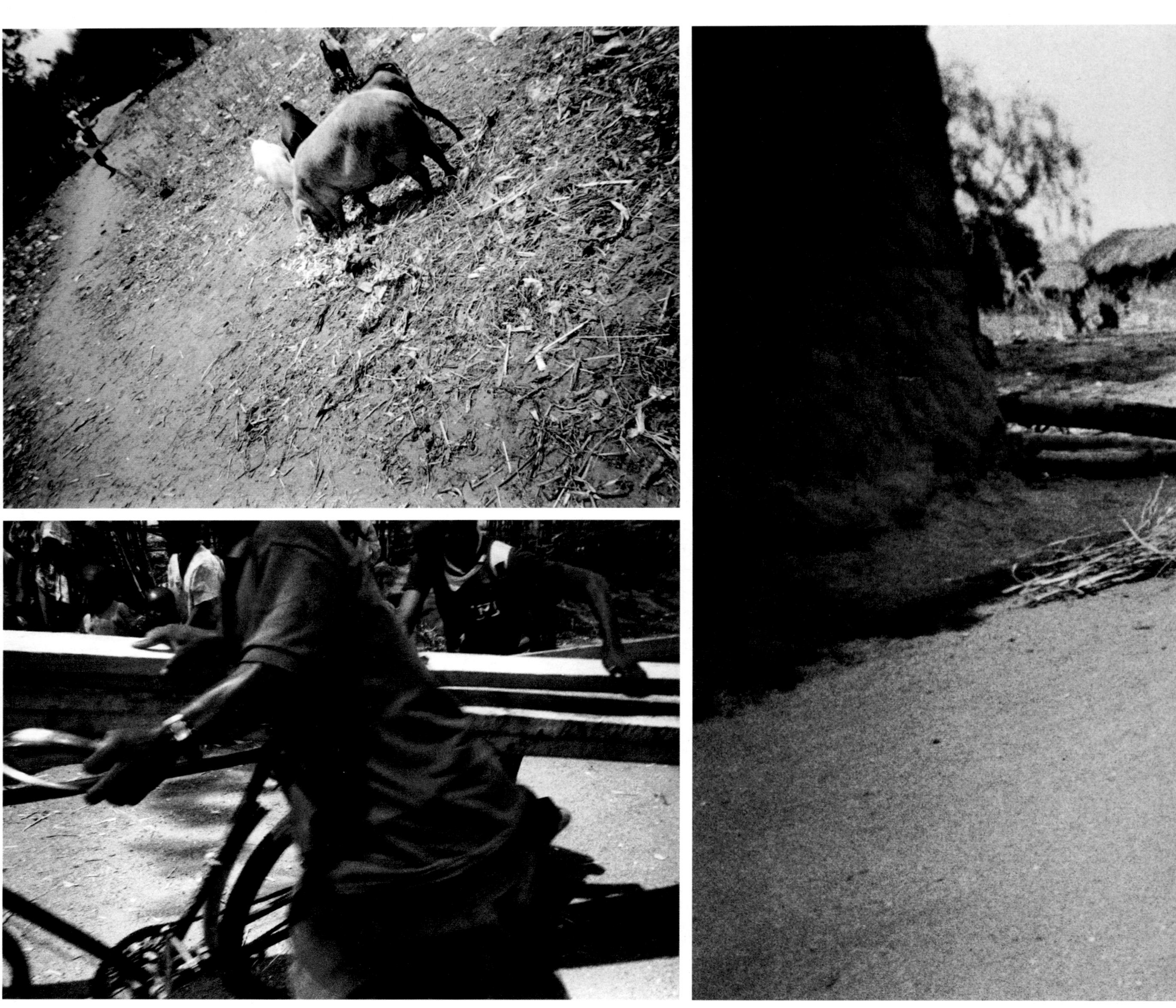

    The Congo Family Album

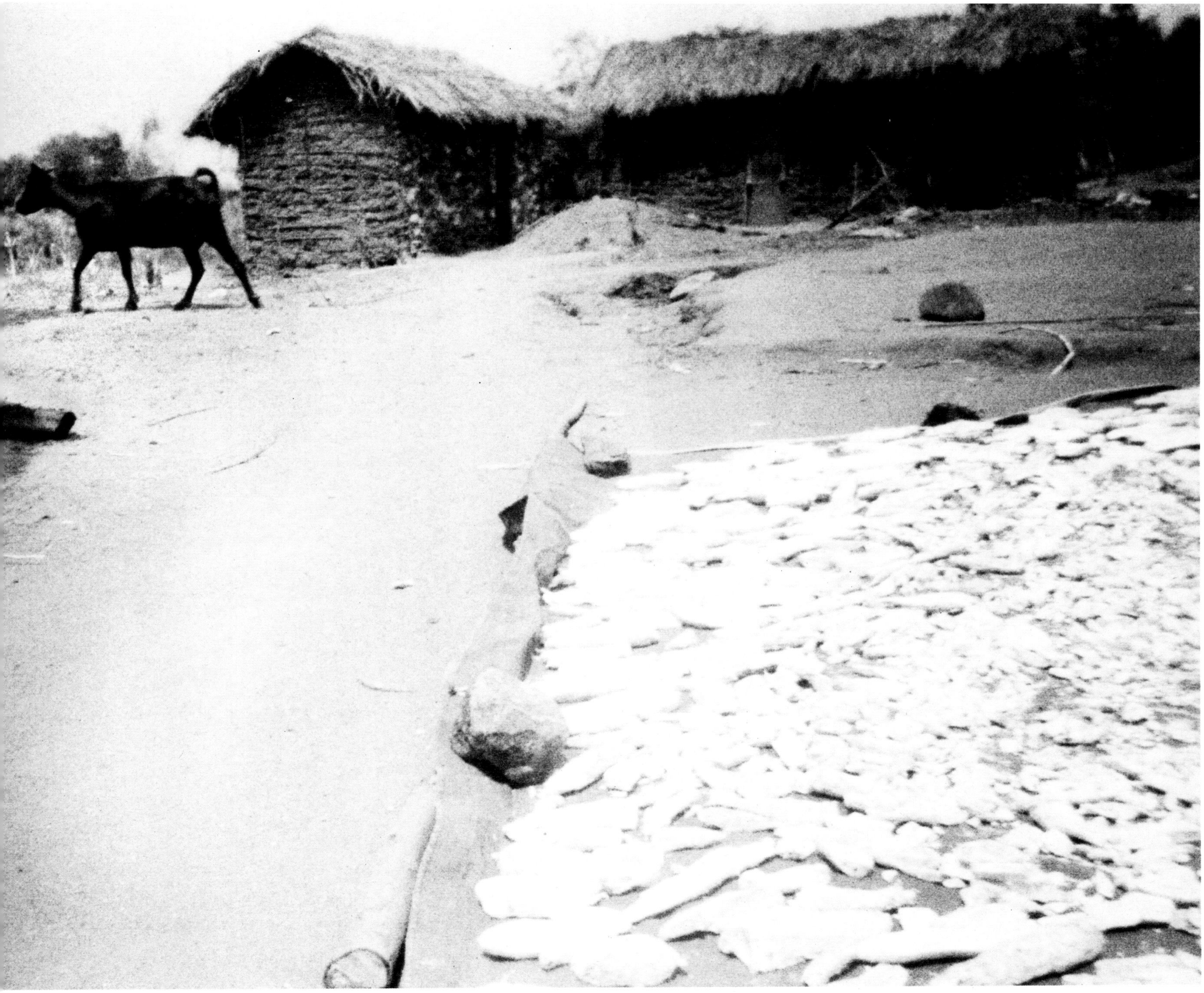

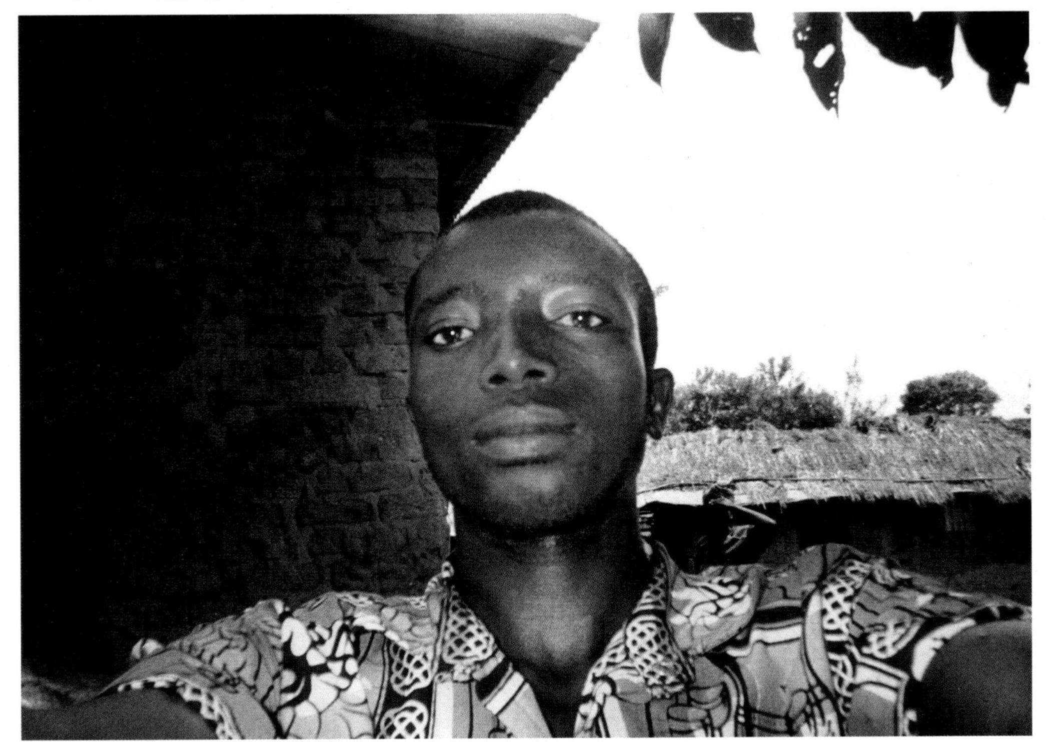

(Below Top)
 – Photograph by Alfredo

"I love this picture.
I like the pose that I'm making.
I look cool."

(Below Middle)
 – Photograph by Buratwa

"I took this picture because
I love water."

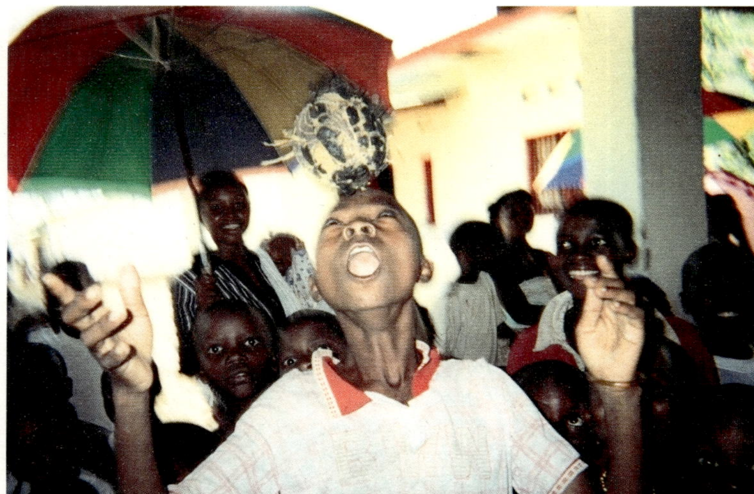

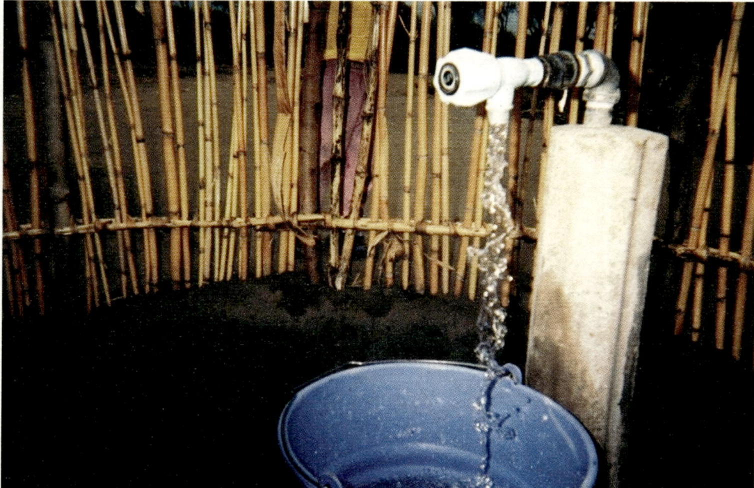

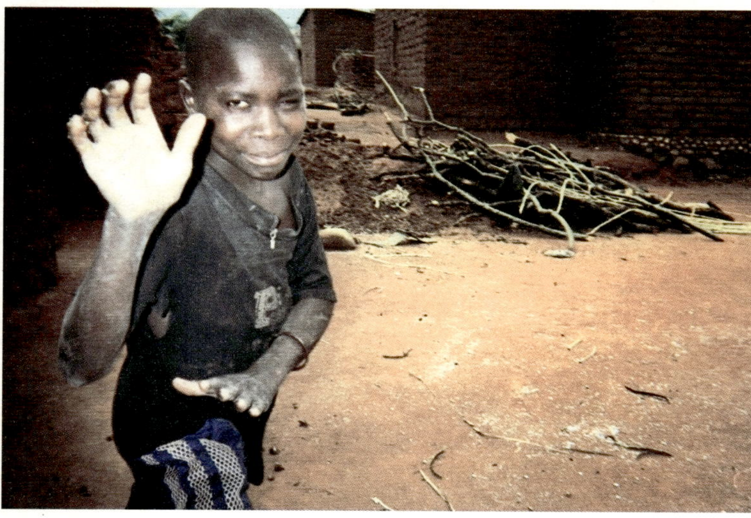

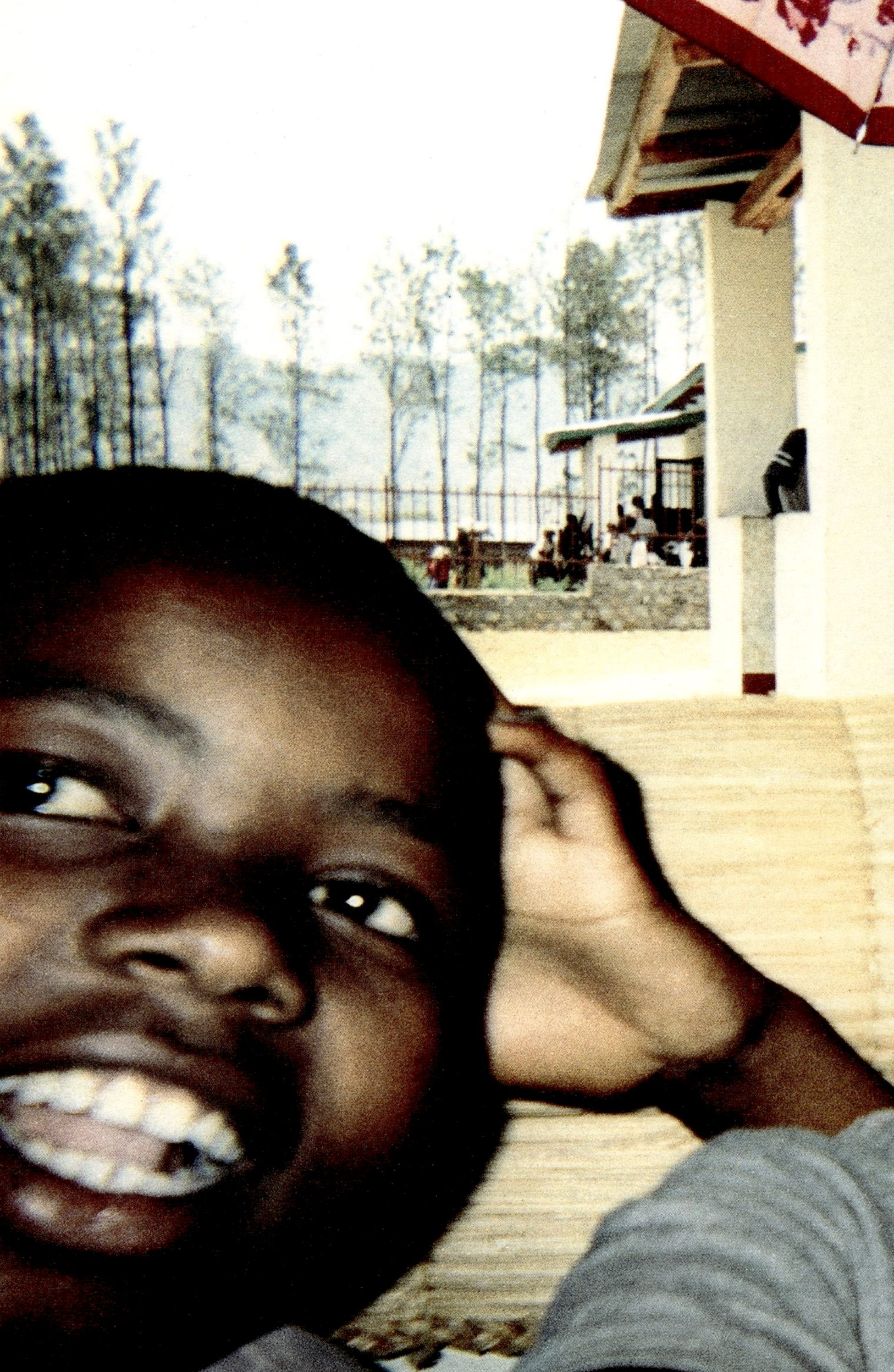

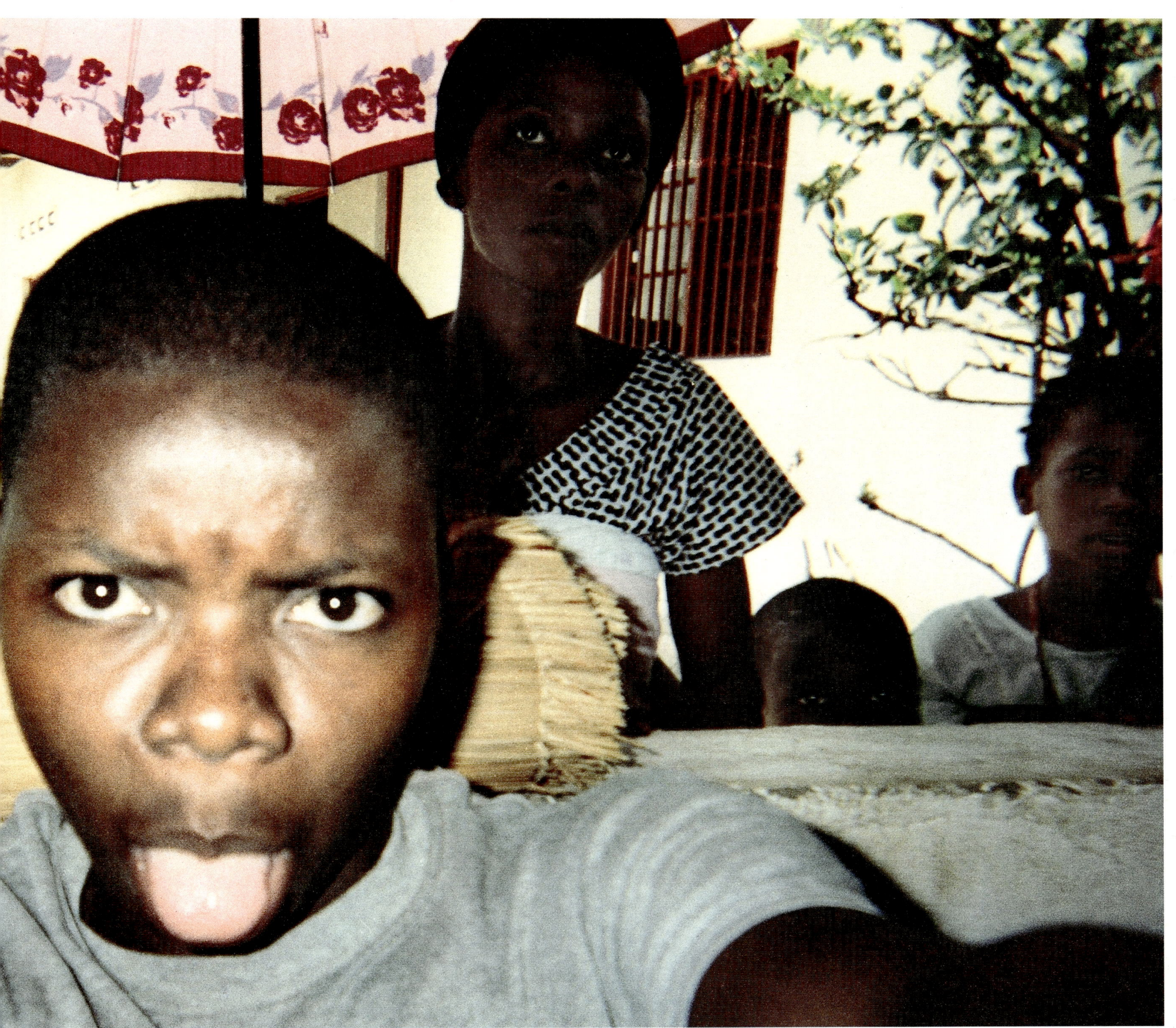

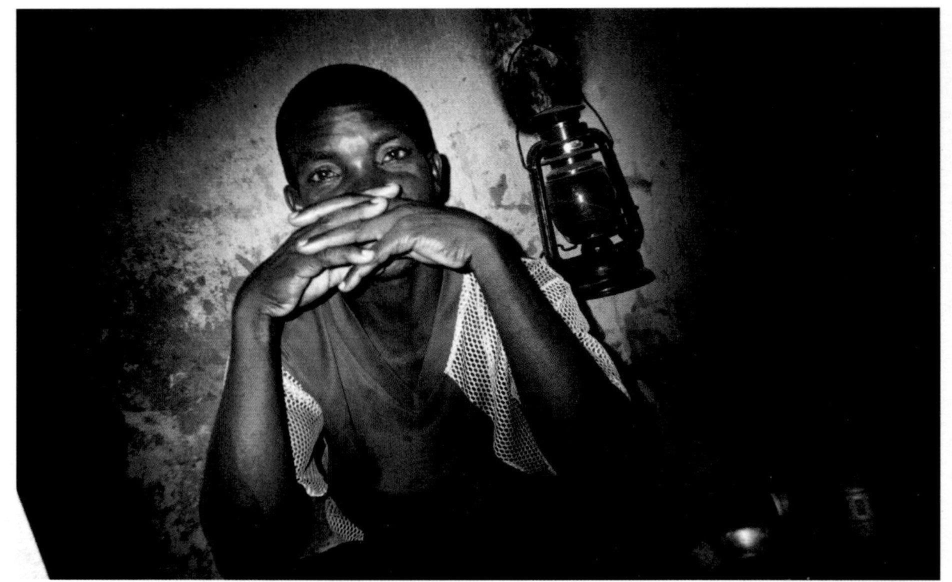

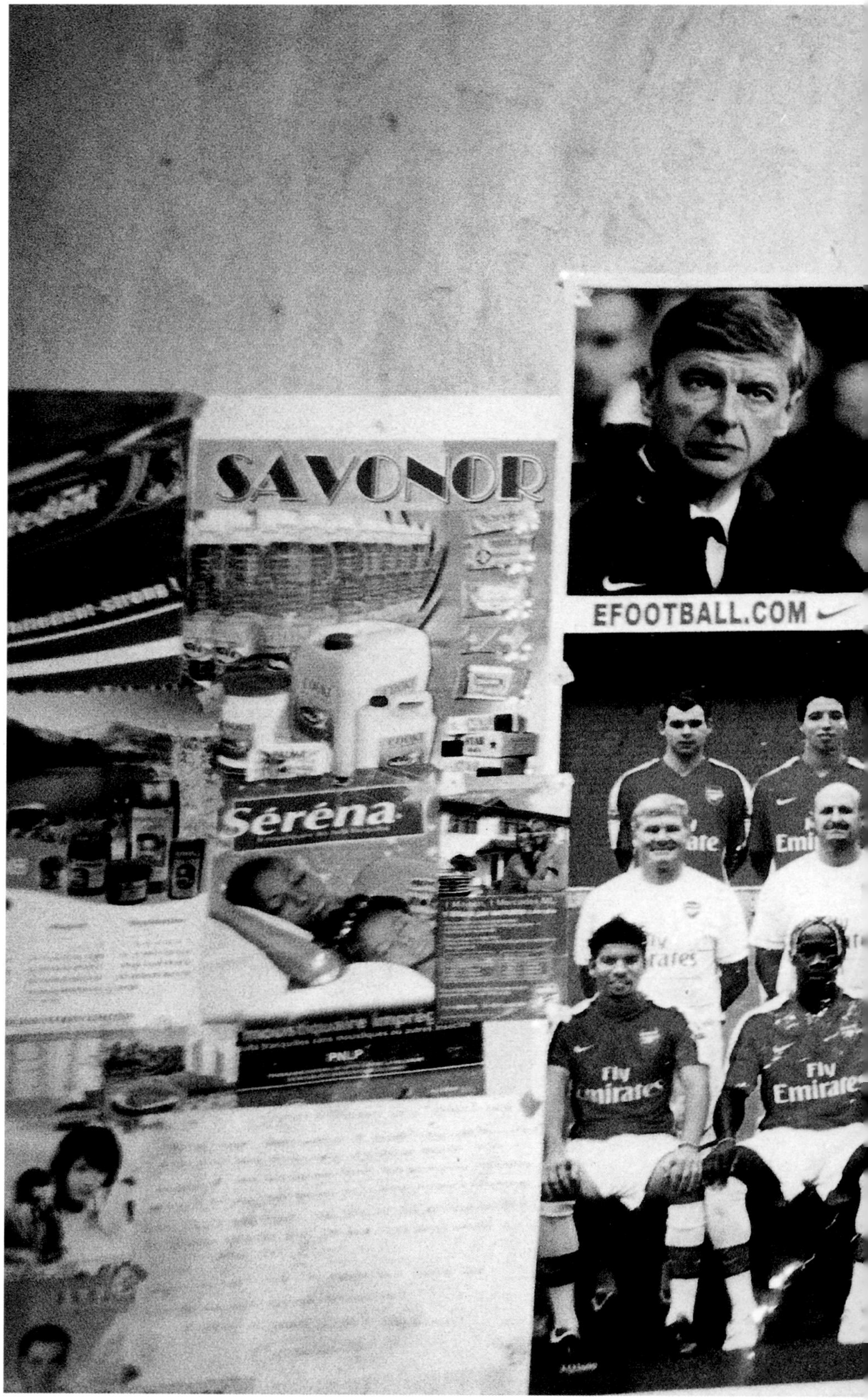

(Right)
– Photograph by Rangombo

"This is the poster I put up on the lounge wall. I am a huge football fan. I am happy because I took this picture really well. I got the whole poster in. I don't have a favourite player. I like all of the team equally. I wouldn't be able to recognise an individual player because I have never seen them. I only listen to the games on the radio."

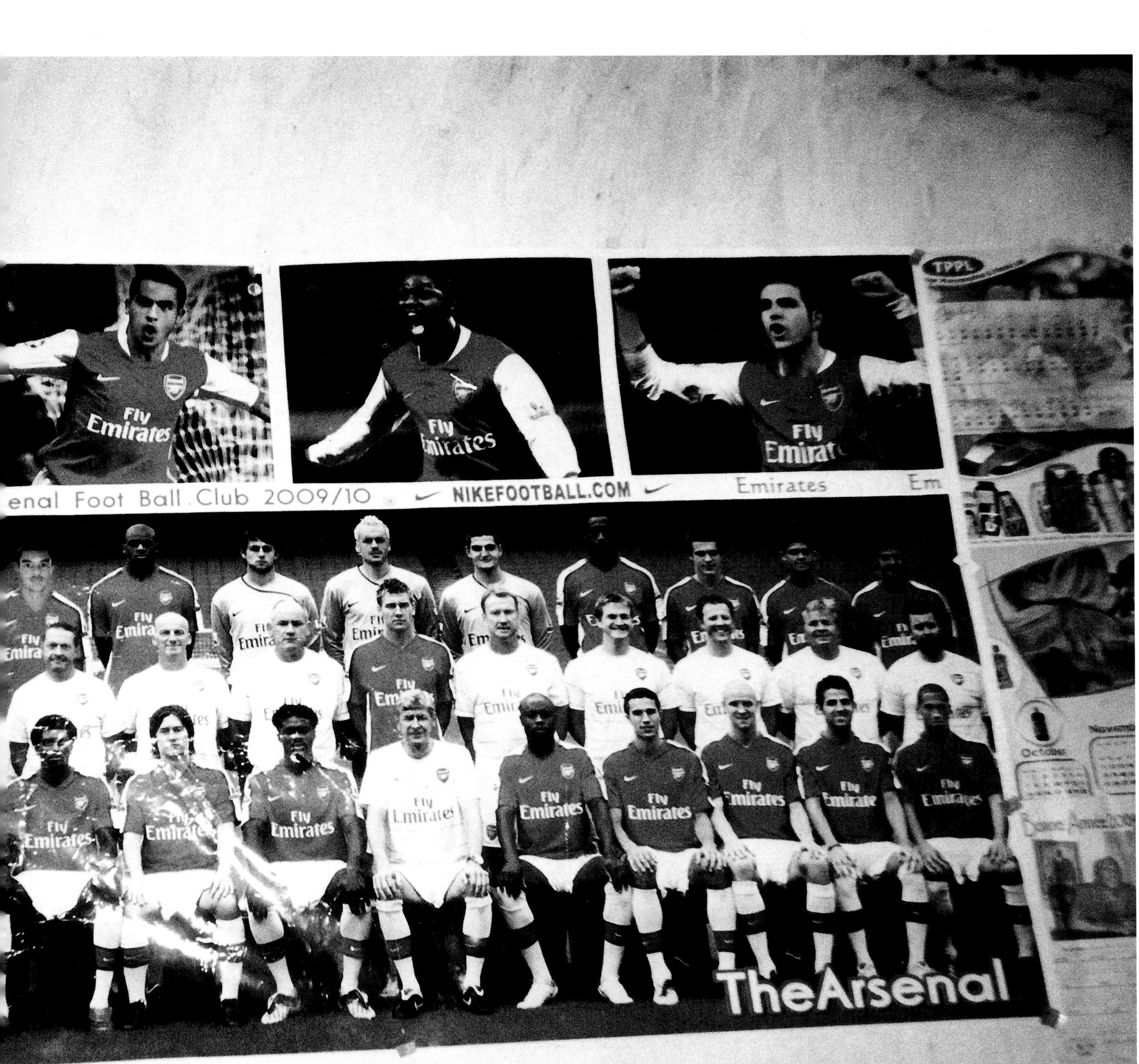

enal Foot Ball Club 2009/10
NIKEFOOTBALL.COM
Fly Emirates
TheArsenal

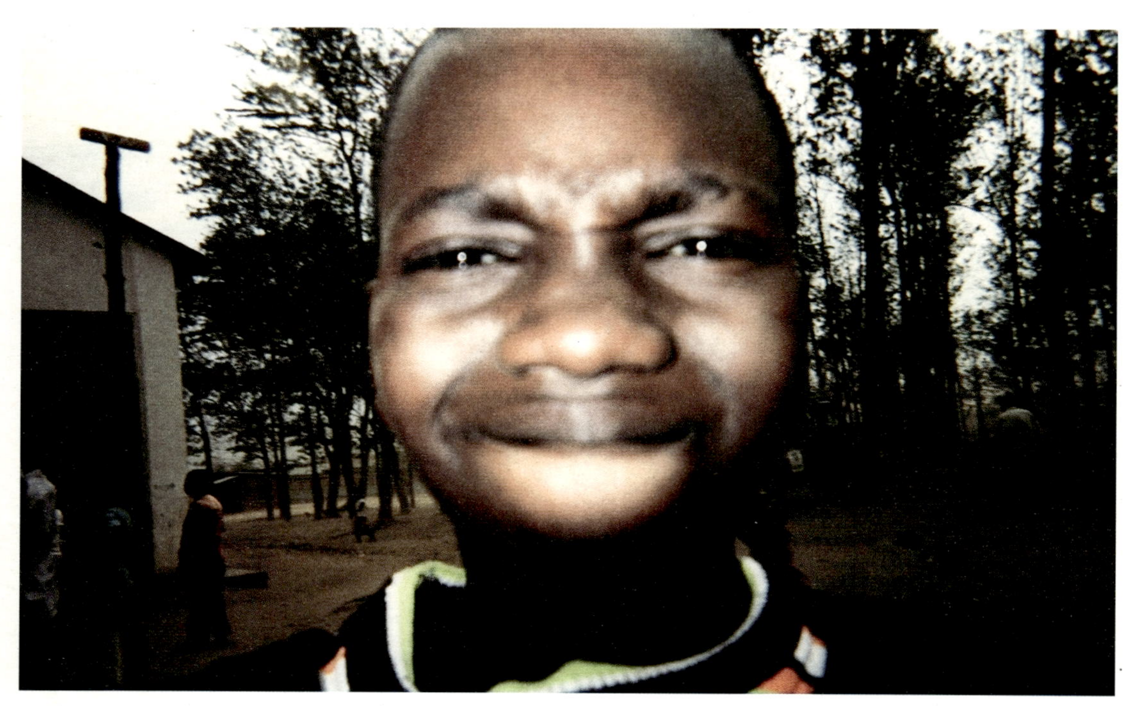

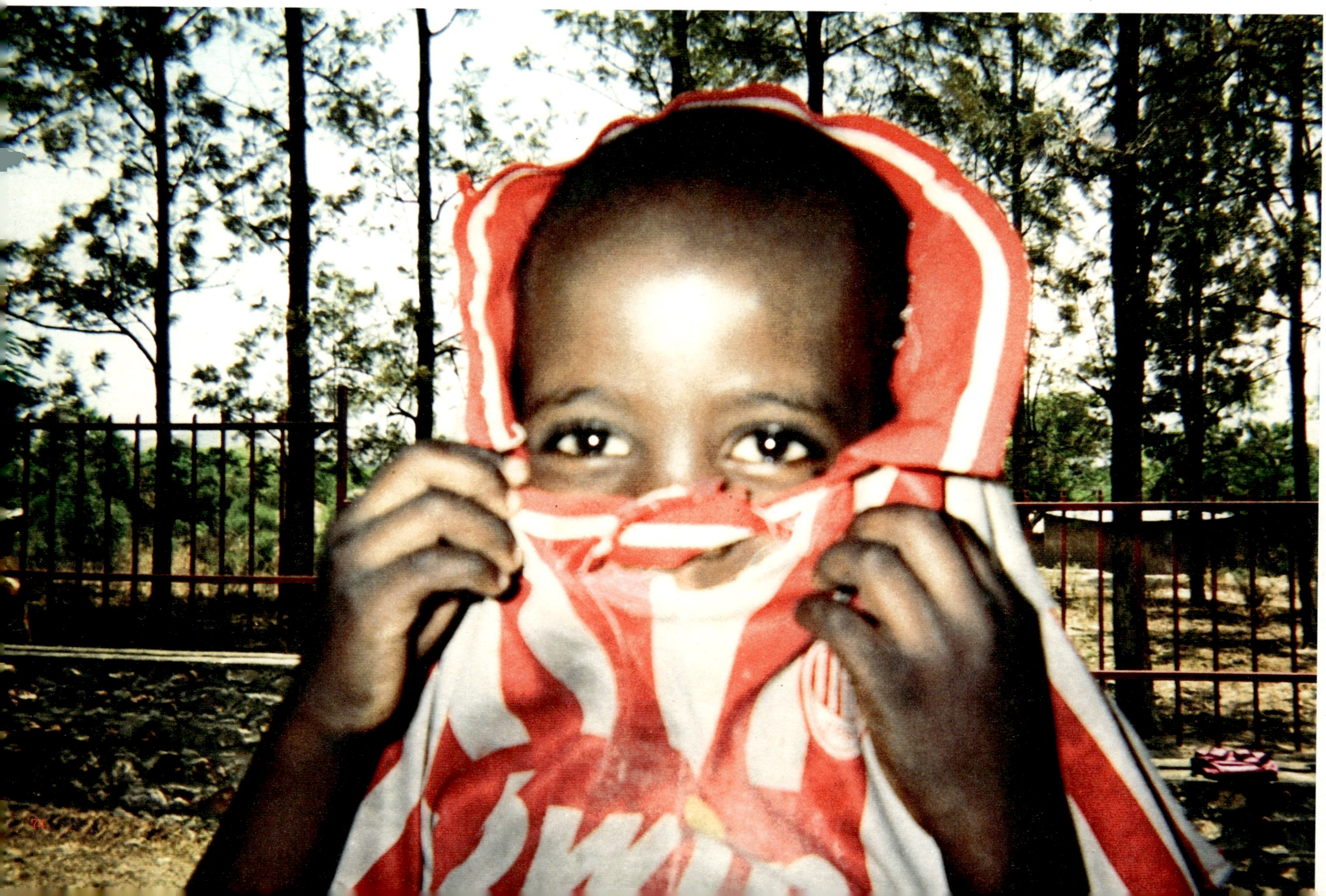

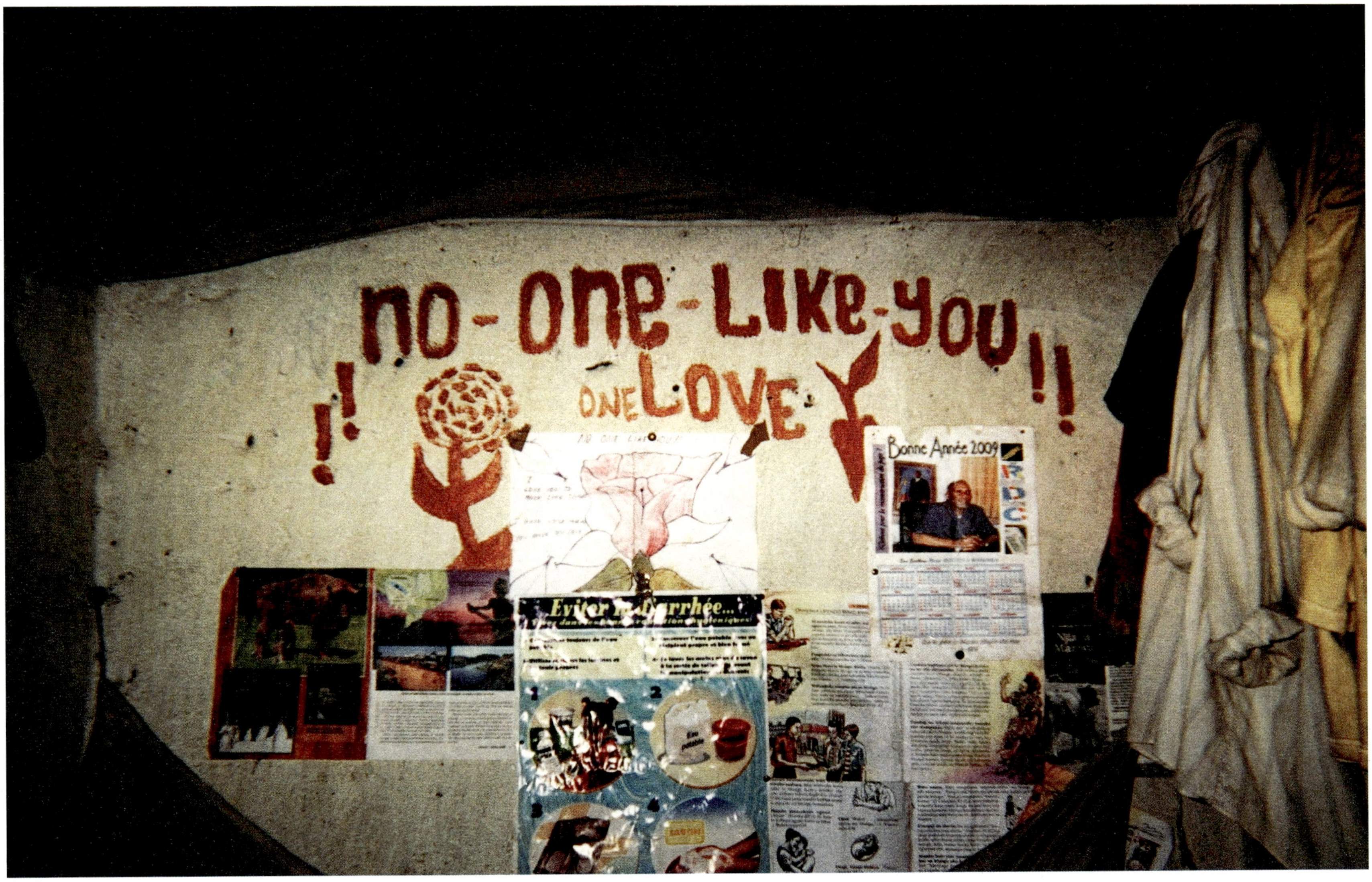

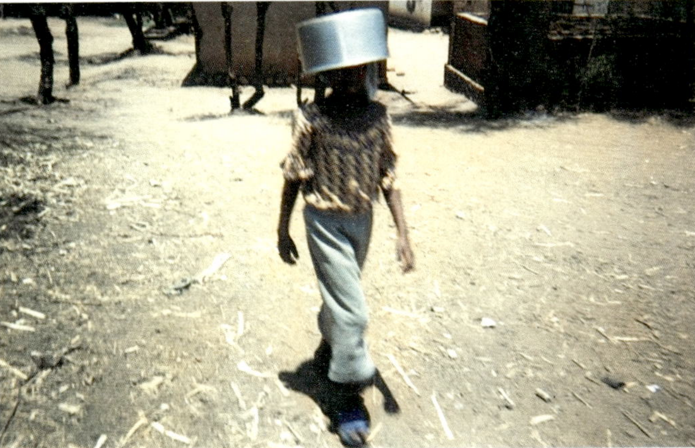

!!no-one-like-you!!
one LOVE
Bonne Année 2009
Eviter la Diarrhée...

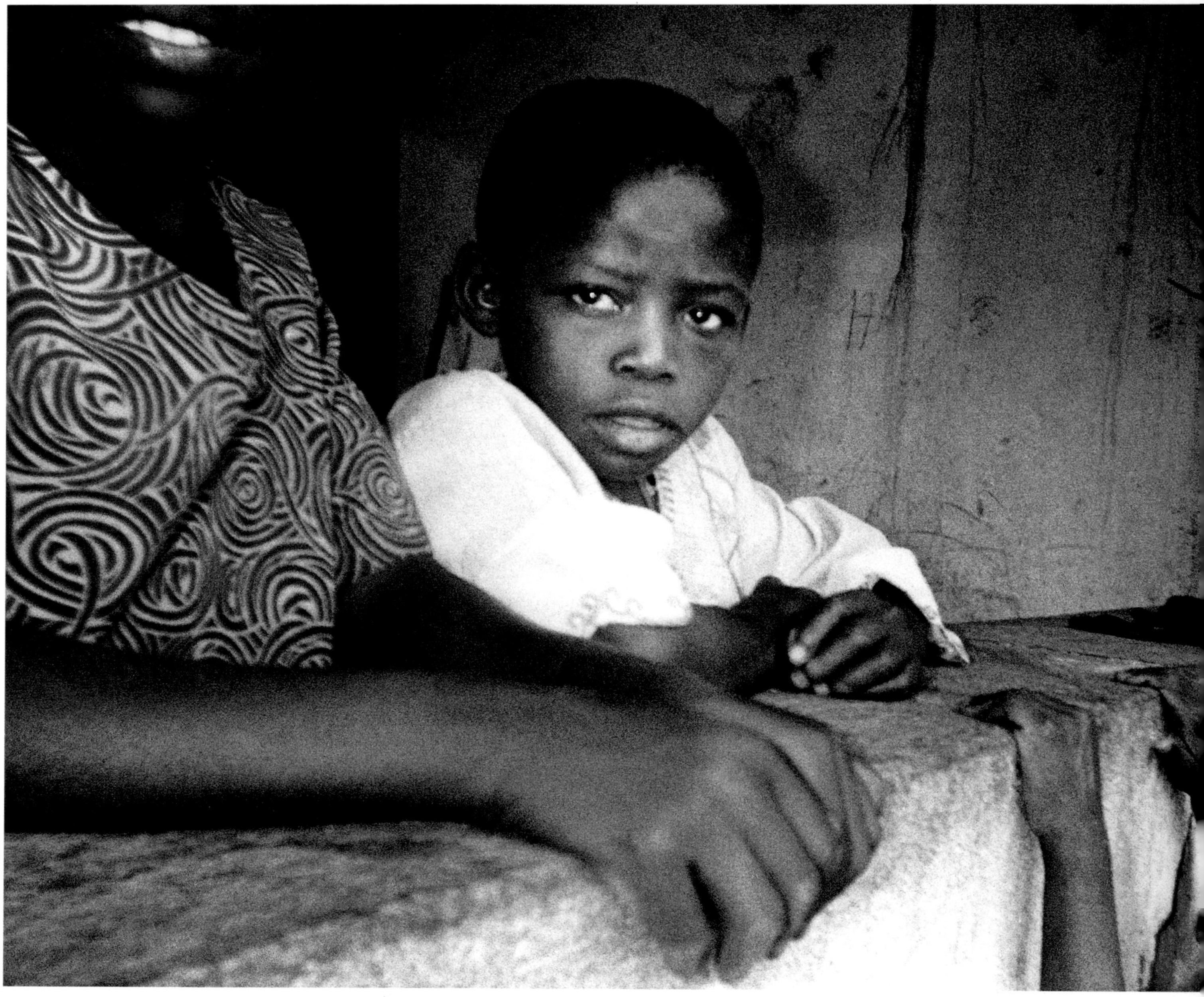

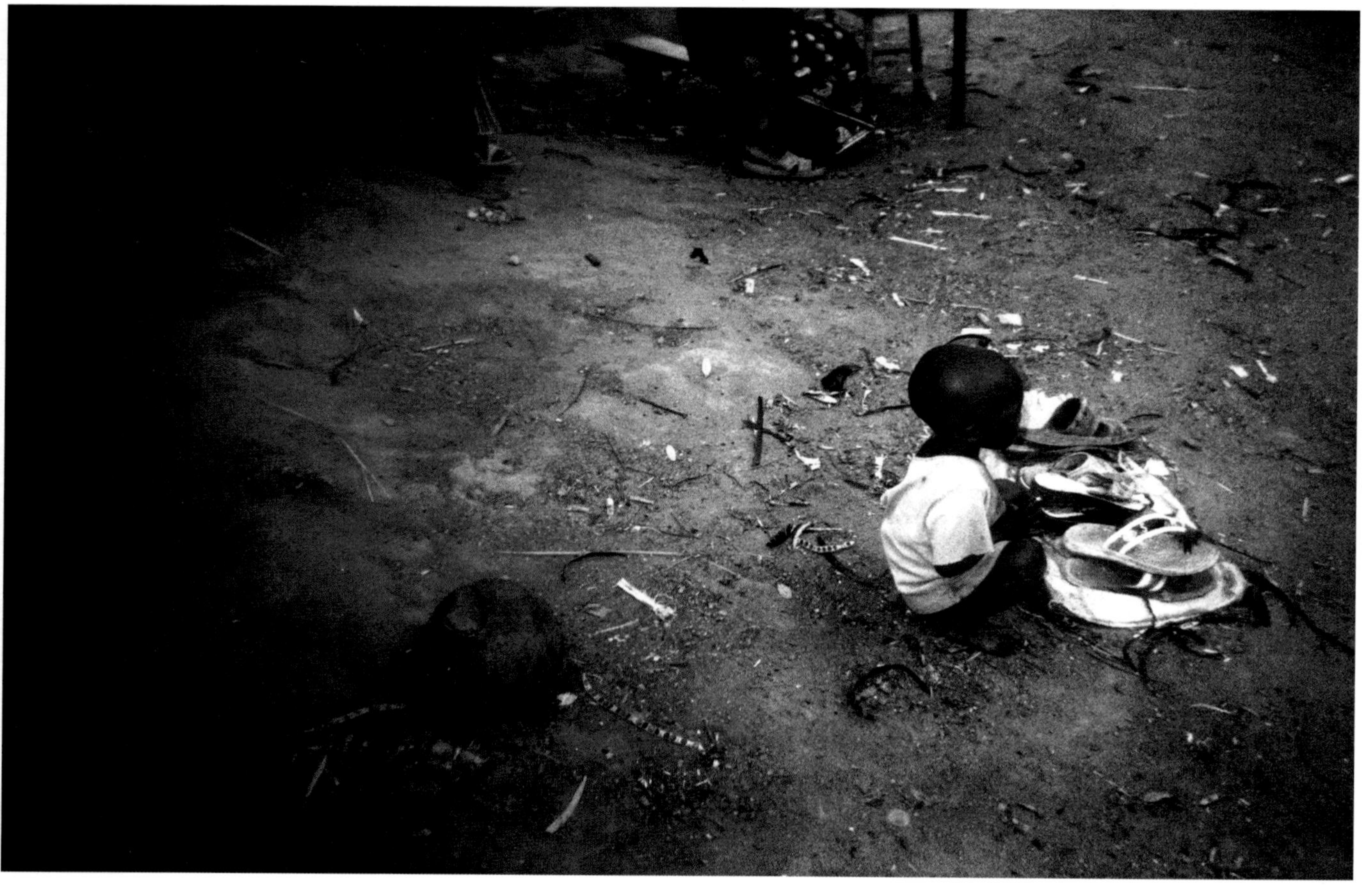

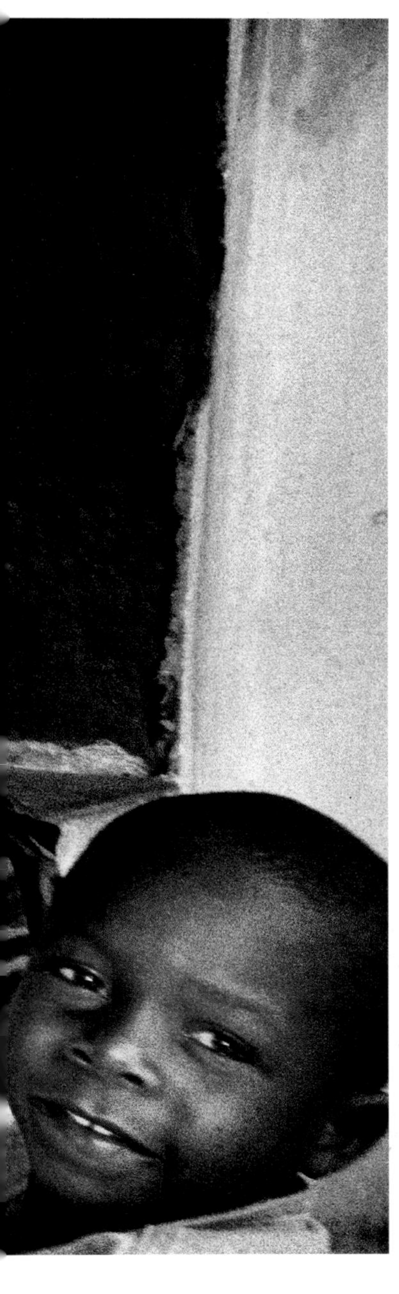
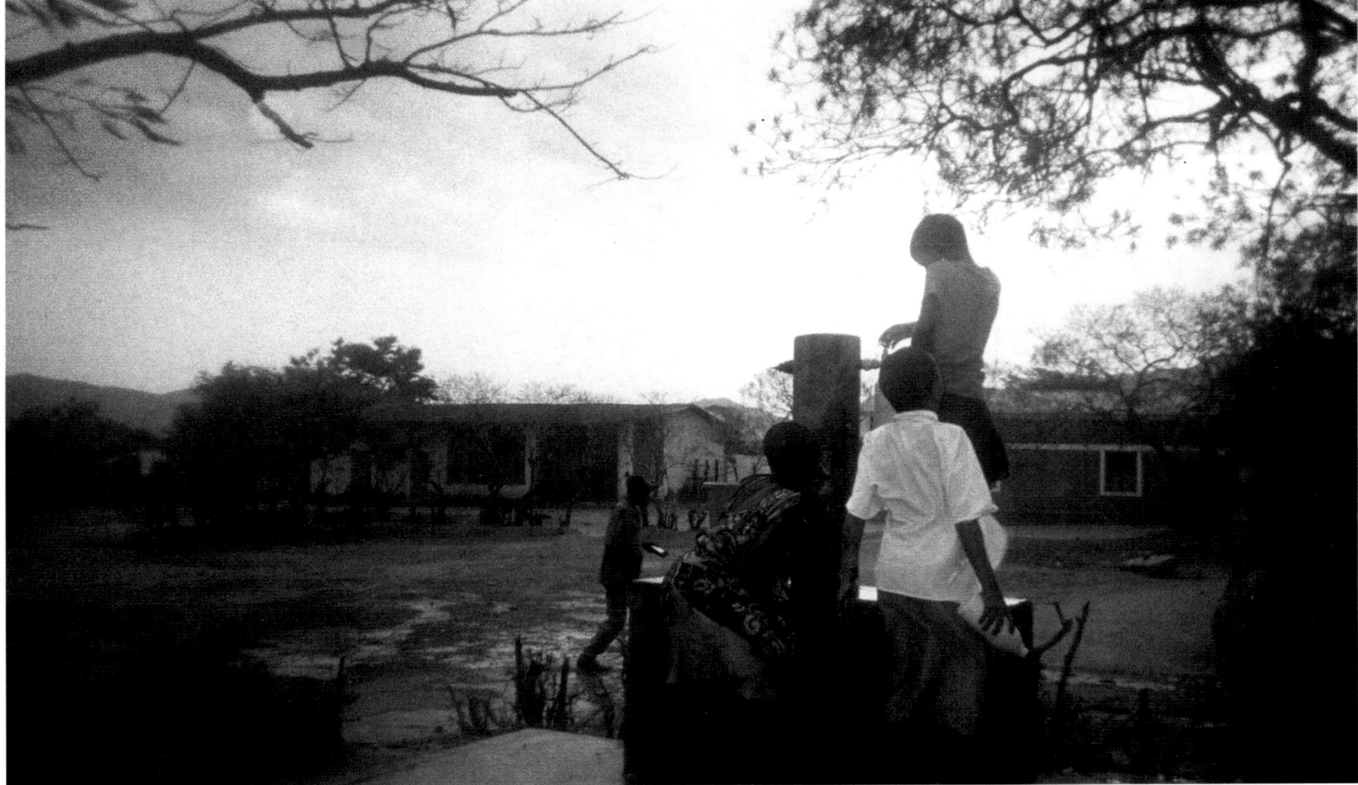
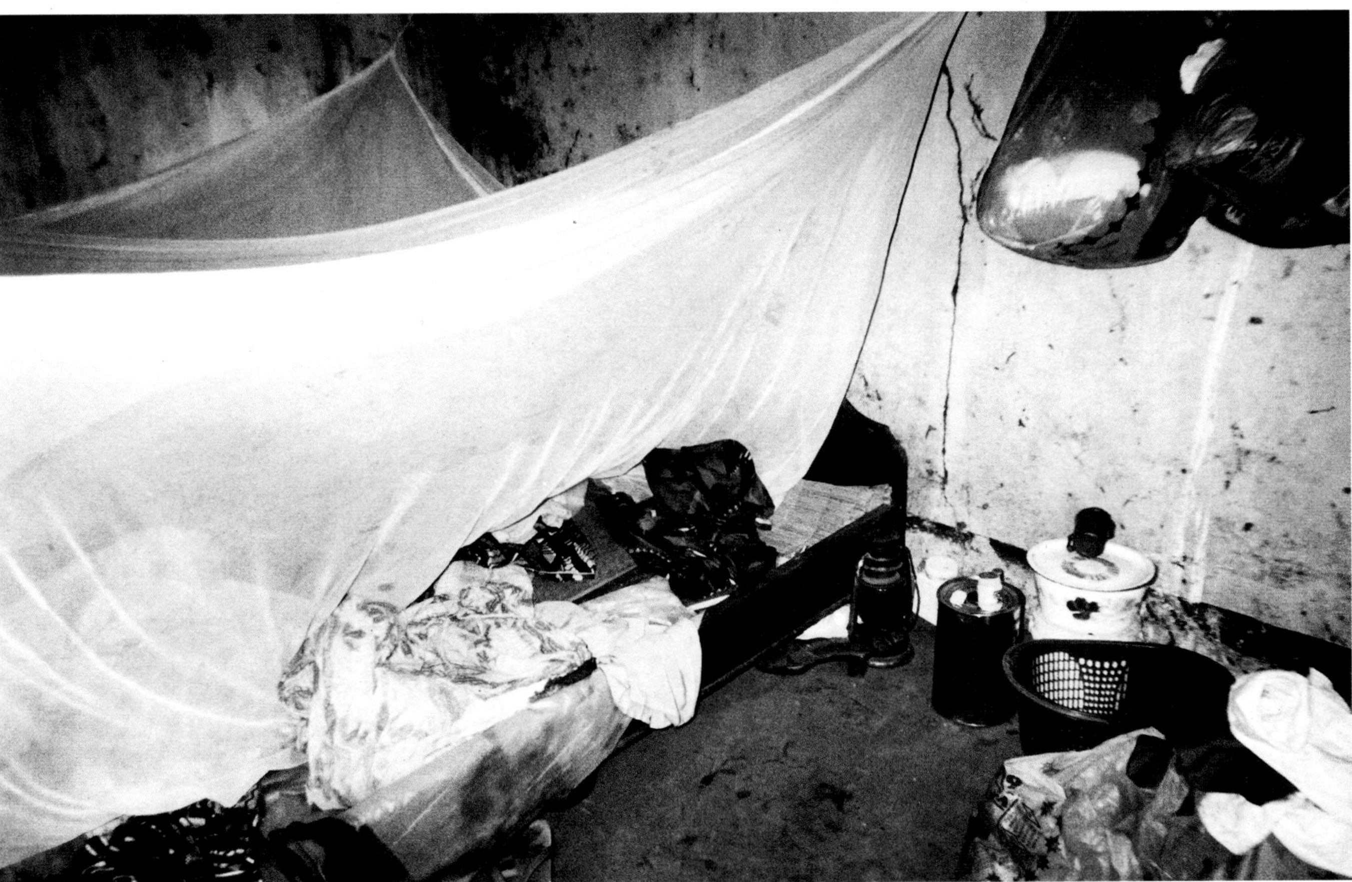

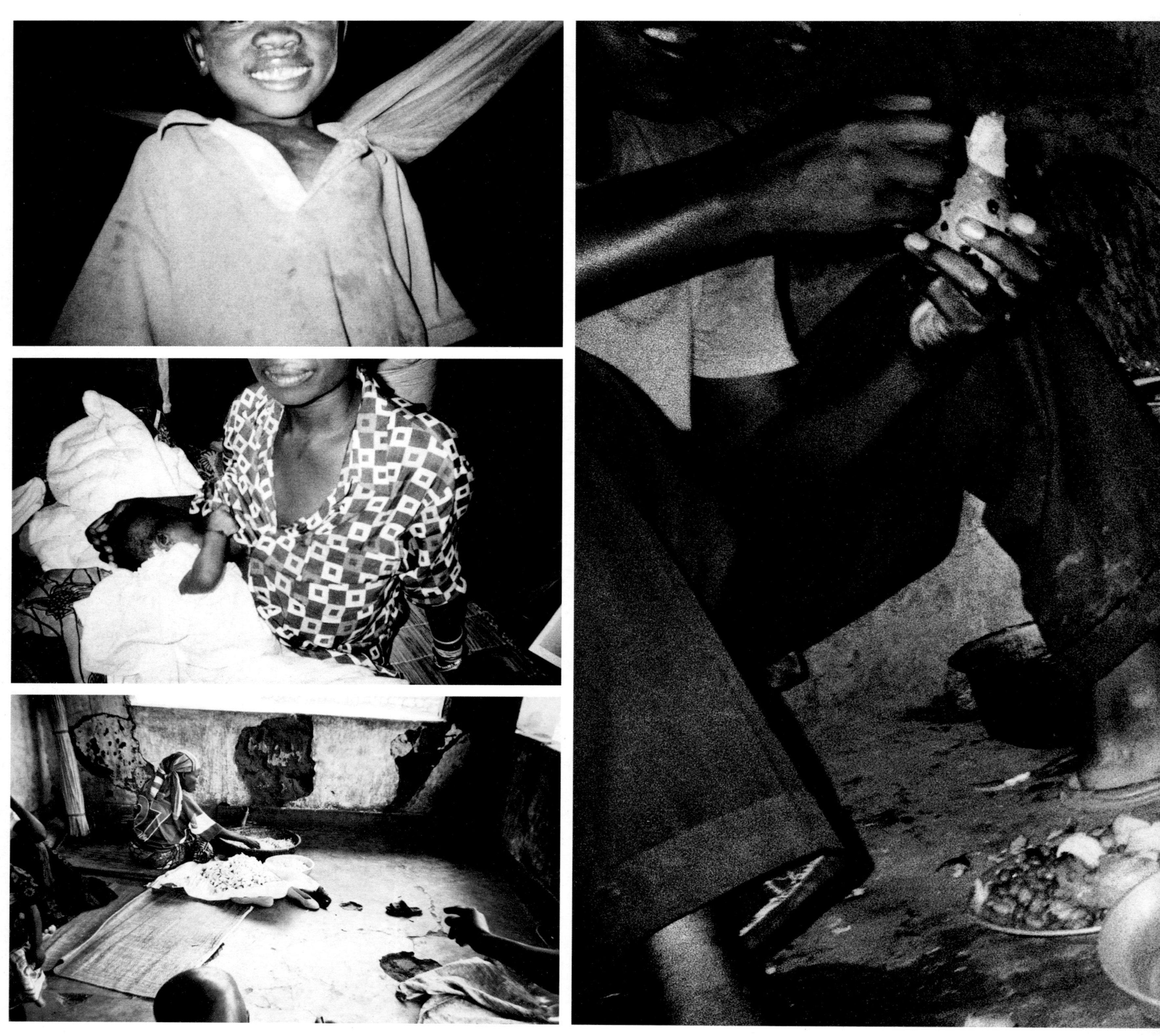

     The Congo Family Album

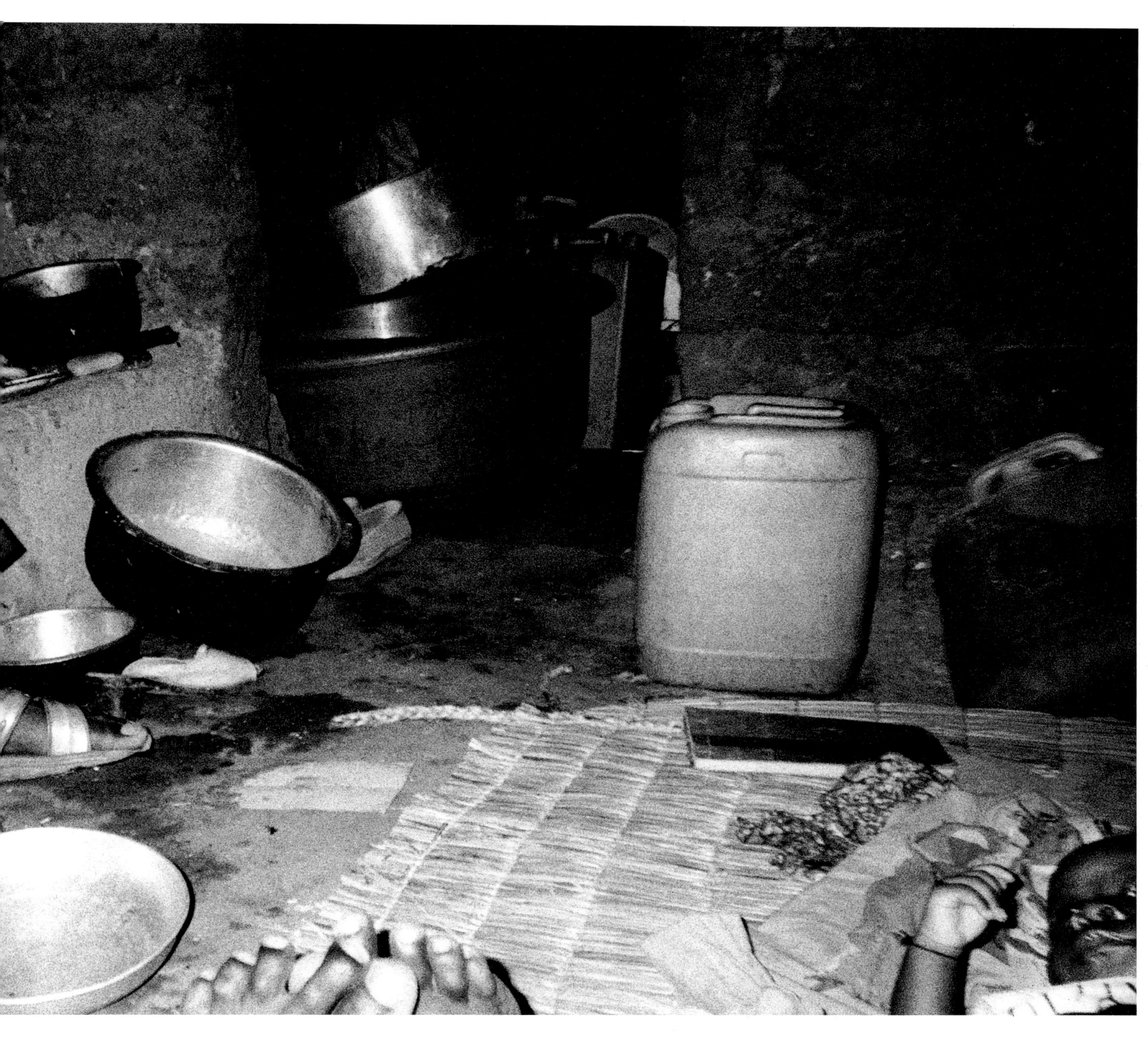

(Below)
 – Photograph by Sikito

"This is a picture of my children.
I took this picture because I love my
children. I think it looks good but I
don't think I am a very good photographer. Look I chopped all of their
heads off!"

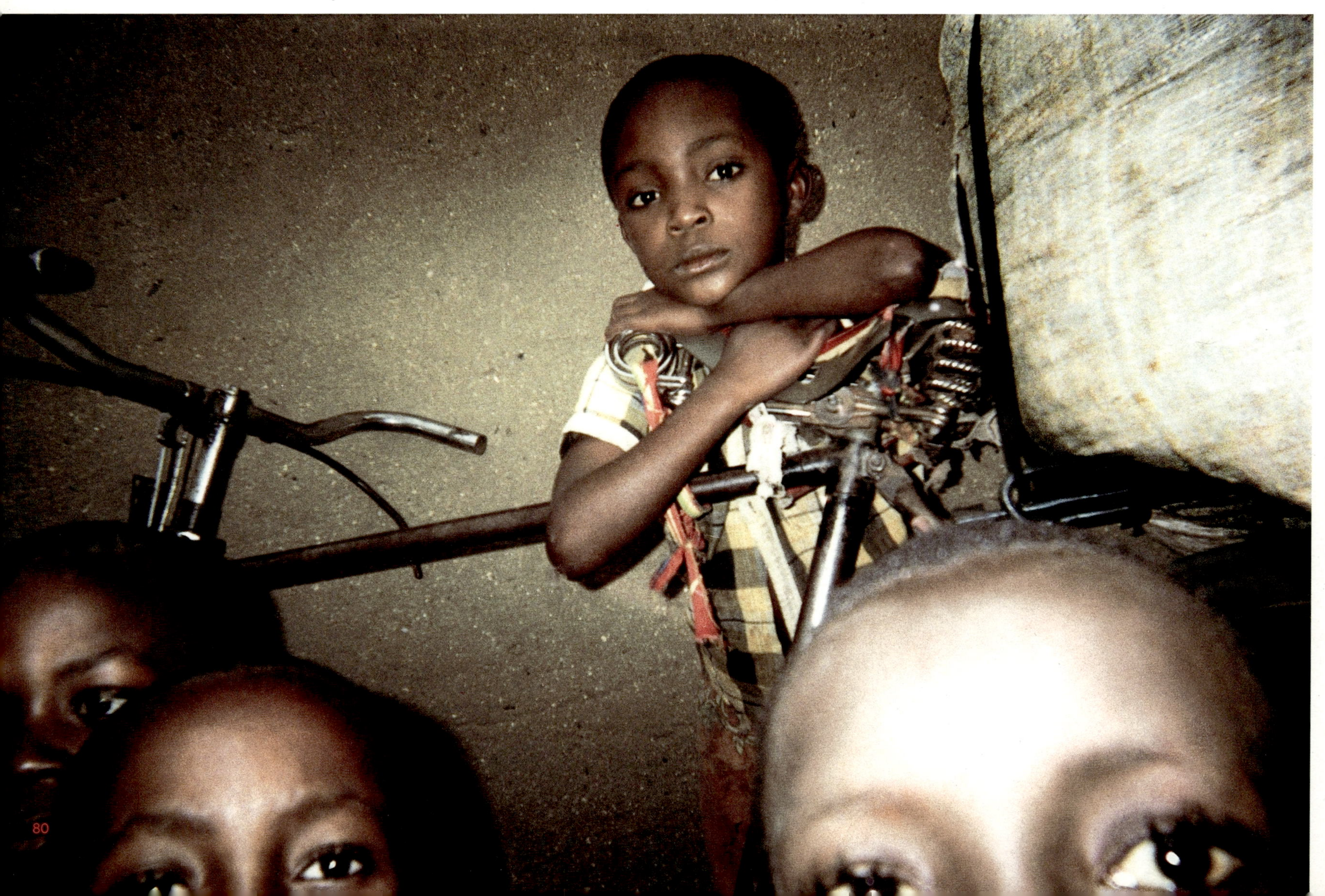

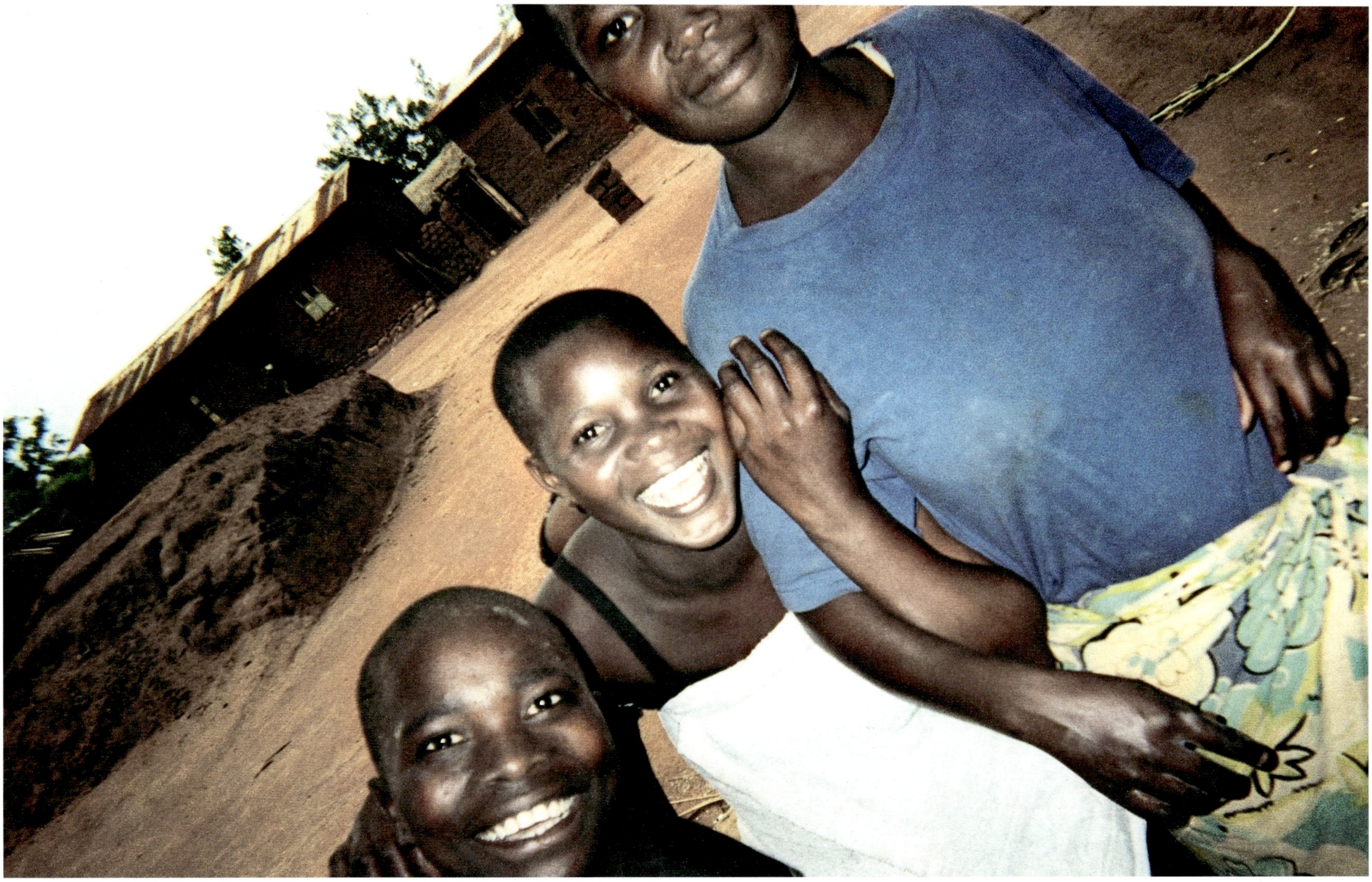

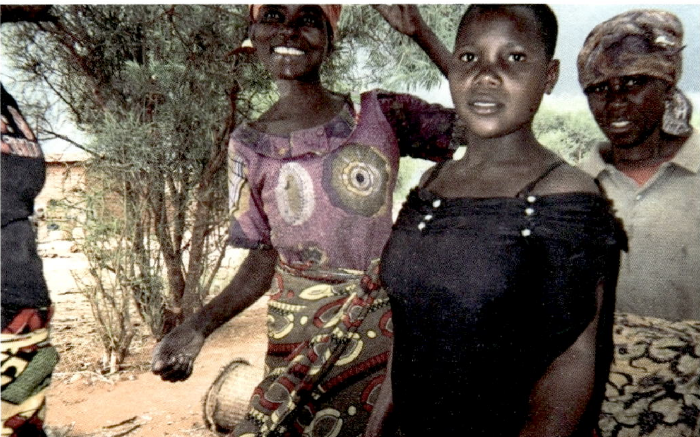

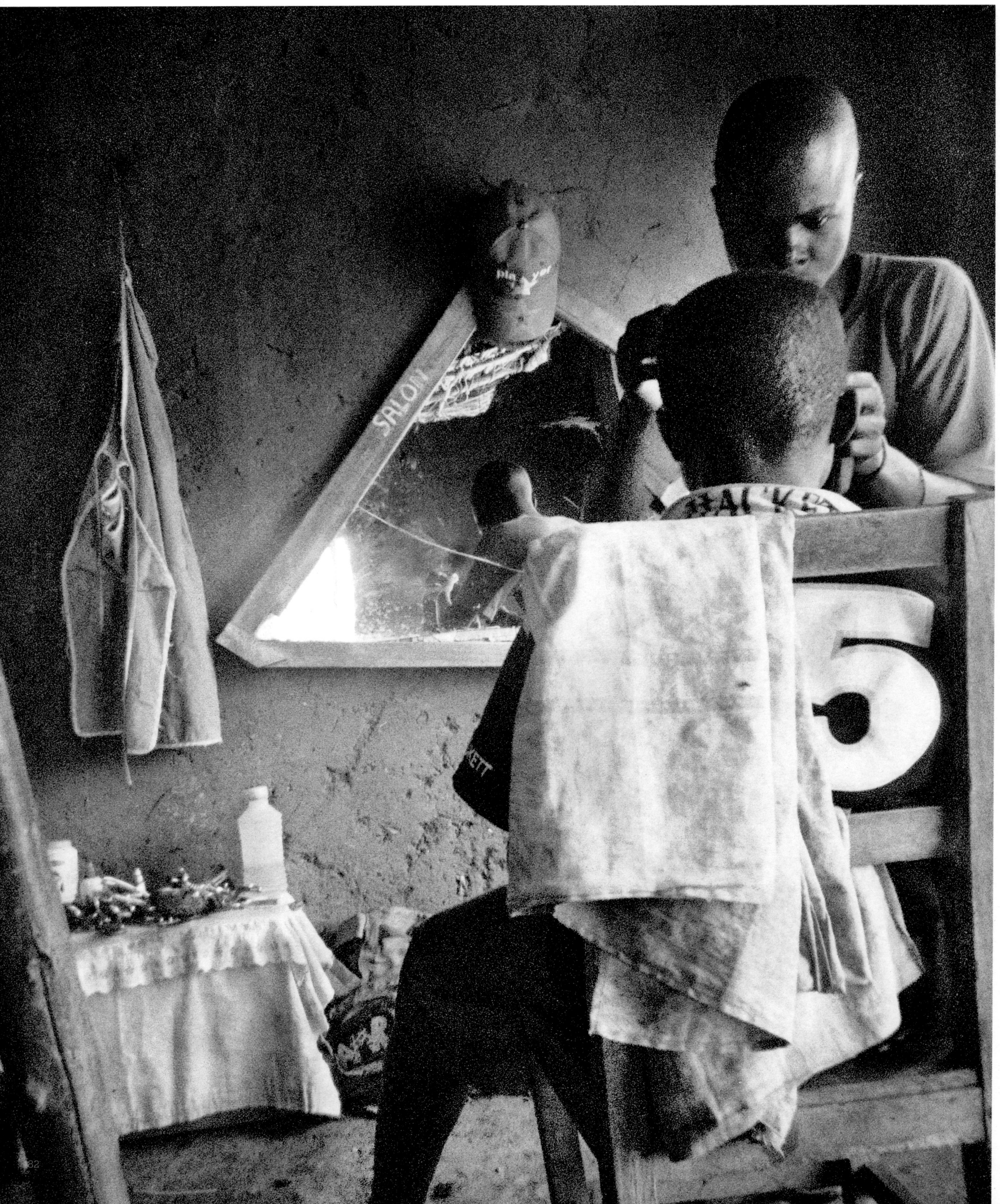

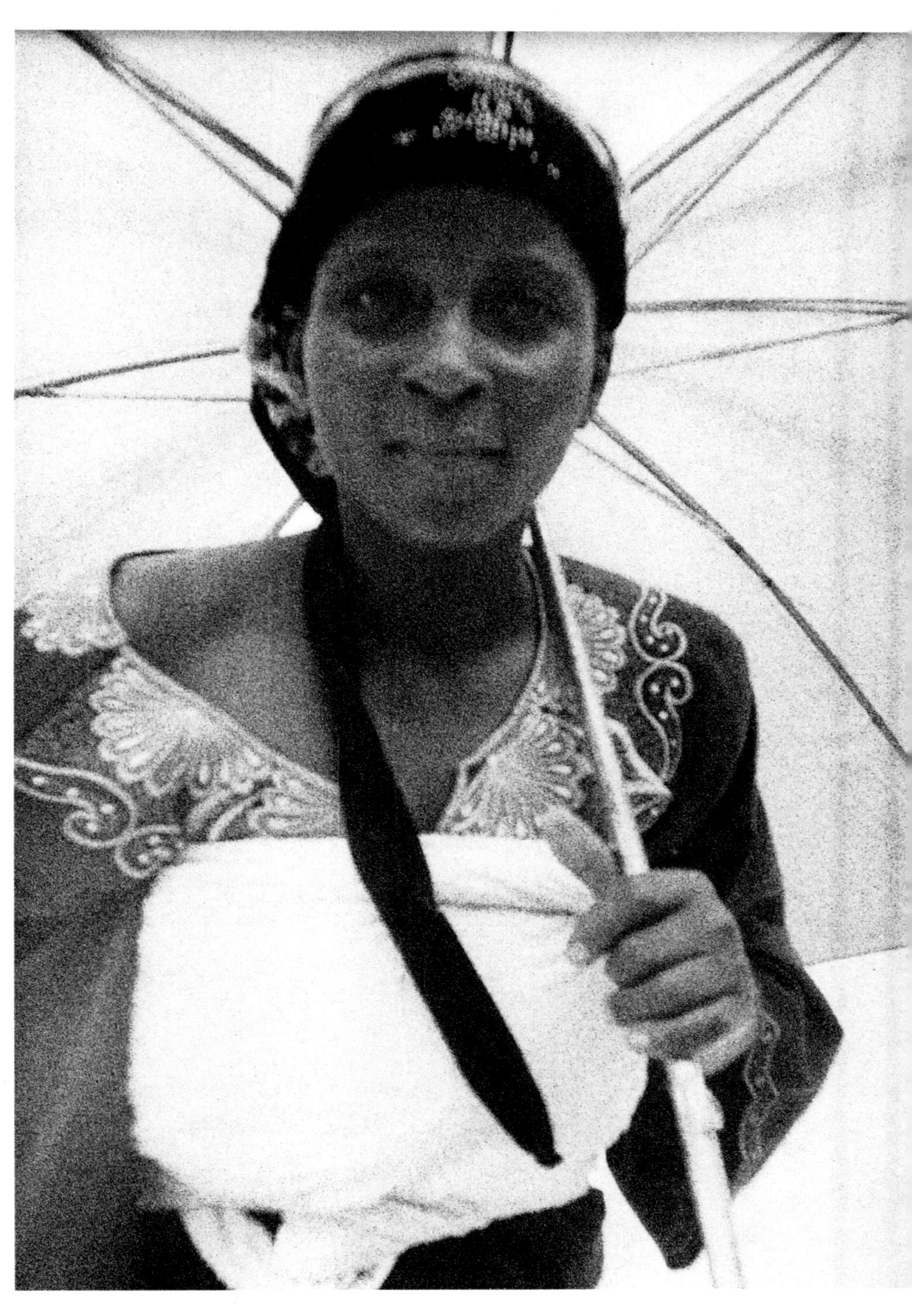

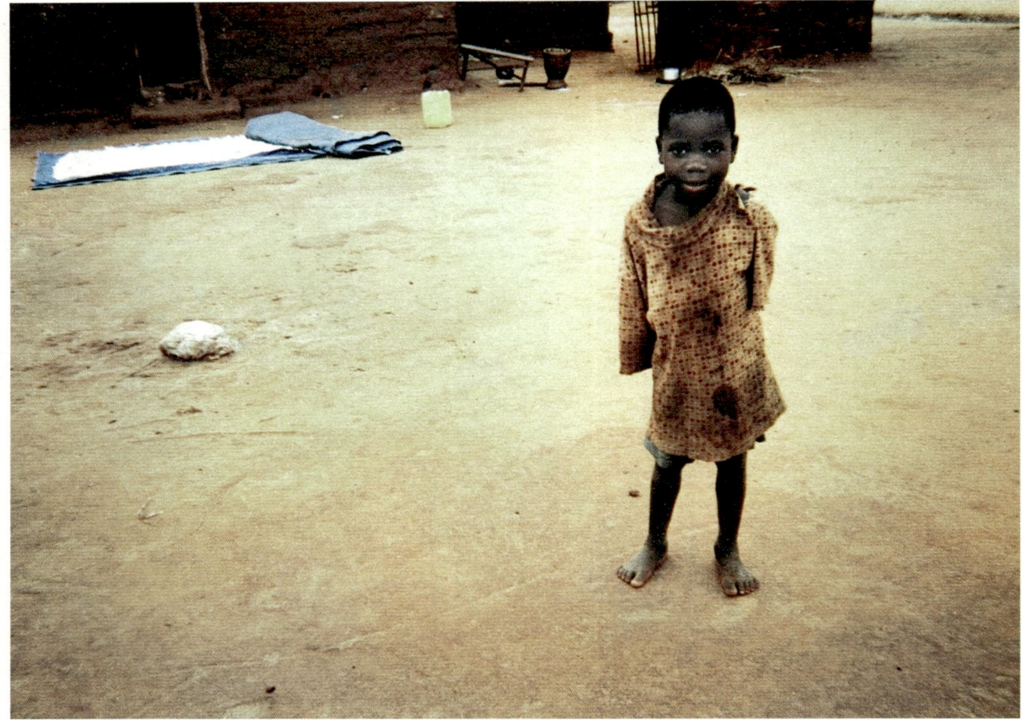

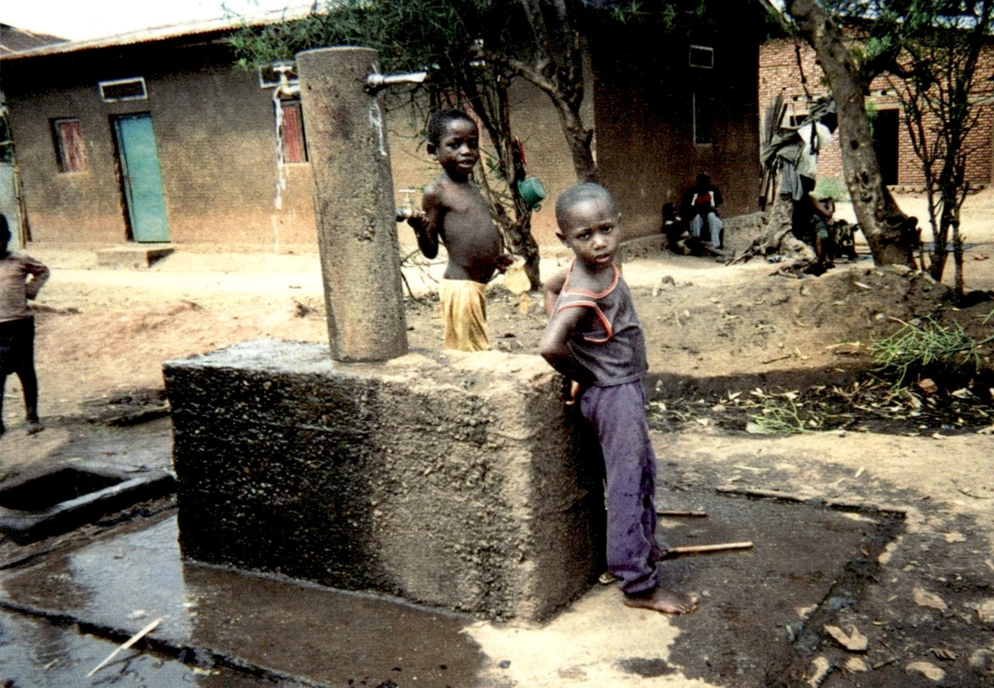

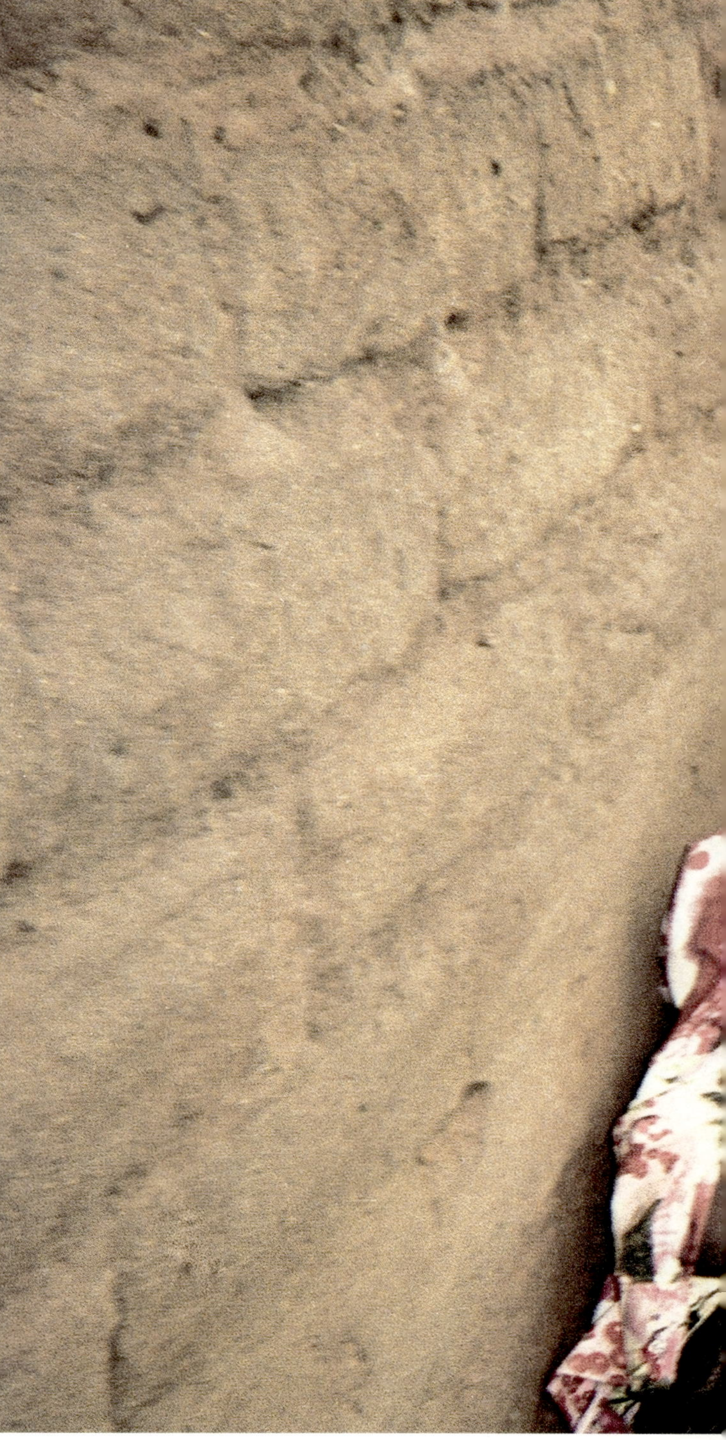

The Congo Family Album

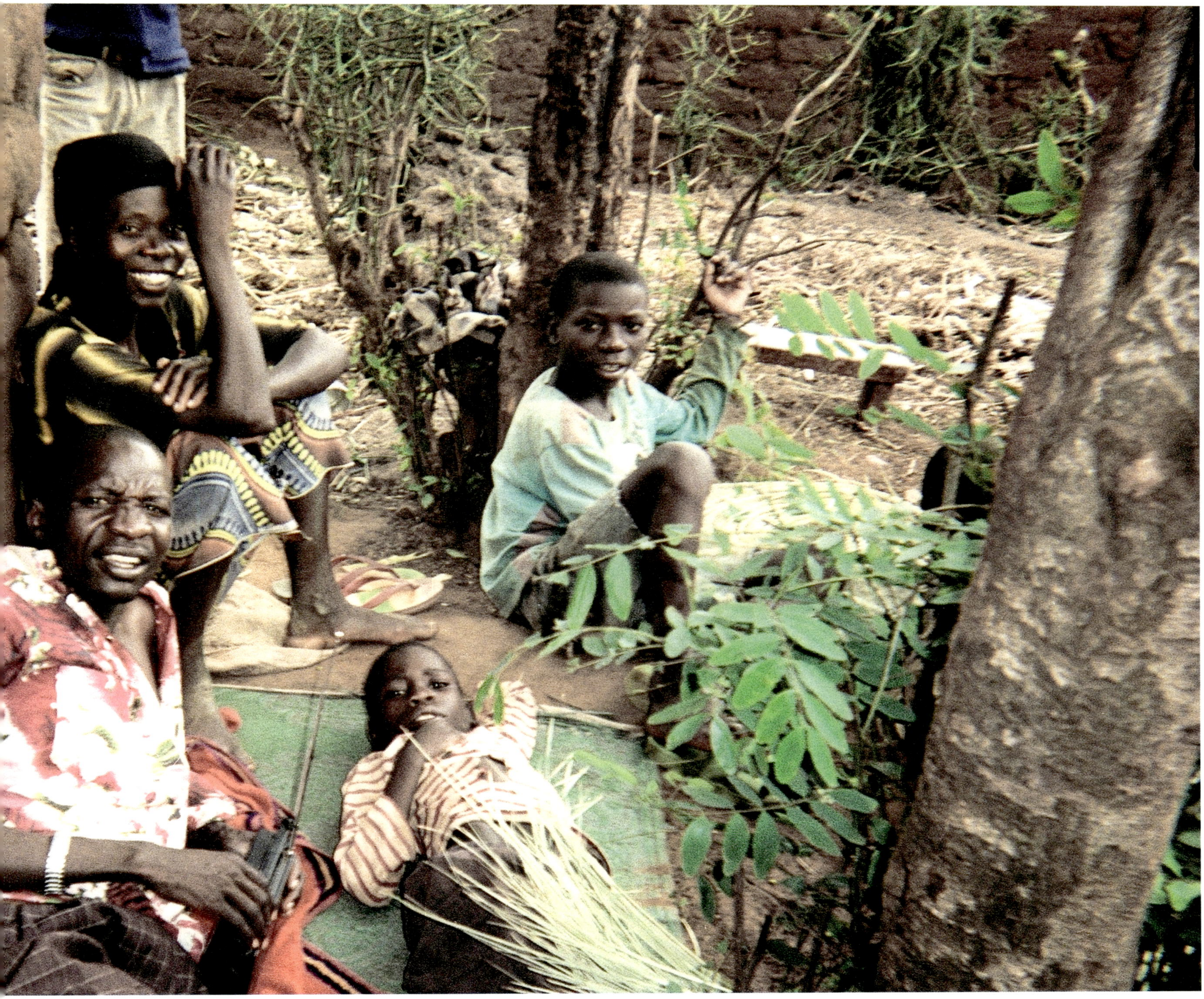

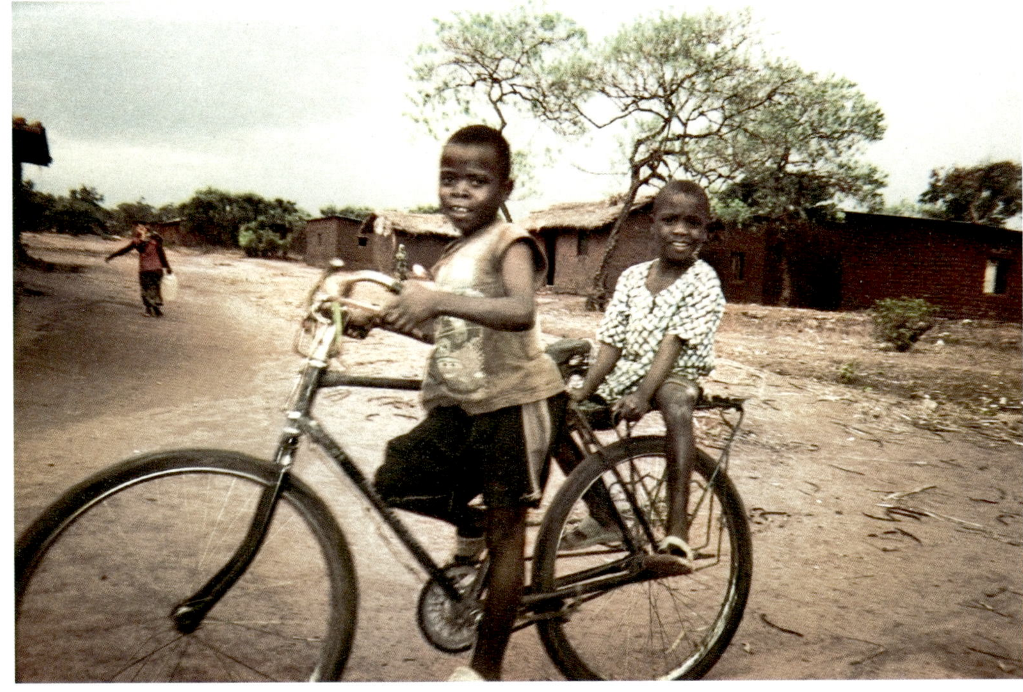

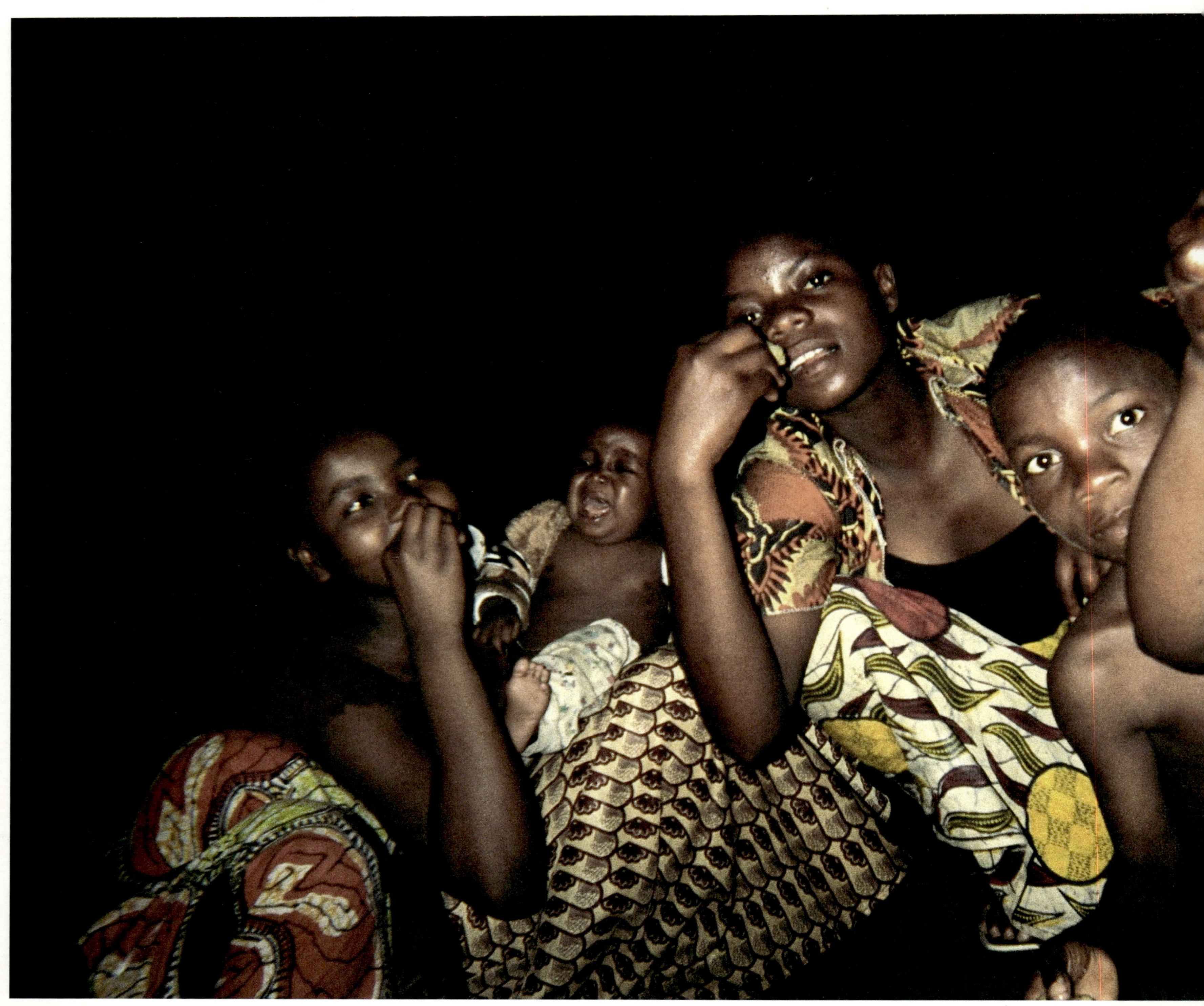

    The Congo Family Album

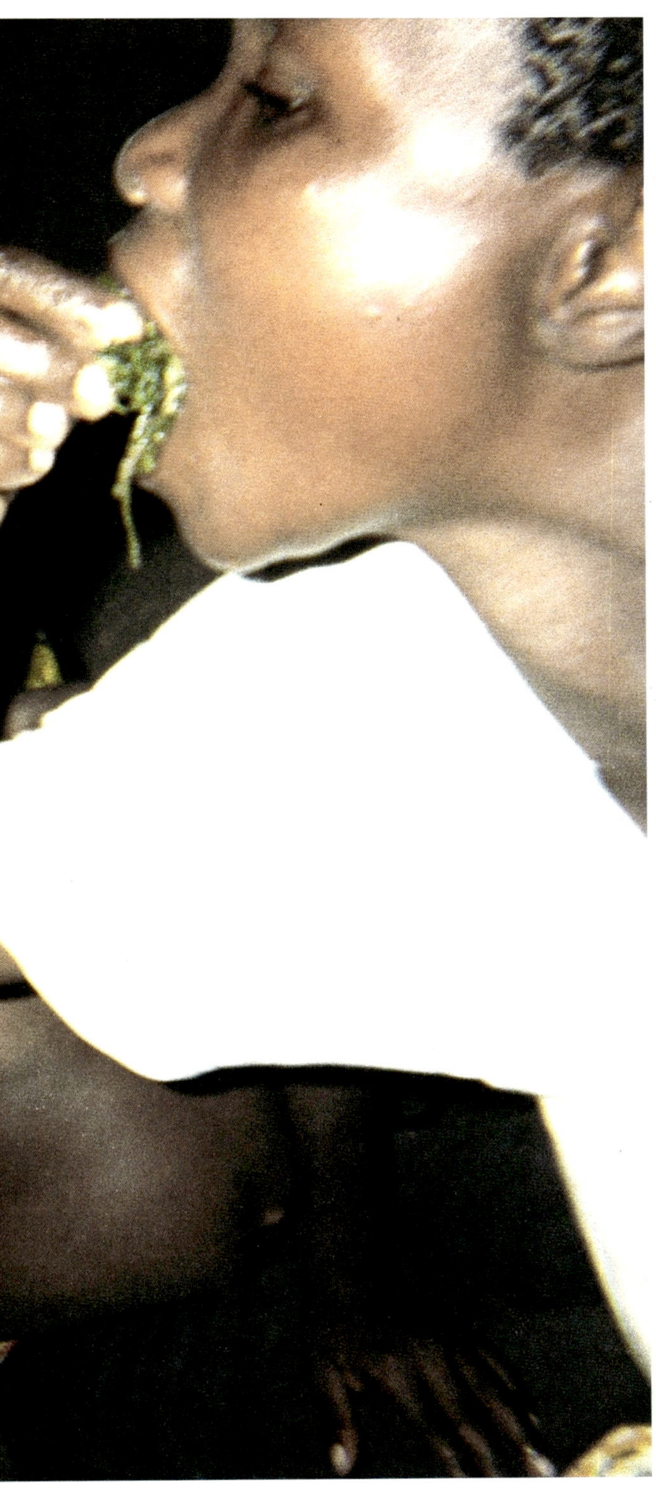

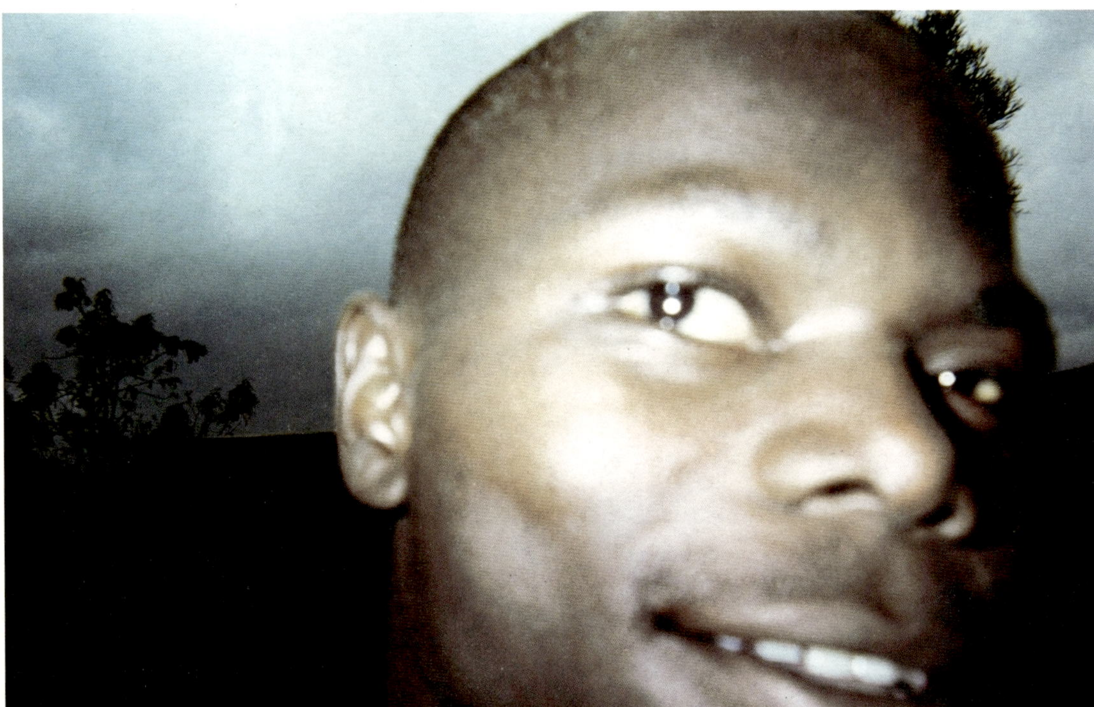

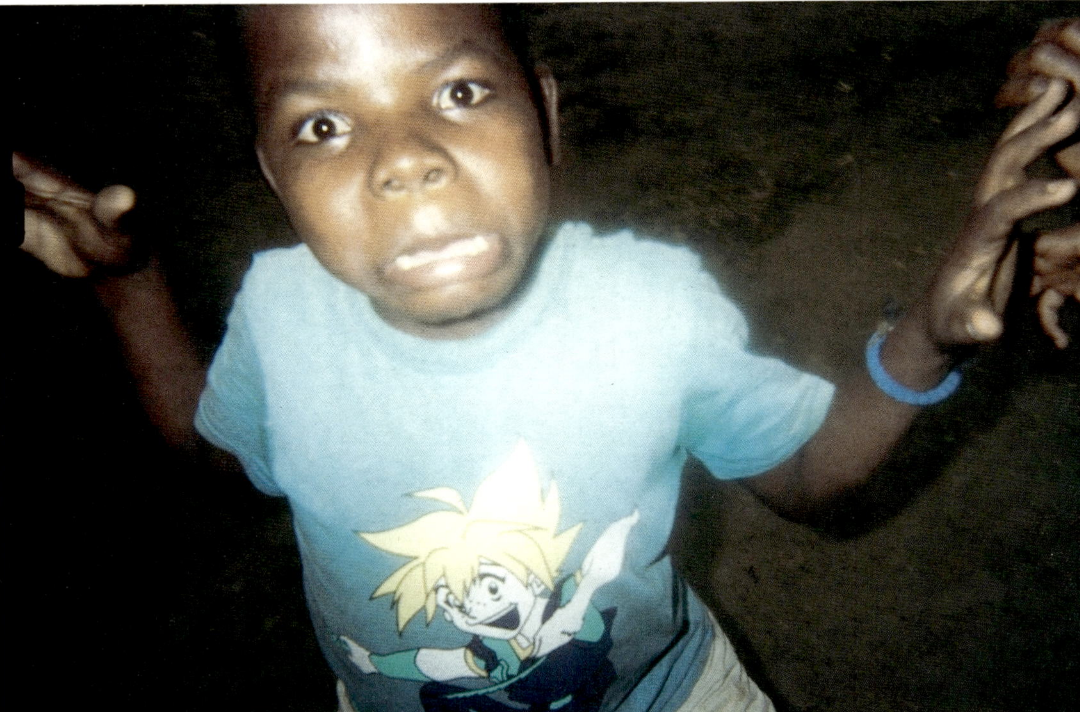

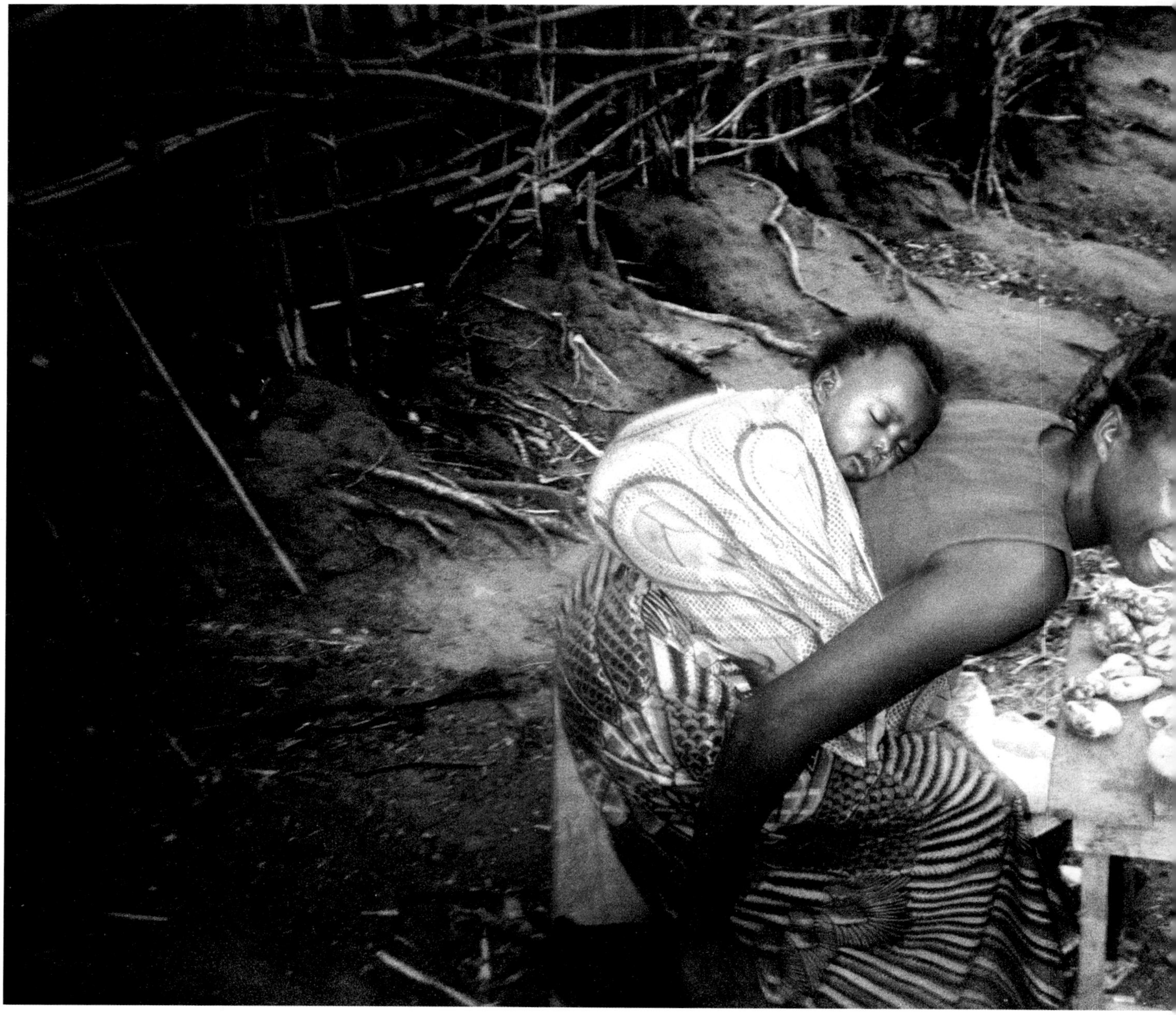

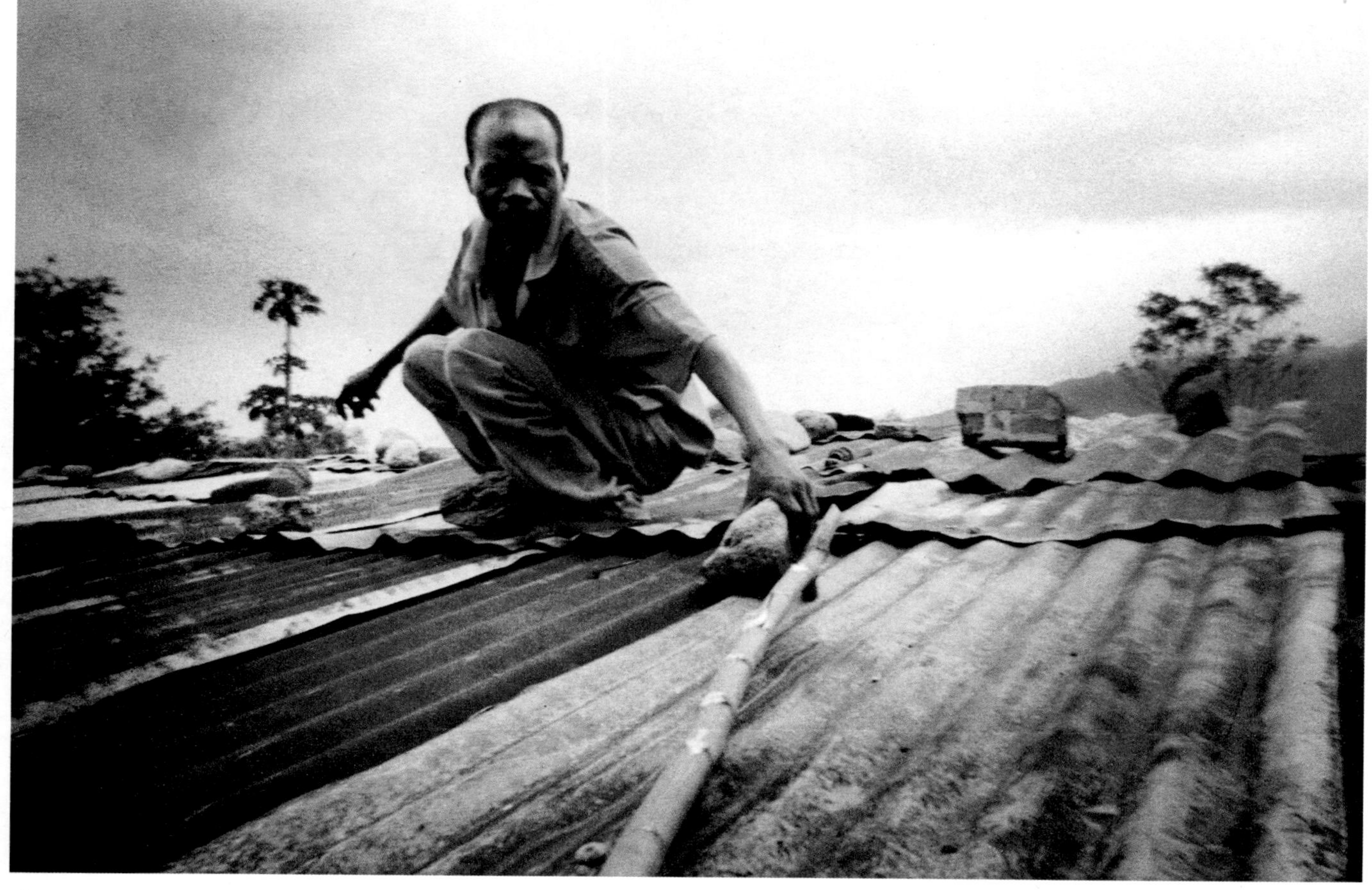

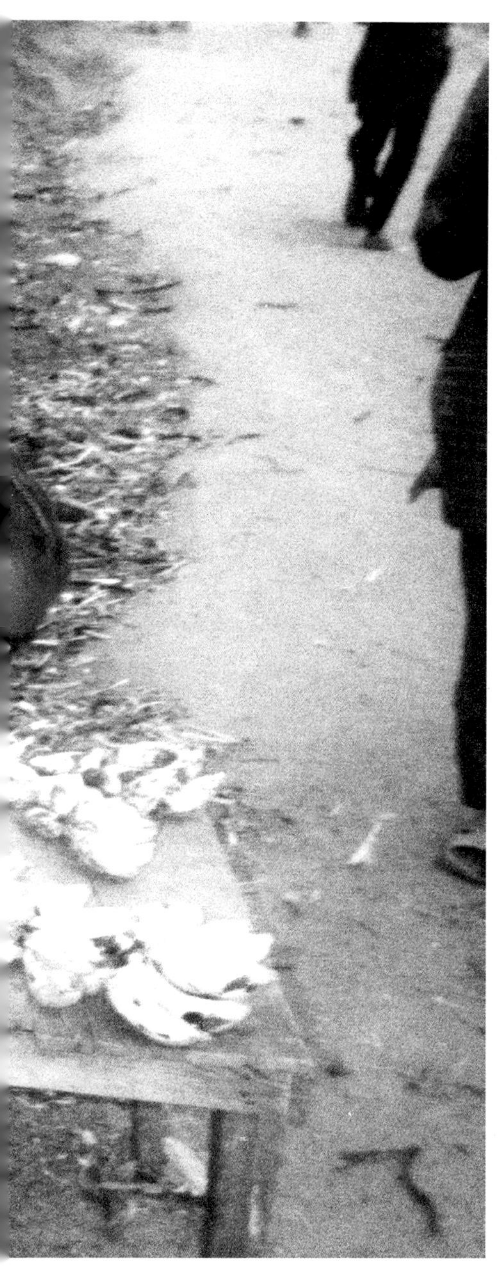

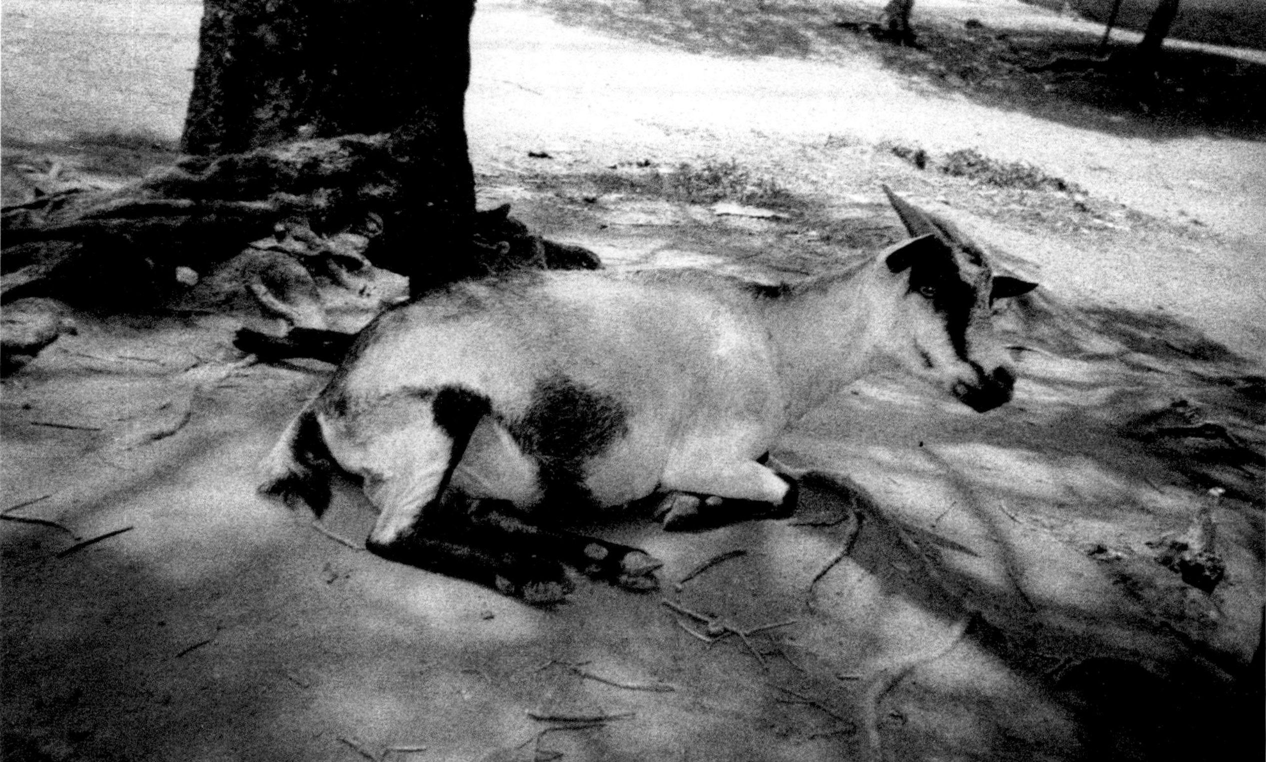

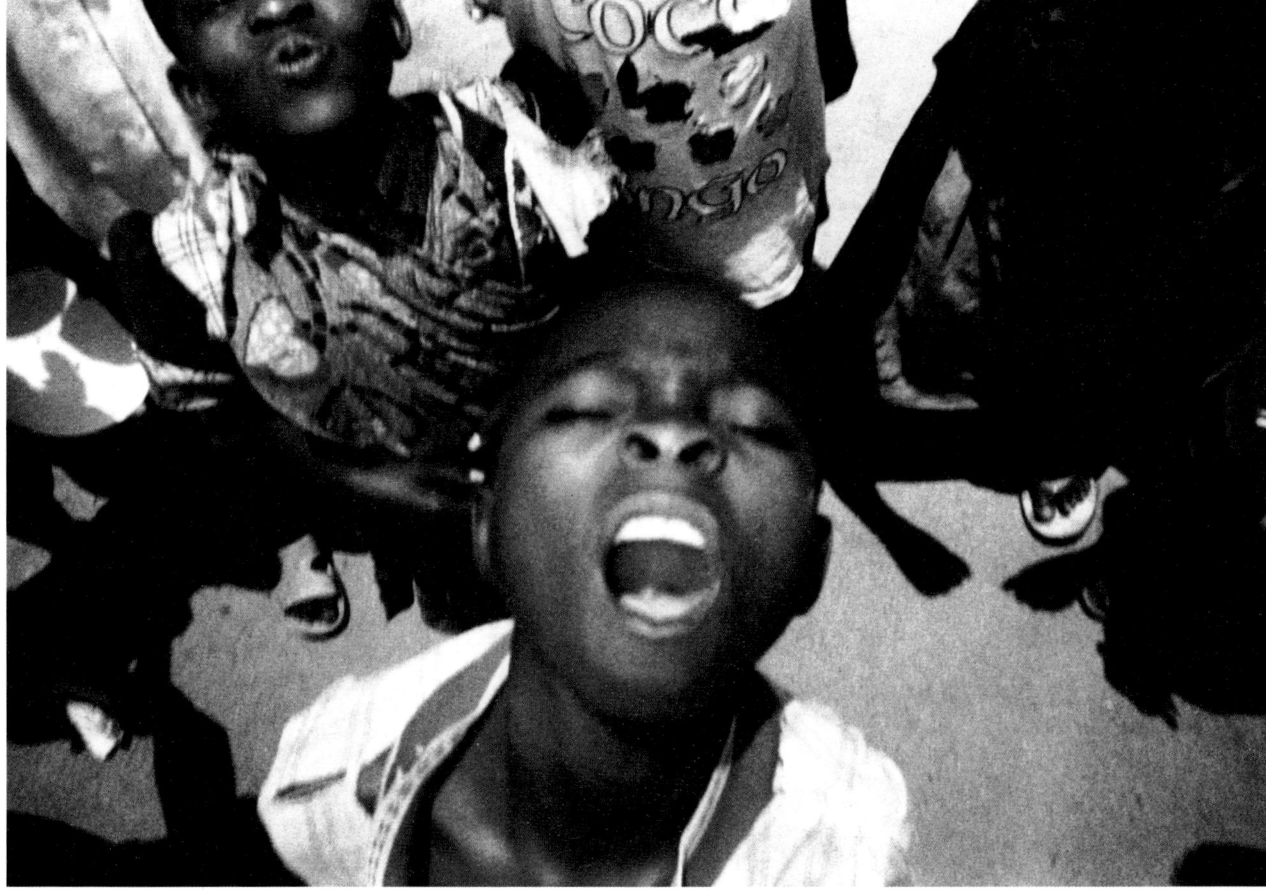

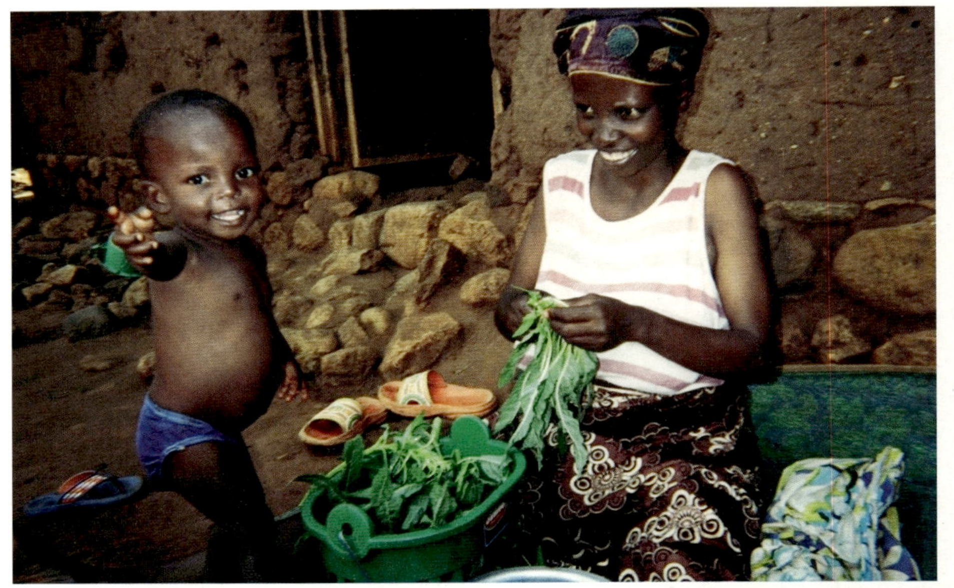

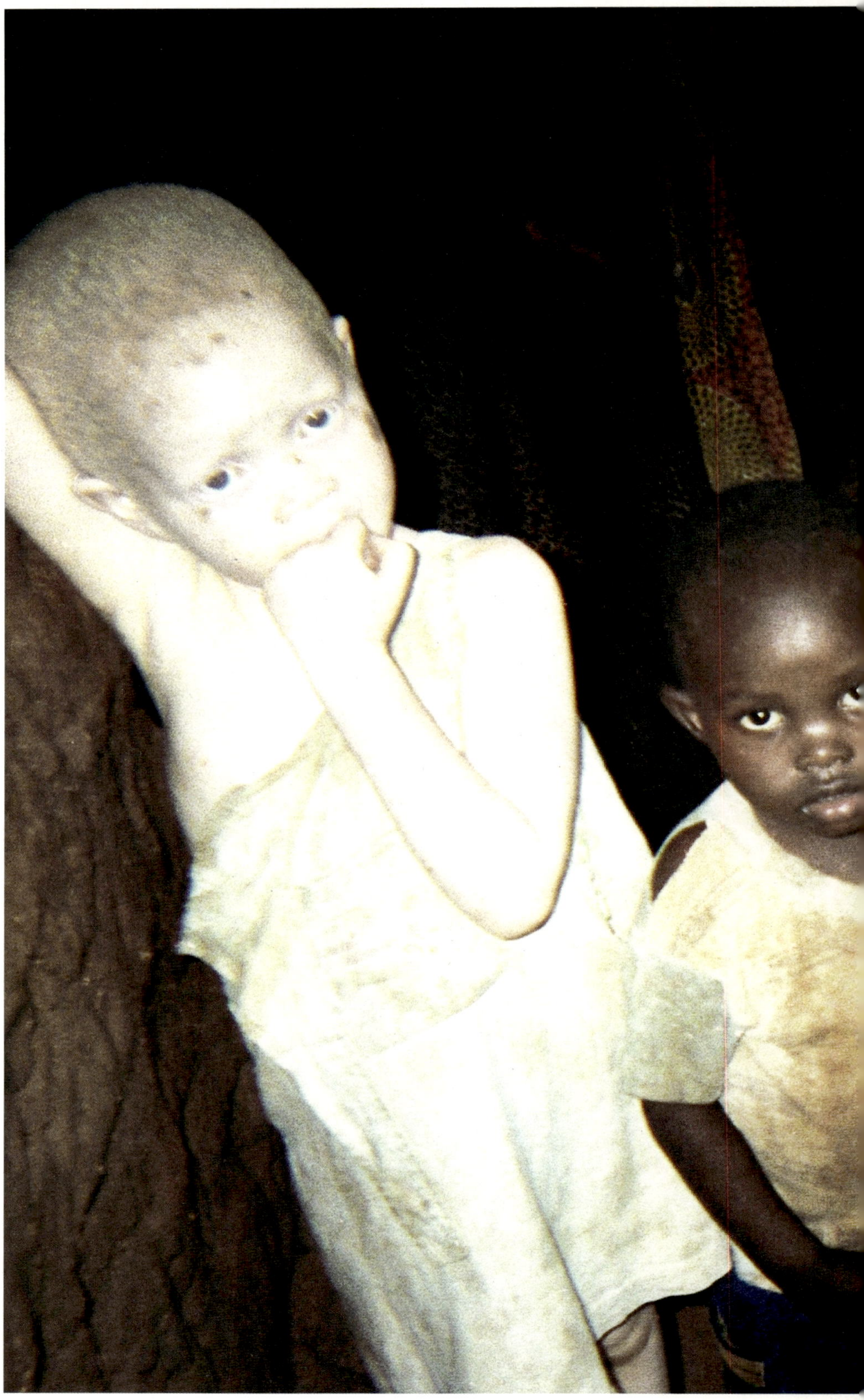

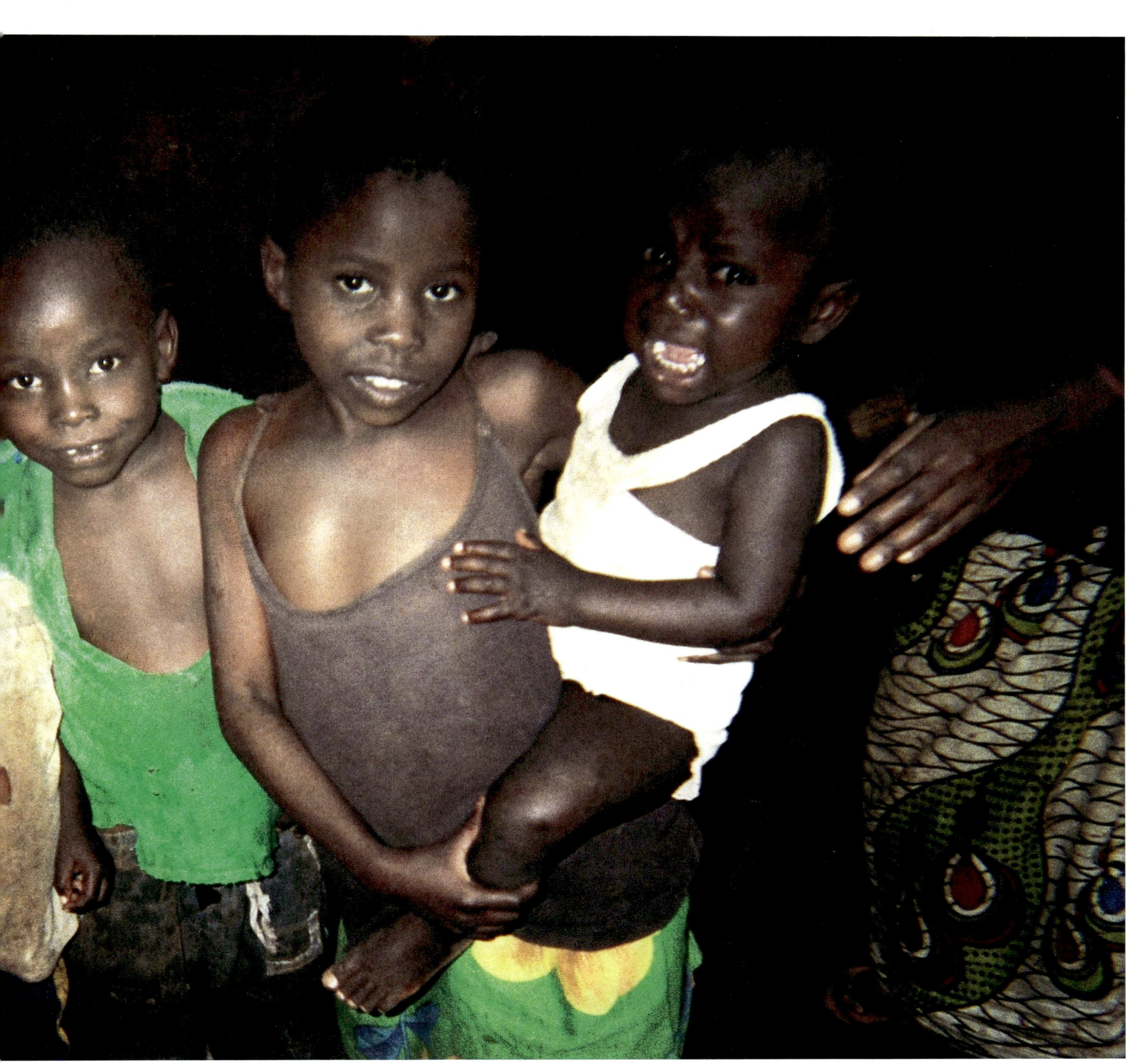

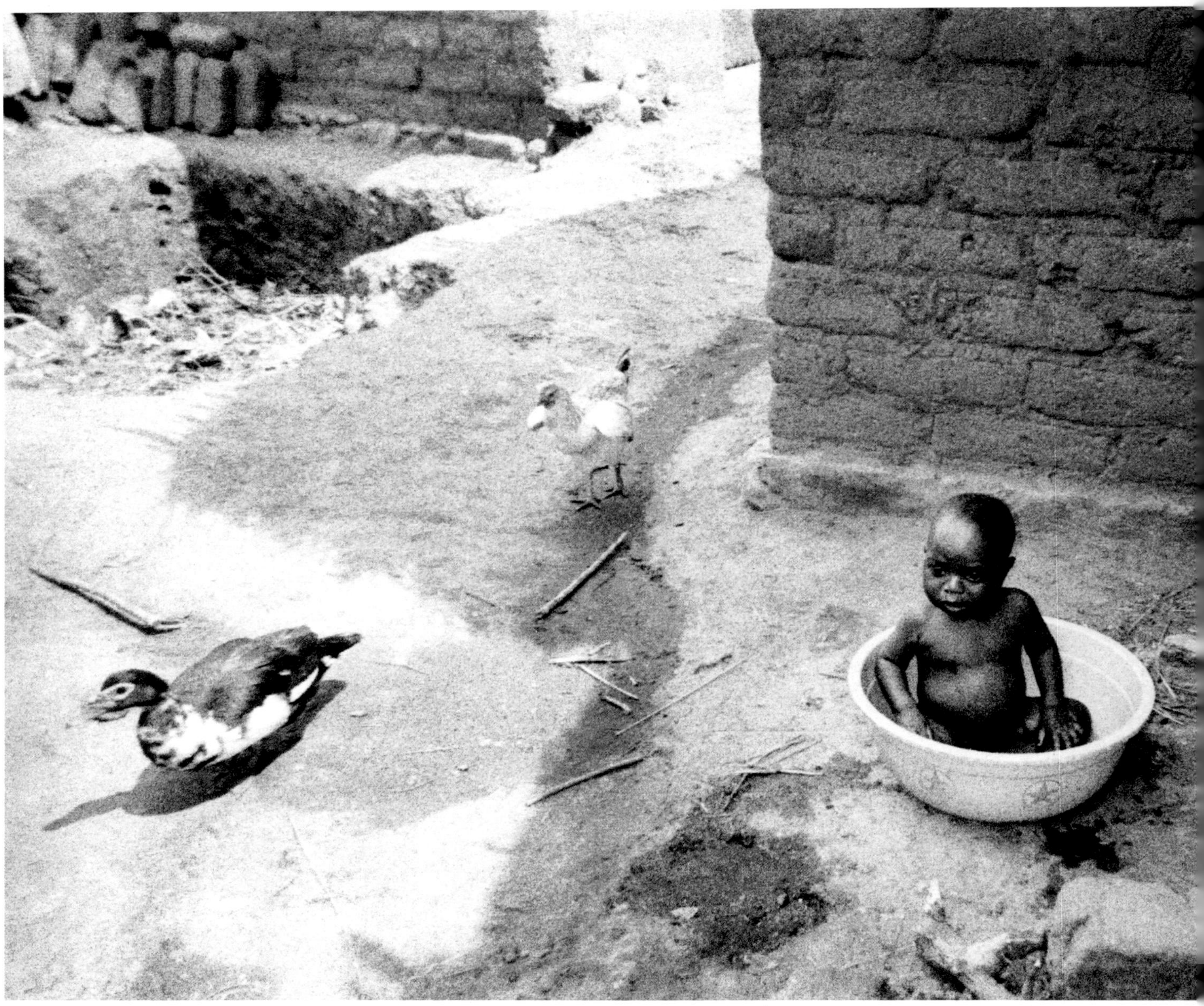

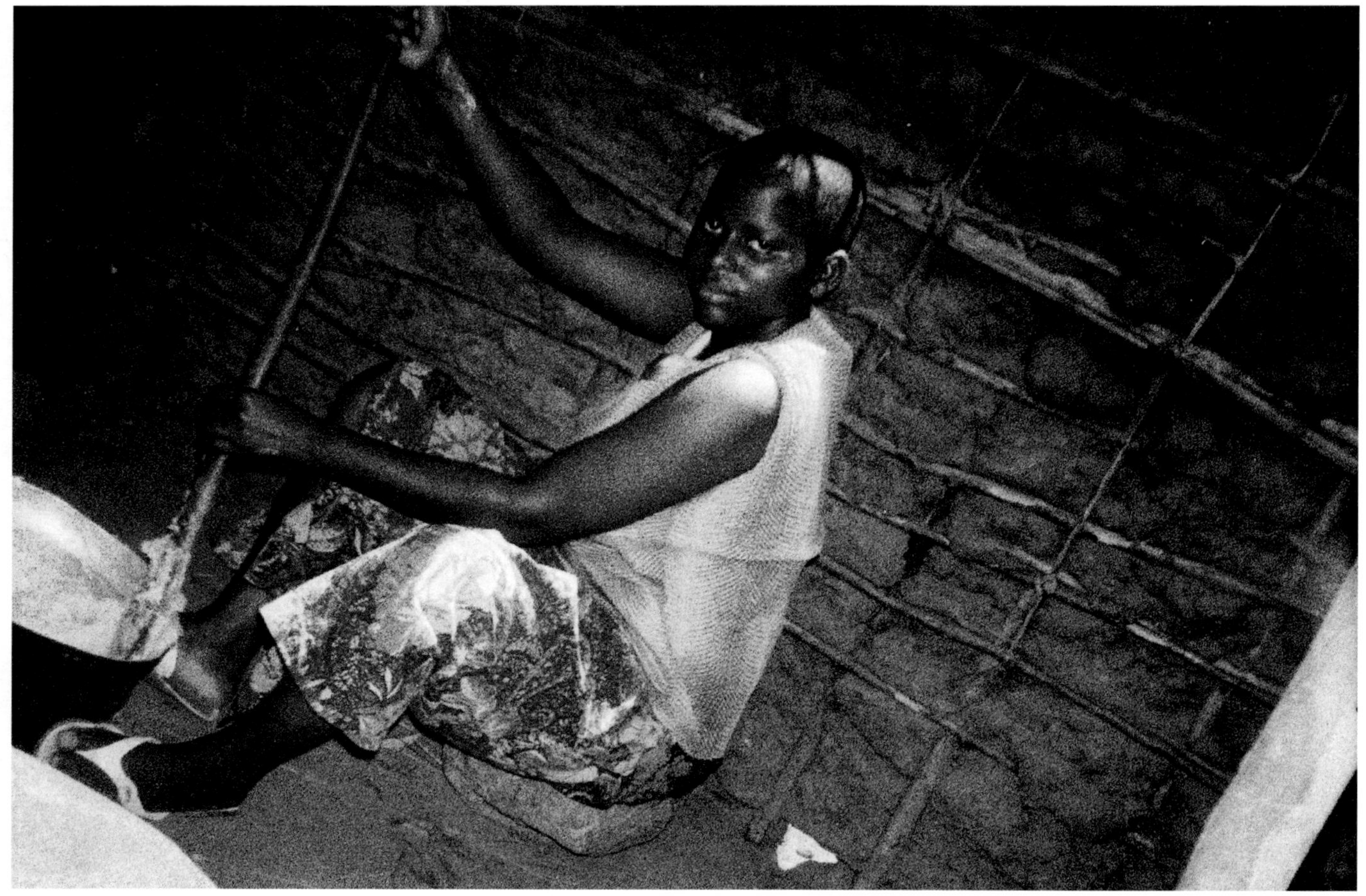

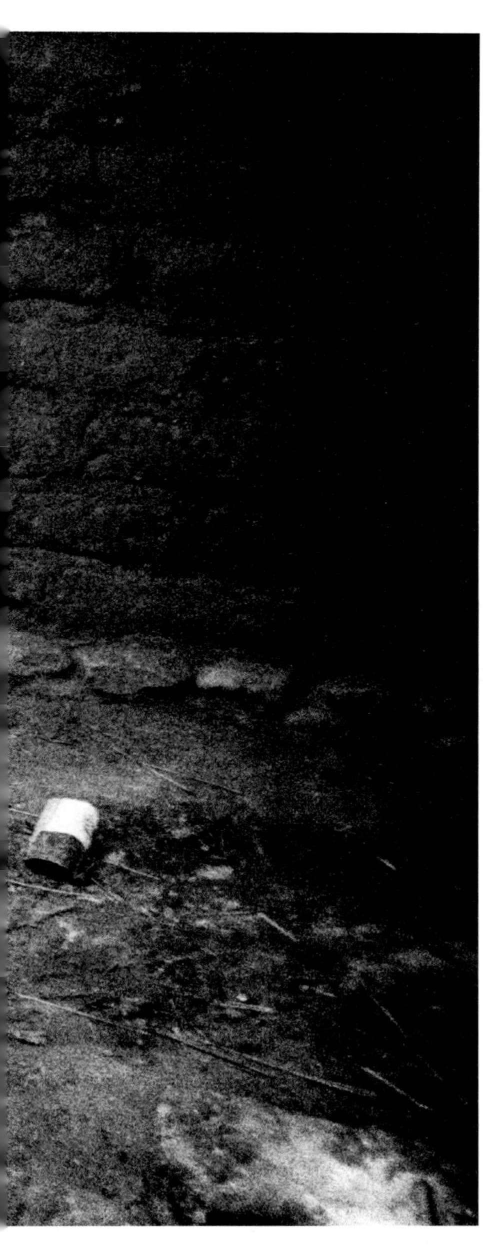

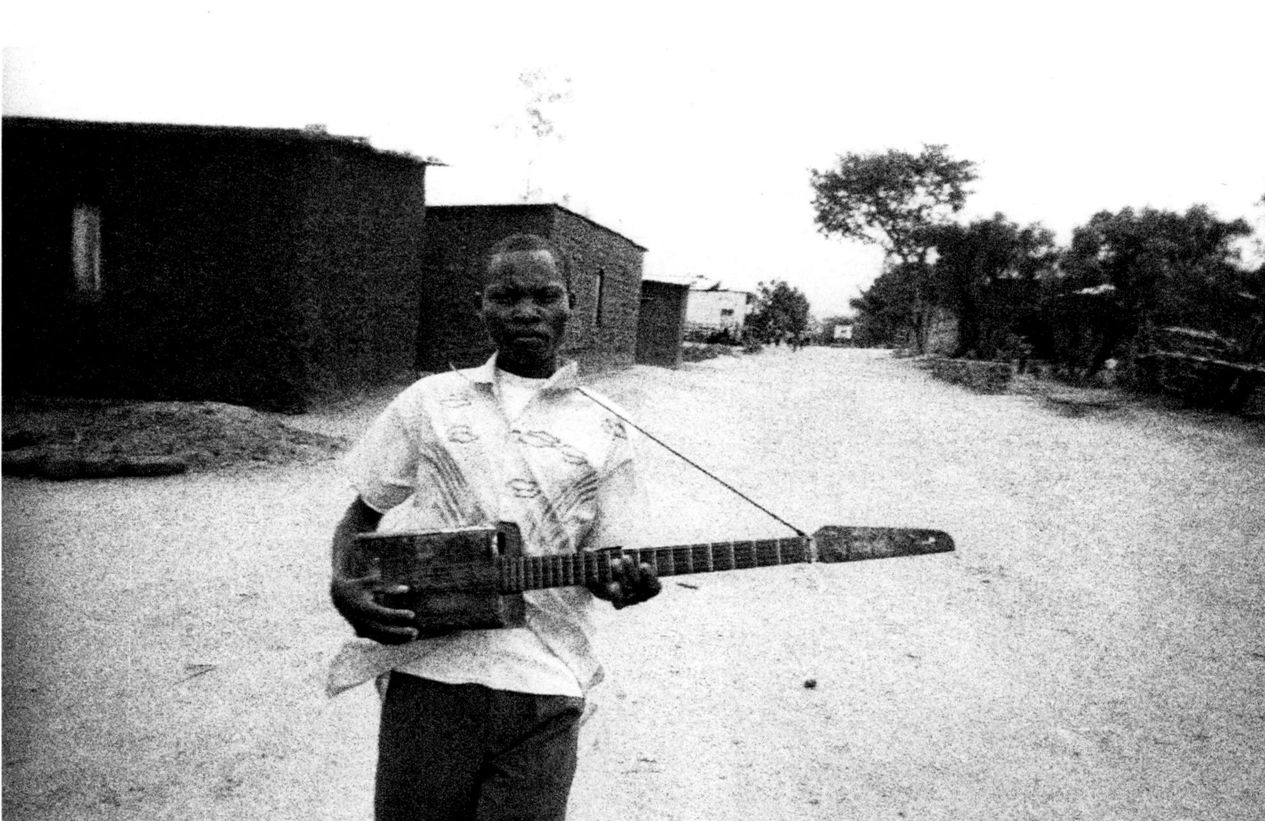

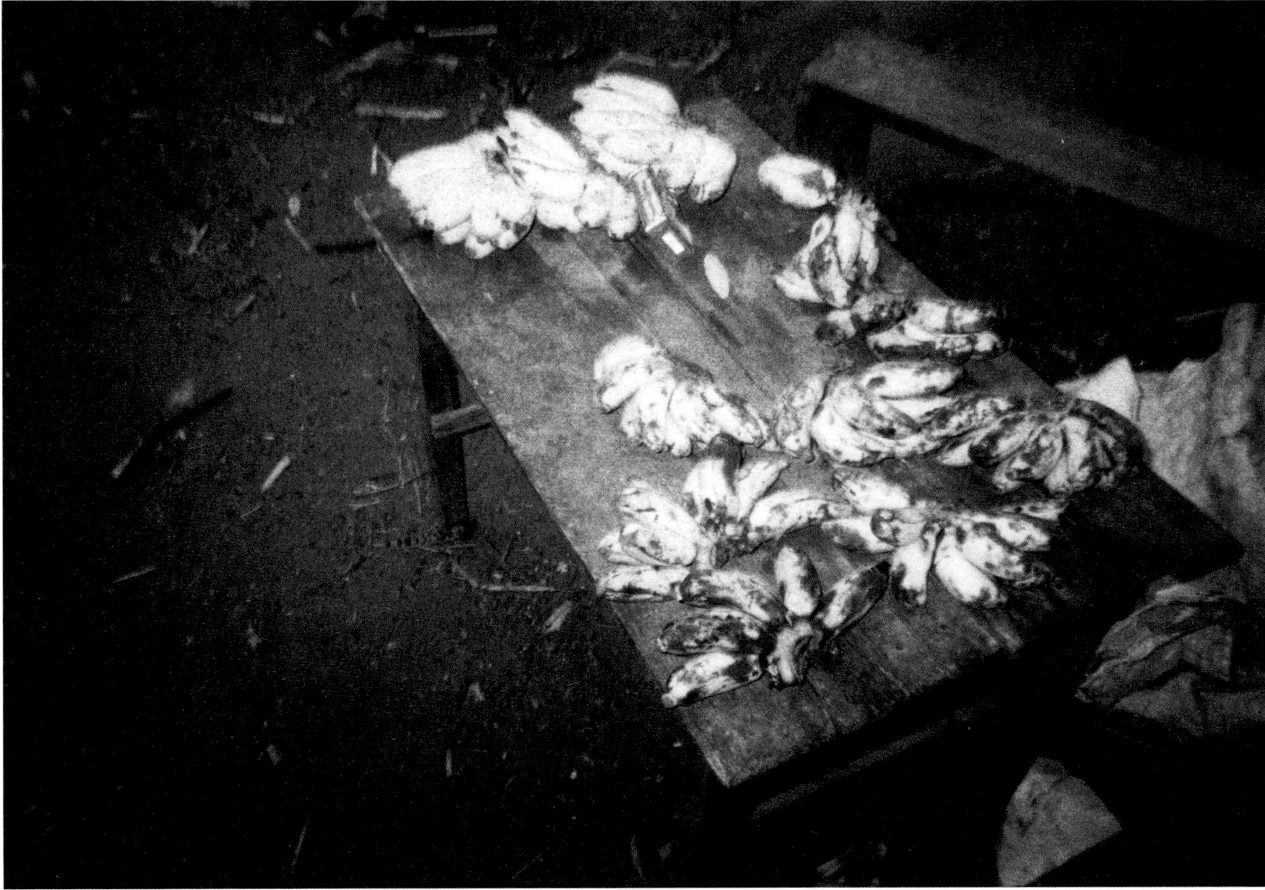

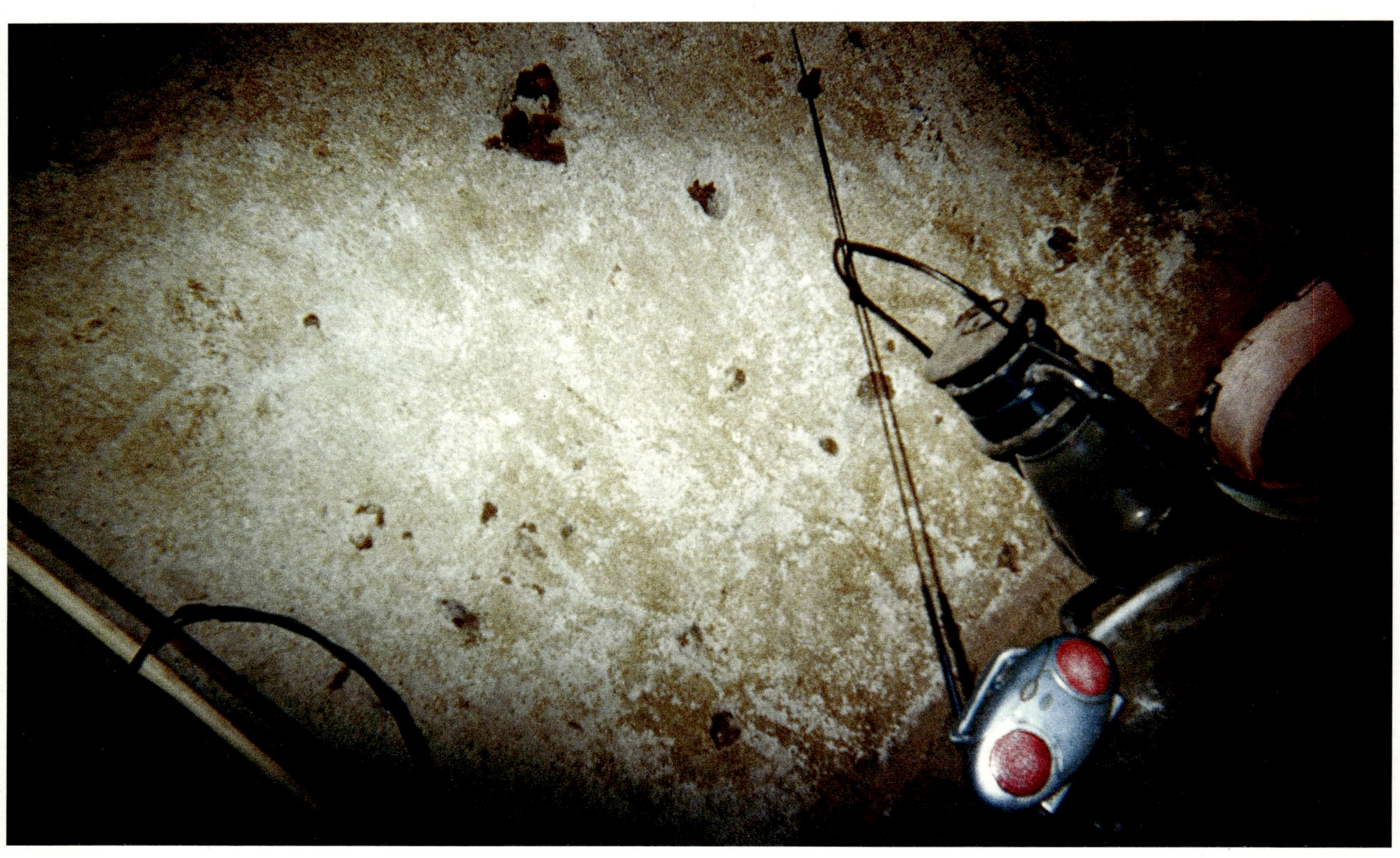

    The Congo Family Album

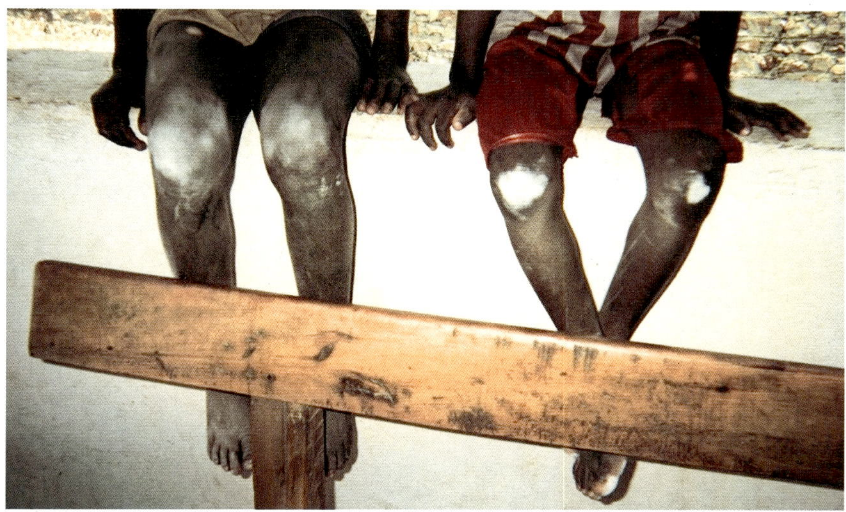

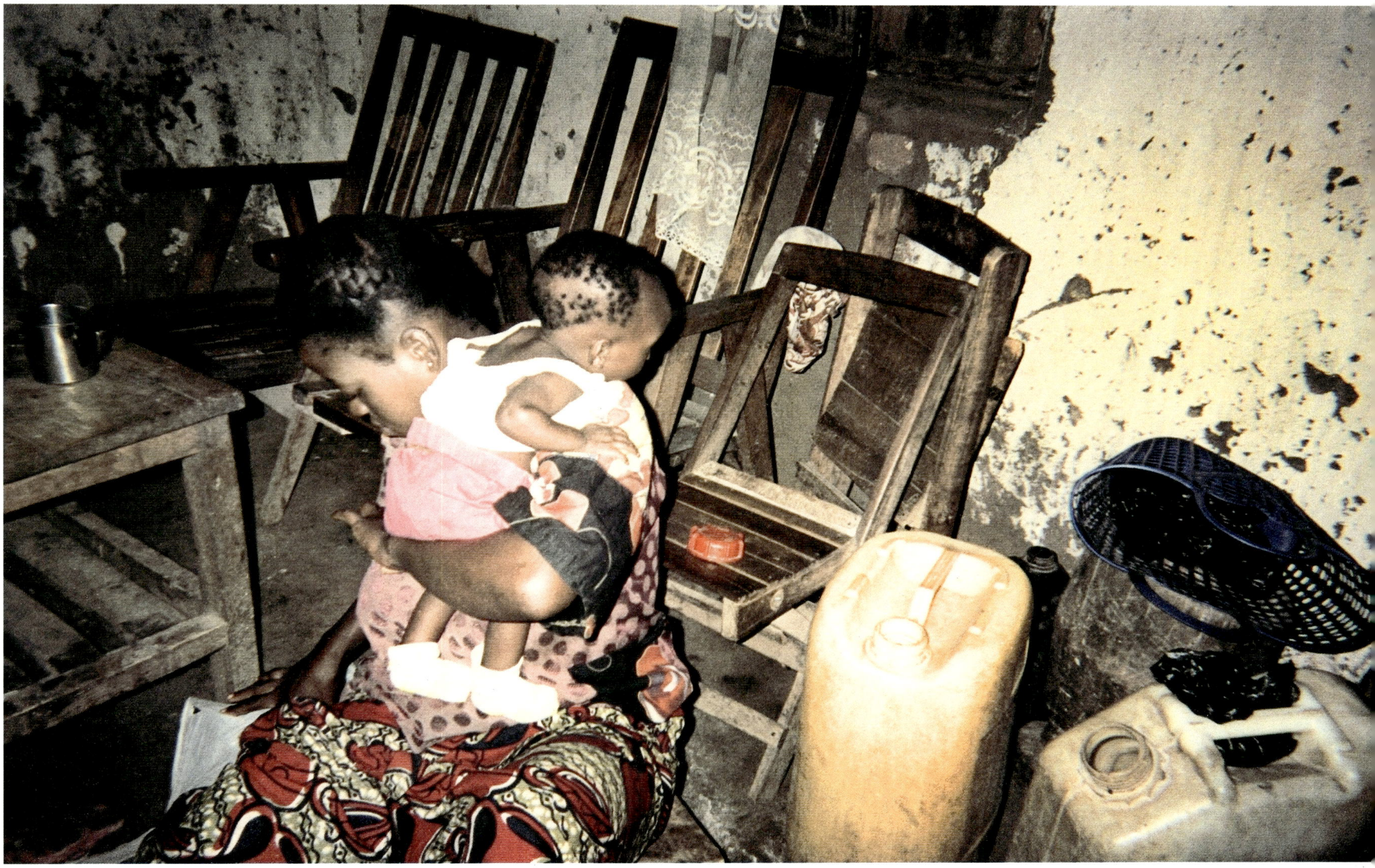

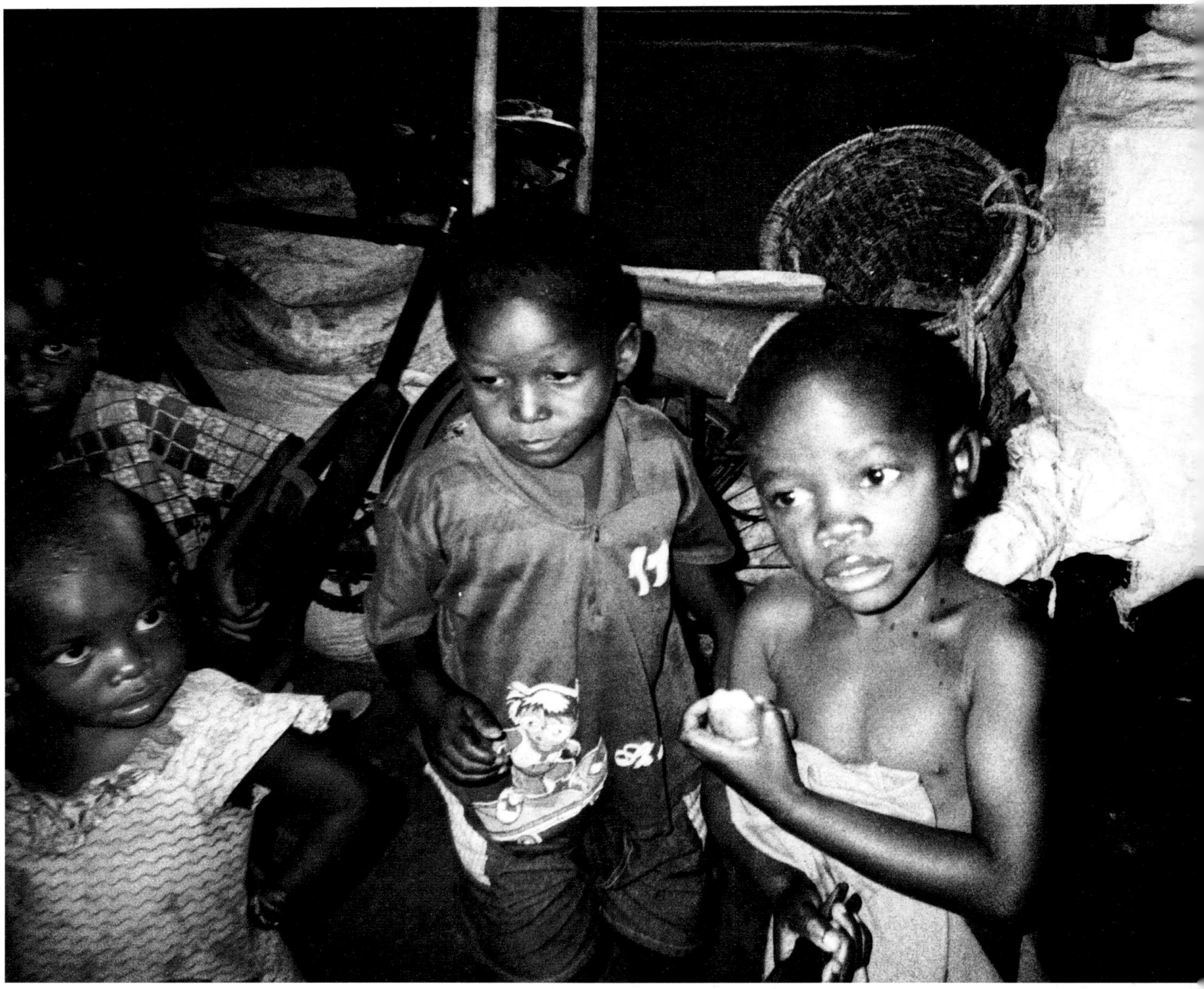

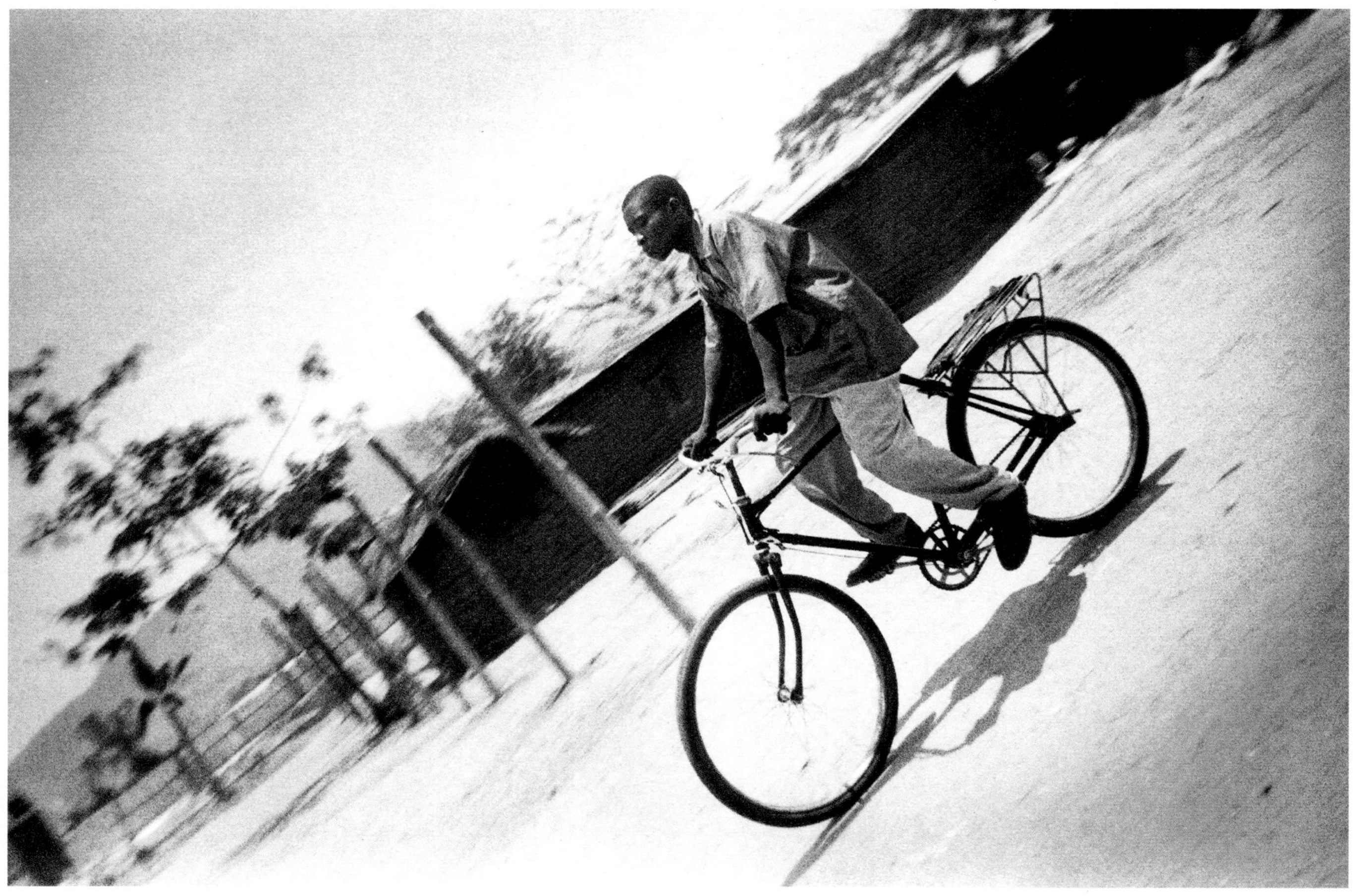

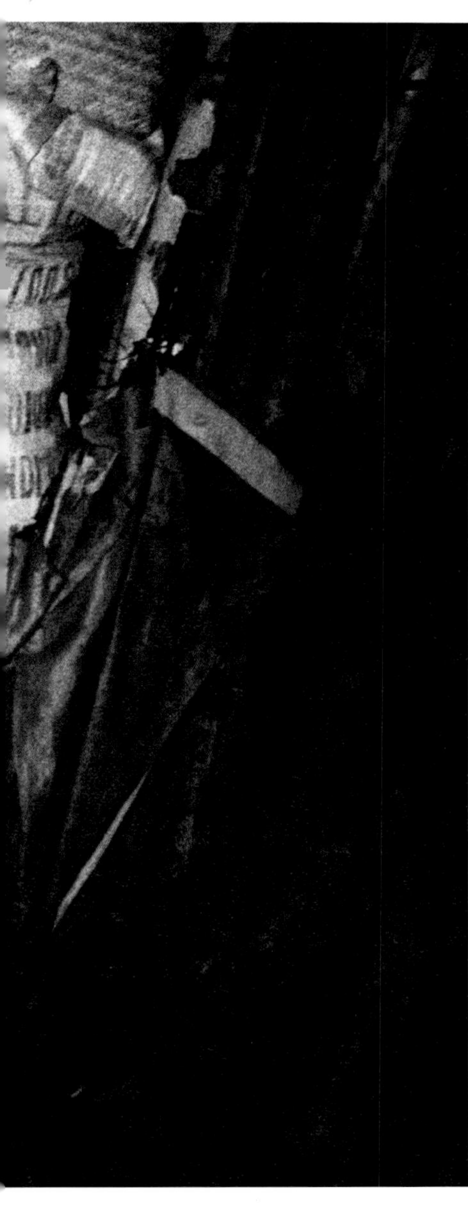

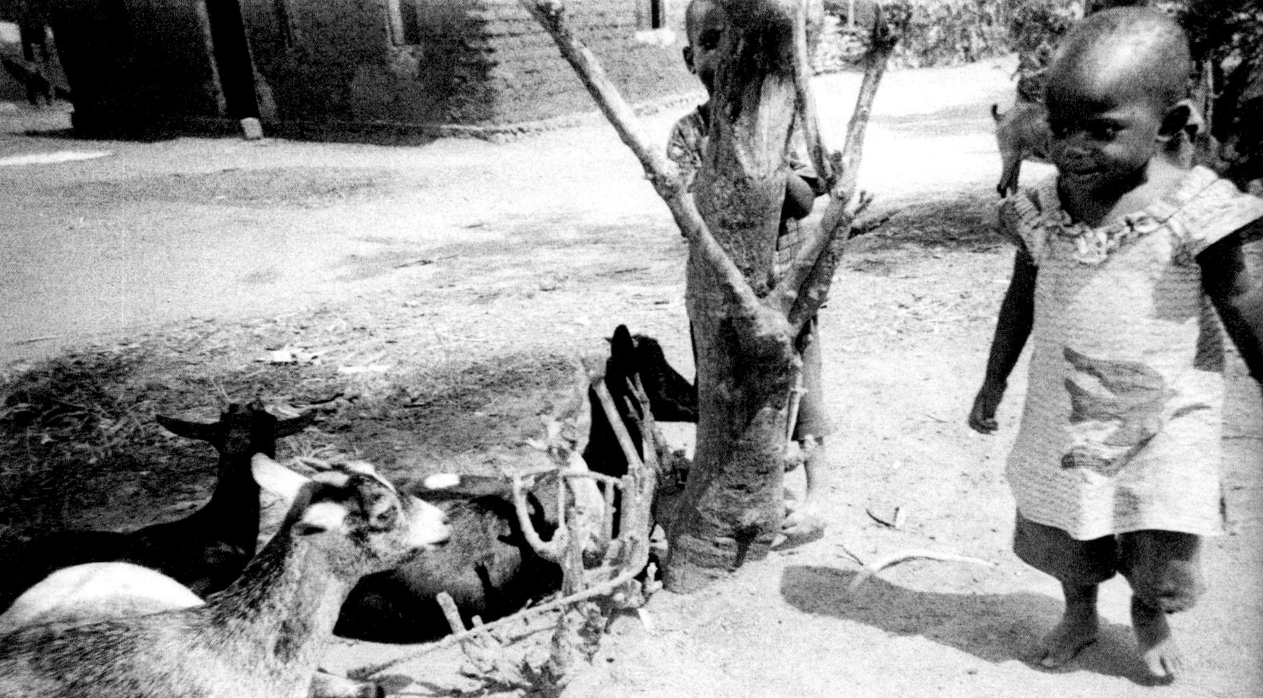

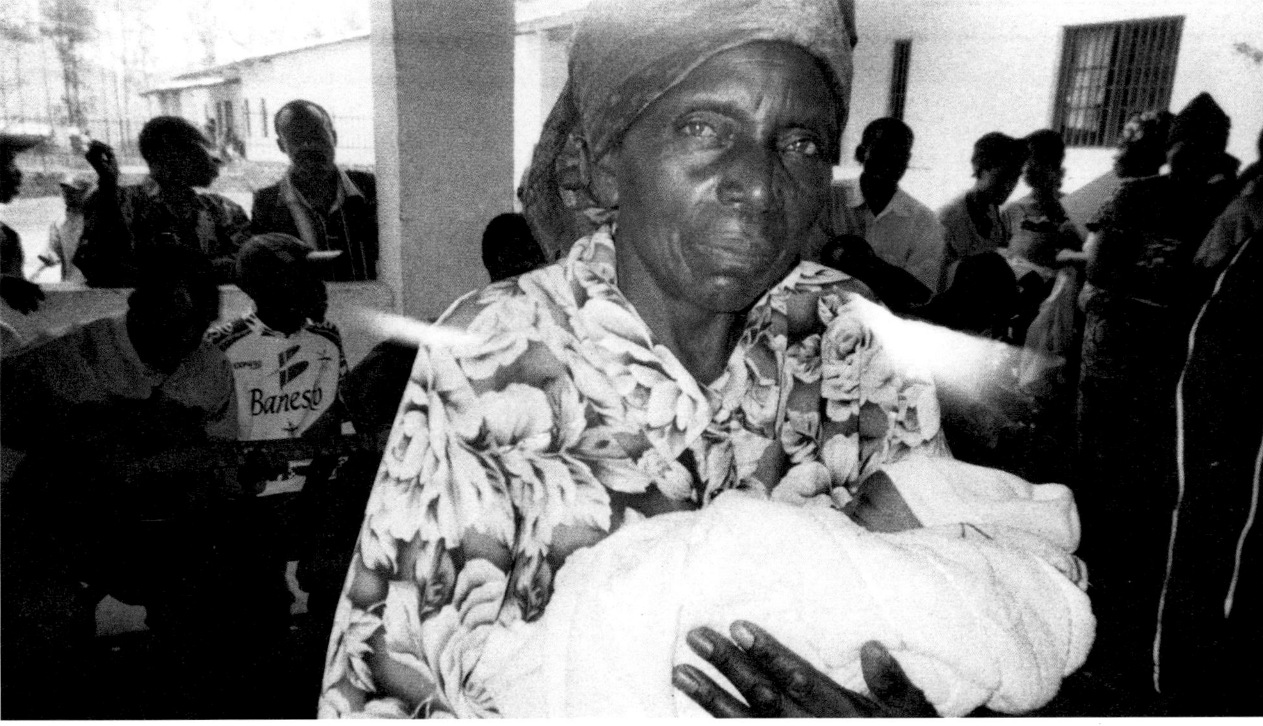

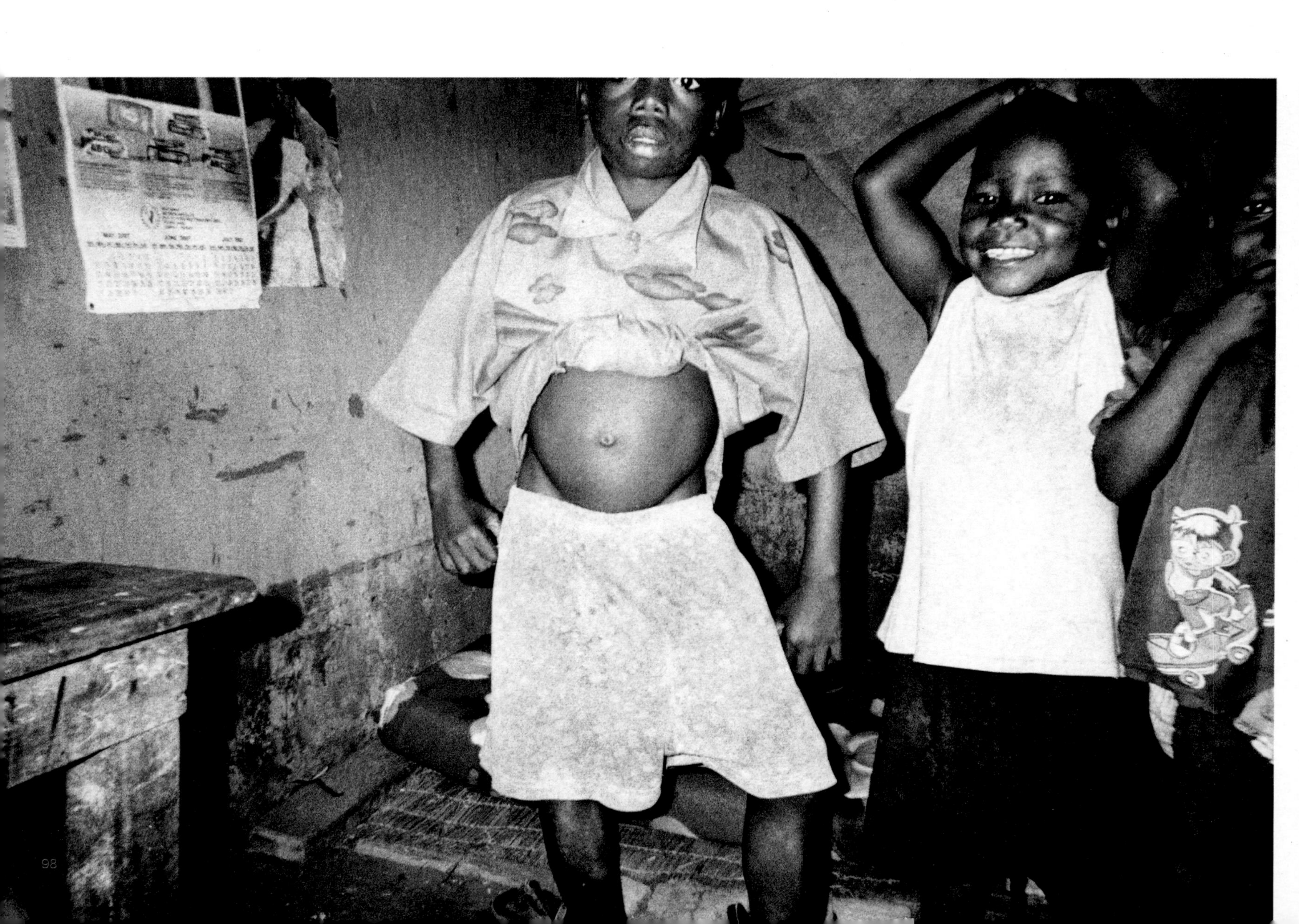

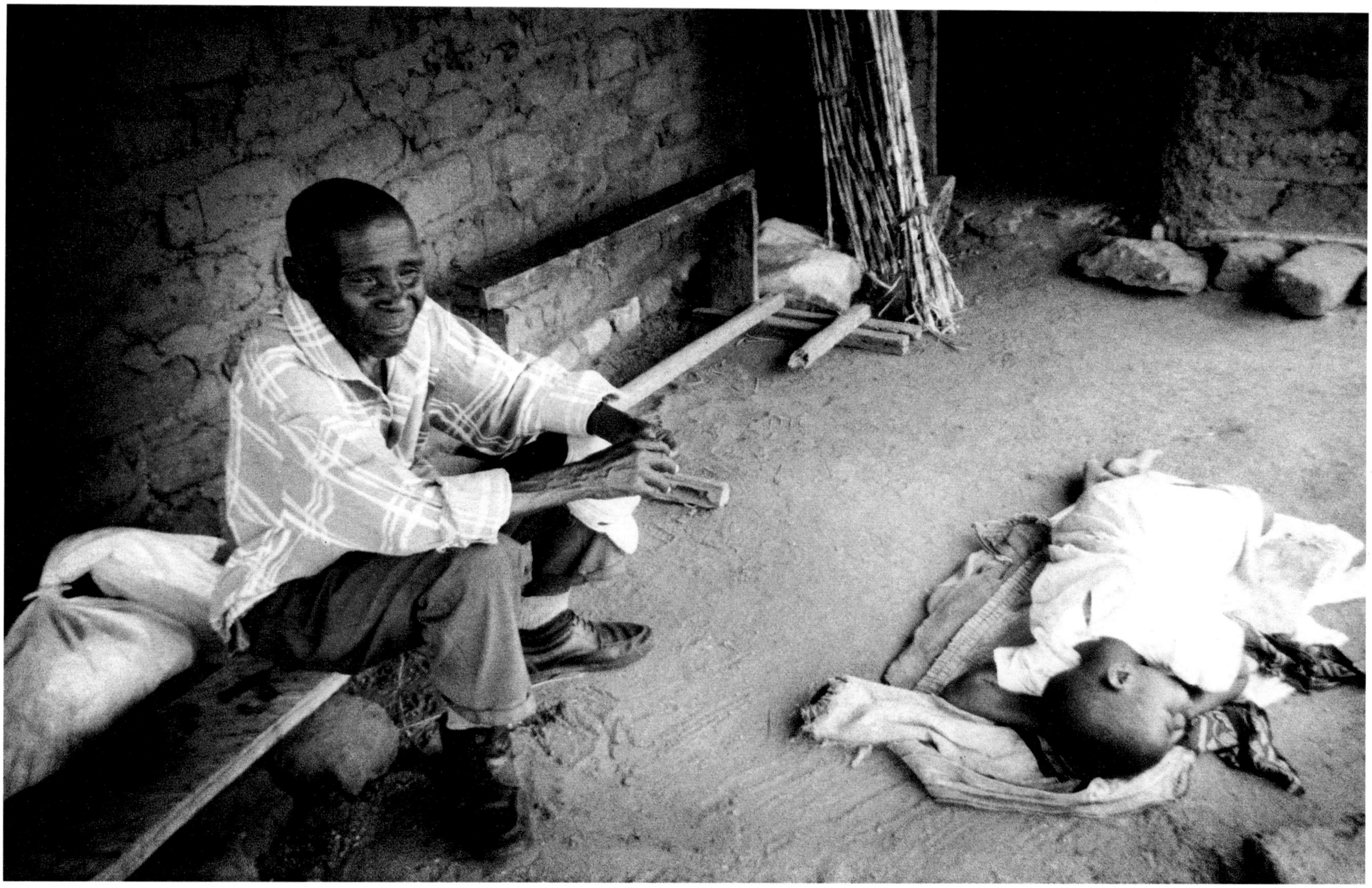

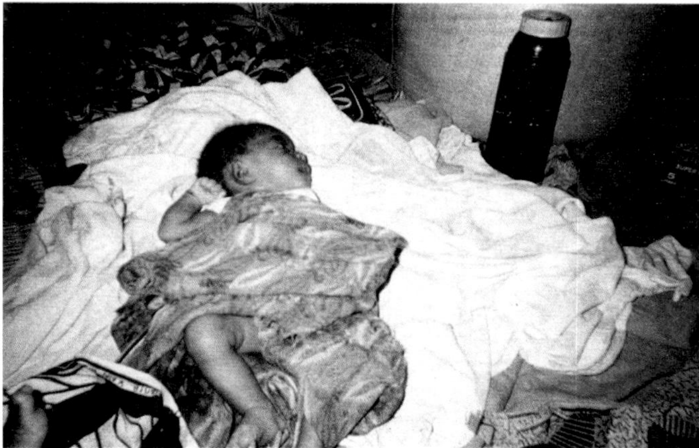

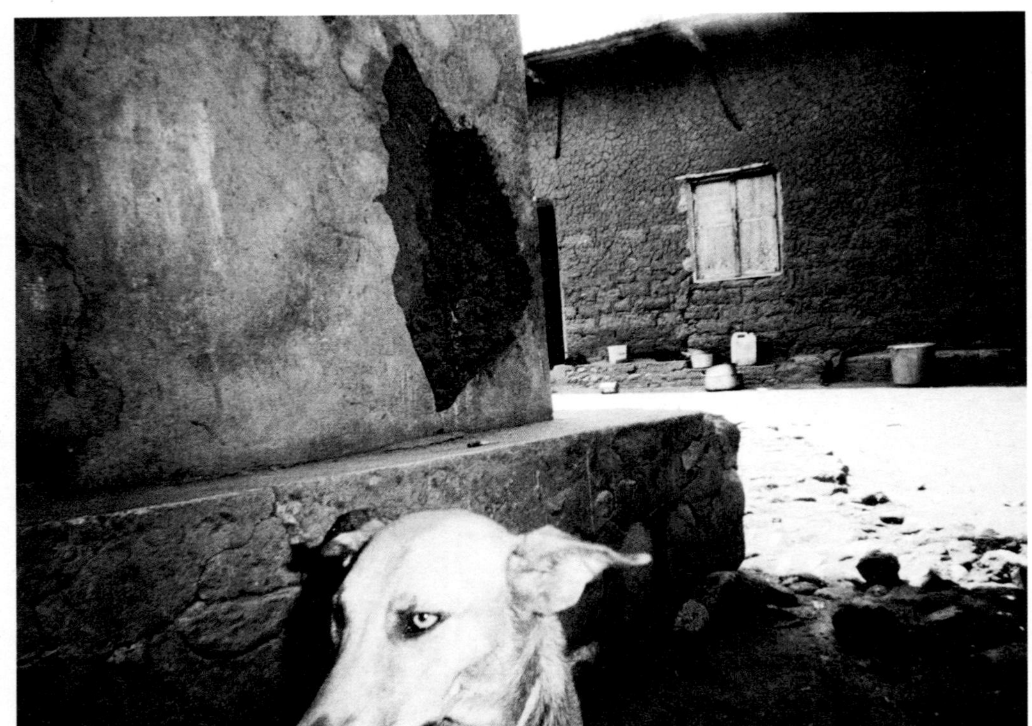
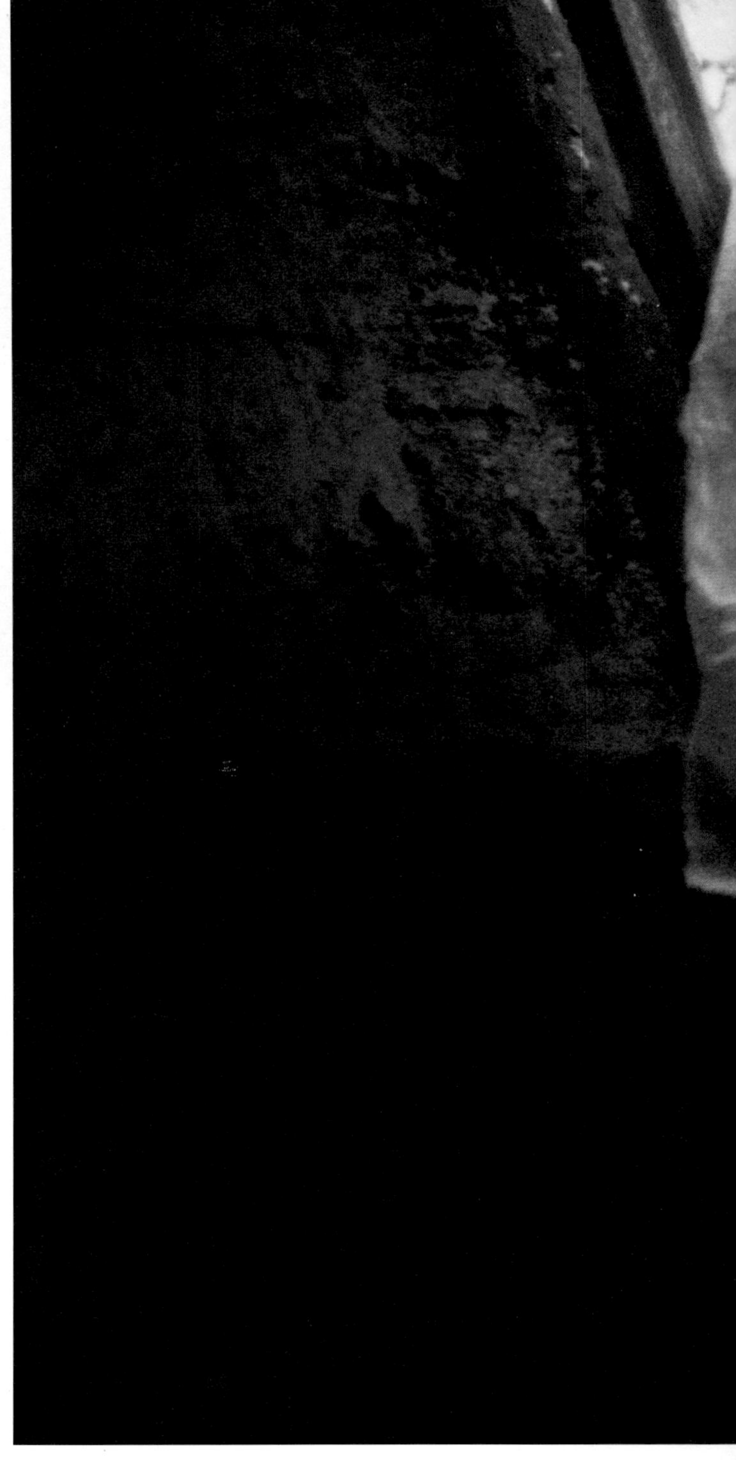

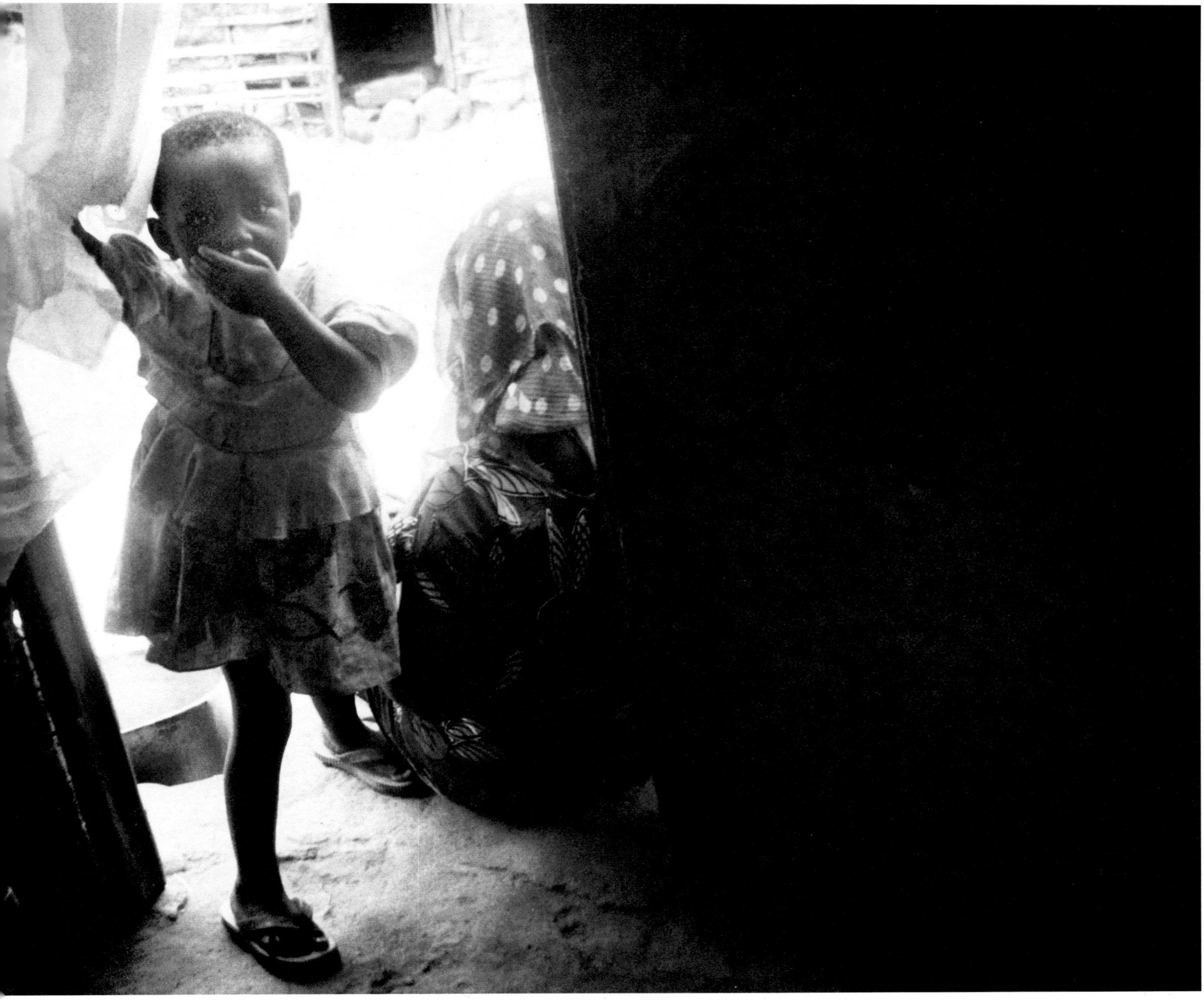

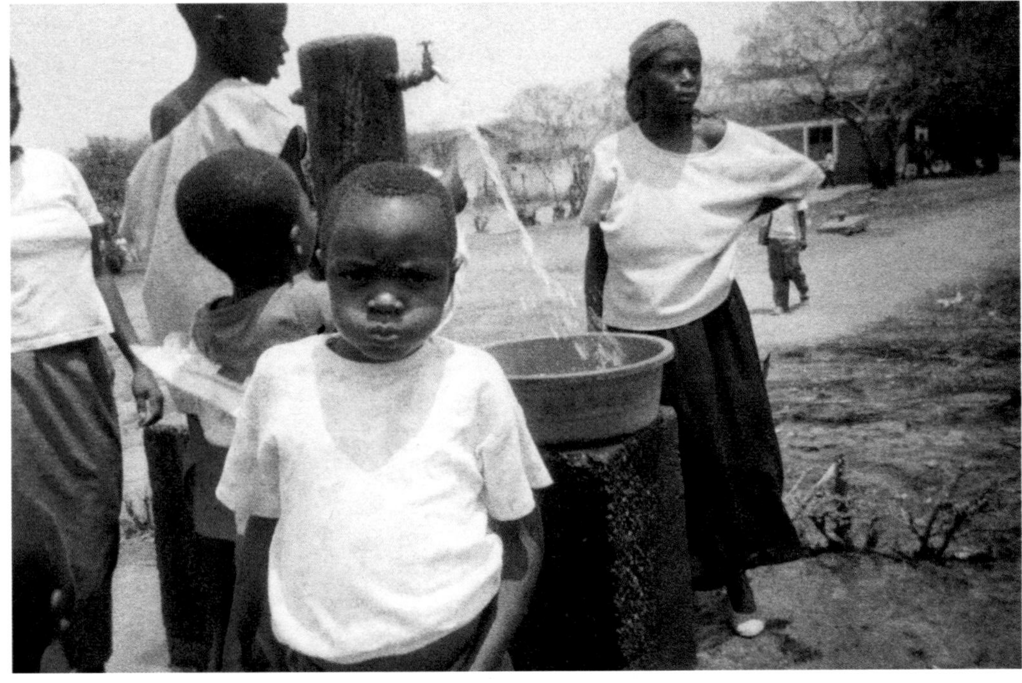

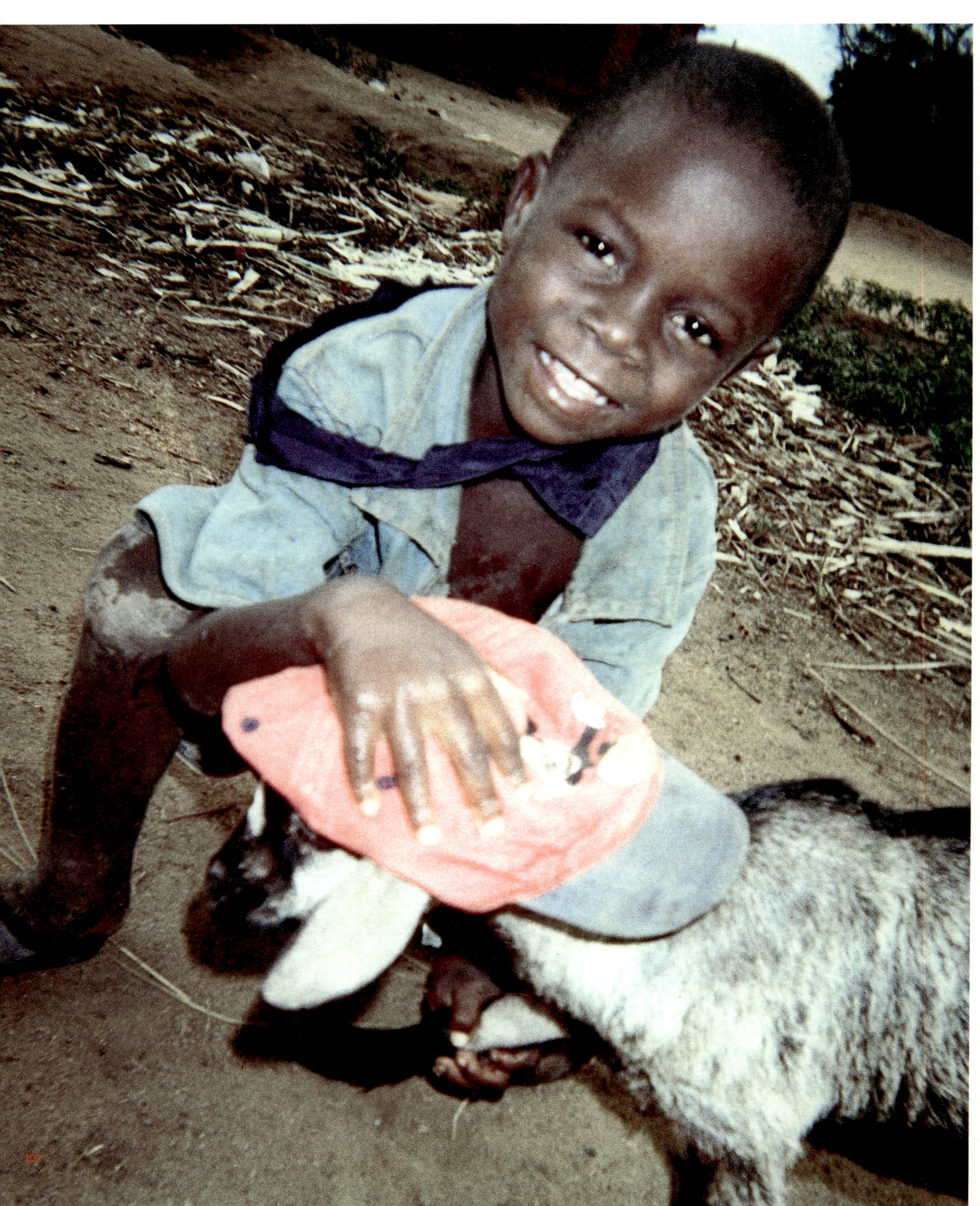

(Left)
– Photograph by Yosia

"I love this goat. I see her often. I think she
is pregnant. We need to look after our ani-
mals because they give us food."

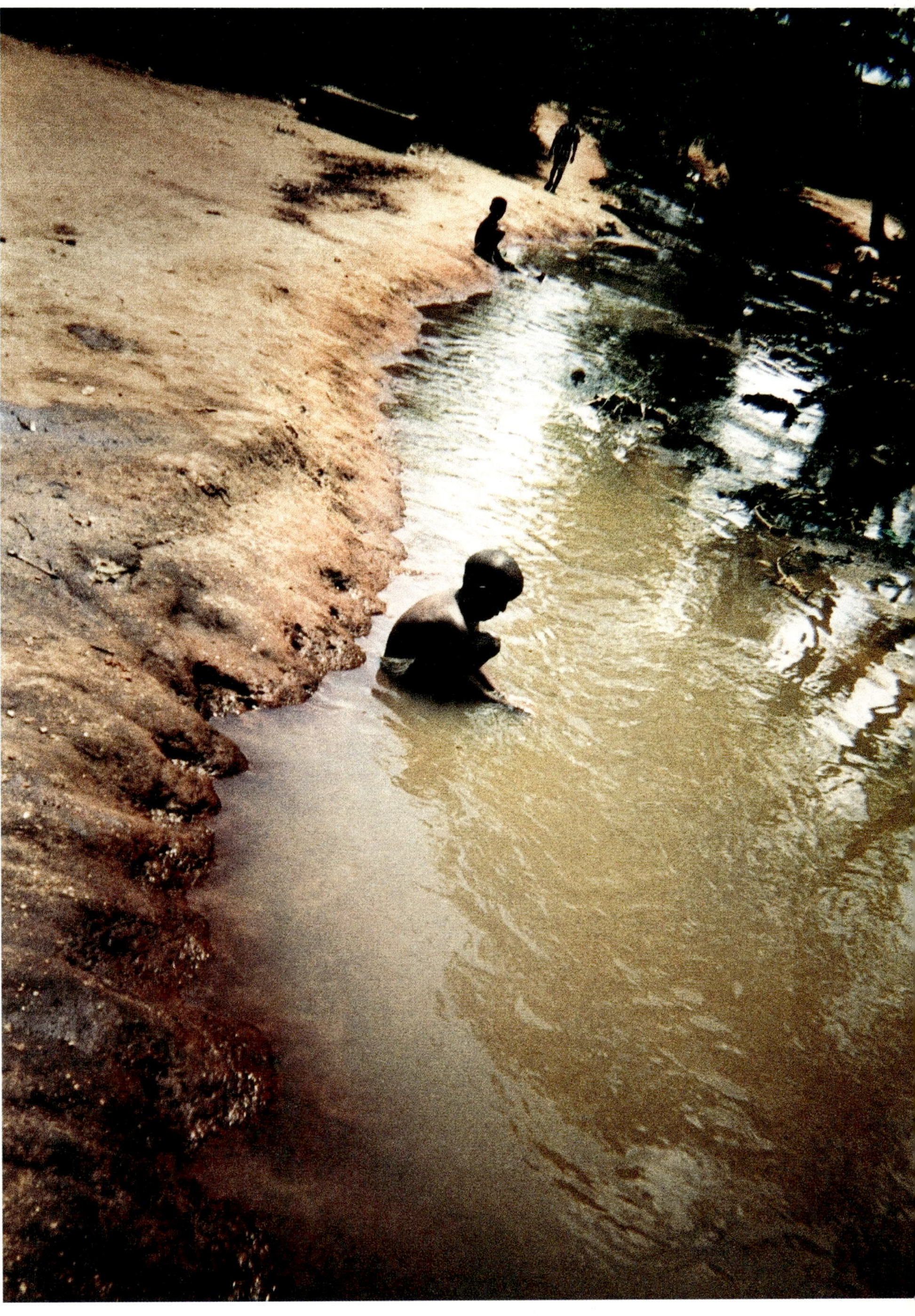

(Above)
– Photograph by Luango

"It's a good natural setting. This guy is
washing here; there are also people col-
lecting water to drink but you can't see
them. Nature is good but I wanted to show
that it is also dangerous. If you drink this
water you may be attacked by a disease like
cholera. It's not good for people to drink
the water they wash in. This picture doesn't
give the message I wanted very well because on the other side was a person col-
lecting water but he doesn't appear in the
photo. I needed to be further away."

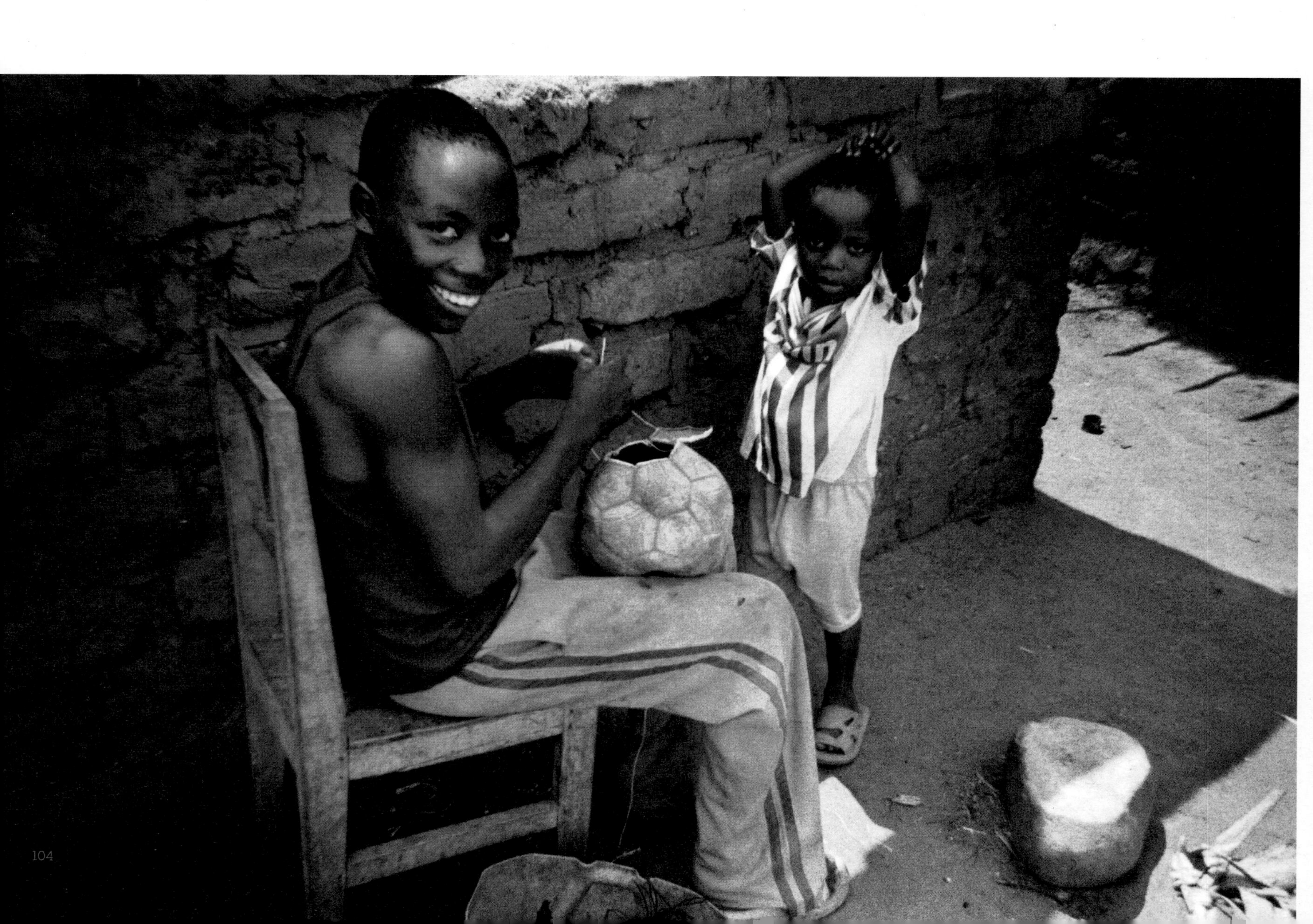

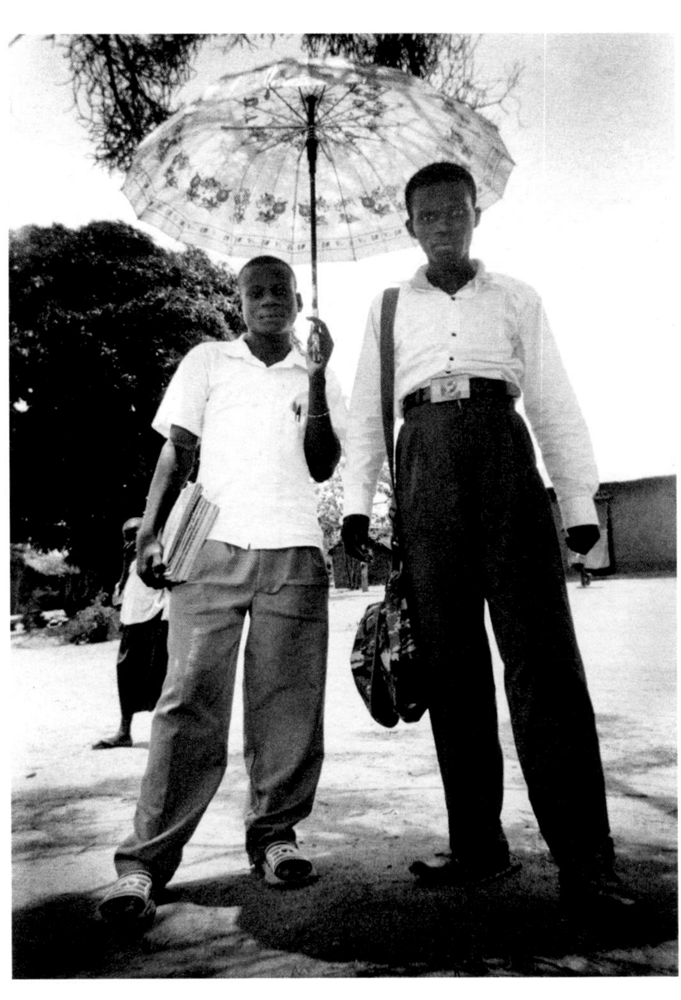

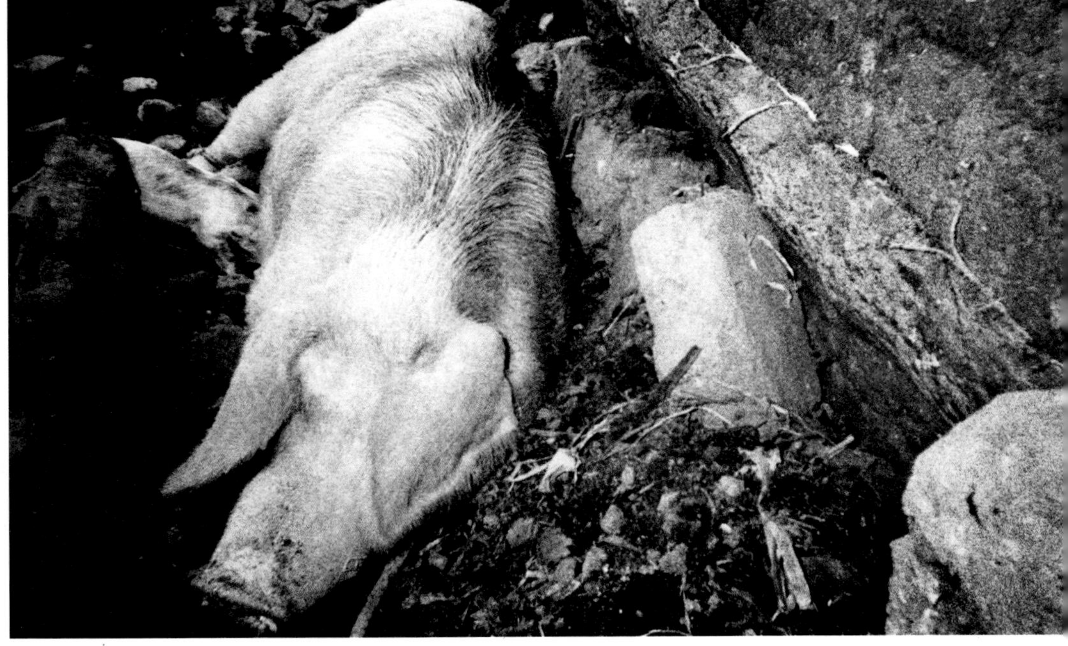

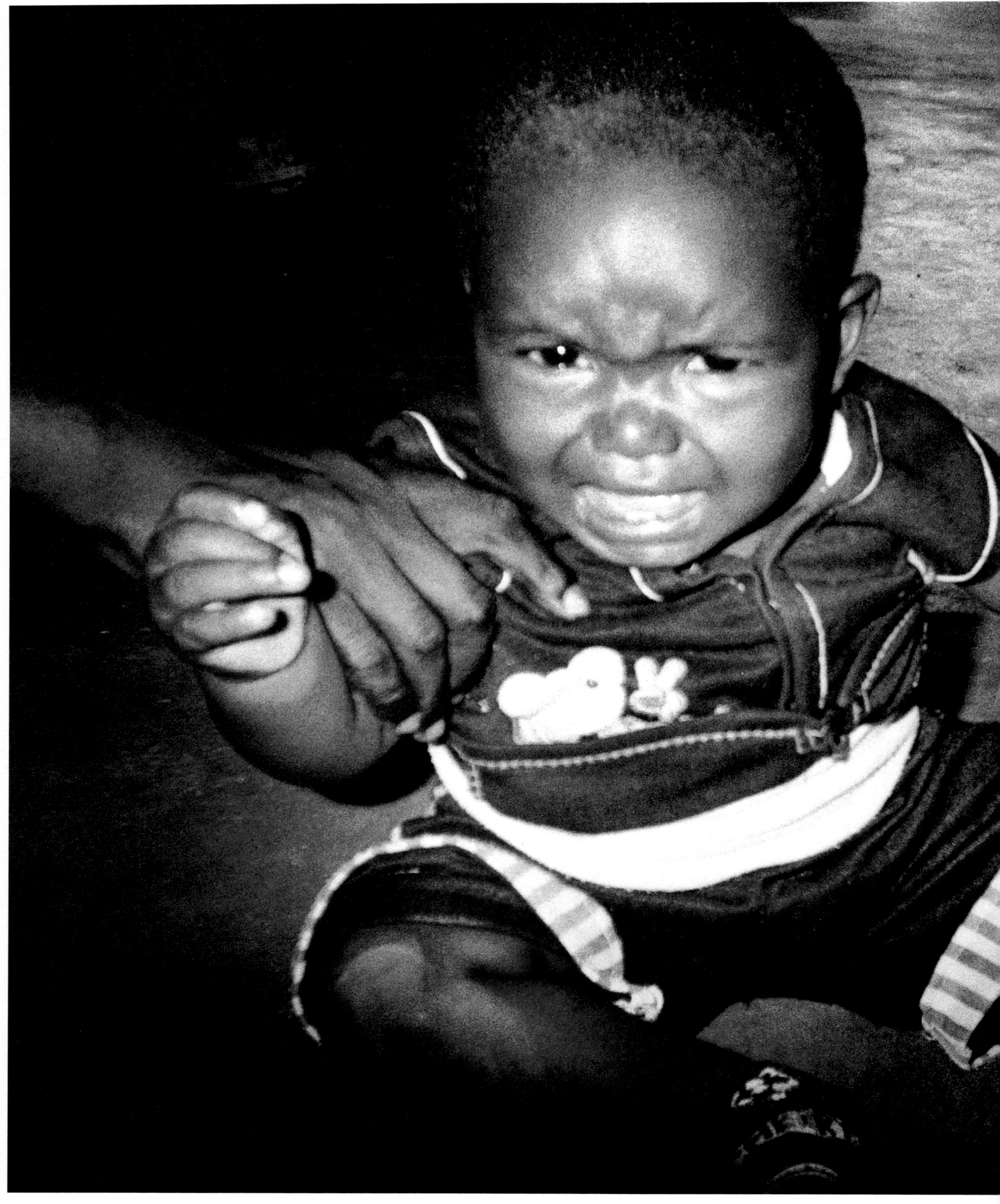

    The Congo Family Album

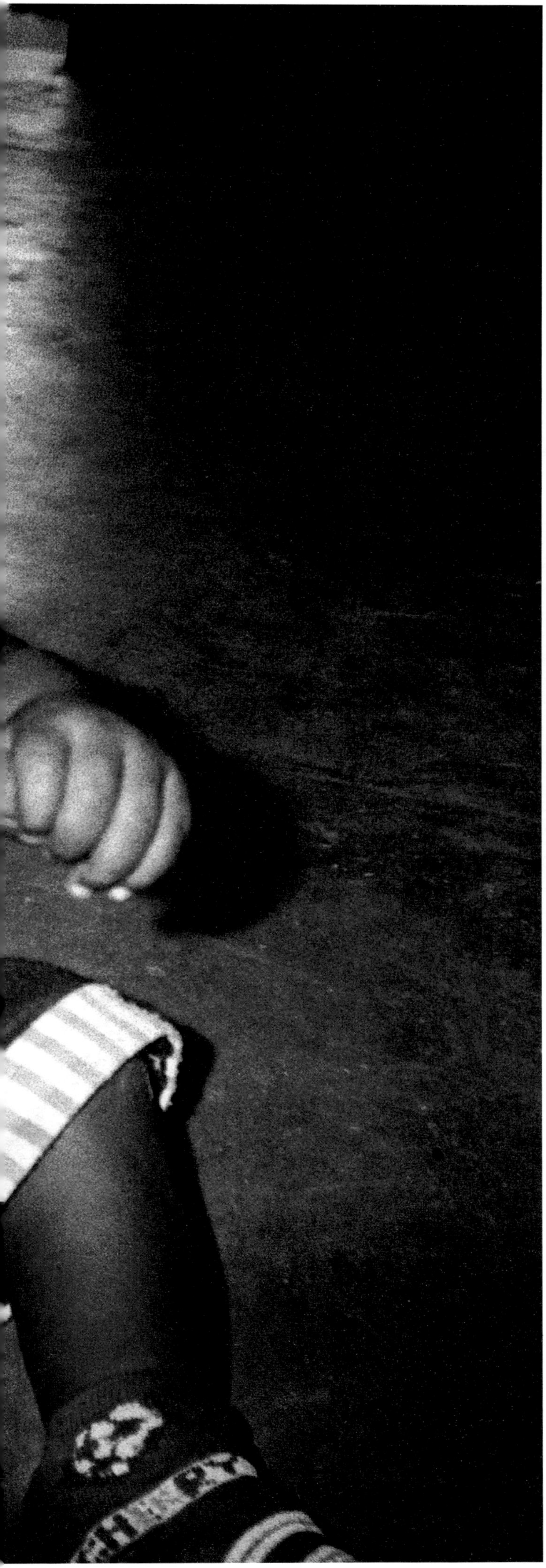

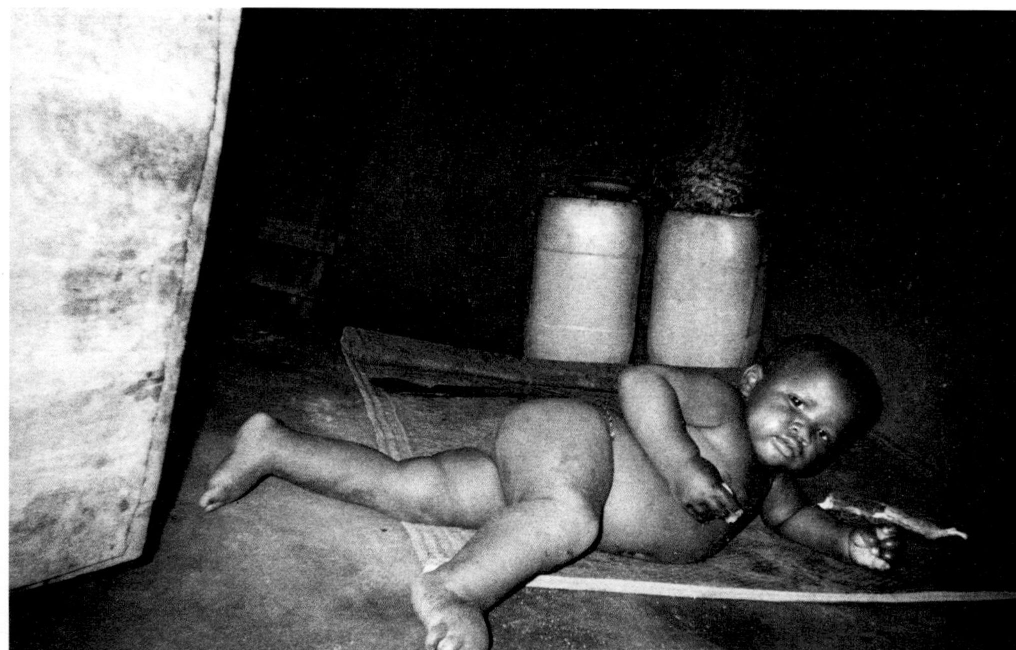

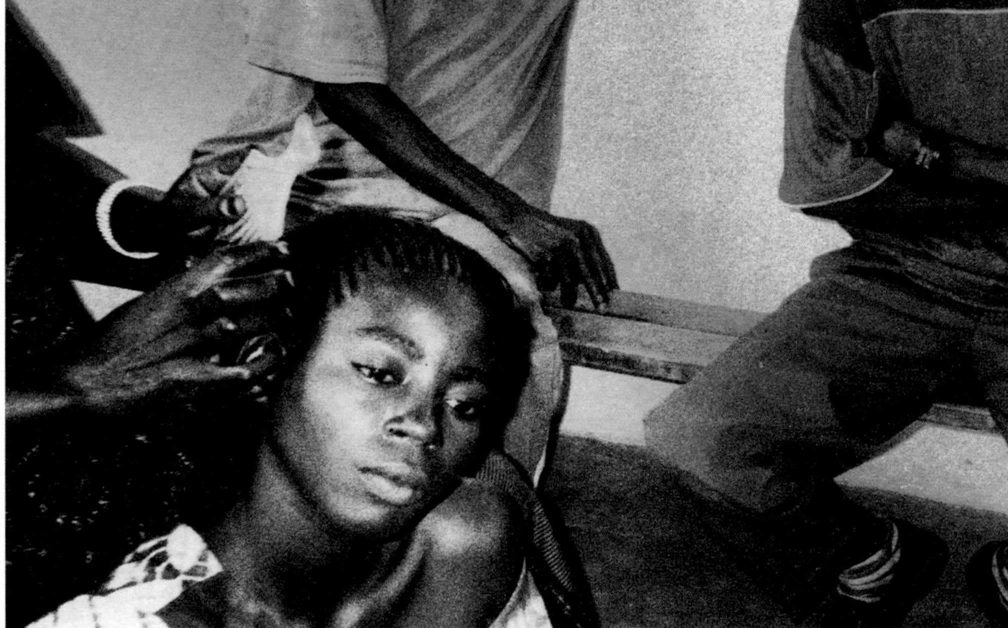

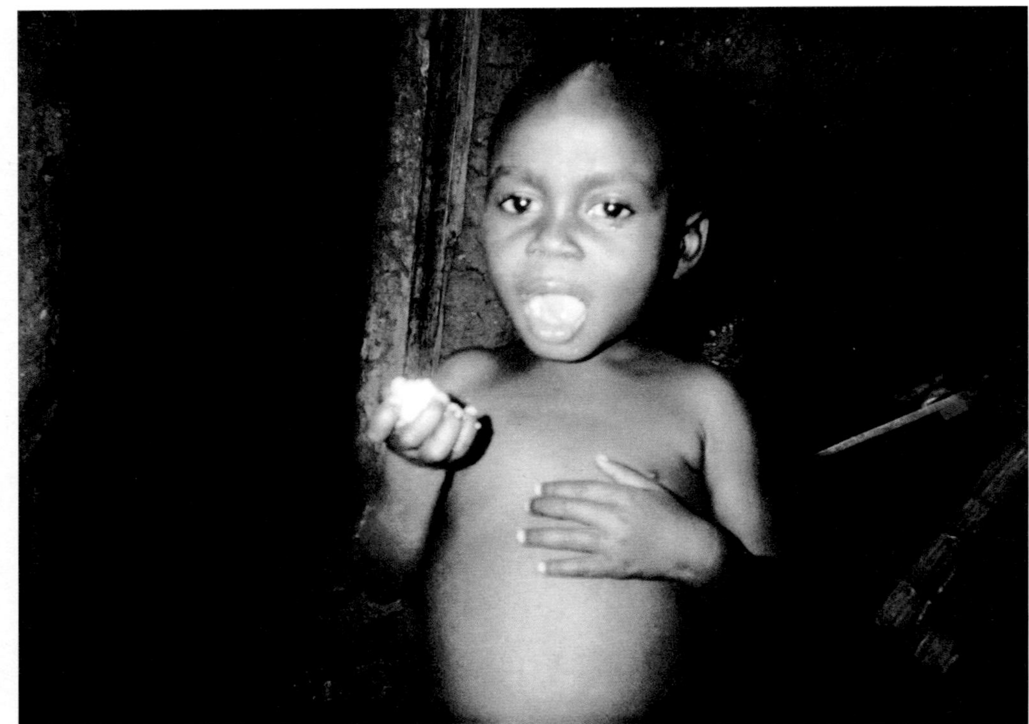

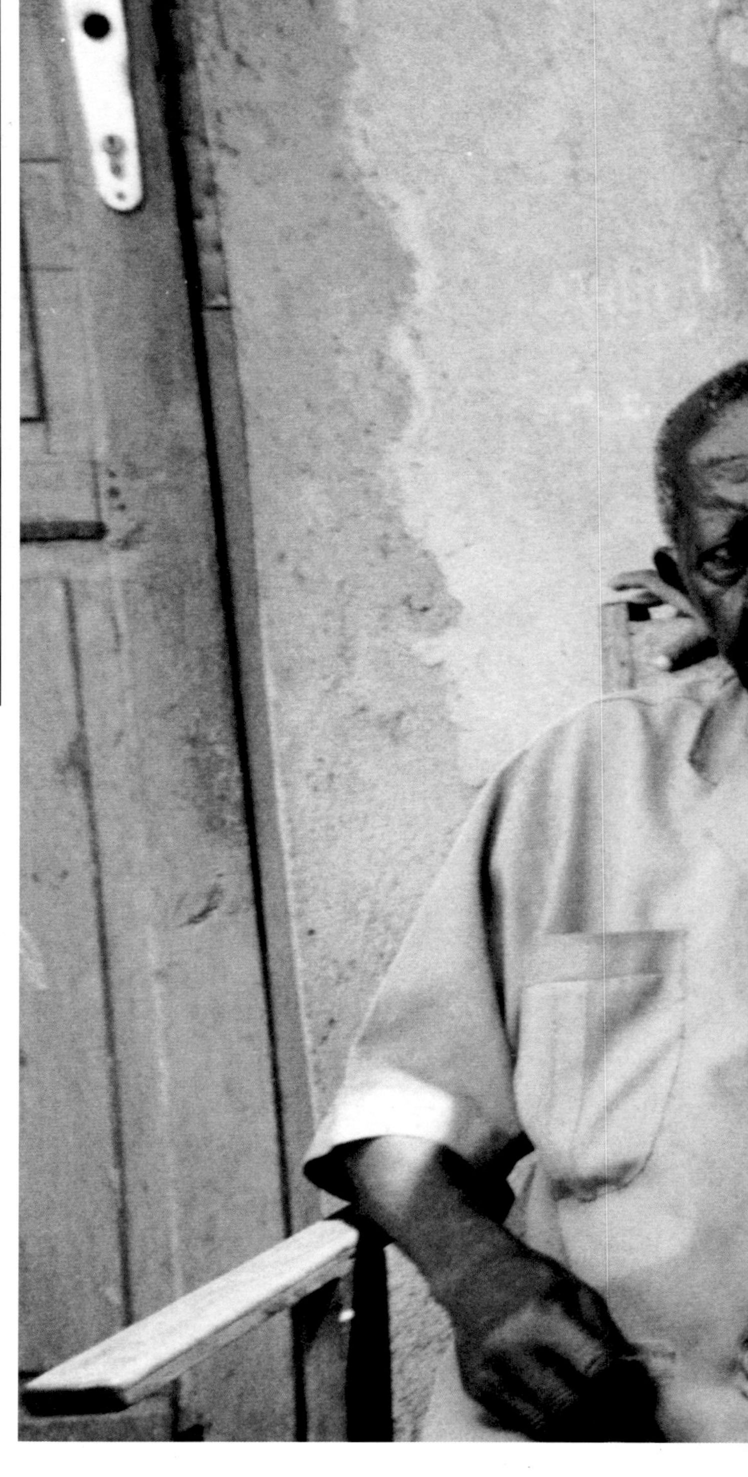

(Top left)
– Photograph by Munwera

"I think it looks great. I took this picture to express the love I have for
my son. He is happy in this picture
because he is eating vegetables."

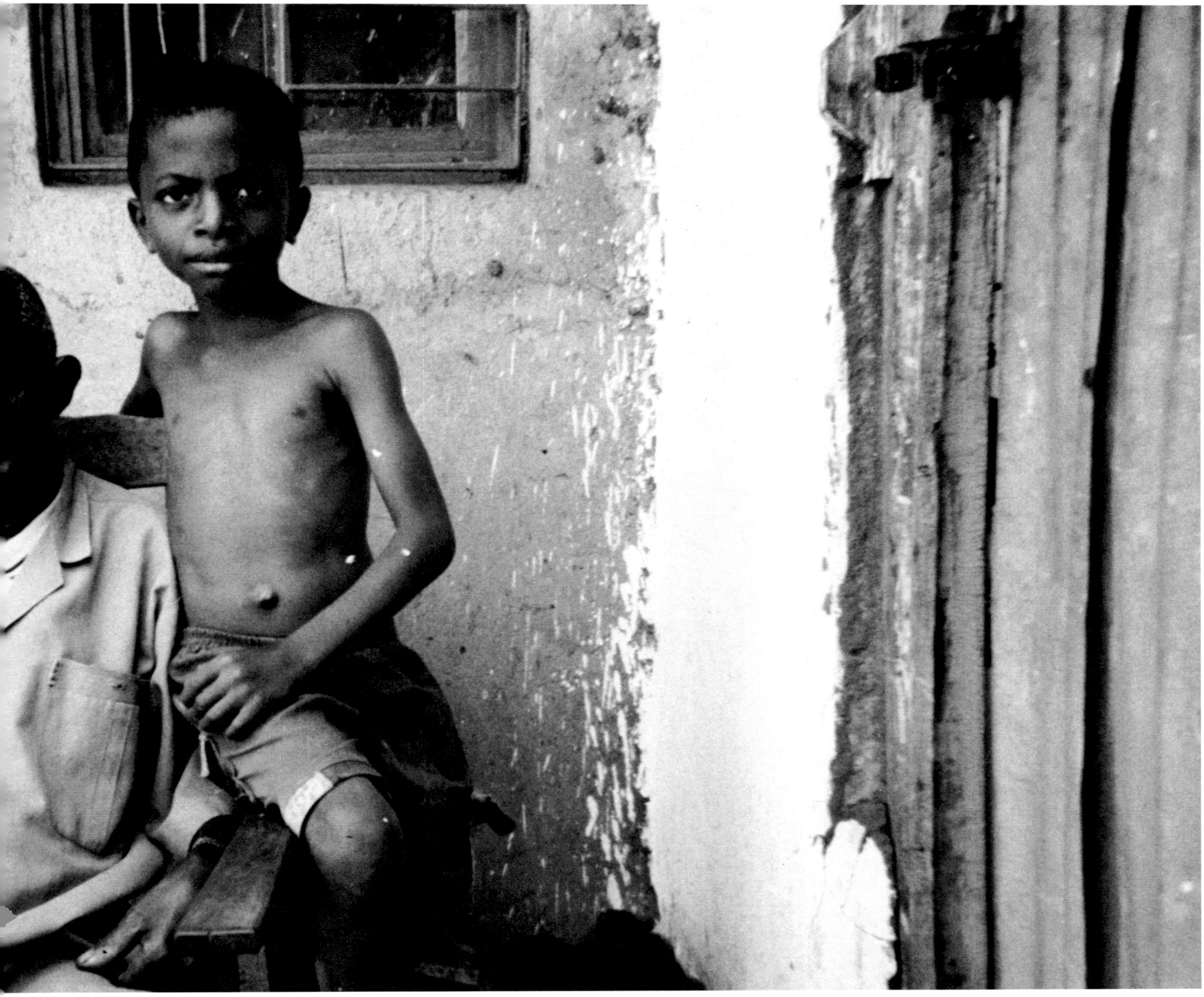

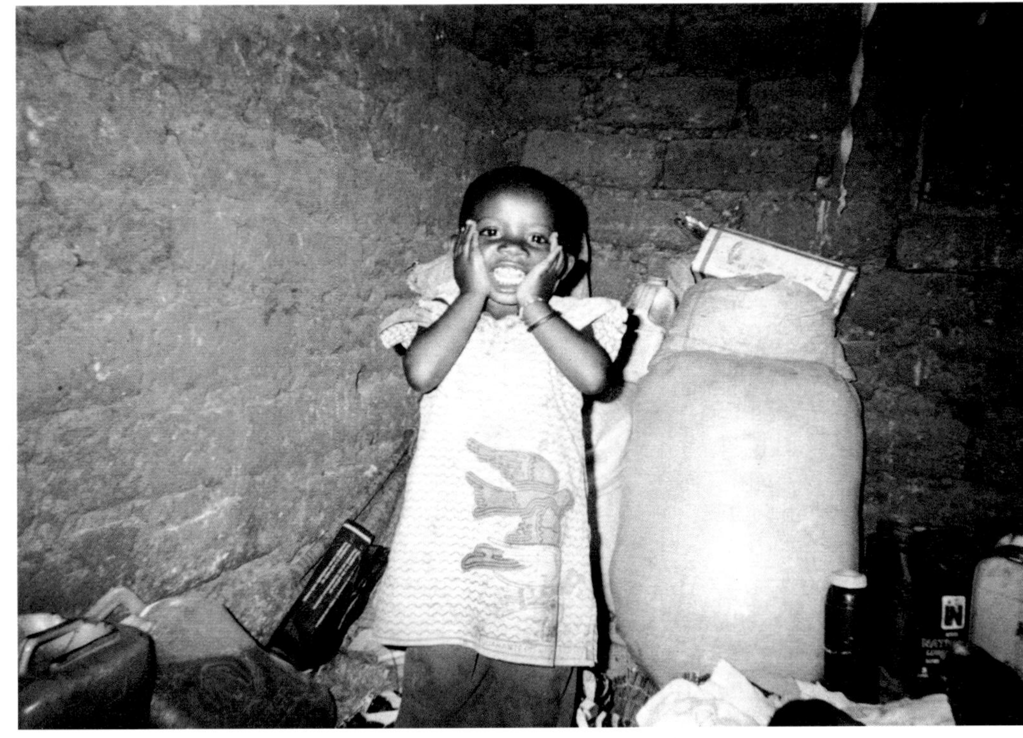

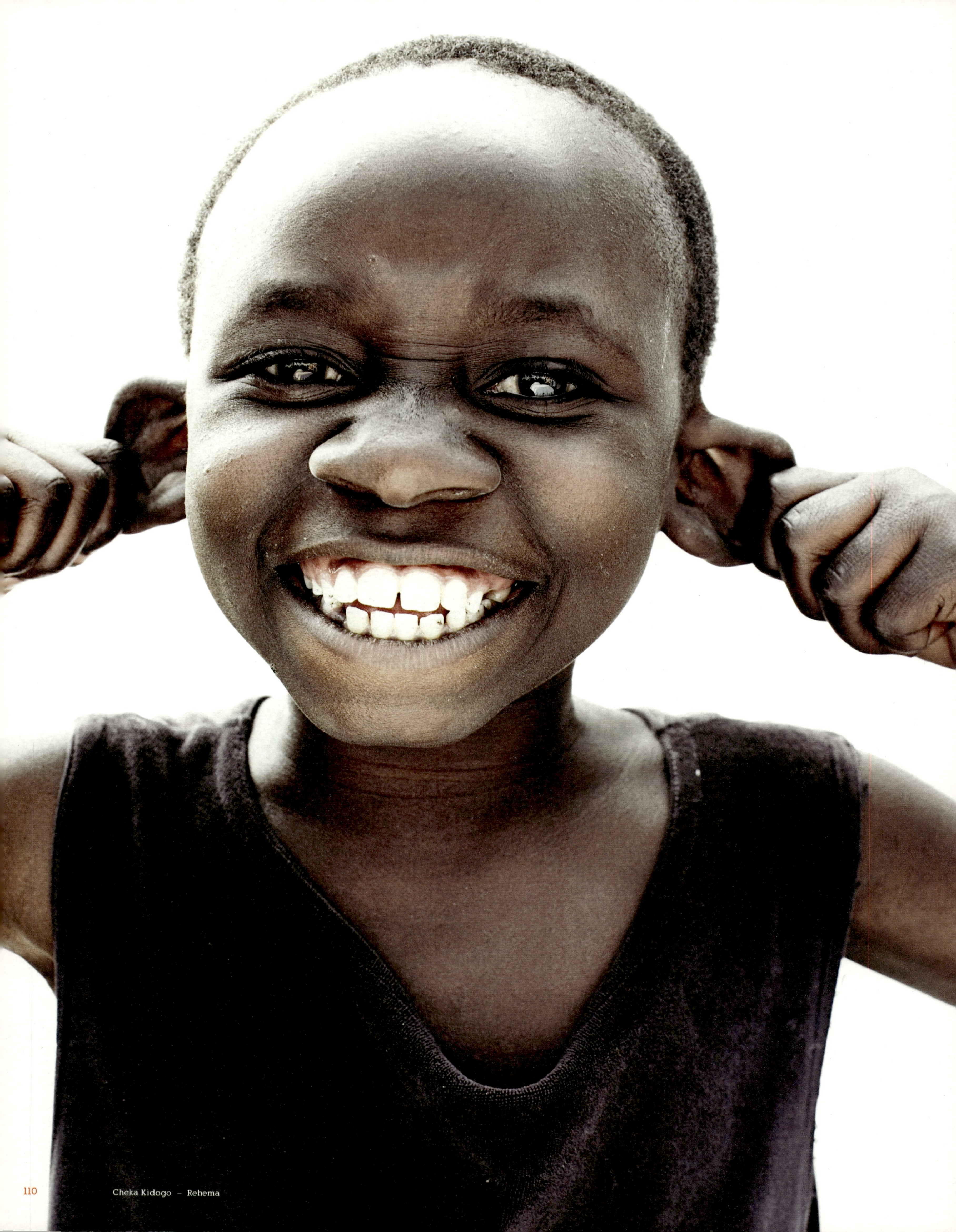

Cheka Kidogo – Rehema

CHEKA KIDOGO
2008

In 2008, Rankin travelled with Oxfam to meet people who had fled conflict and were living in Mugunga Camp, in the DRC's Goma Region. His photographs capture the bravery, humanity, strength and determination of the people who live there – and their desire for peace. The name of the collection, Cheka Kidogo, means 'Laugh a Little' in Swahili. Rankin chose it after hearing people calling the phrase out to friends who were being photographed. It also celebrates the spirit of the people he met. Worldwide, 139 million people have seen these images. So far, they have helped to raise more than £1 million for Oxfam's emergency work in the DRC.

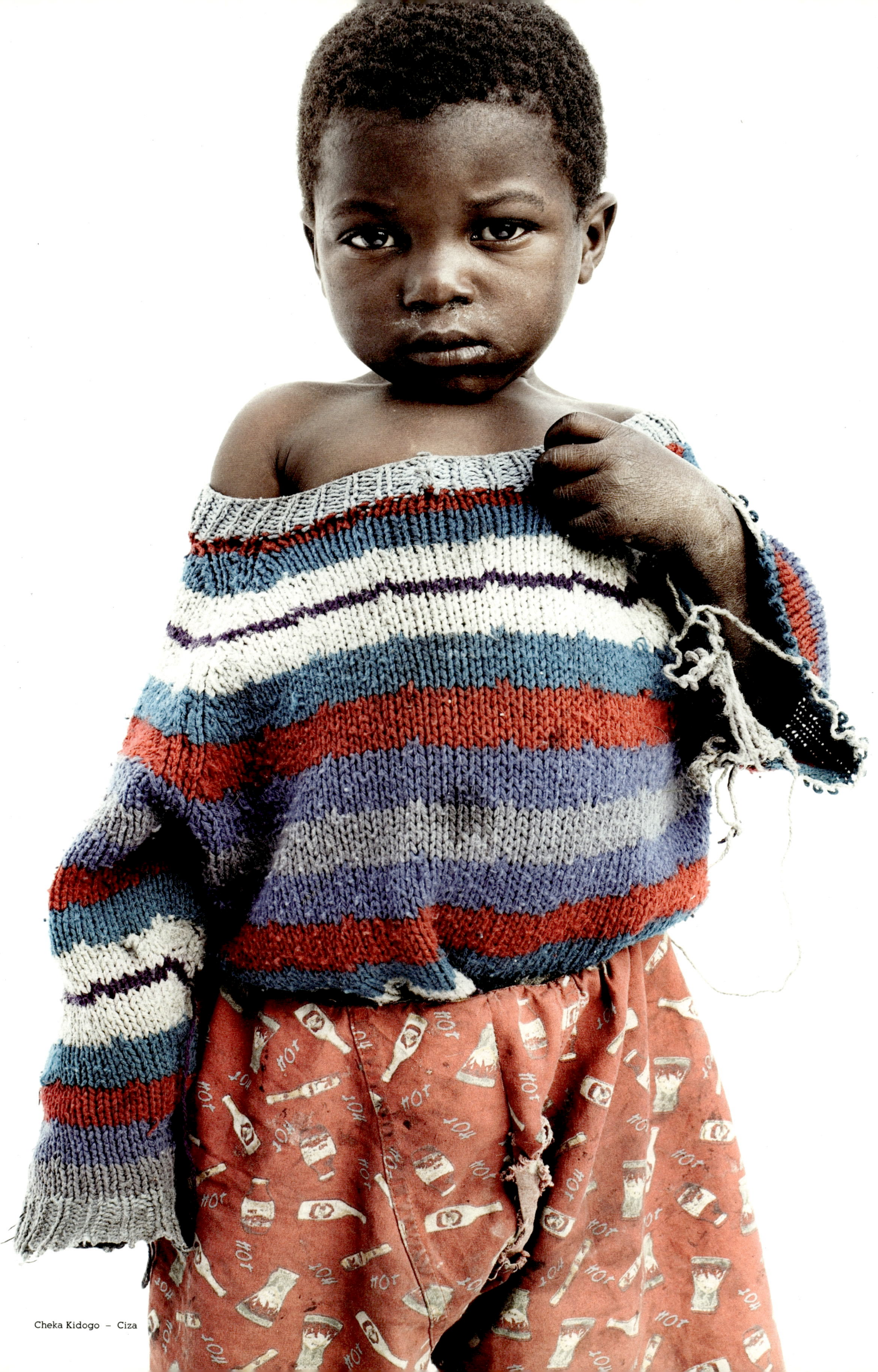

   Cheka Kidogo – Ciza

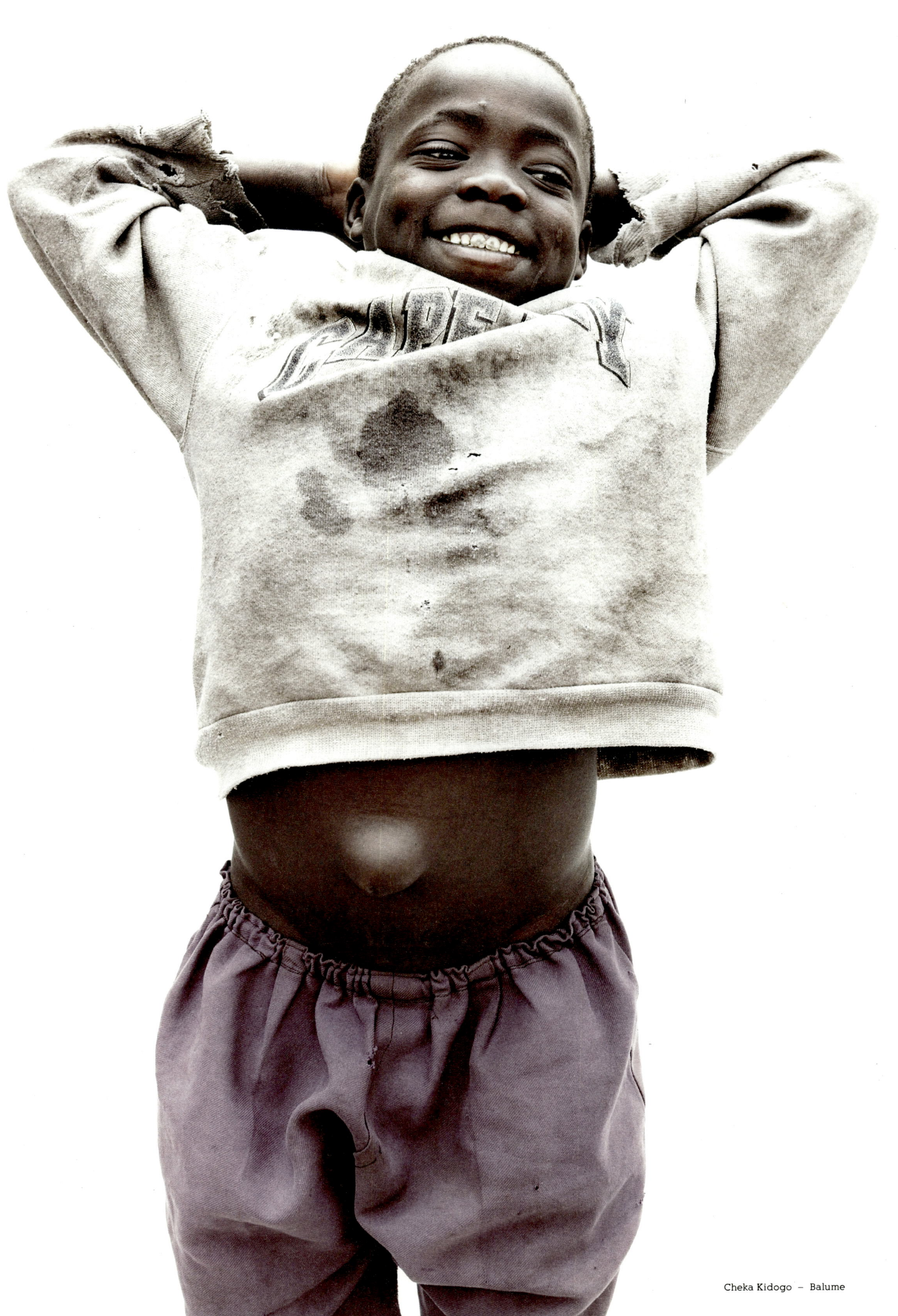

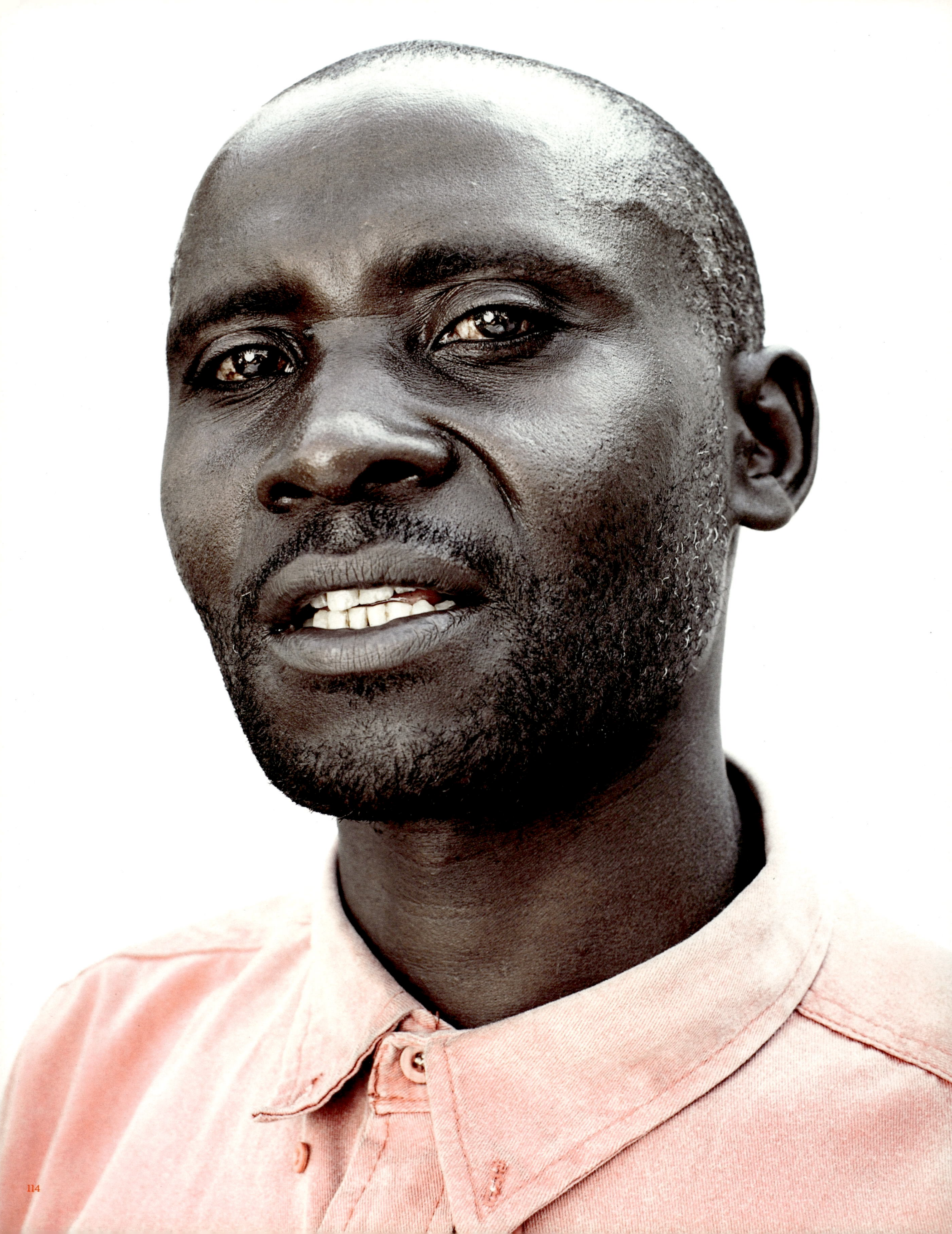

"They are killing our men, kidnapping our children – and the women live in constant fear of being raped. I used to teach in a primary school. But there are no schools here. So now I don't have a job. I am just waiting and praying for peace – because we are all suffering here. My ten children and I are living in one small hut. We need peace, but I have to tell you that things are getting worse. Only God knows if we will ever be able to return to our village."

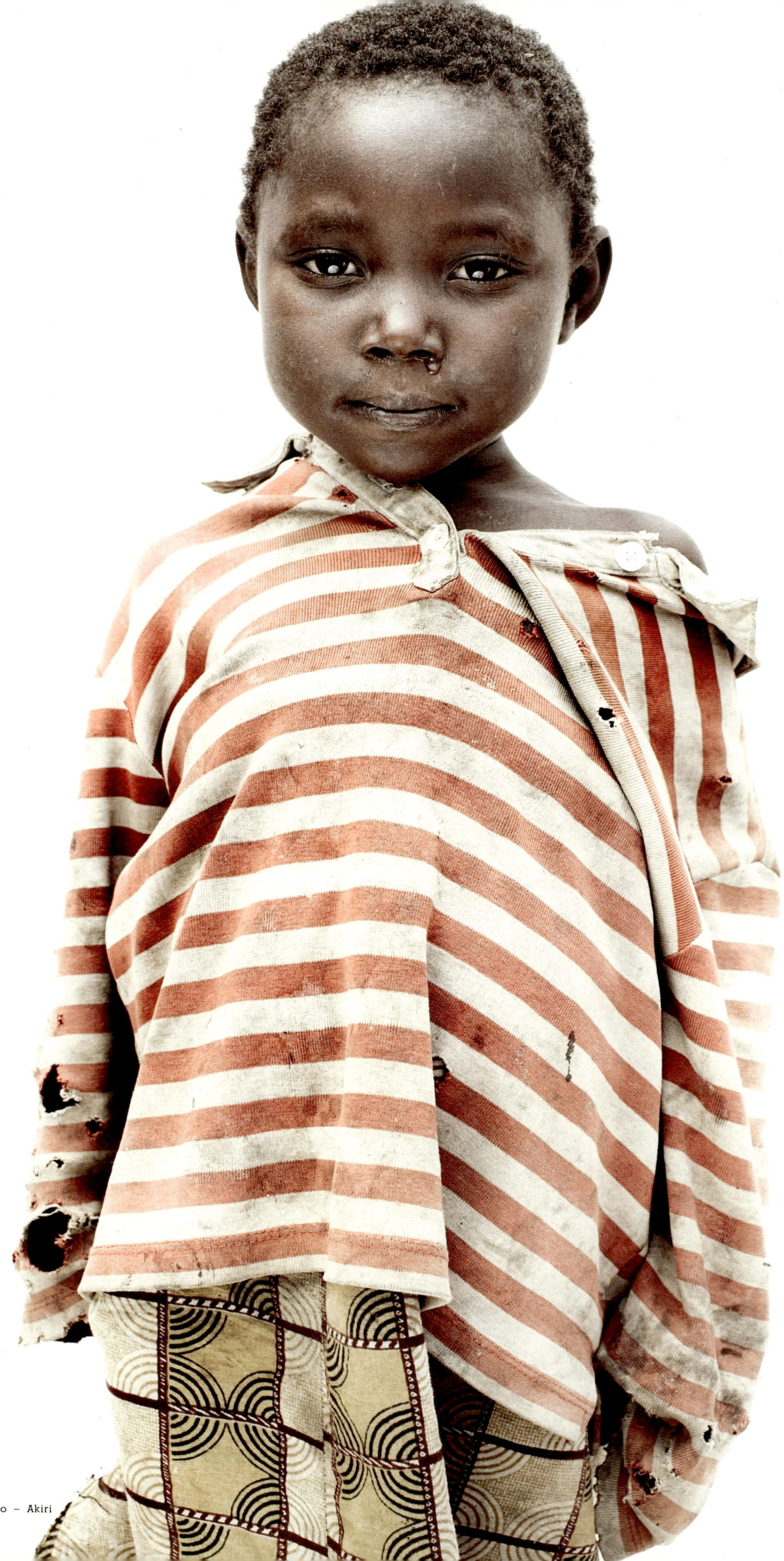

Cheka Kidogo – Akiri

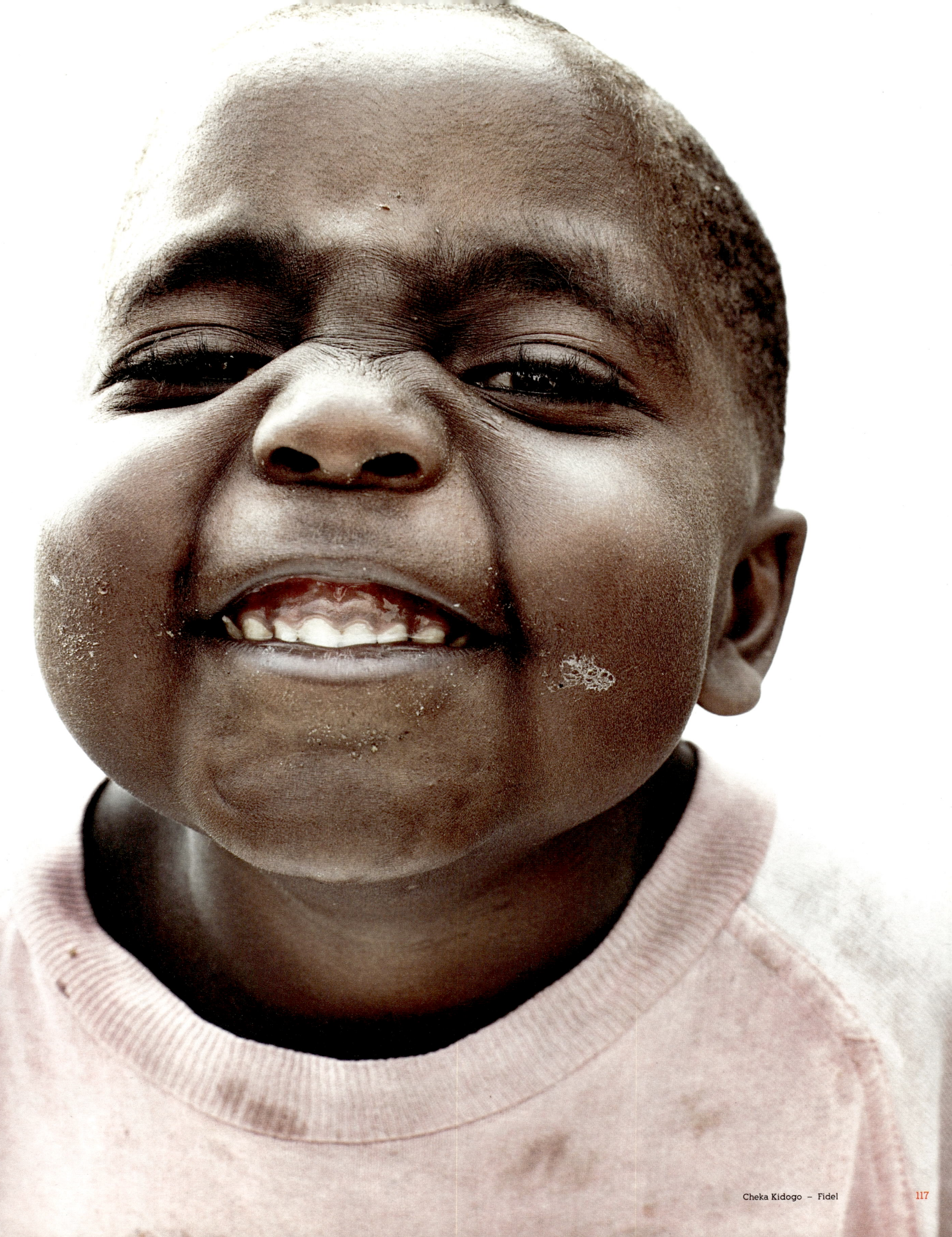

Cheka Kidogo – Fidel

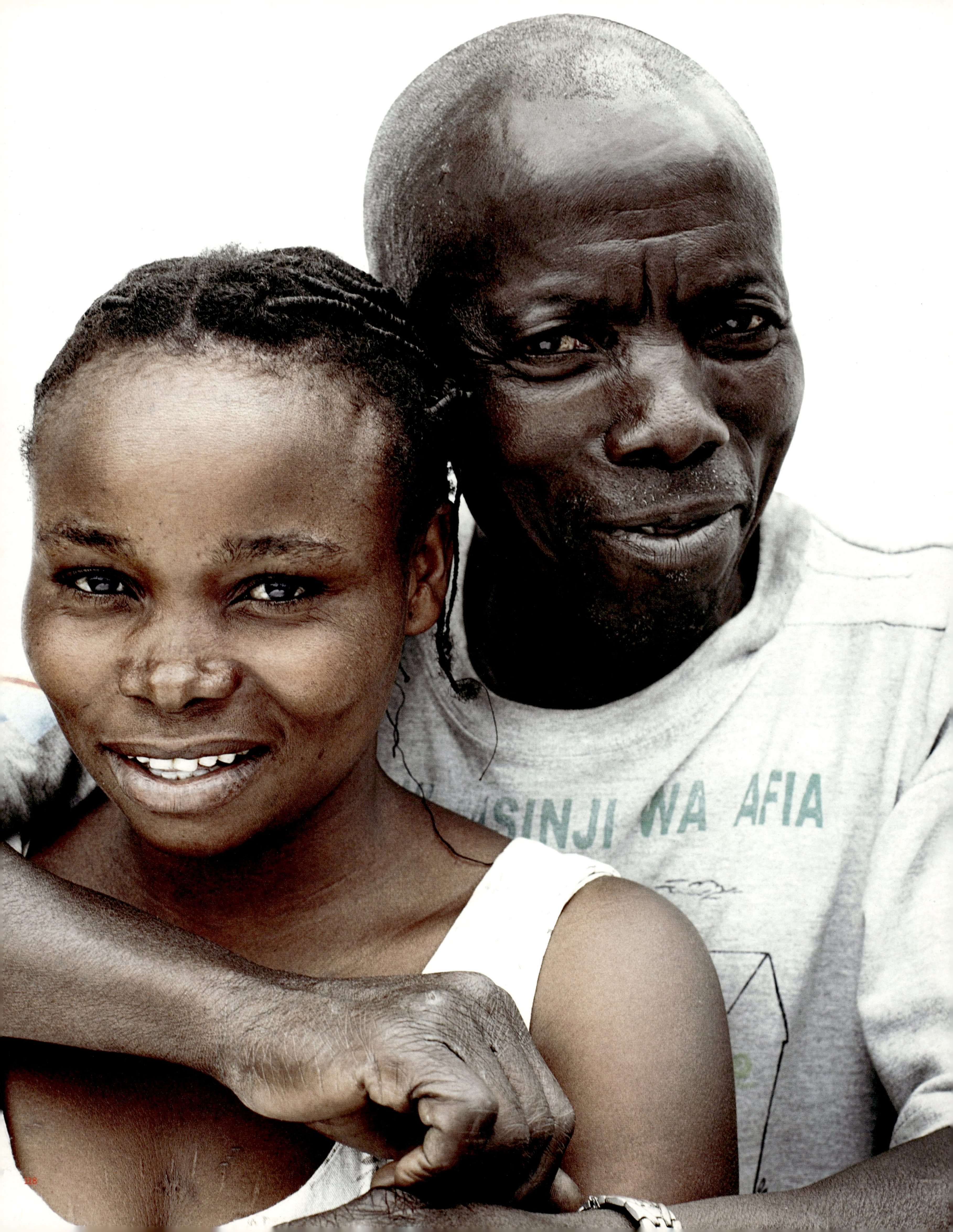
...SINJI WA AFIA

"I know someone from my village who was castrated by the rebels. This war has scared us a lot – it has really affected us. I can't say if we will ever return home. We are afraid that if we go back we will be killed."

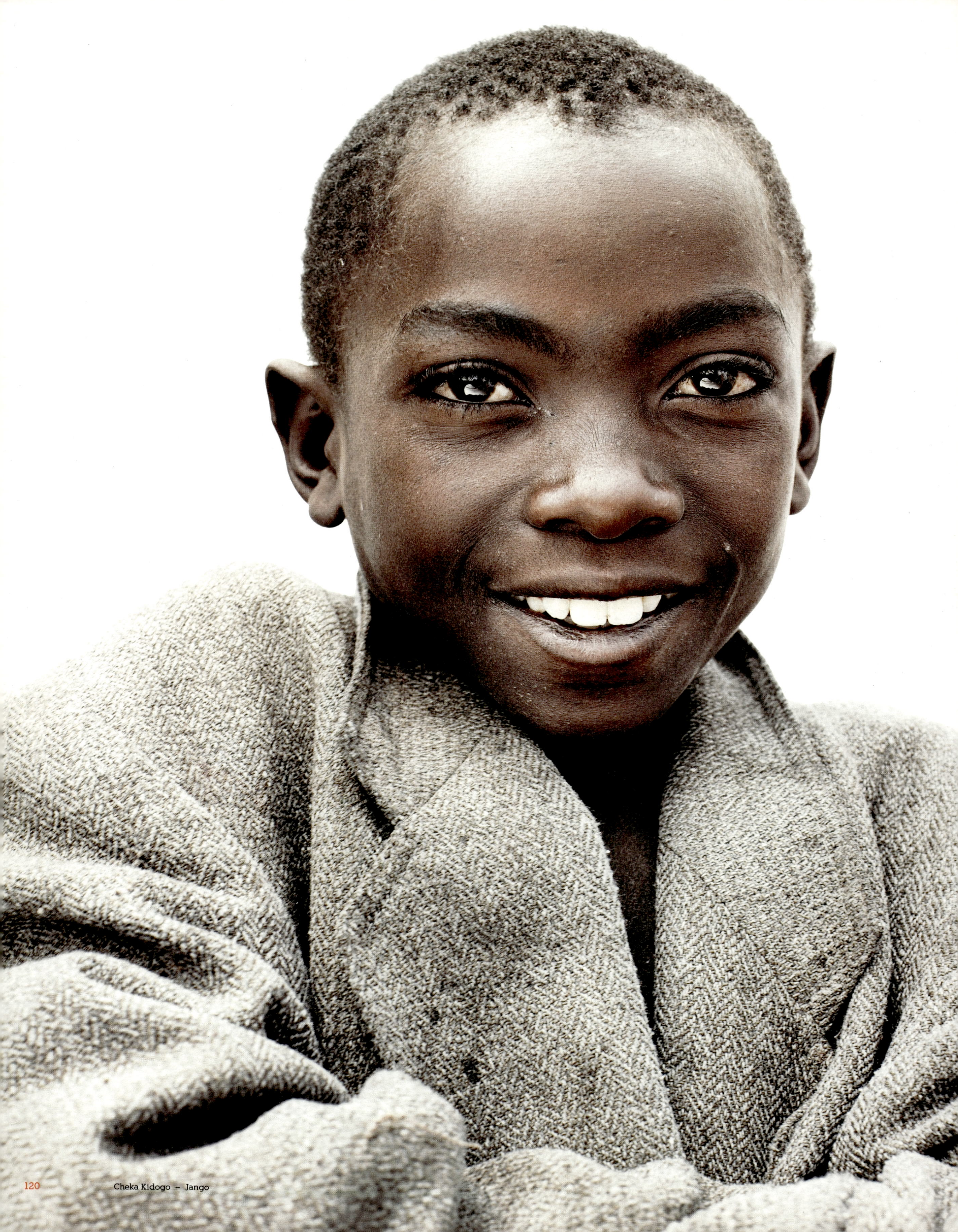

Cheka Kidogo – Jango

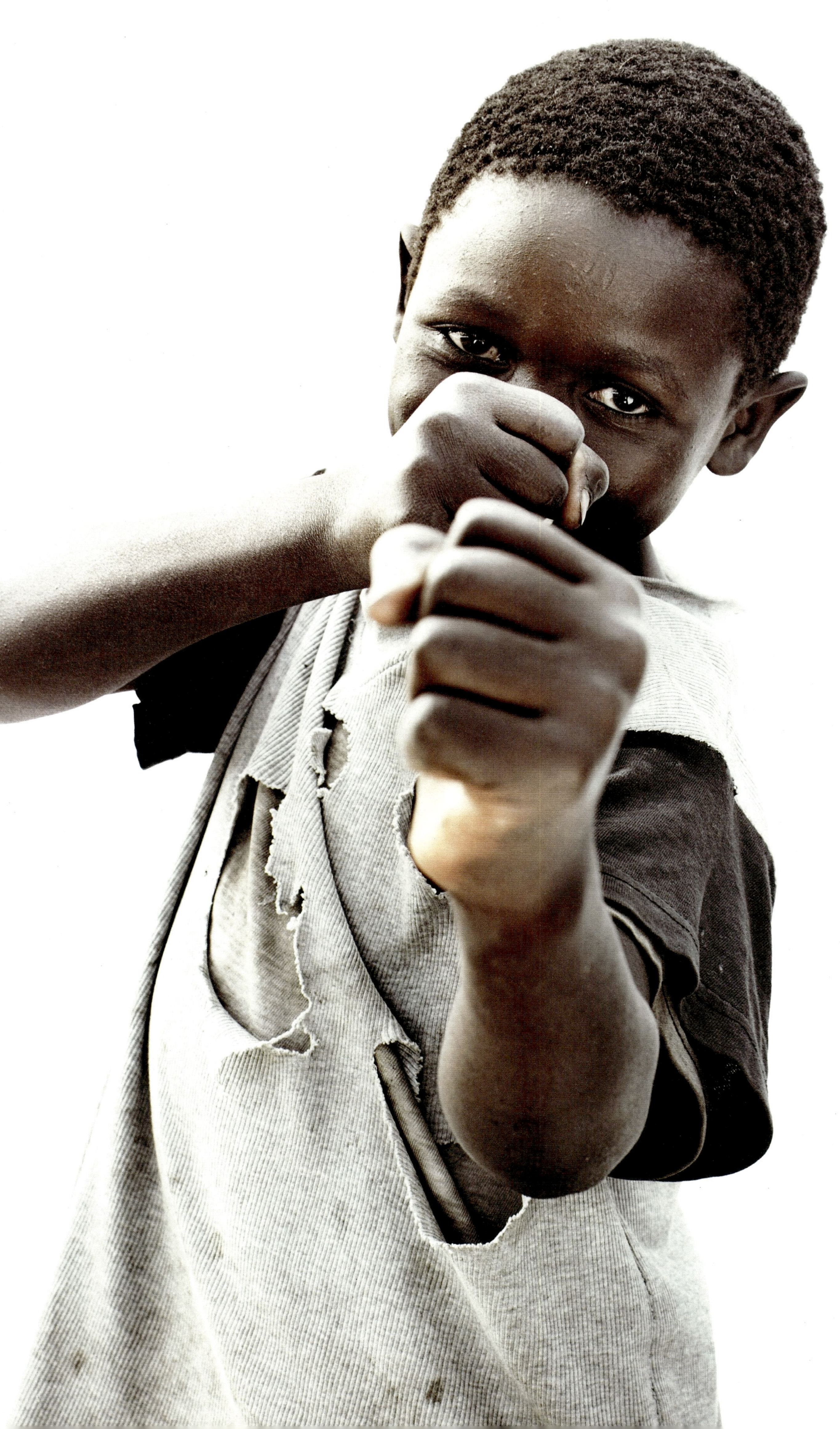

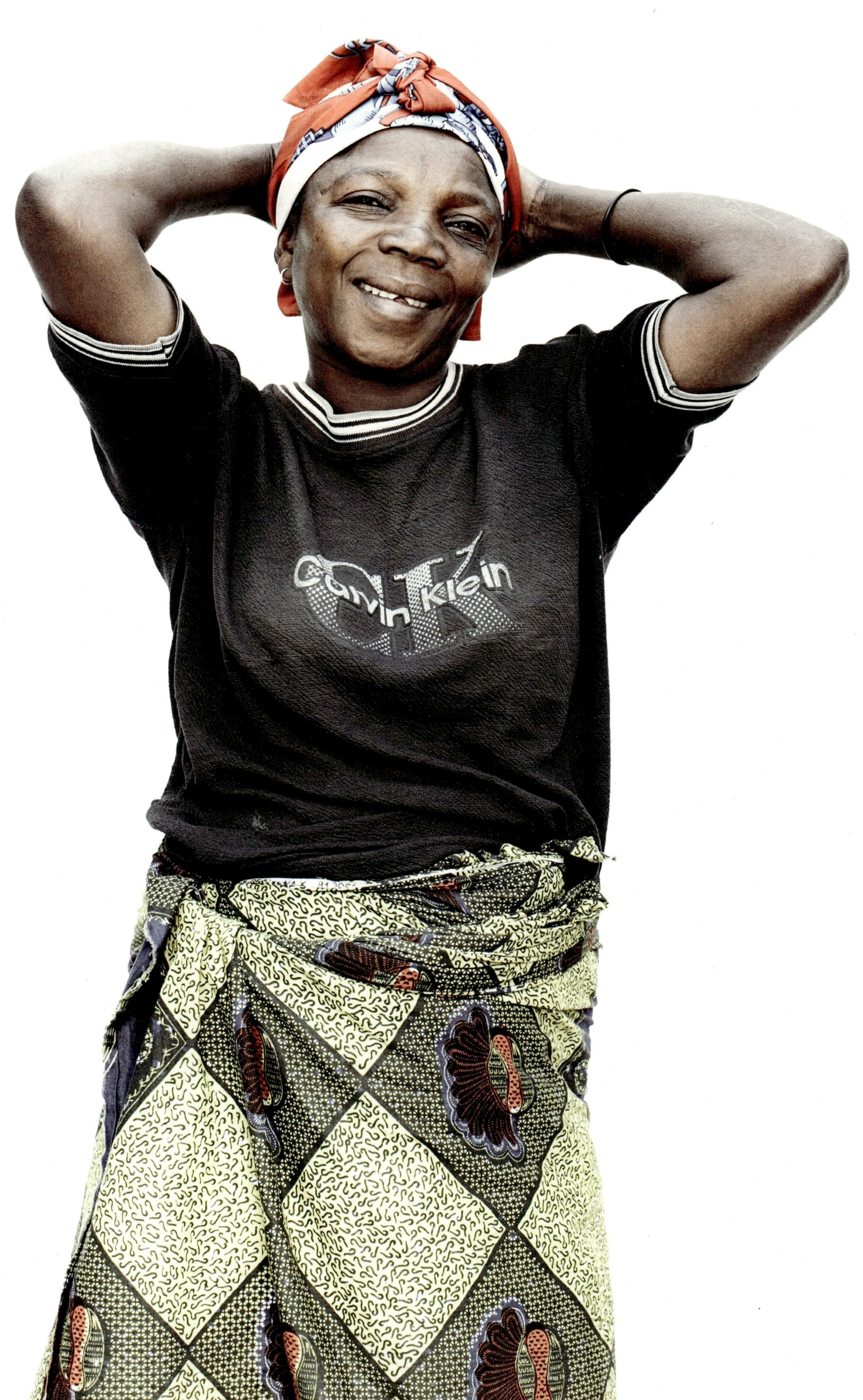

"I lost my husband and four of my children because of this war. As the fighting started, I ran into the bush with some of the children. My husband stayed behind with the others. When we returned to the village, there were dead bodies everywhere. As I entered my house, I found the dead bodies of my husband and my four eldest children – all shot in the head. That day, 175 people from my village were murdered. Then, as I was running away, I was struck down by a spear. A priest found me and took me to hospital in Goma. He rescued my children, told them what had happened to me, and brought them to this camp. Two days later that priest was killed. His name was Mwamba. He was killed because he helped us."

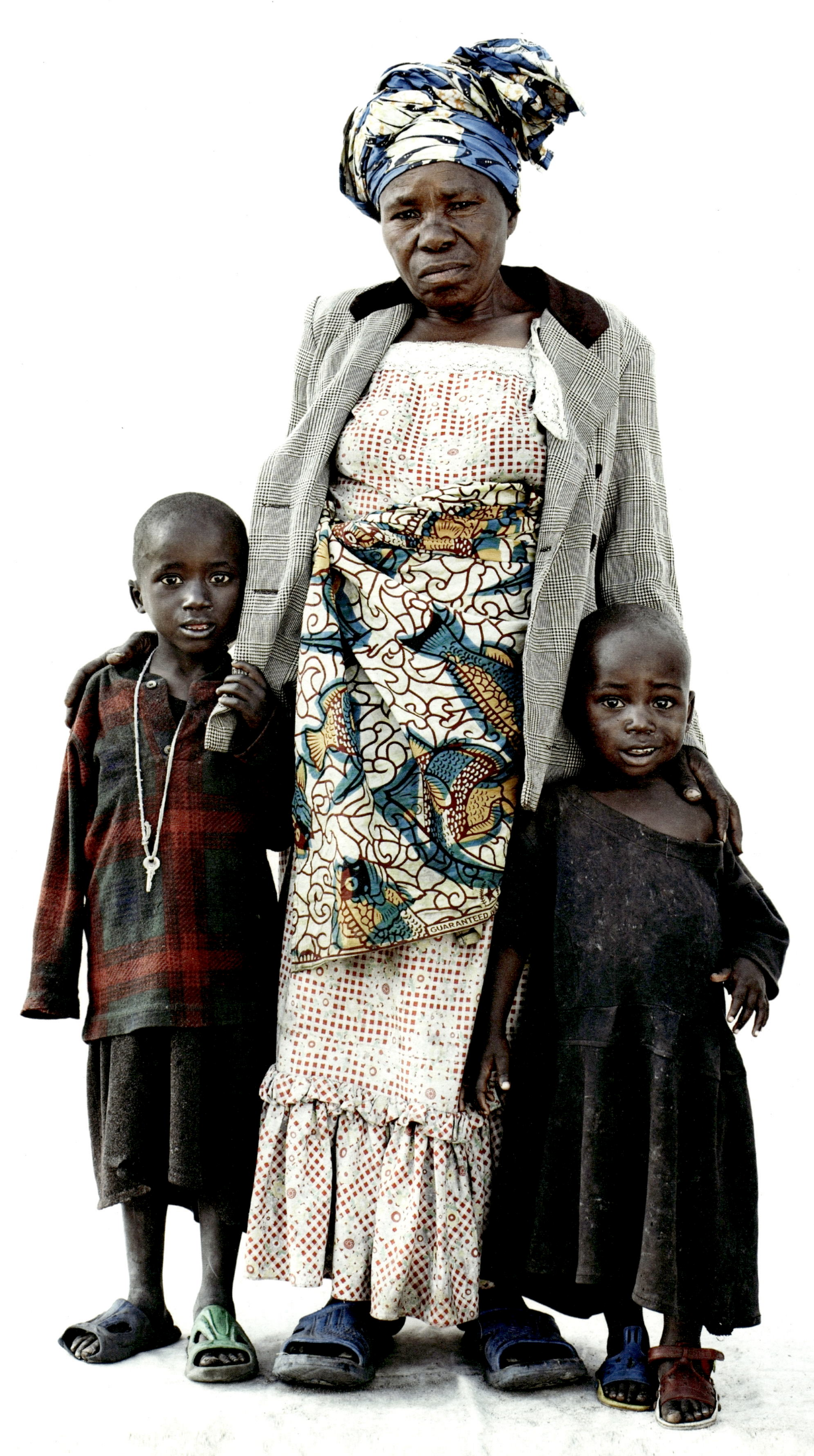

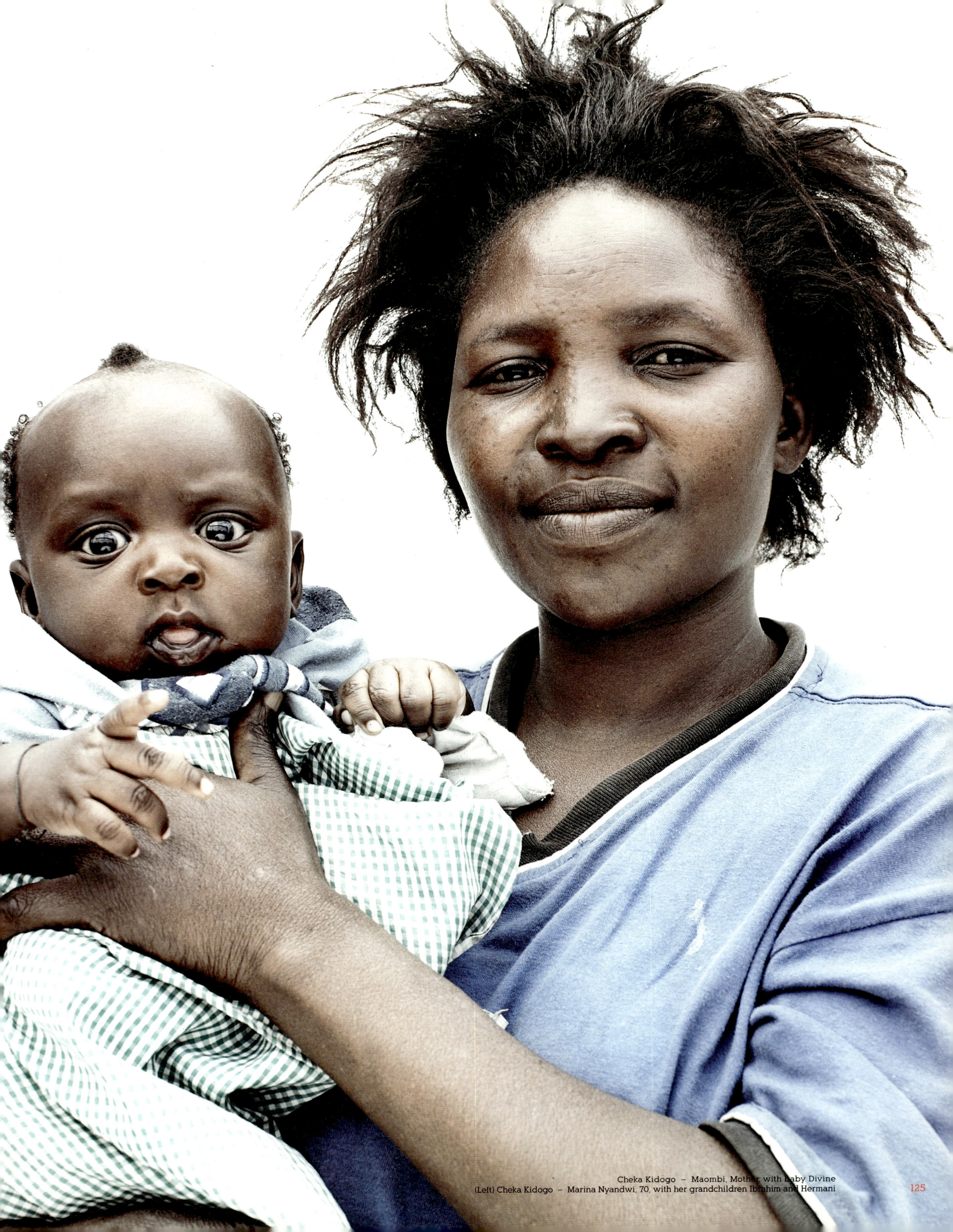

Cheka Kidogo – Maombi, Mother with Baby Divine
(Left) Cheka Kidogo – Marina Nyandwi, 70, with her grandchildren Ibrahim and Hermani

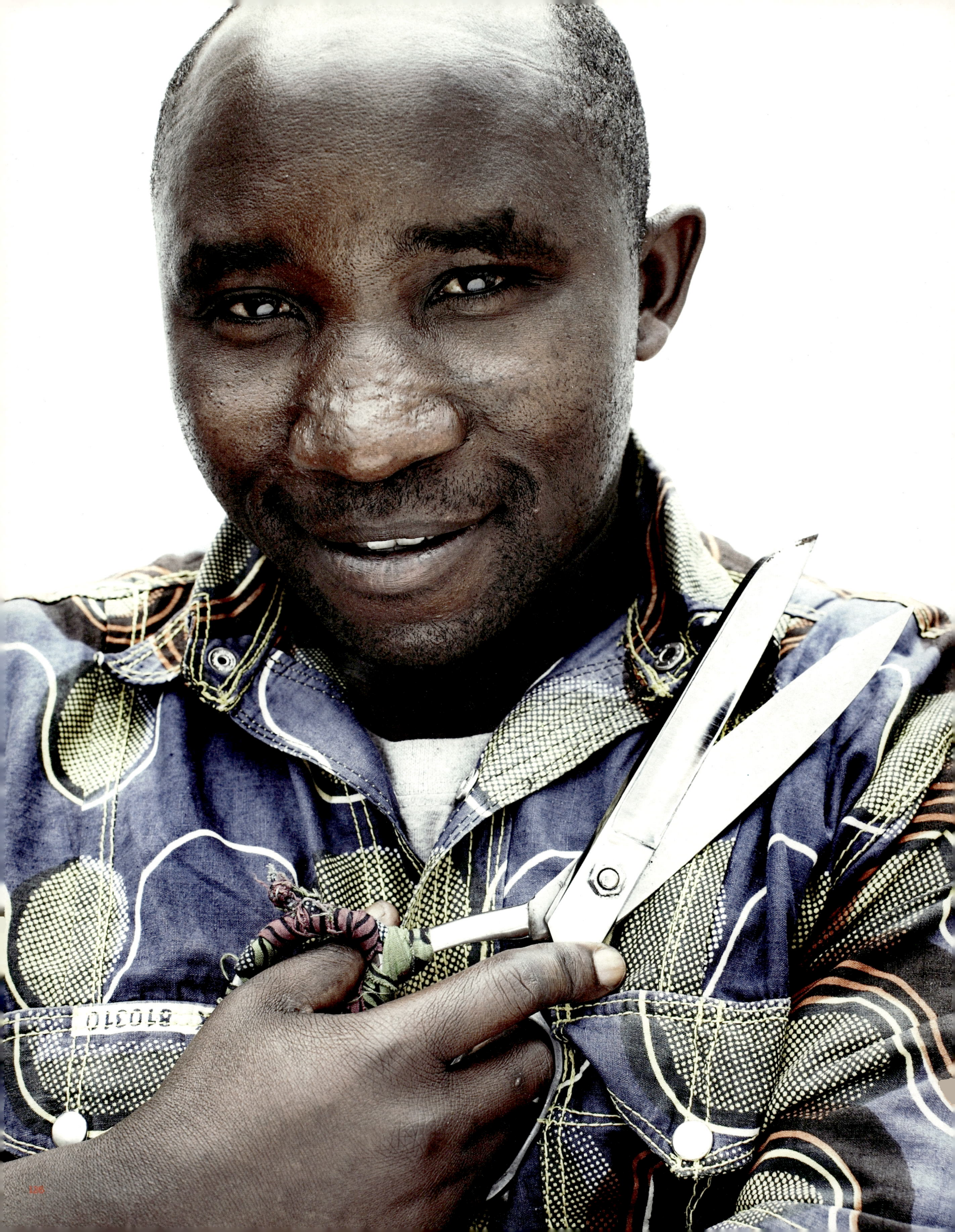

"I am a tailor without a sewing machine. I couldn't carry it when I ran from my village. I had to carry my children. At night, when the men with guns were patrolling, we hid in the bush. We could hear the beating and killing. One of my neighbours was castrated – it's a warning to others. The children were screaming. And someone who tried to help him was killed the next day. I haven't seen my brothers for several months and I haven't had any news from them. We lost each other as we were fleeing. They ran one way and I ran another. I came here in January 2008, with my four children. I want to go back to my home. If the warlord is kicked out of the area and there is peace, we will go back and we will sleep again."

"It takes two weeks to make a basket – but it only sells for 260 francs (25p). How can you work for two weeks to make 25p? If I can sell a basket then I can eat. I come from Karuba. I fled when the war came. People were throwing bombs into our houses. I was living with my son. He and his wife were killed. I remember the troops started shooting, people scattered, and then he was dead. I fled with my two grandsons. One is 15 and the other 13. They are orphans now. The men who killed my son are still there in the village. They stayed there. That's why we can't go home."

     Cheka Kidogo – Furaha Vumilia, 65. Basket Maker

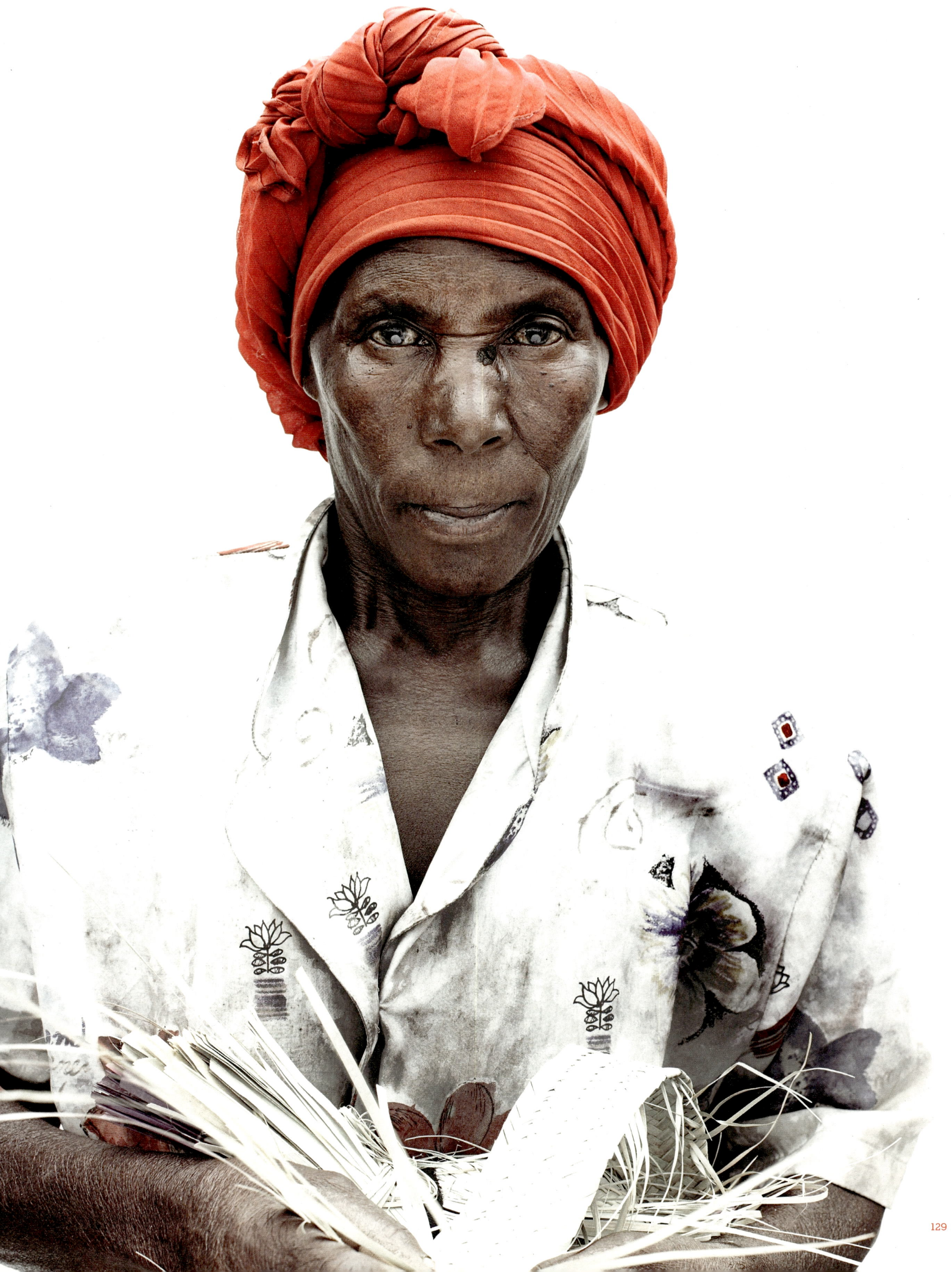

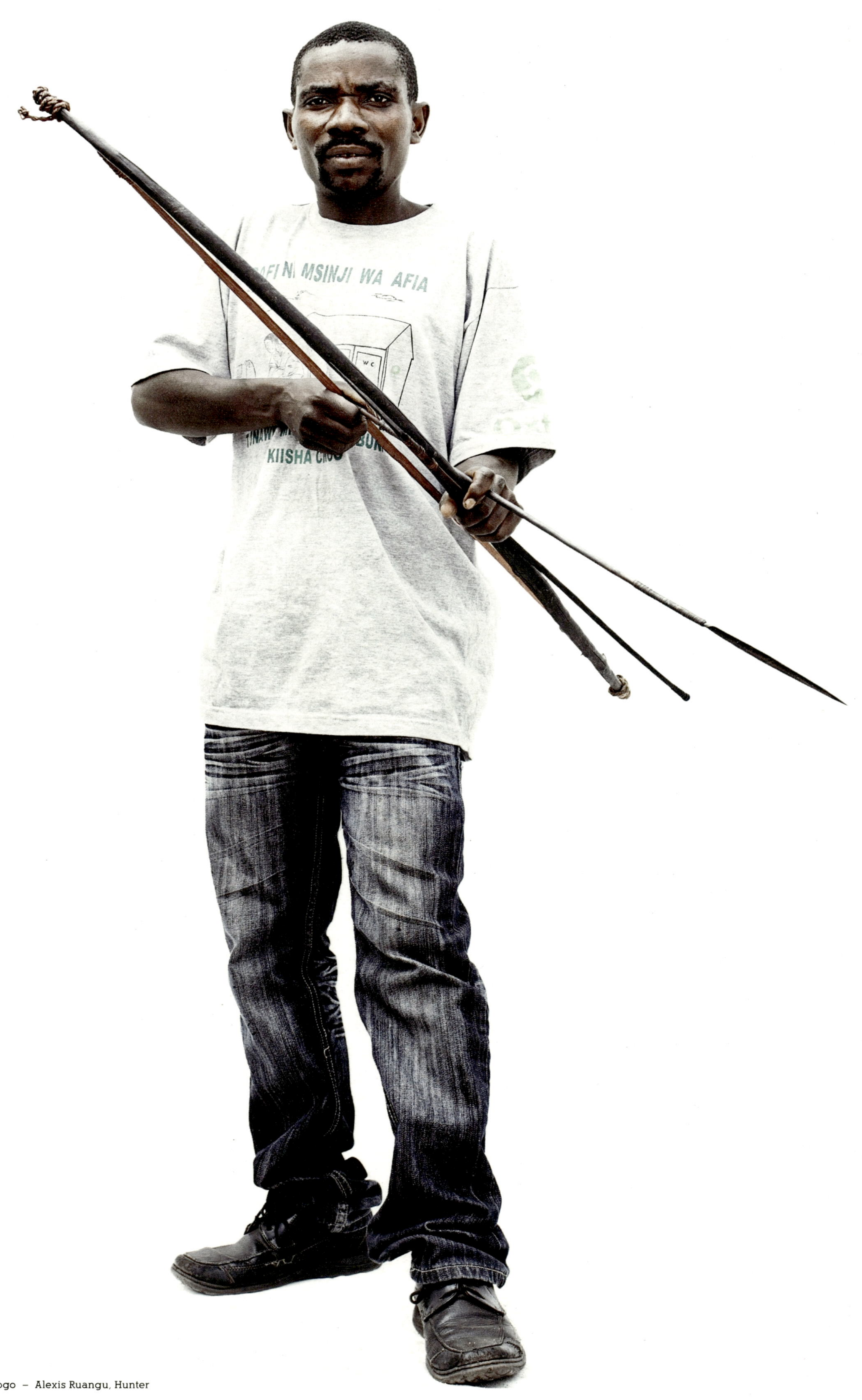

   Cheka Kidogo – Alexis Ruangu, Hunter

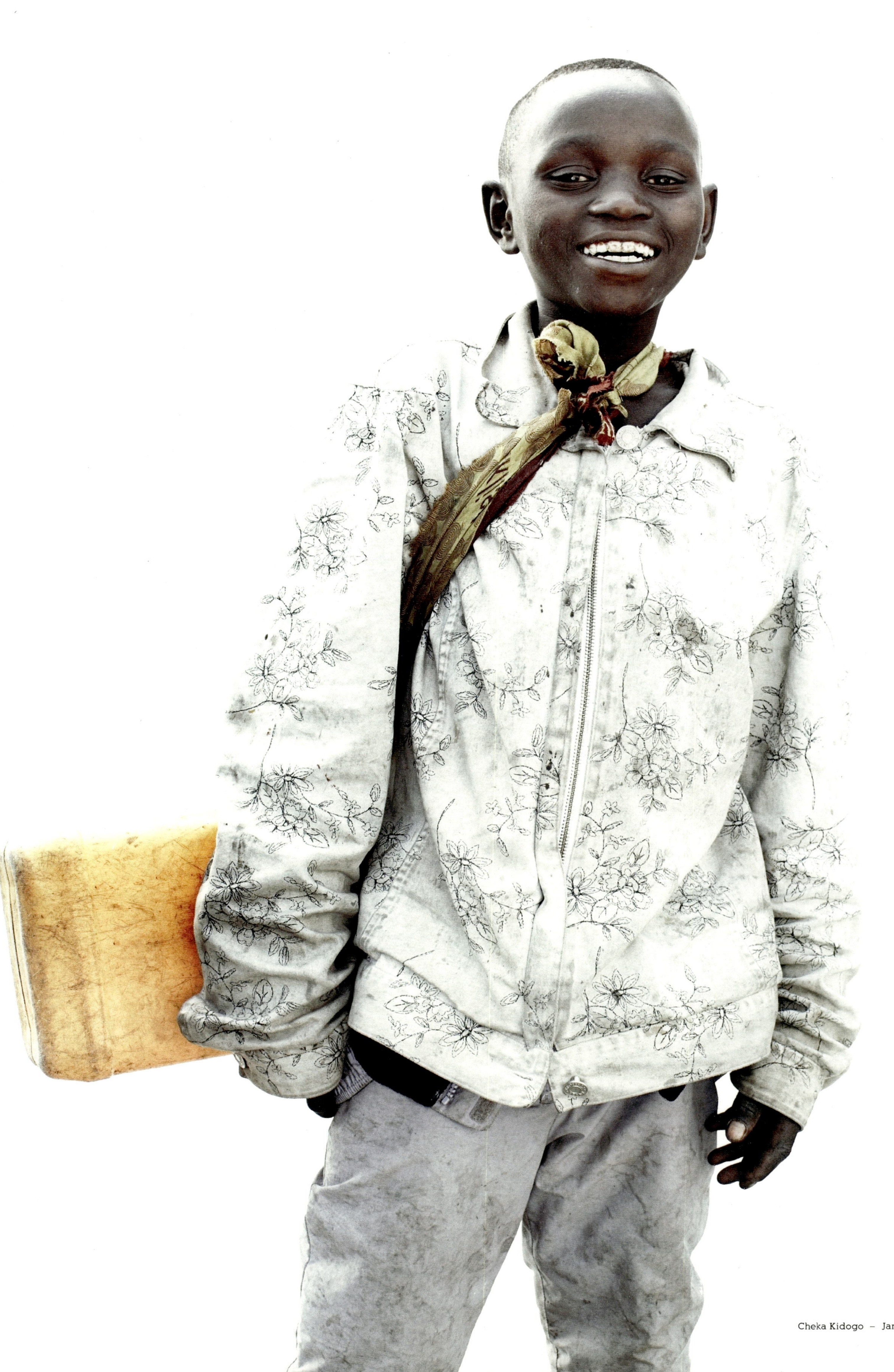

"I arrived in May 2007. I have been here for one year and four months. I have eight children and 12 grandchildren. My husband was a businessman. He is dead. I had to flee due to the war and sexual violence. My husband and some of my relatives were killed. Some of my friends were raped.

One night those men entered the village. They were assaulting us, shooting people, and setting fire to our homes. My husband was shot. I found his body on the street. I didn't attempt to bury him. I couldn't. I had to run.

I will forgive those armed men. What else can I do? The only thing I hope for now is peace. I want to find a place to settle with my family. I want my grandchildren to go to school. We have nothing to do here. We get up early in the morning and when the sun sets we go to sleep."

   Cheka Kidogo – Antoinette, 70, Wife and Granny

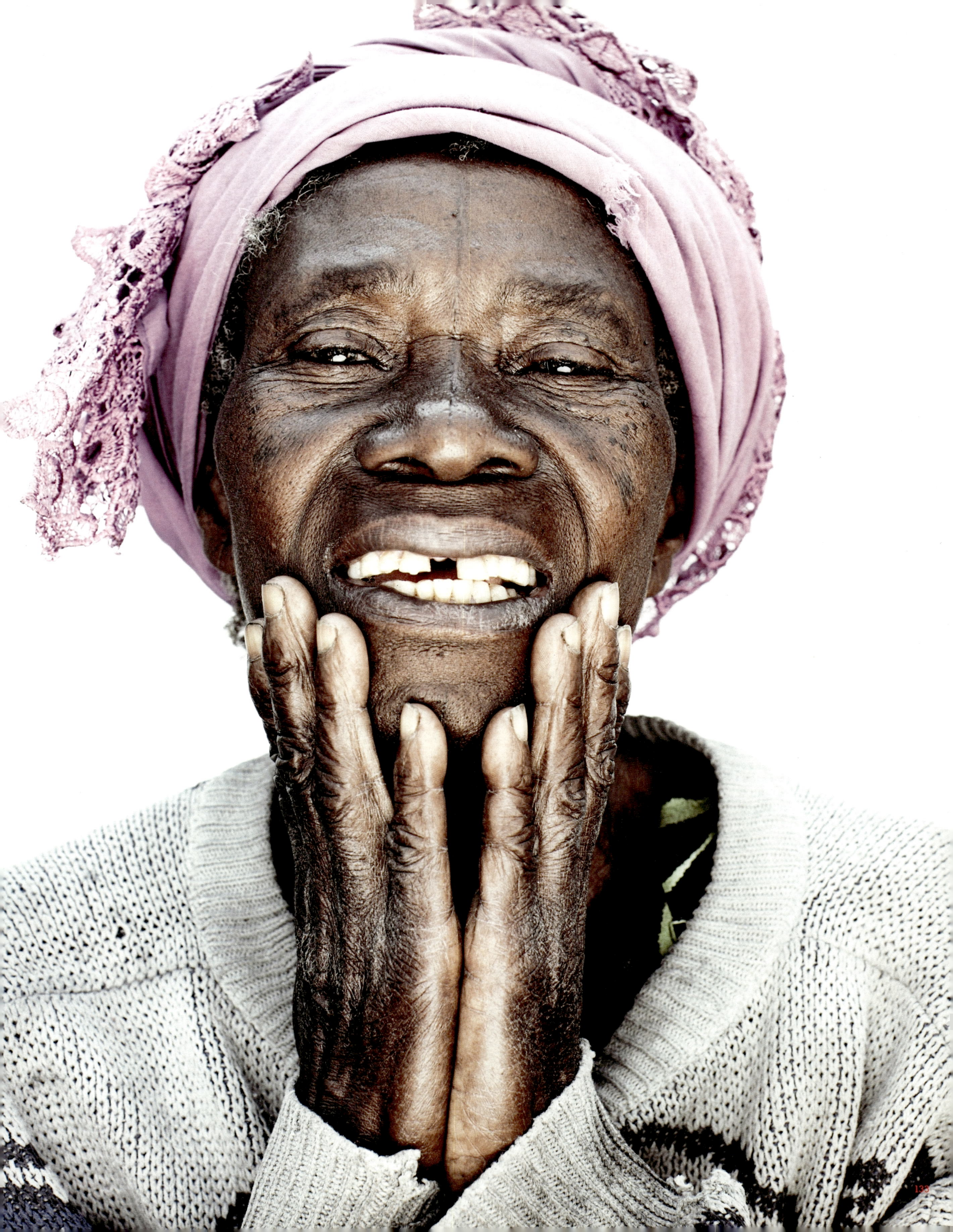

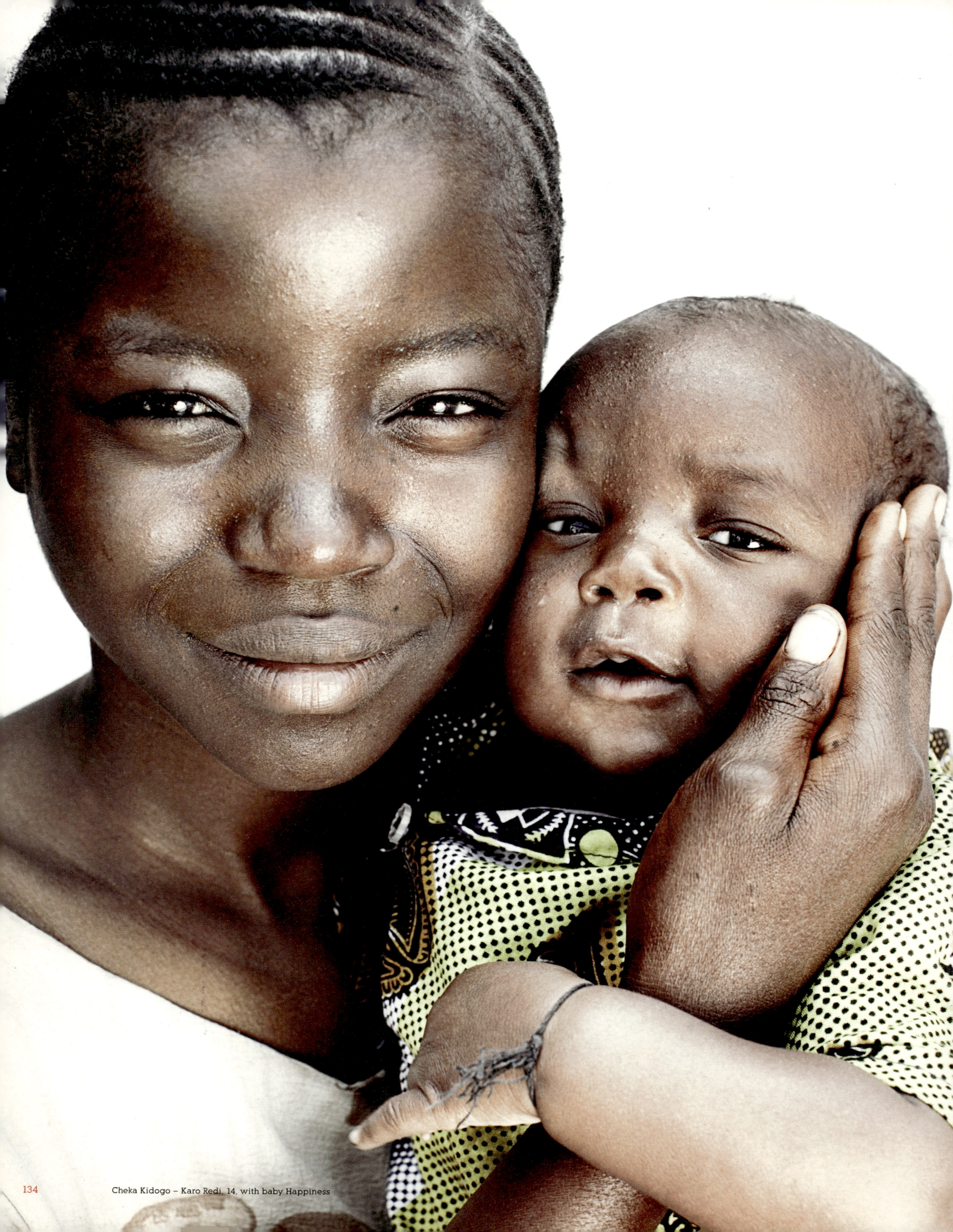

Cheka Kidogo – Karo Redi, 14, with baby Happiness

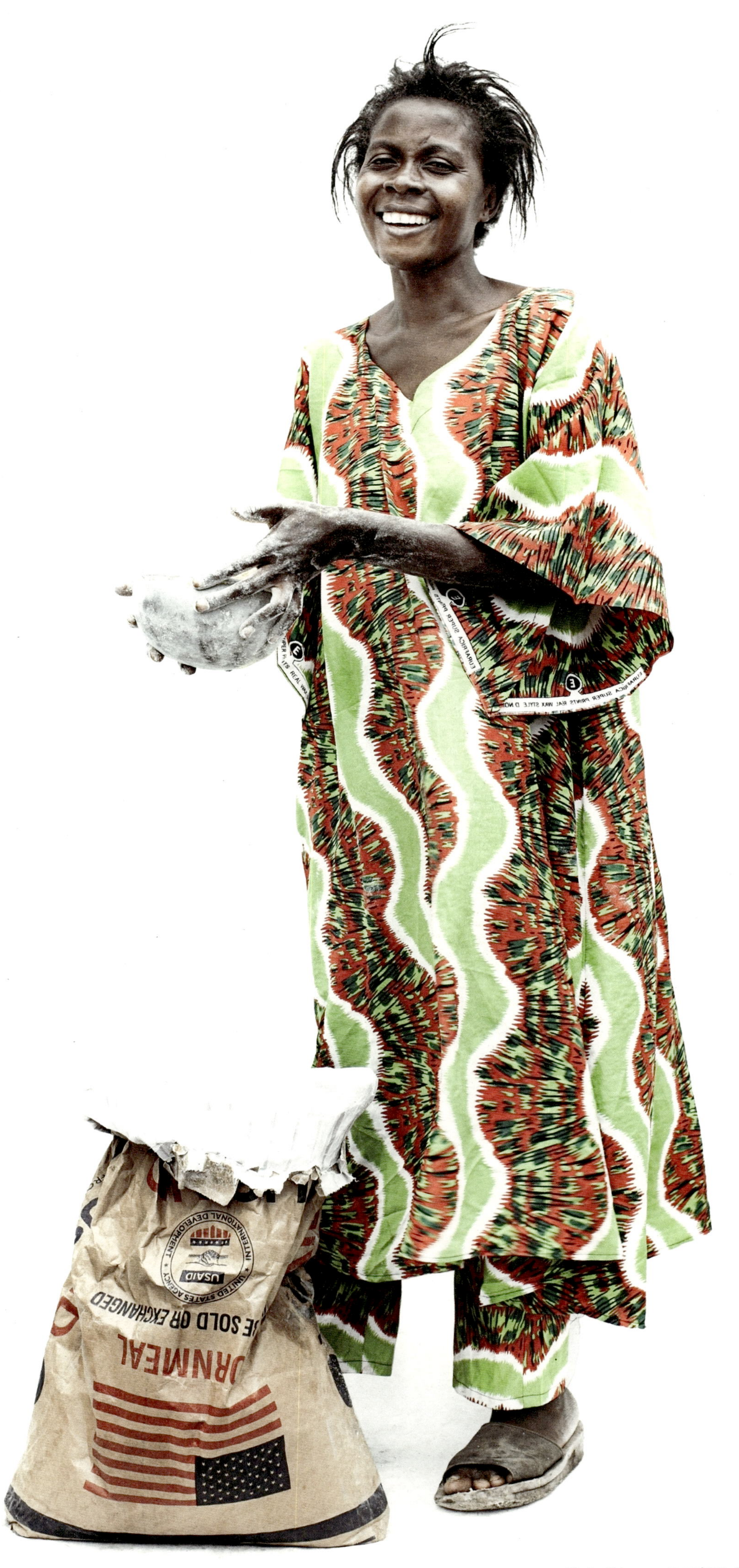

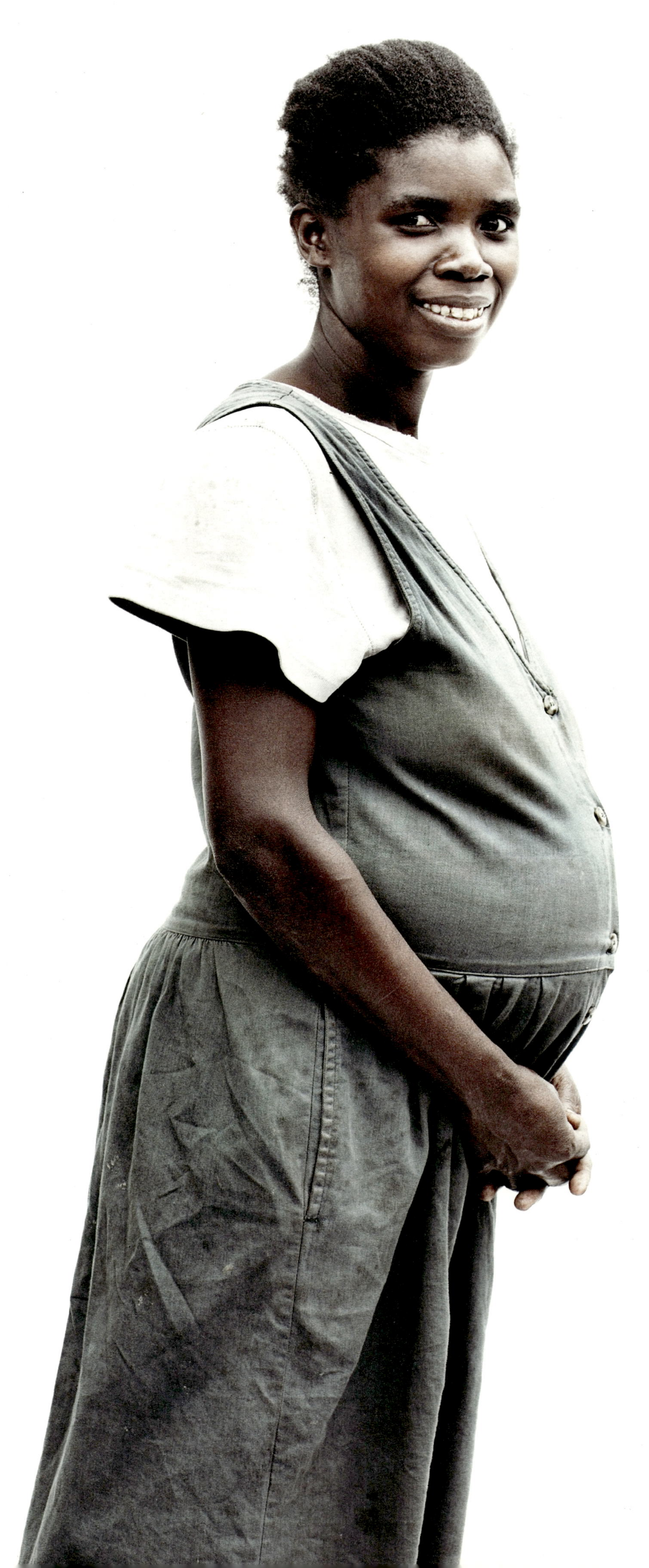

"I am here with my husband and our five children. The sixth is due any day now. We came here from Kinchanga village in September 2007. Almost every night people were coming, shooting and killing. We often had to hide in the bush. It was very cold spending the night outside. Sometimes, these men would kill you in the fields anyway. My uncle was killed in the fields. And my brother was sitting under a tree when he was hit in the head by a bullet. So we decided we had to leave. My eldest daughter and my husband each carried one of the younger children. I carried one on my back and the other could just about walk by herself. All I want is peace, so we can go back to our village. Nothing will remain there. We will have to restart our lives, rebuild our homes, and plant new crops to feed us."

Jean's baby son arrived, in the camp's health centre, just a few hours after this photograph was taken. She asked us to name him. Rankin suggested Cheka (Swahili for 'smile').

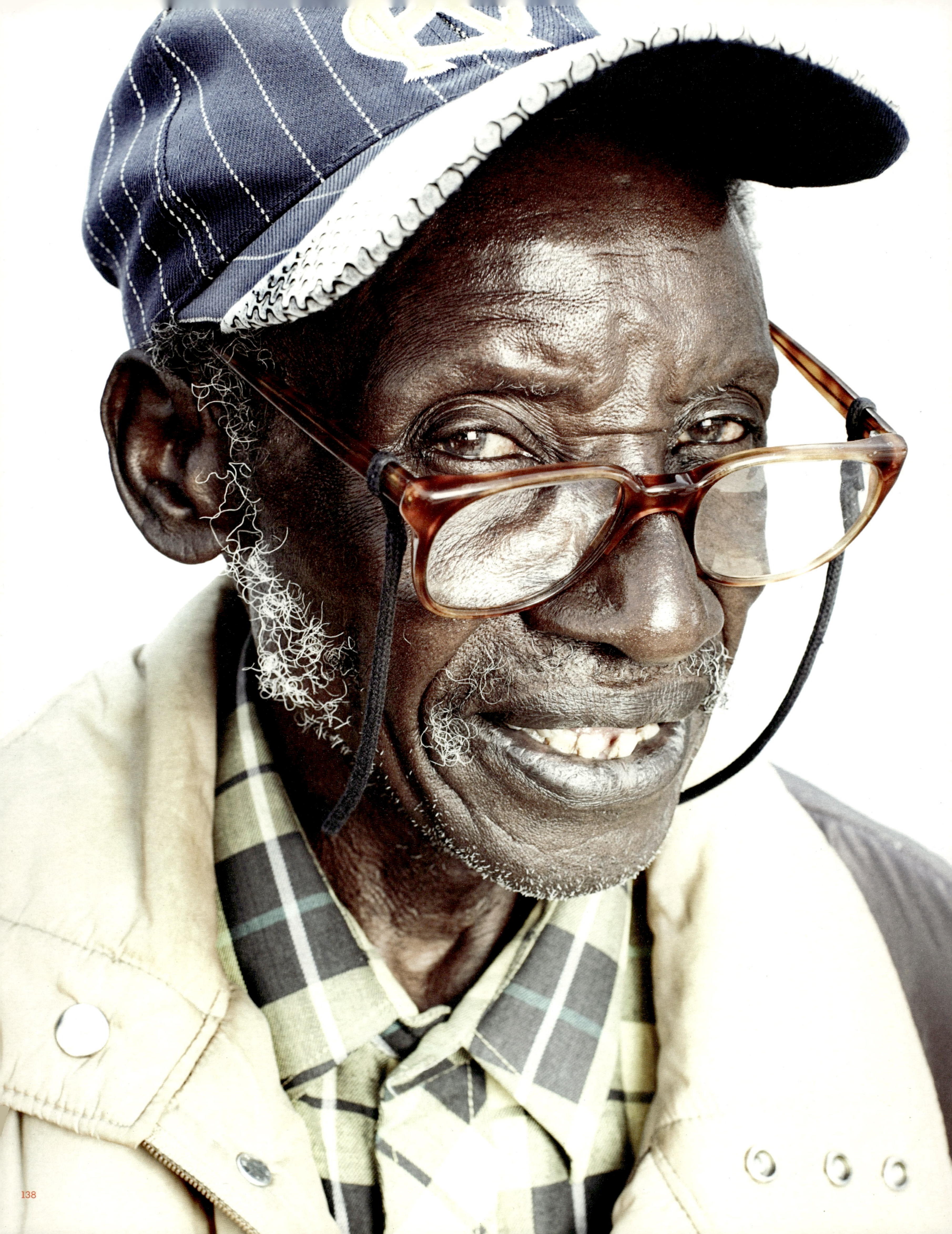

Cheka Kidogo – Charles Kimanuka, 78. Chef

"There are 24 of us in the camp, living in four small huts. In our village we had four big houses. Only one is still standing. The men who drove us away are living in it. They smashed our other houses and used them for firewood. We fled when we heard the shooting in the middle of the night, and we walked for four days. People from other villages saw us approaching and gave us bananas. And they welcomed us into their homes to rest for the night.

The worst moment in my life is right now. We want peace. That's all. Peace so that we can go back home. We want you people to talk to the politicians and ask them to stop this war."

    Cheka Kidogo – Banza Masamba, 47. Hairdresser

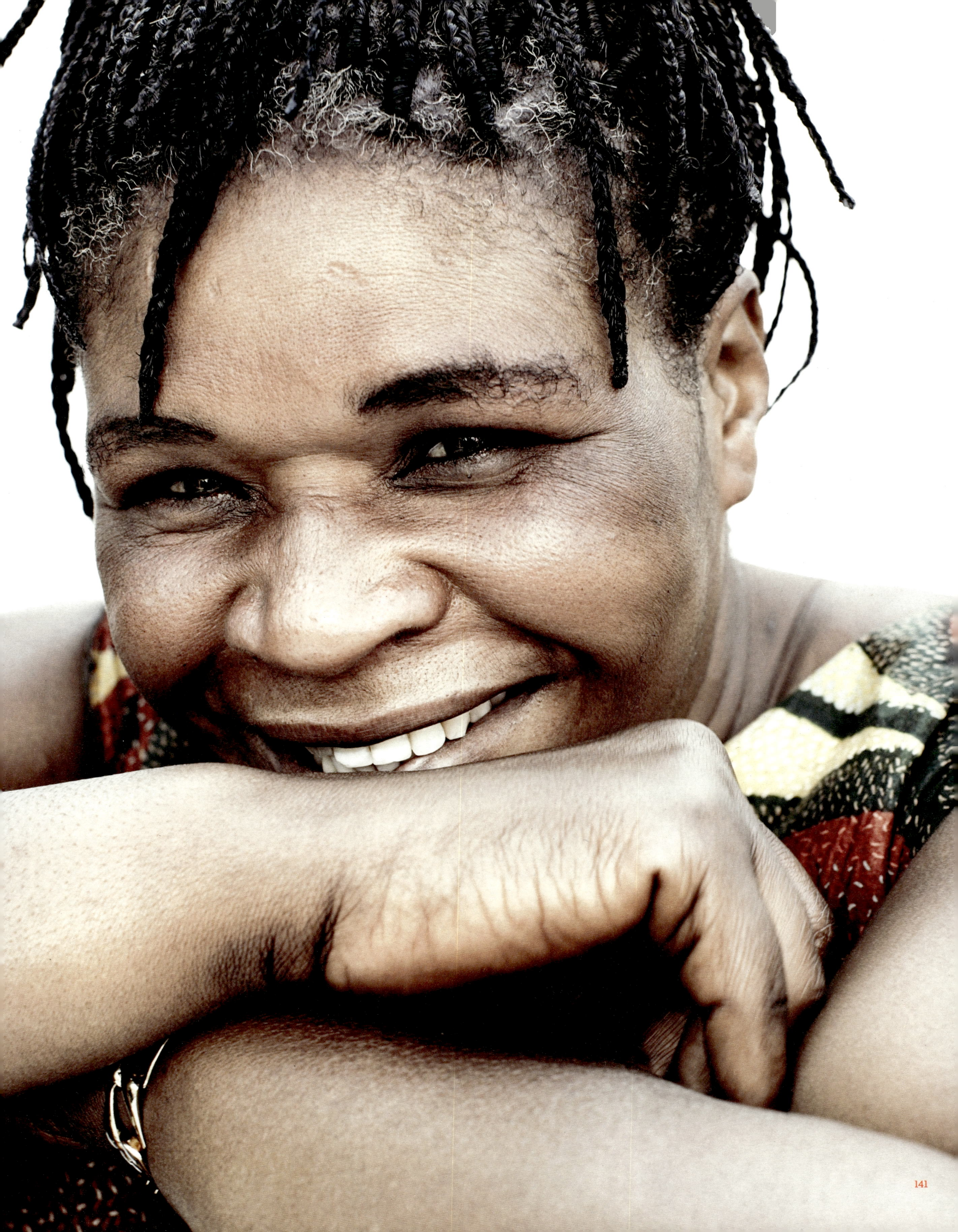

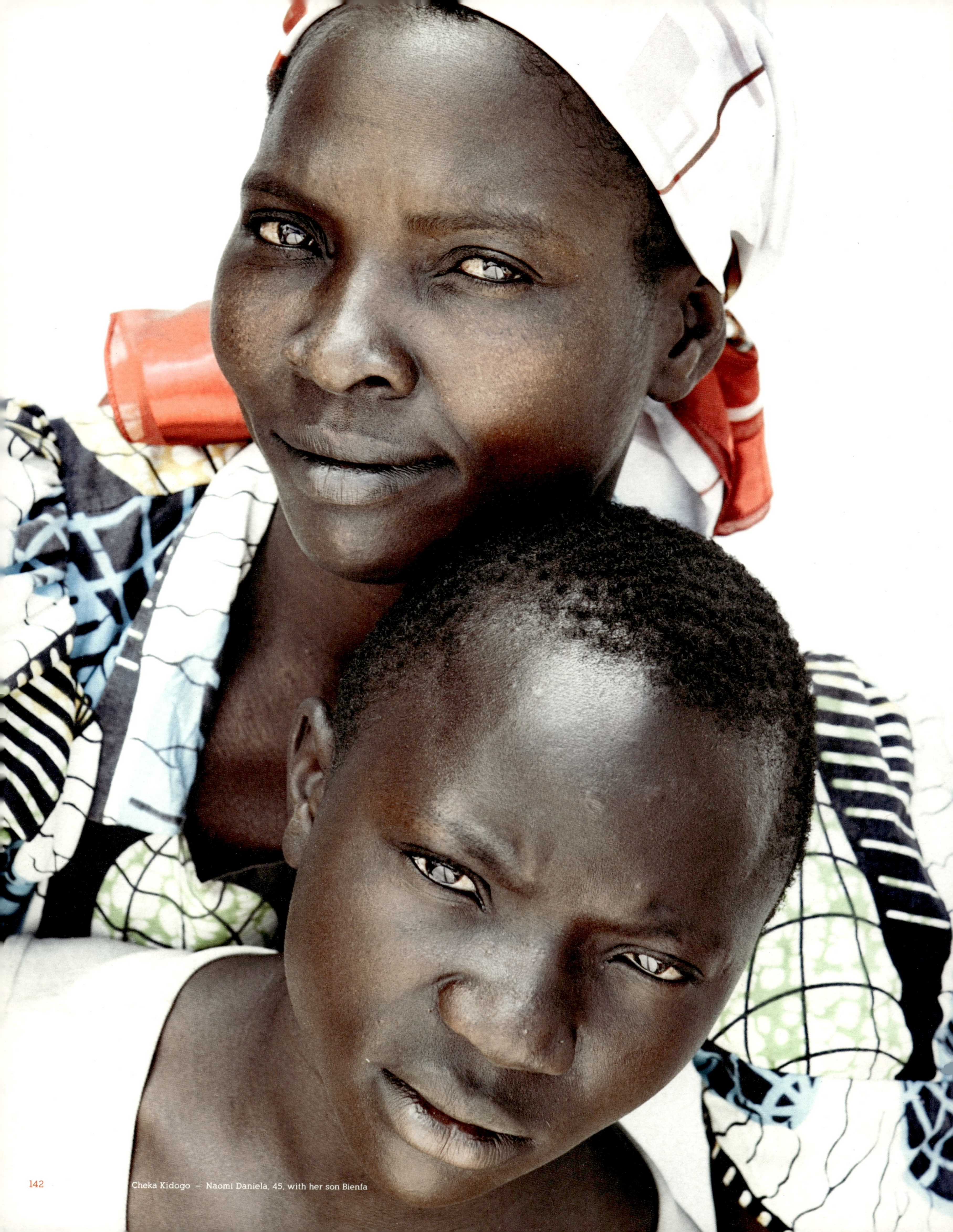

Cheka Kidogo – Naomi Daniela, 45, with her son Bienfa

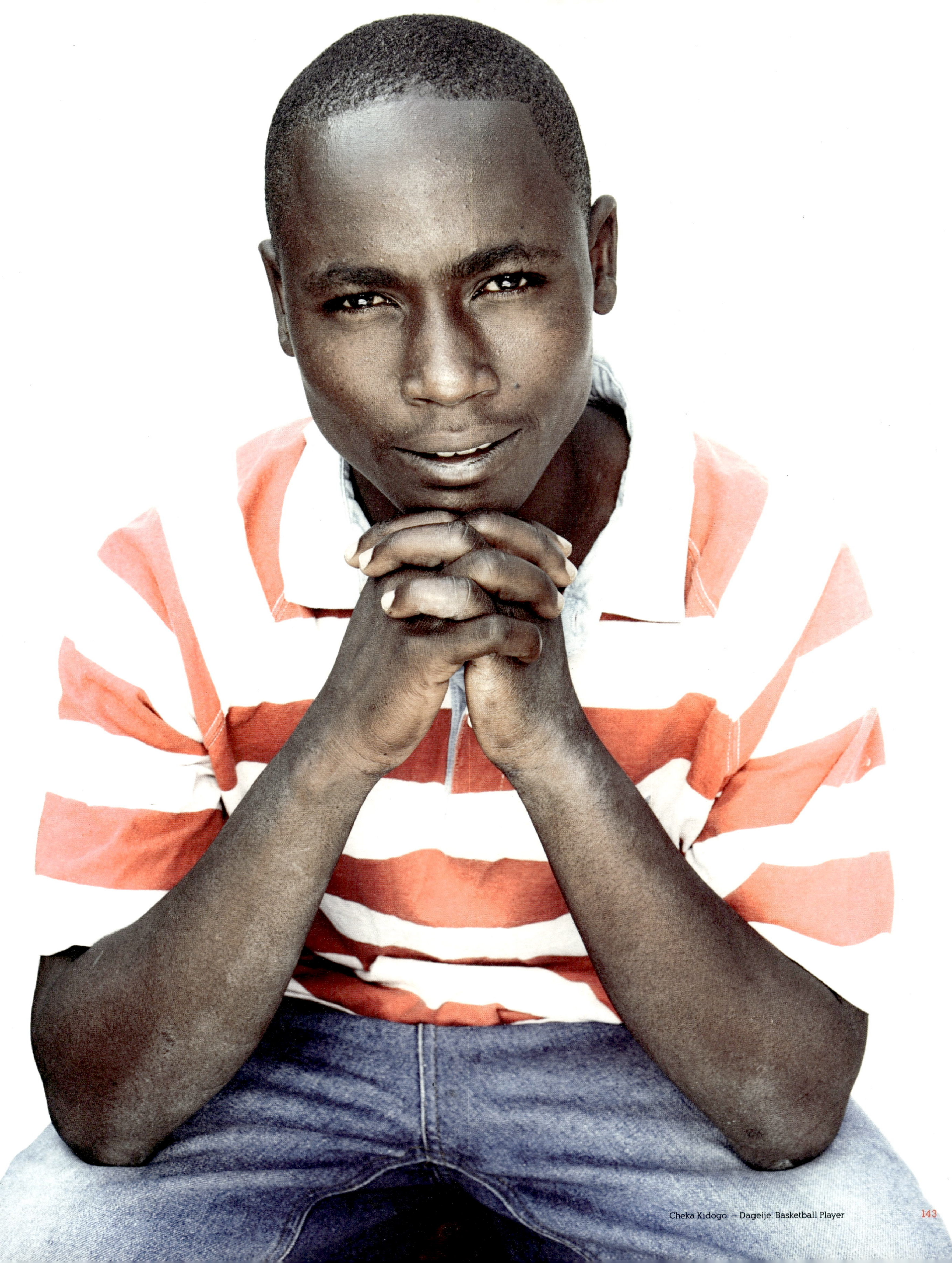

Cheka Kidogo – Dageije, Basketball Player

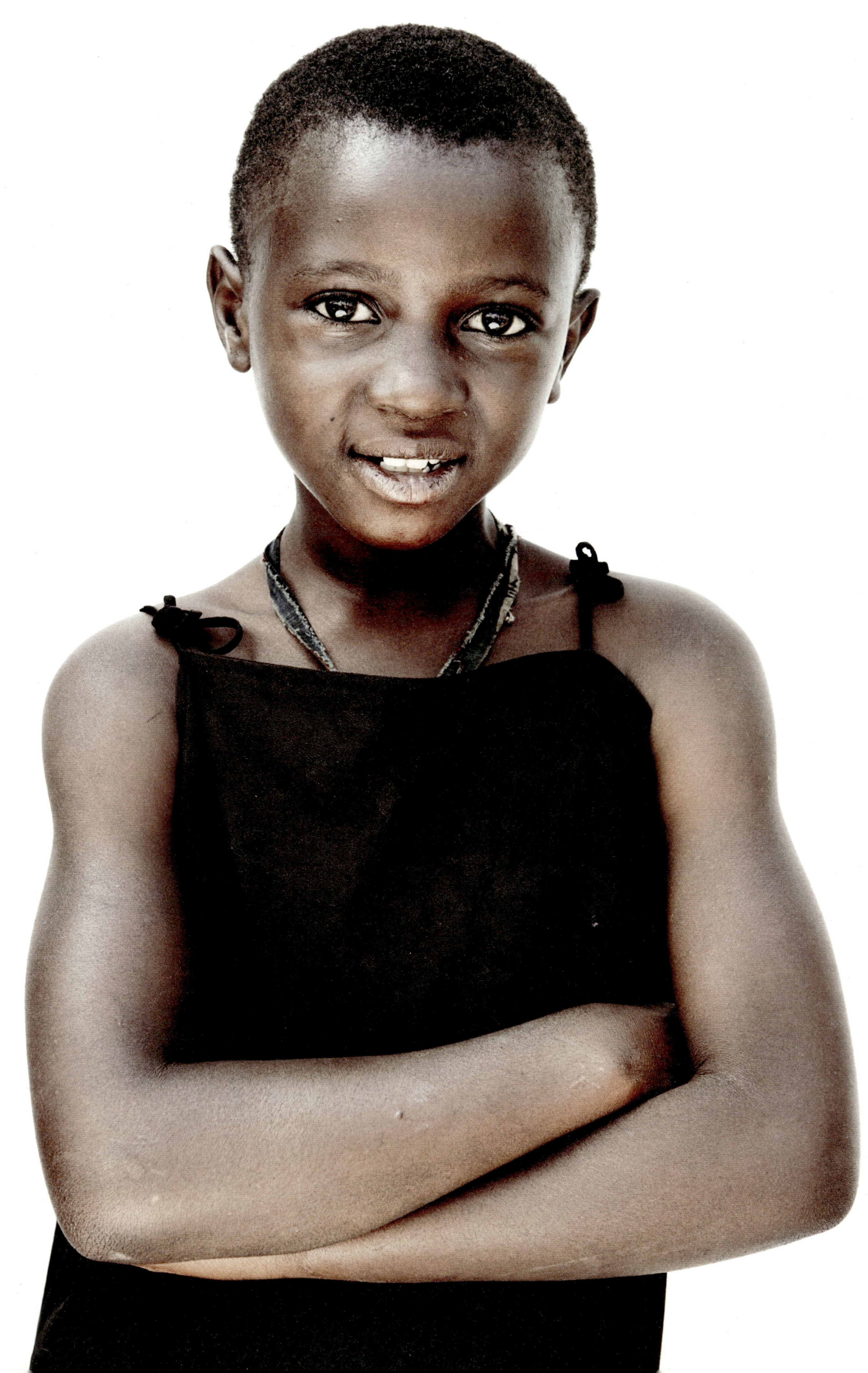

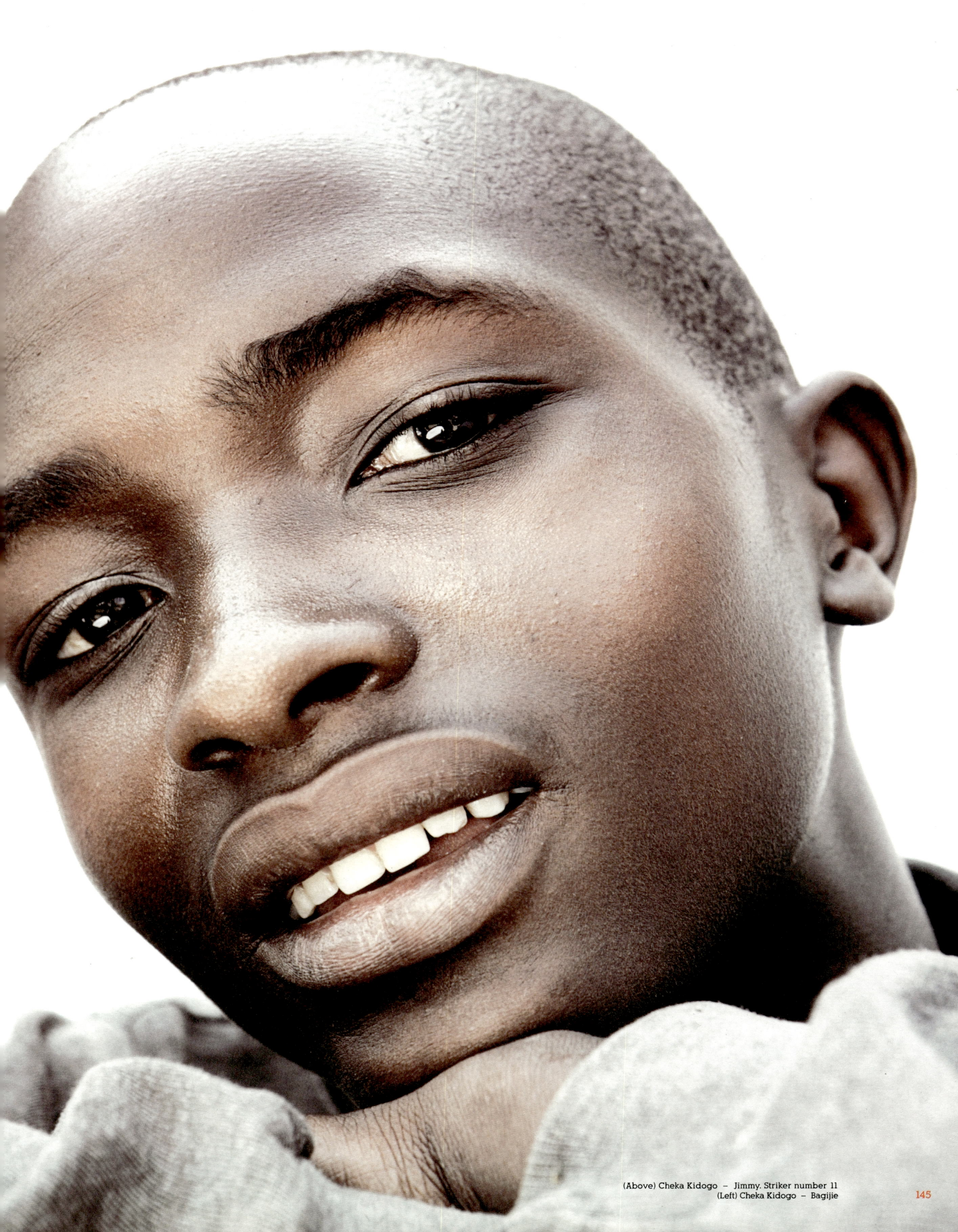

(Above) Cheka Kidogo – Jimmy. Striker number 11
(Left) Cheka Kidogo – Bagijie

145

"It's war. There's no security in our village. We were forced out – my wife and I with our seven children and 12 grandchildren. Many houses were set on fire. Many people were killed.

I used to make shoes for everyone. I loved my work. I had special tools and thread but I had to leave everything behind when we fled. There are four shoemakers here in the camp. We don't make new shoes any more. No one has any money. So we just repair old ones. We charge 200 francs (19p) to mend a pair of shoes, but it's hard to get hold of all the materials we need. It's not great business."

Cheka Kidogo – Kalimbiro Shamavu, 75. Cobbler

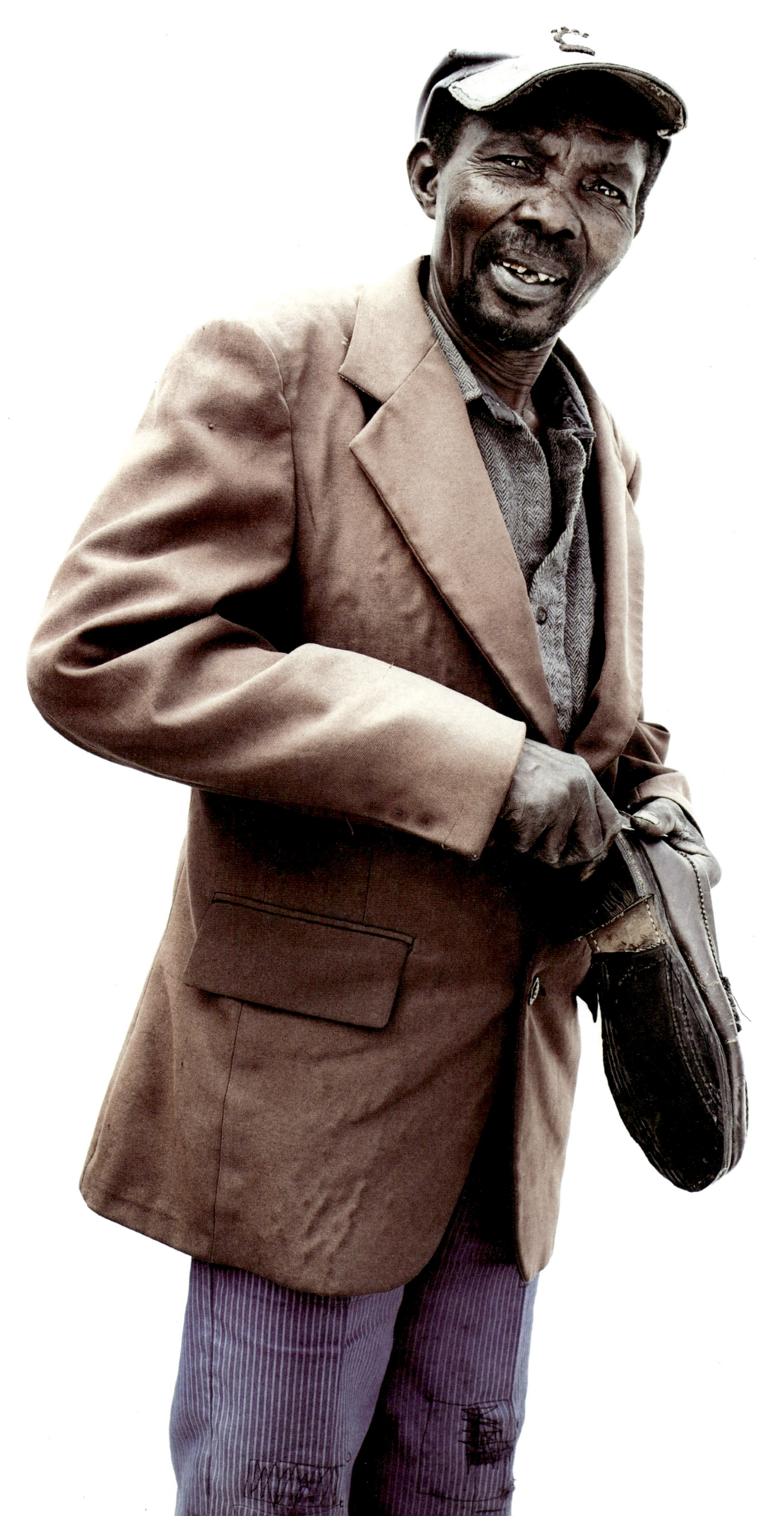

"I am strong. I used to be a farmer but there is no work here. I'm here with my two grown up sons. We had to run from our village when they started the killing. I was running in a large group. Ten people were shot in the back as we were running. One man went back to help his wife he was trying to carry her when he was shot too. I don't know how I reached this camp. I was running helplessly. Just running and running."

     Cheka Kidogo – Eupraise. Farmer

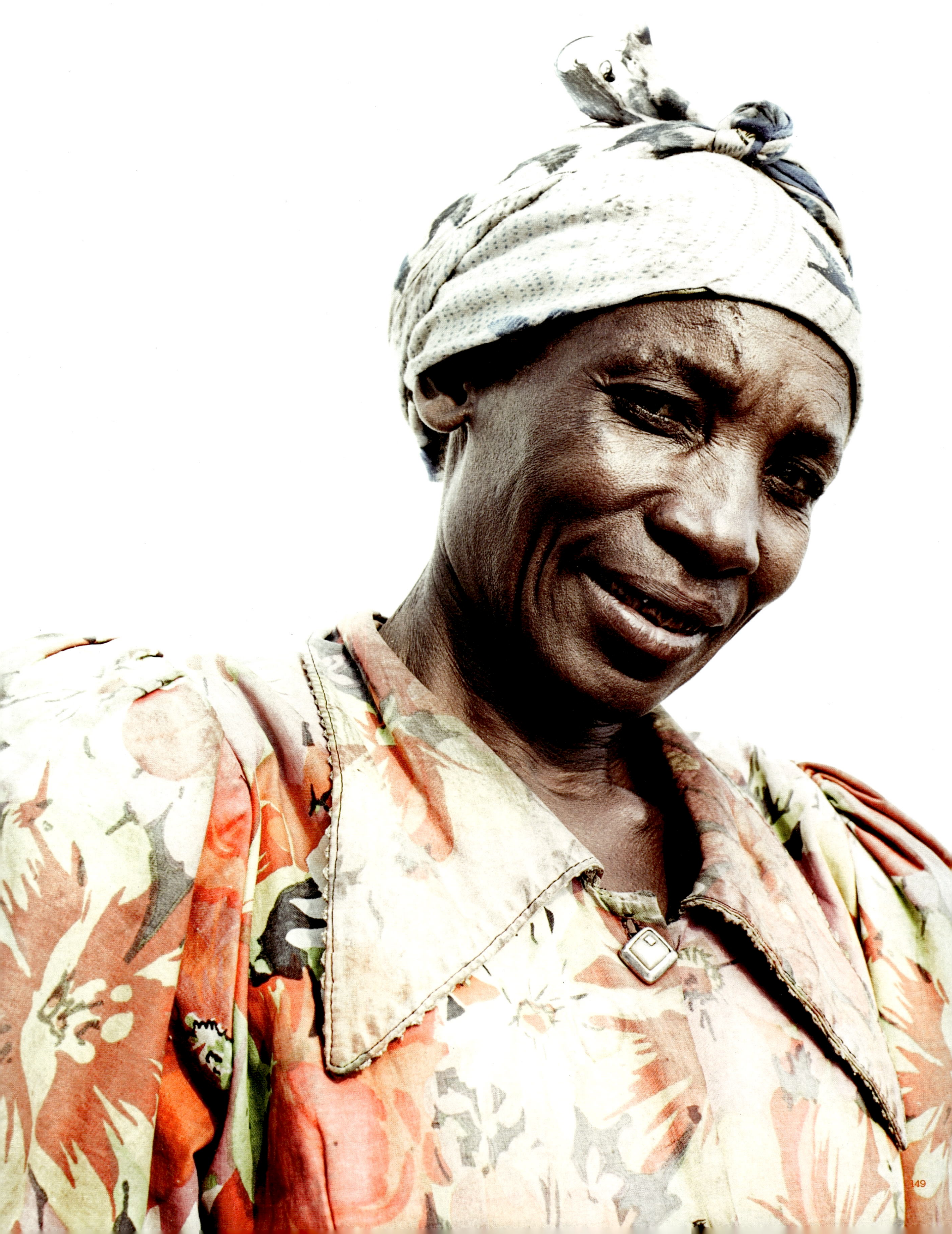

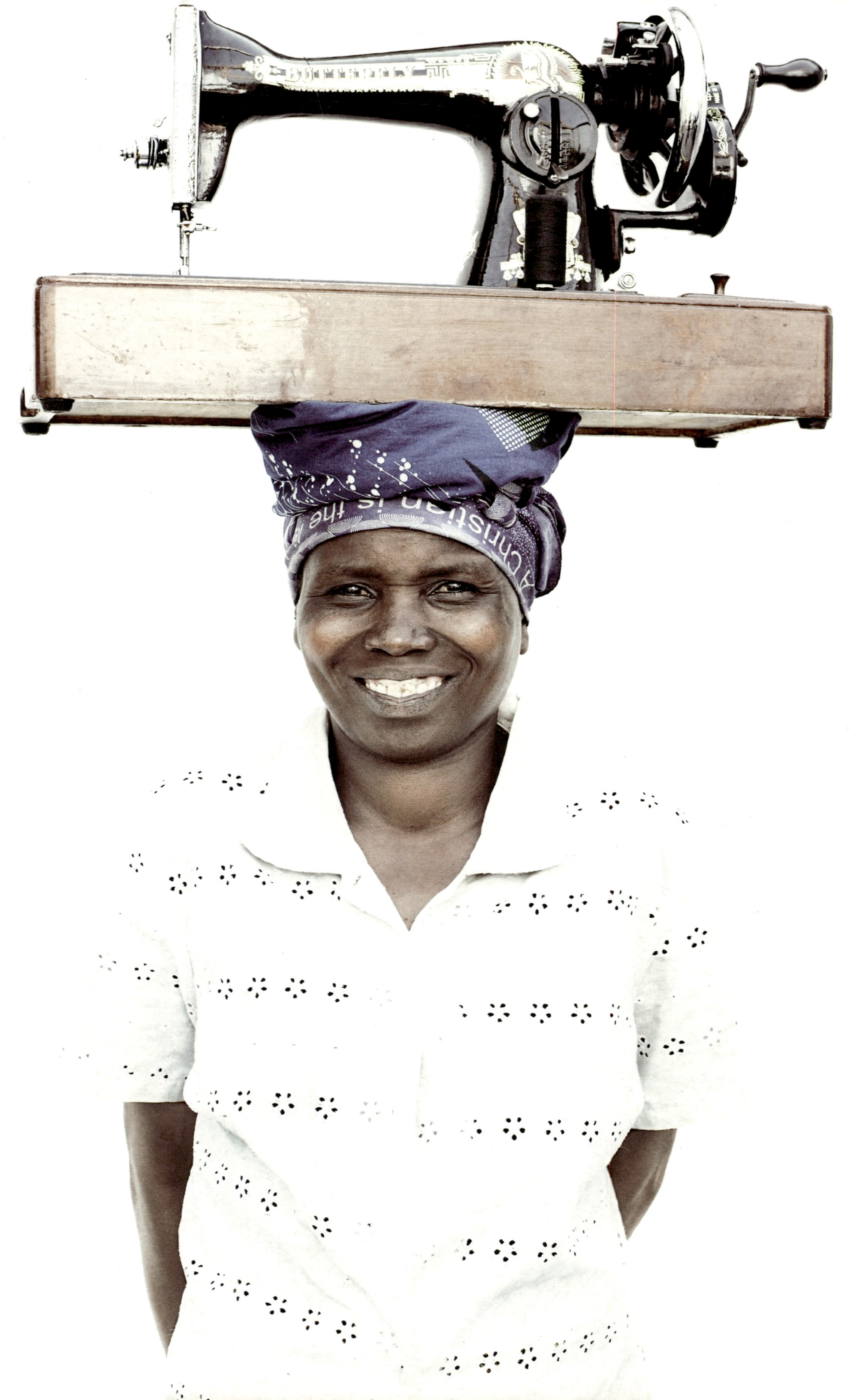
A Christian is the M

"This sewing machine is all I could take with me. It was heavy, difficult to carry, but I couldn't leave it behind. I make women's dresses, and sell them in the camps and on the roadside. This sewing machine feeds my eight children and me. I have eight children. If someone were to take this from me, they would be taking my life. We have been here since September 2007. Every- one in Karuba village decided to leave together – in the middle of the night – when we heard gunfire so close to our homes. We had no time to gather food. We were running for our lives. Many villagers were killed – Victor Materina and his wife were run- ning next to me when they were shot dead."

A PANORAMIC PORTRAIT OF THE MUGUNGA CAMP

On the last day of Rankin's 2008 visit to DRC, Oxfam held an exhibition of Rankin's photographs in the heart of the camp. Over a hundred A4 printed portraits were pegged to a washing line and strung up through the market place. It created massive excitement, as 100s clamored for a peek of their photos. What's more, those who hadn't had their photo taken were eager to get in on the action, too. Faced with an enormous, raucous crowd, Rankin grabbed his camera and improvised, directing people to make one long line. In reality this colourful line went on for over 100 metres; you can watch it unfurl over the next 32 pages. And look out for faces that pop up more than once – some people kept running ahead so they could be photographed again....

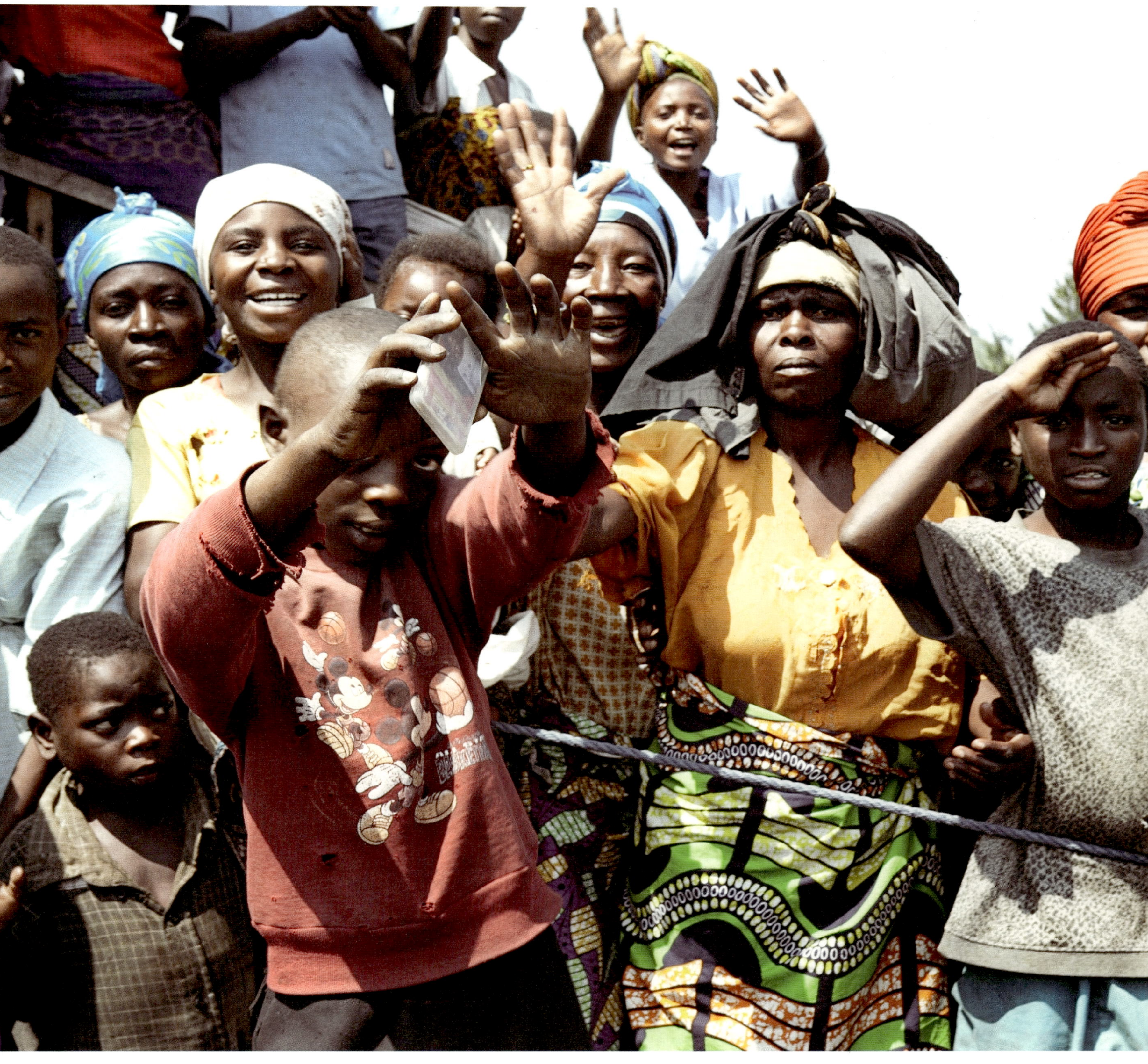

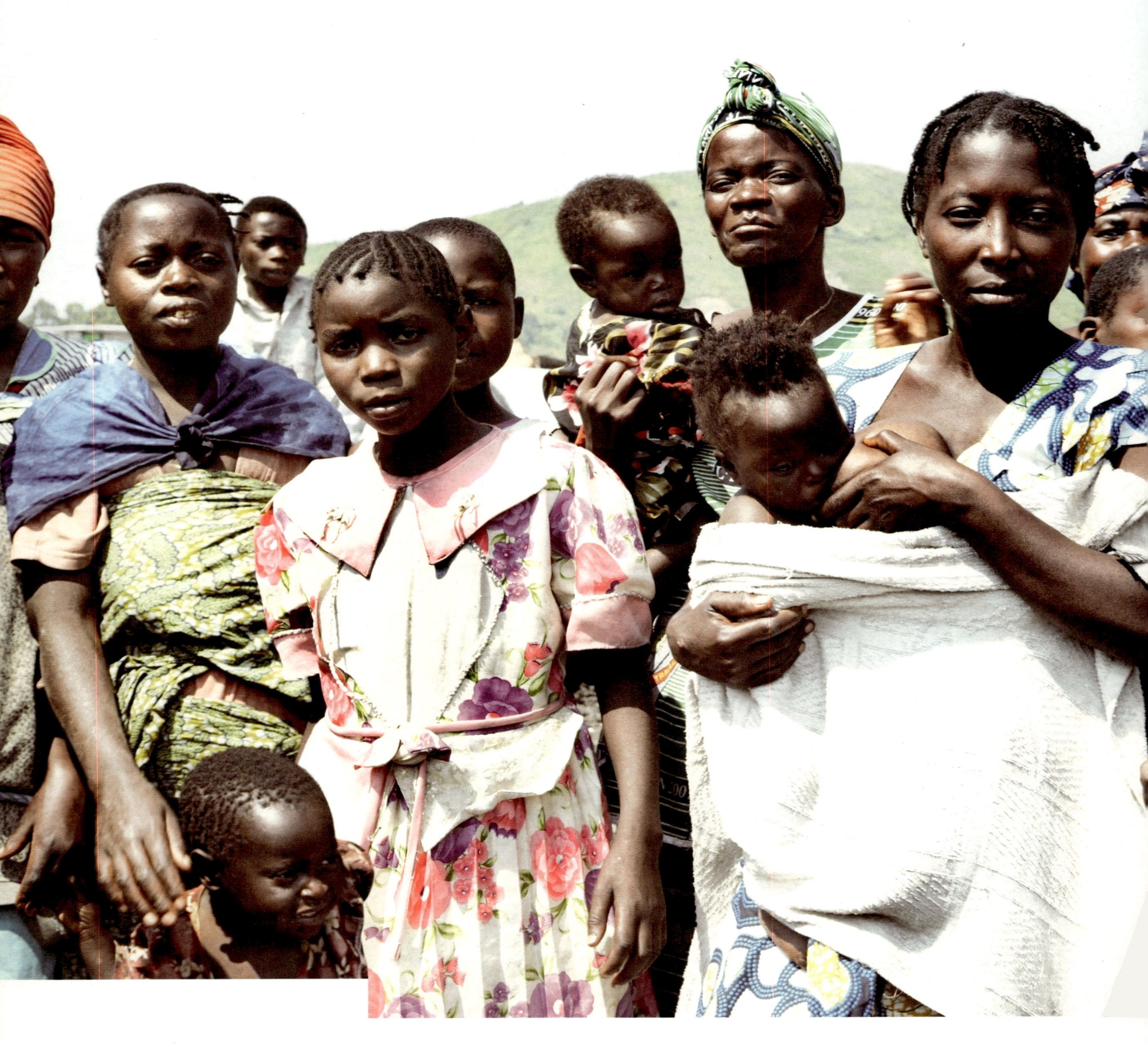

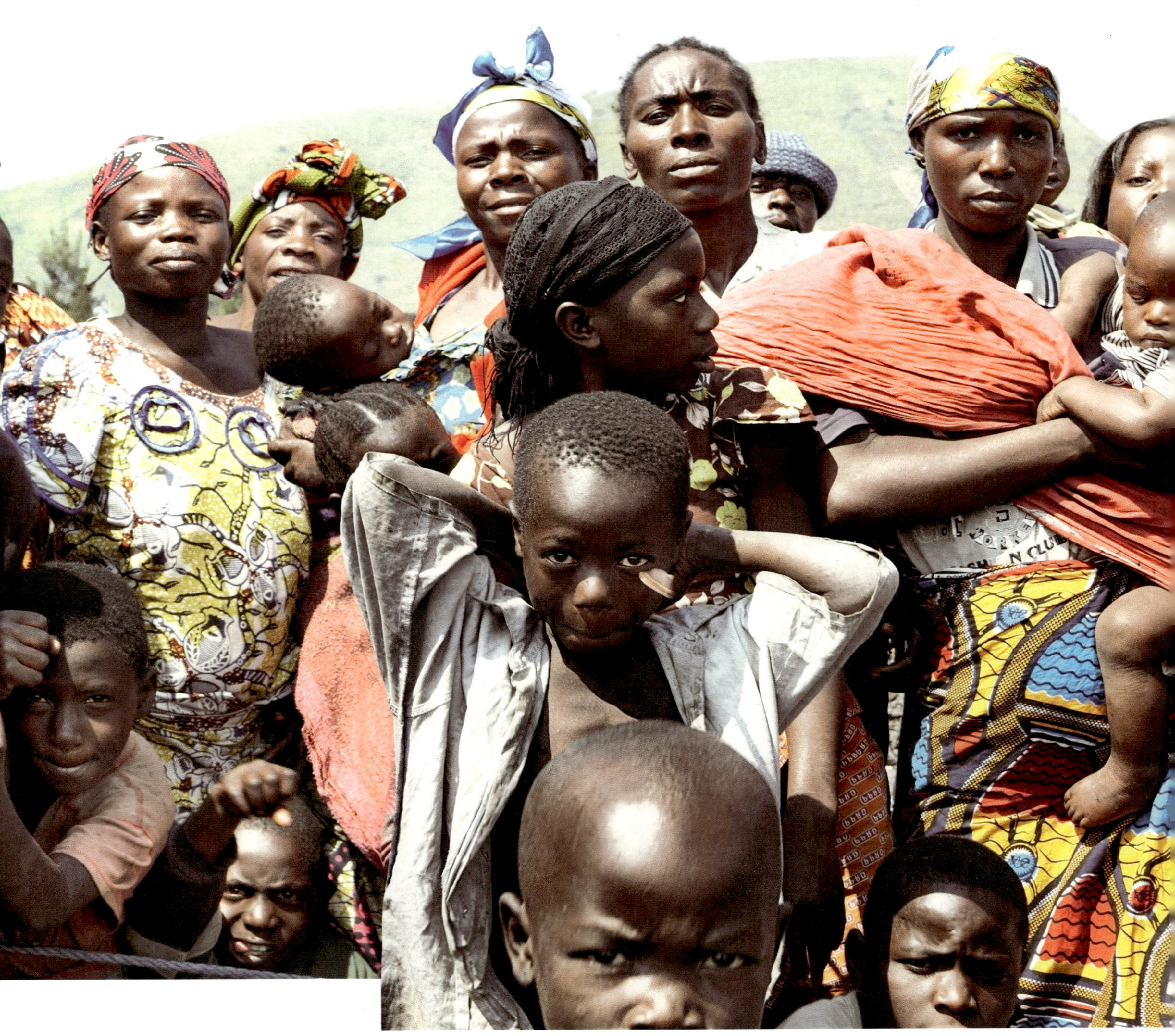

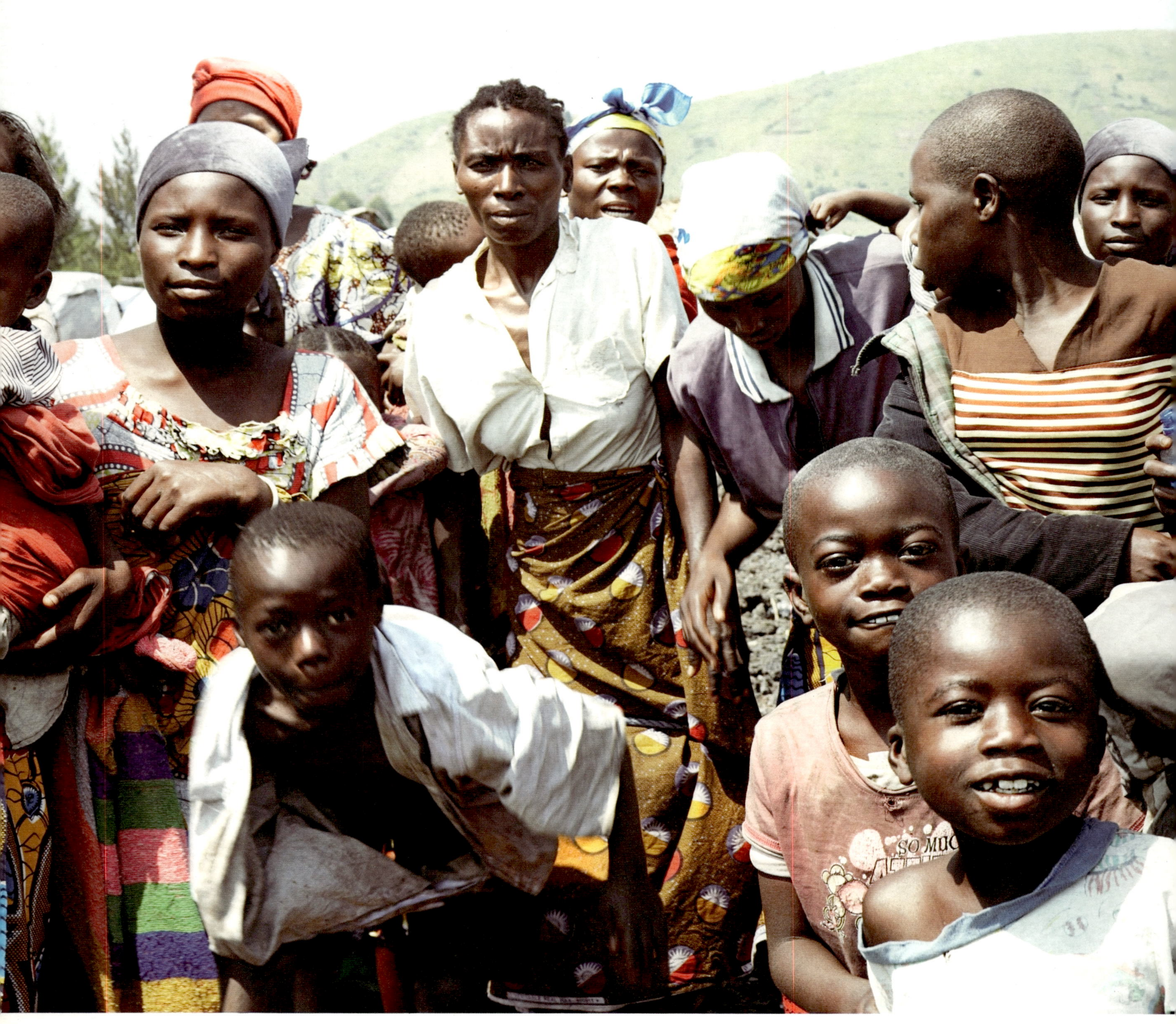

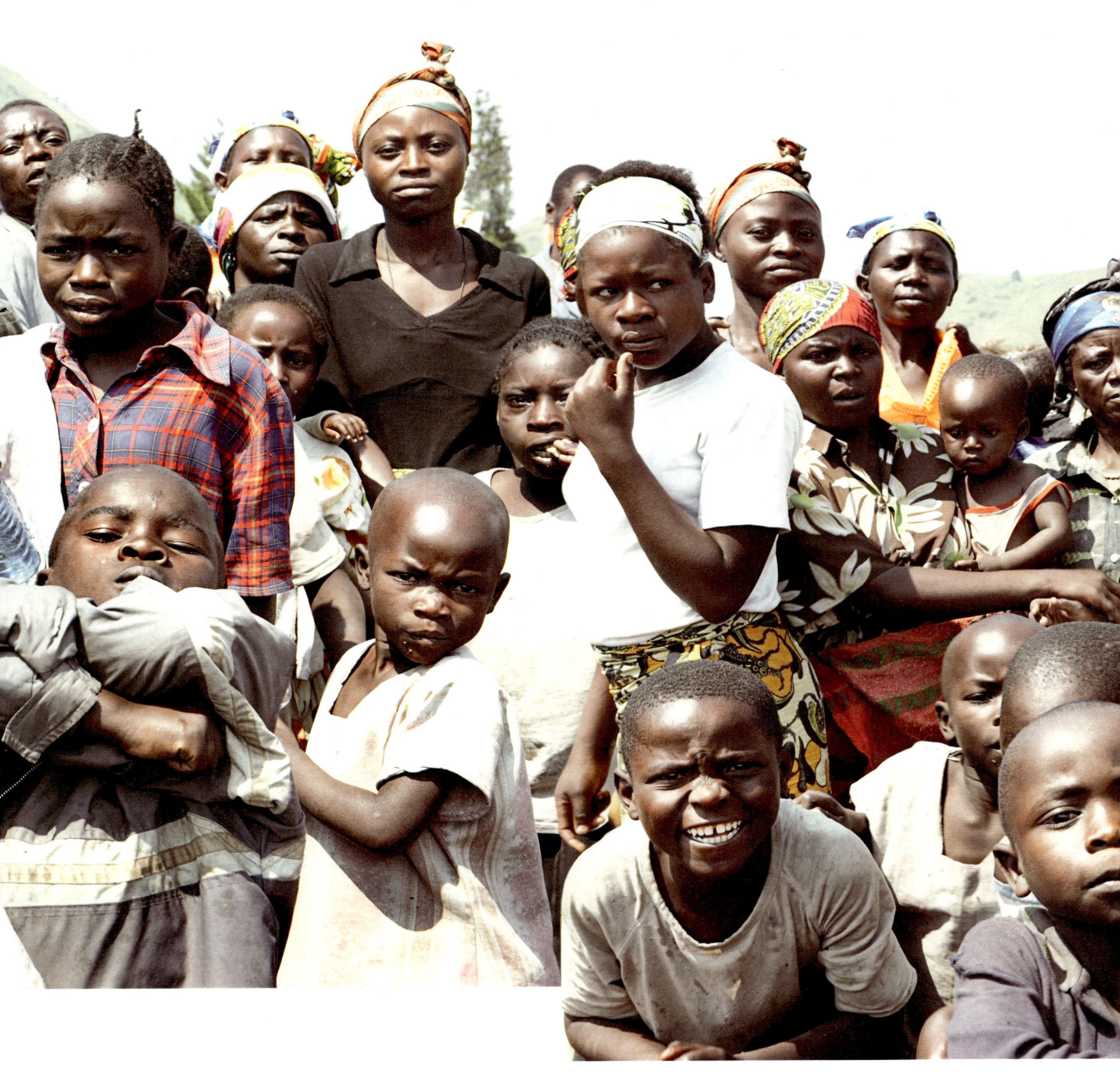

A Panoramic Portrait of the Mugunga Camp

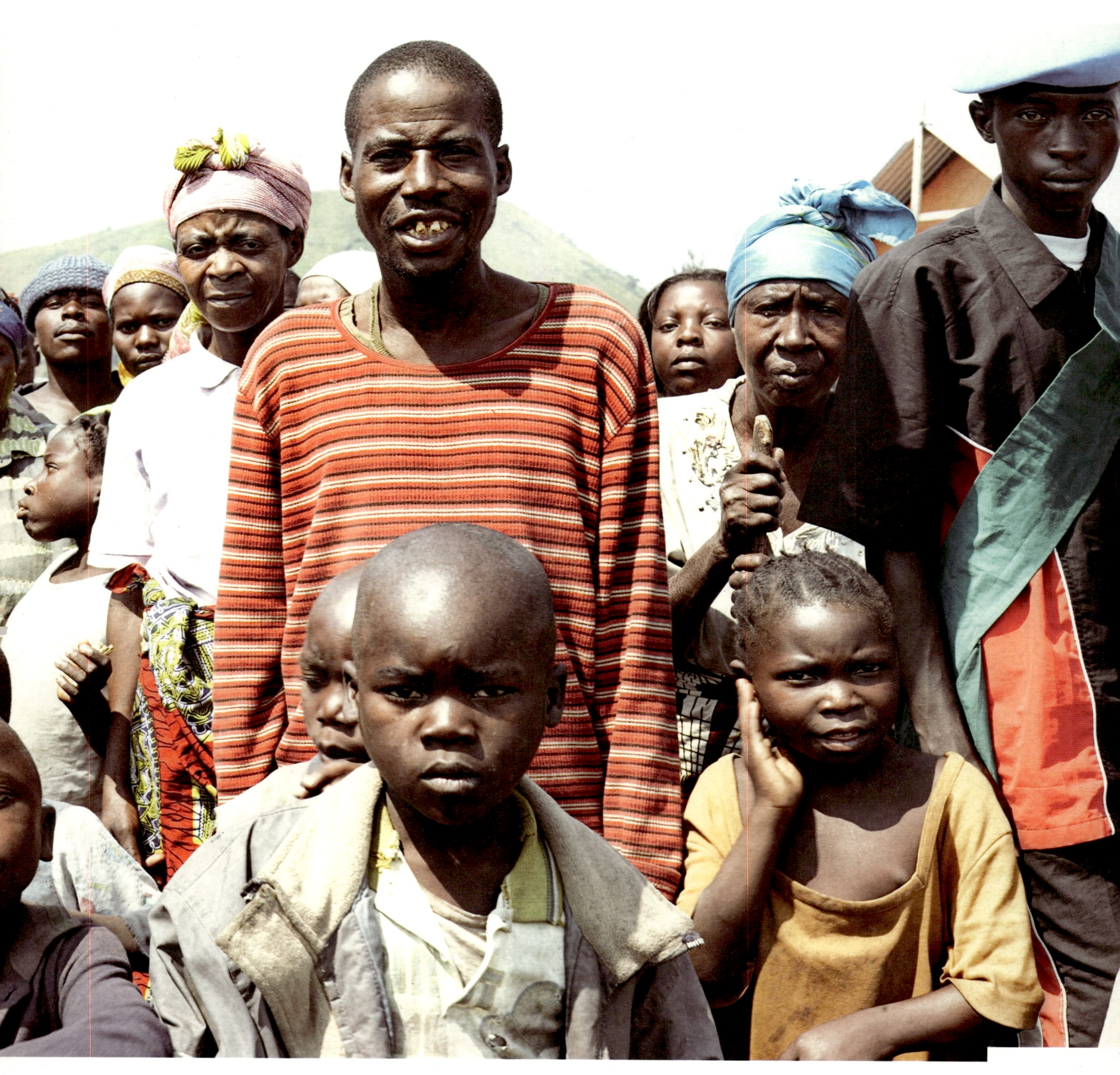

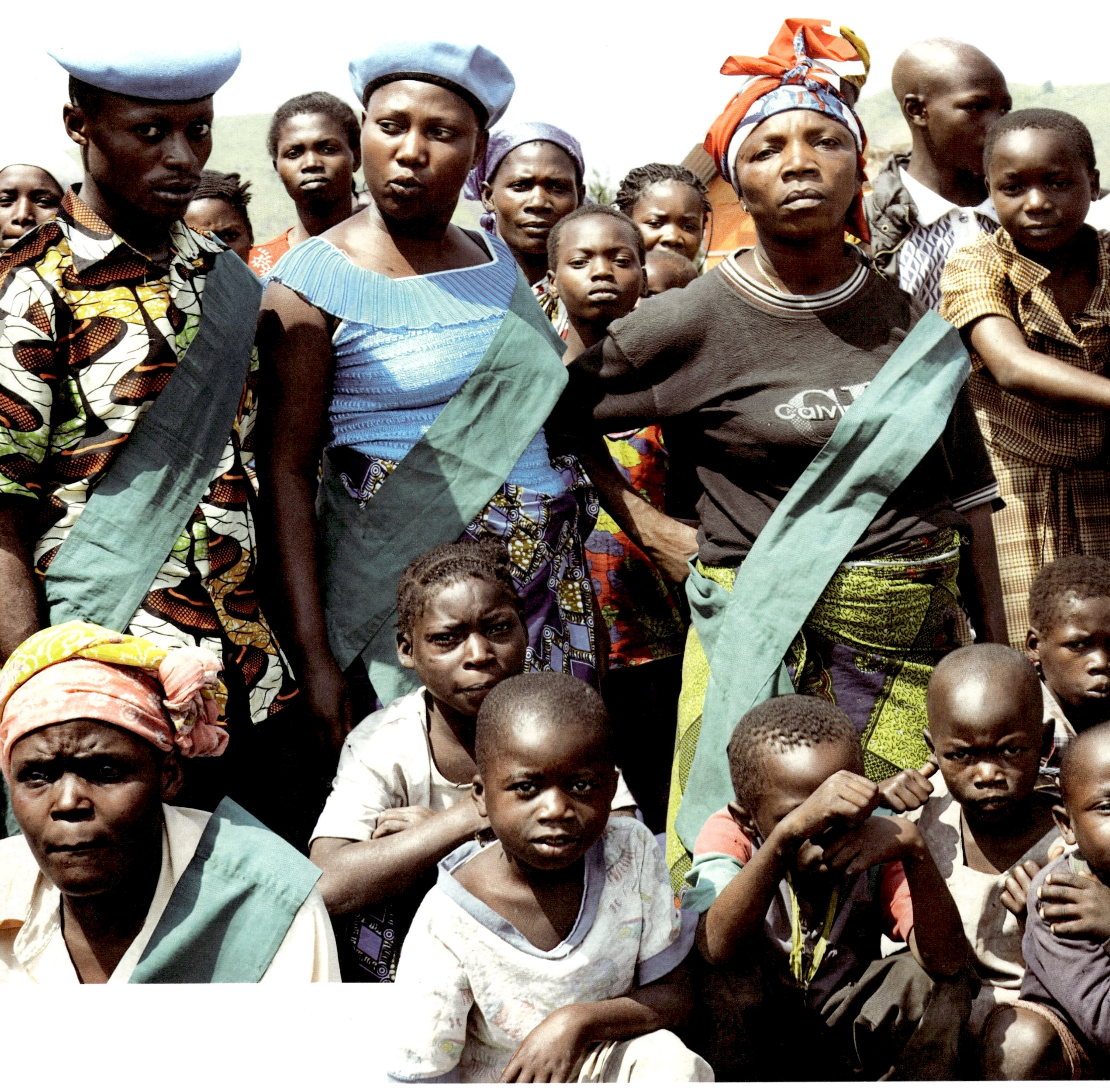

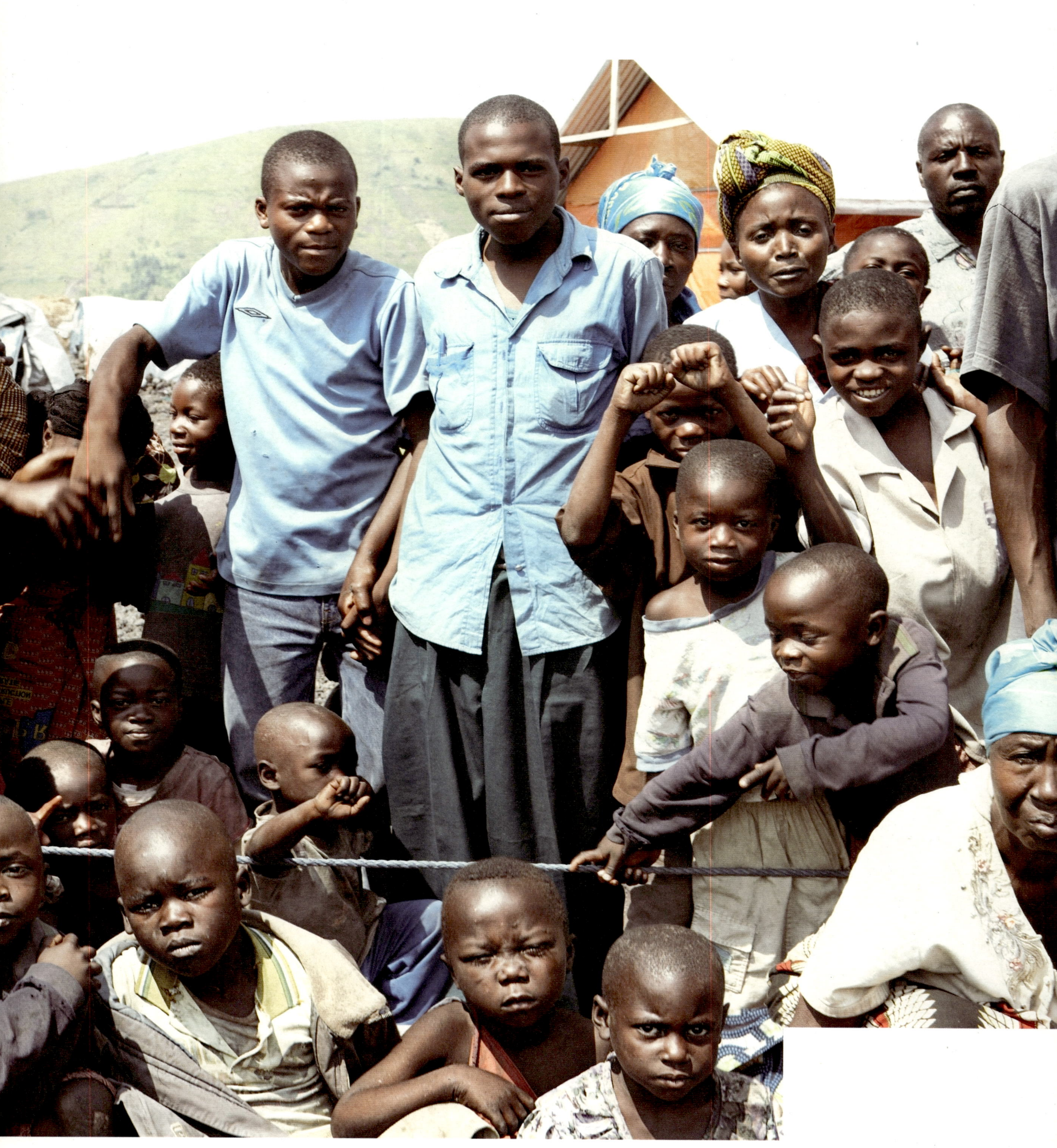

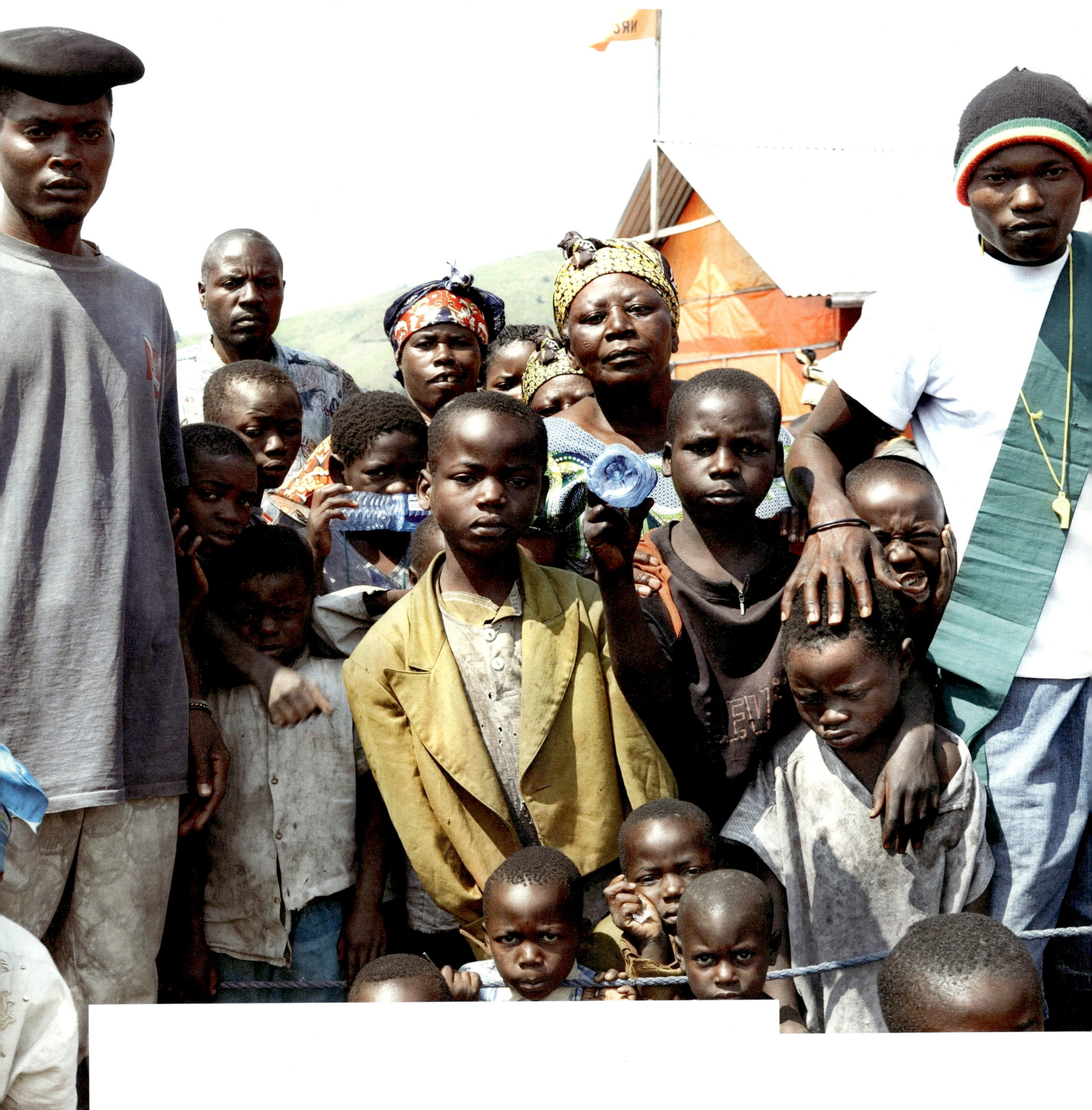

A Panoramic Portrait of the Mugunga Camp

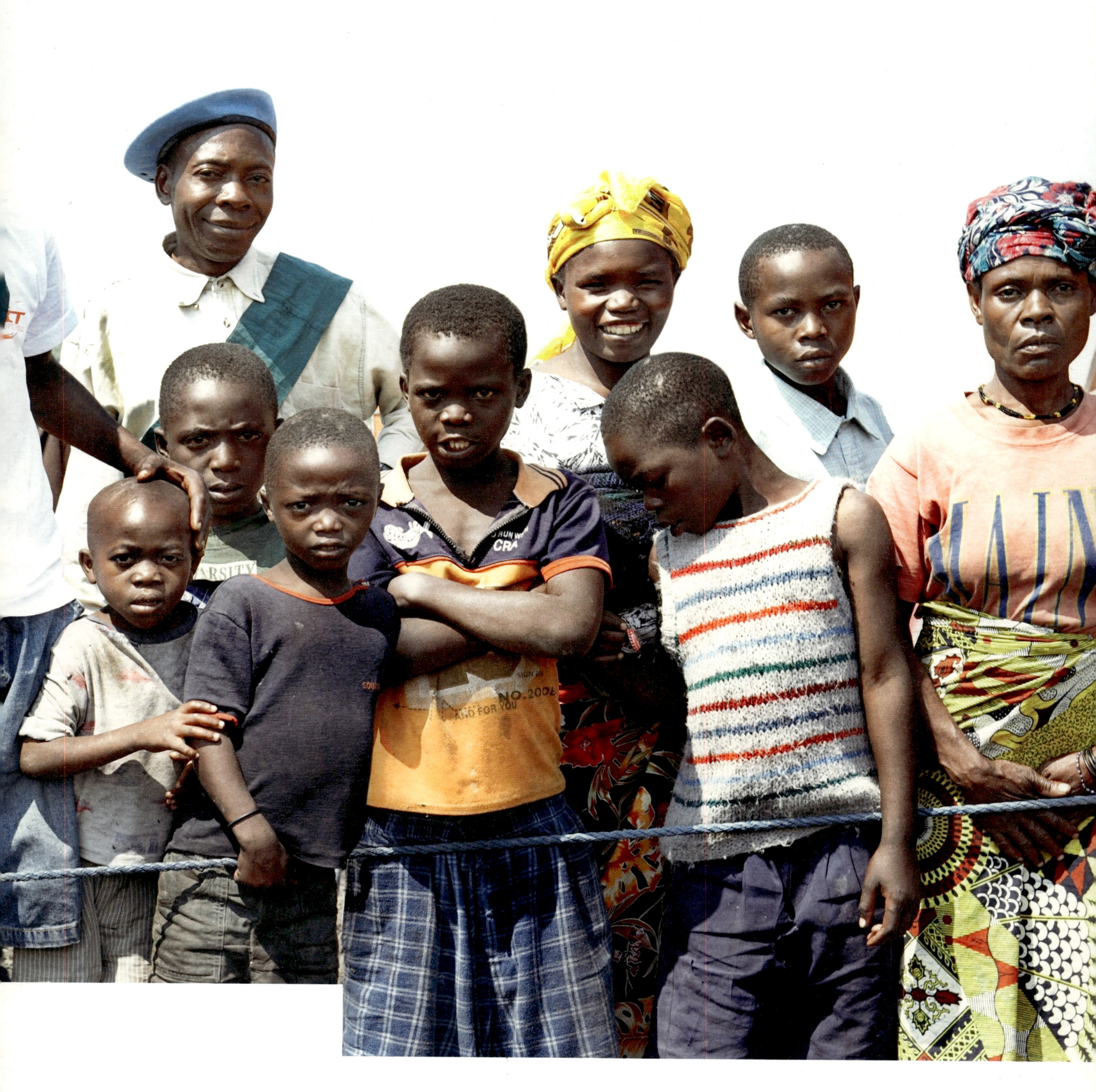

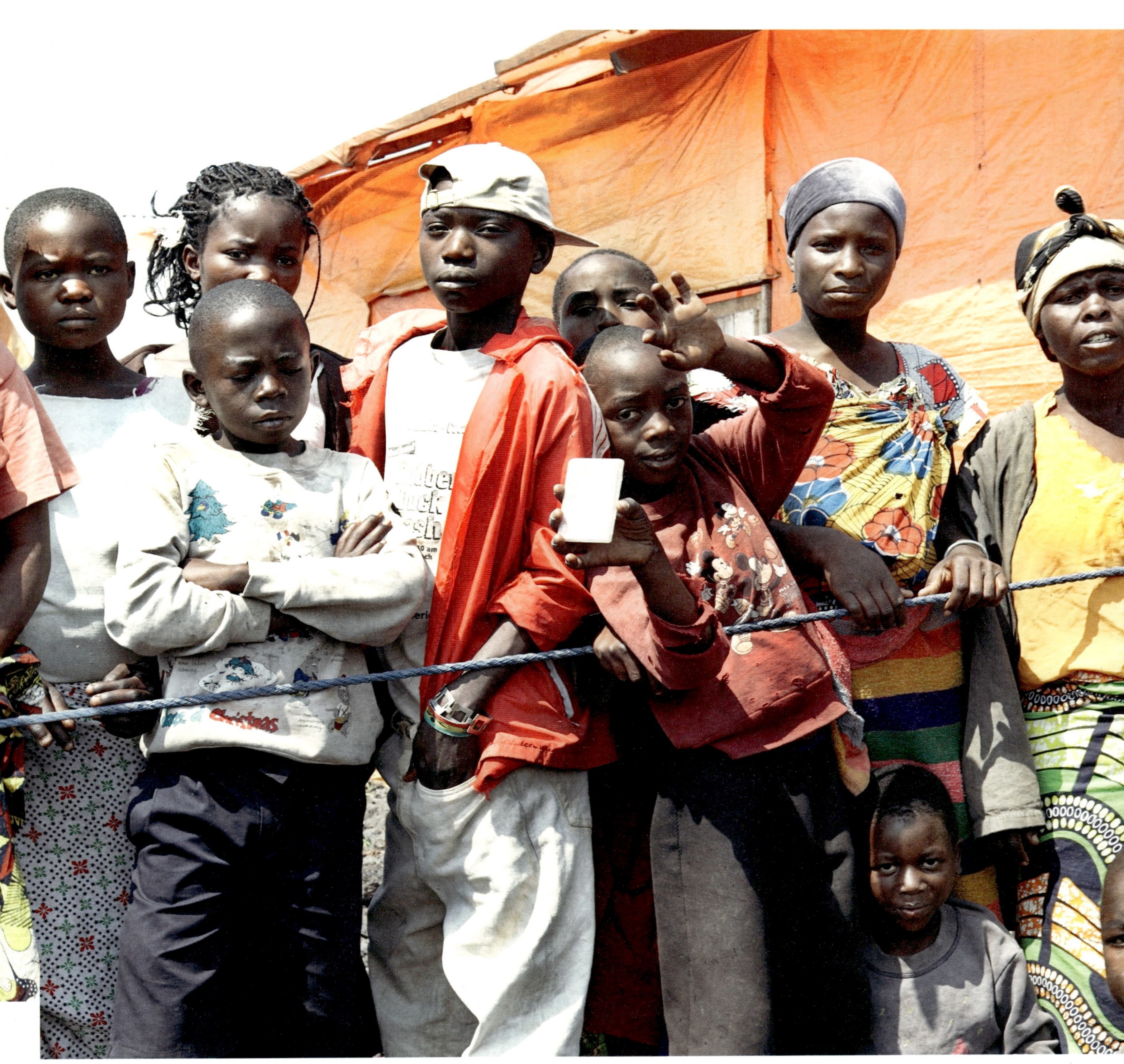

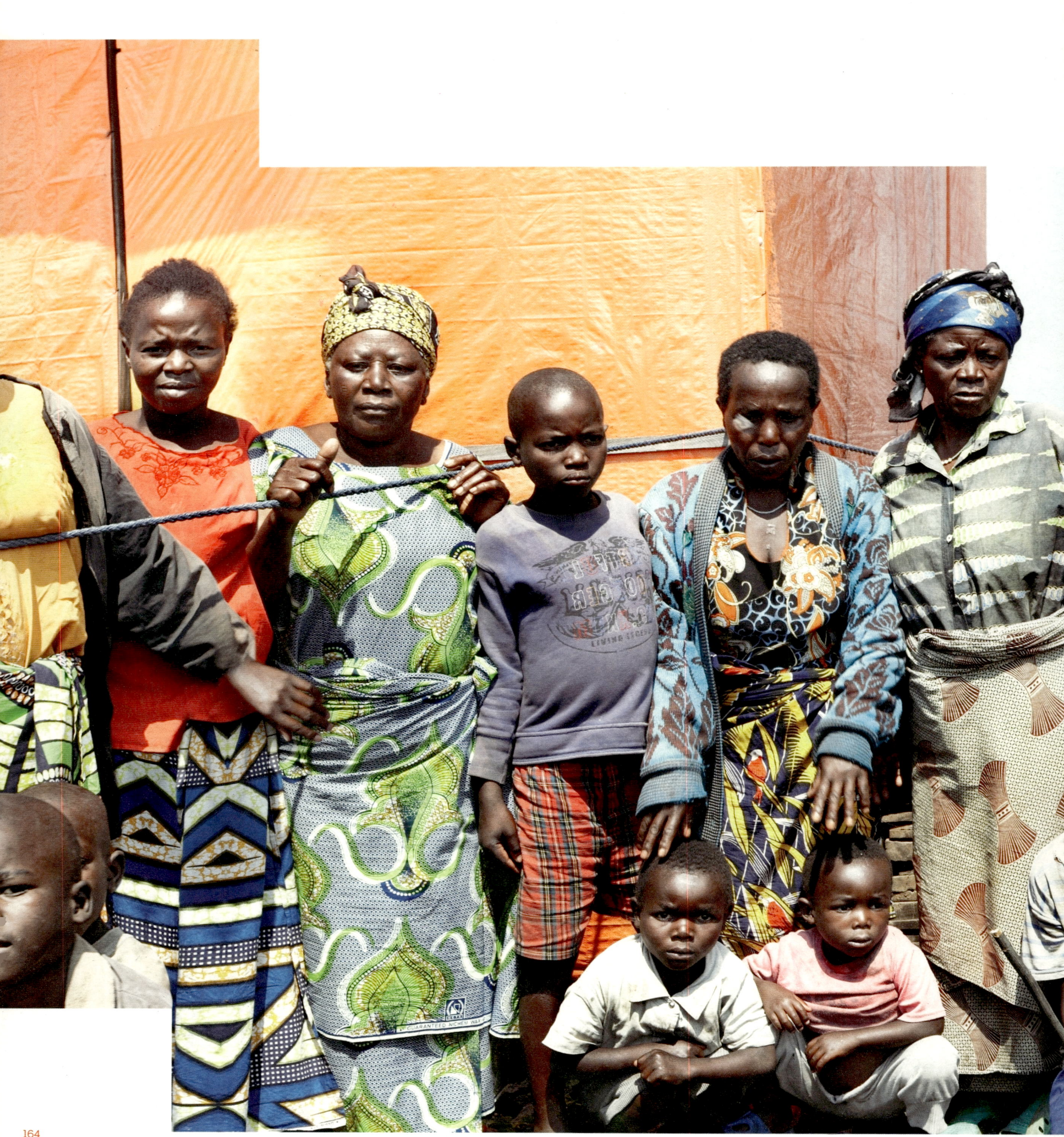

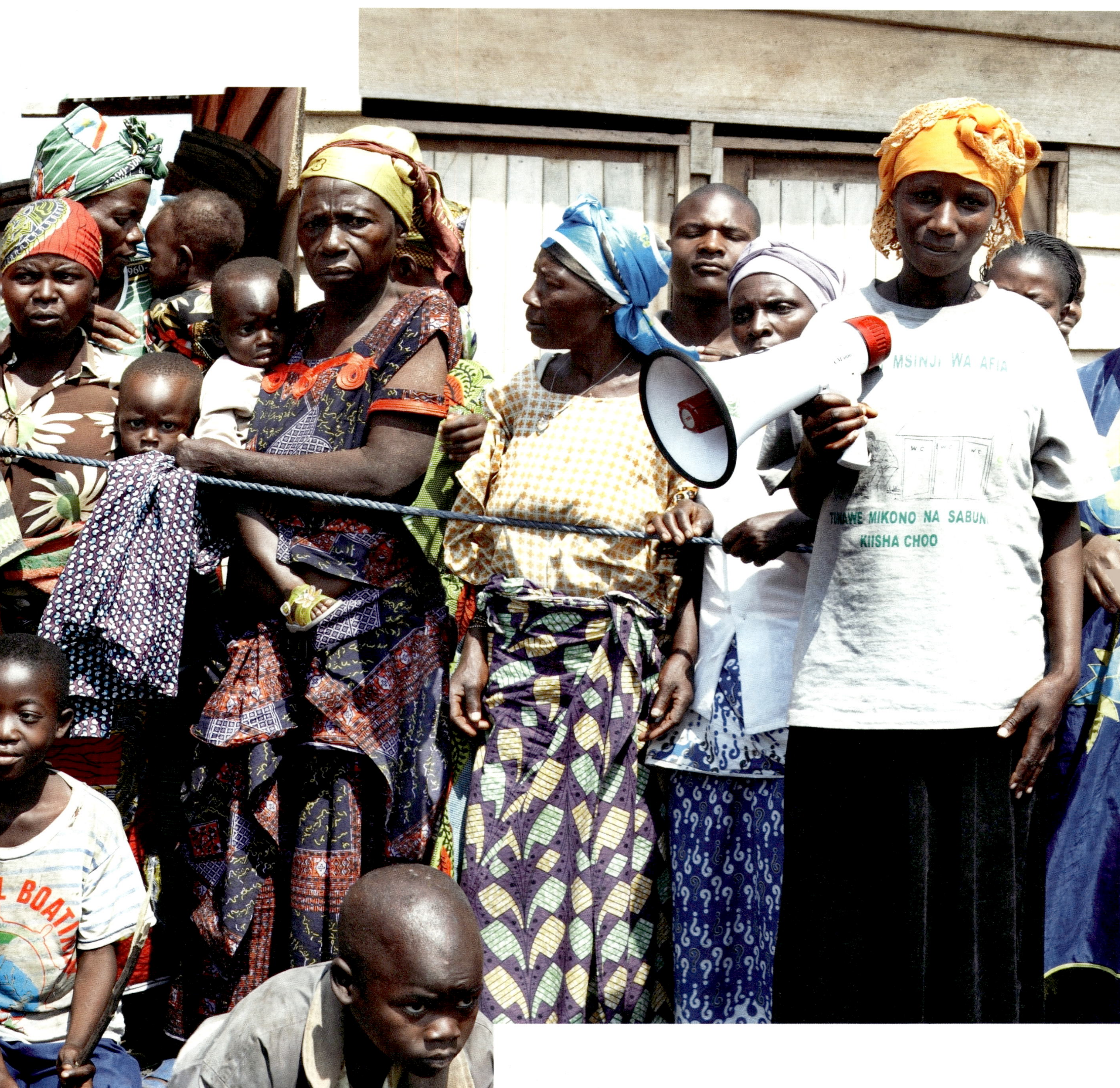

A Panoramic Portrait of the Mugunga Camp

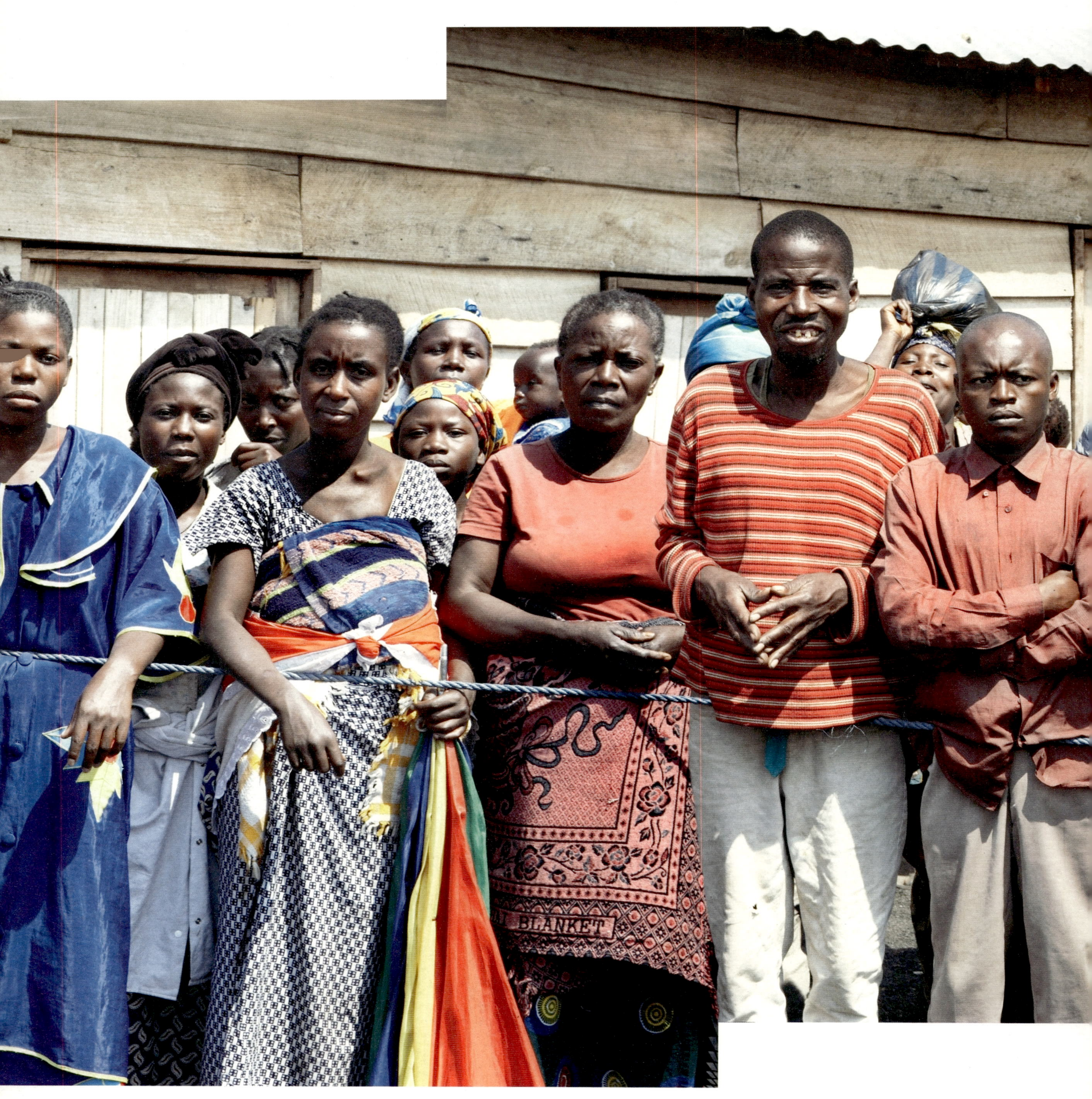

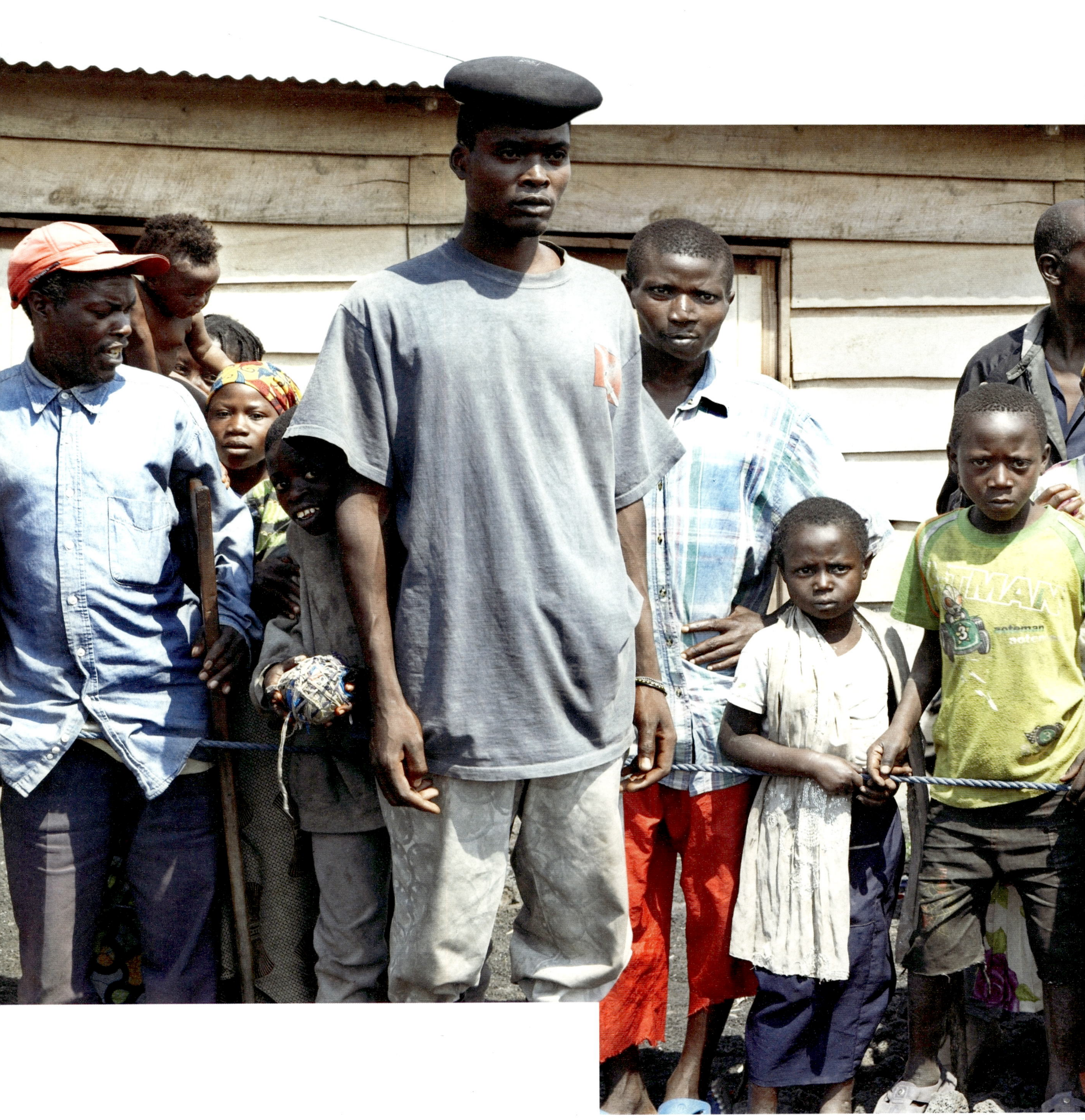

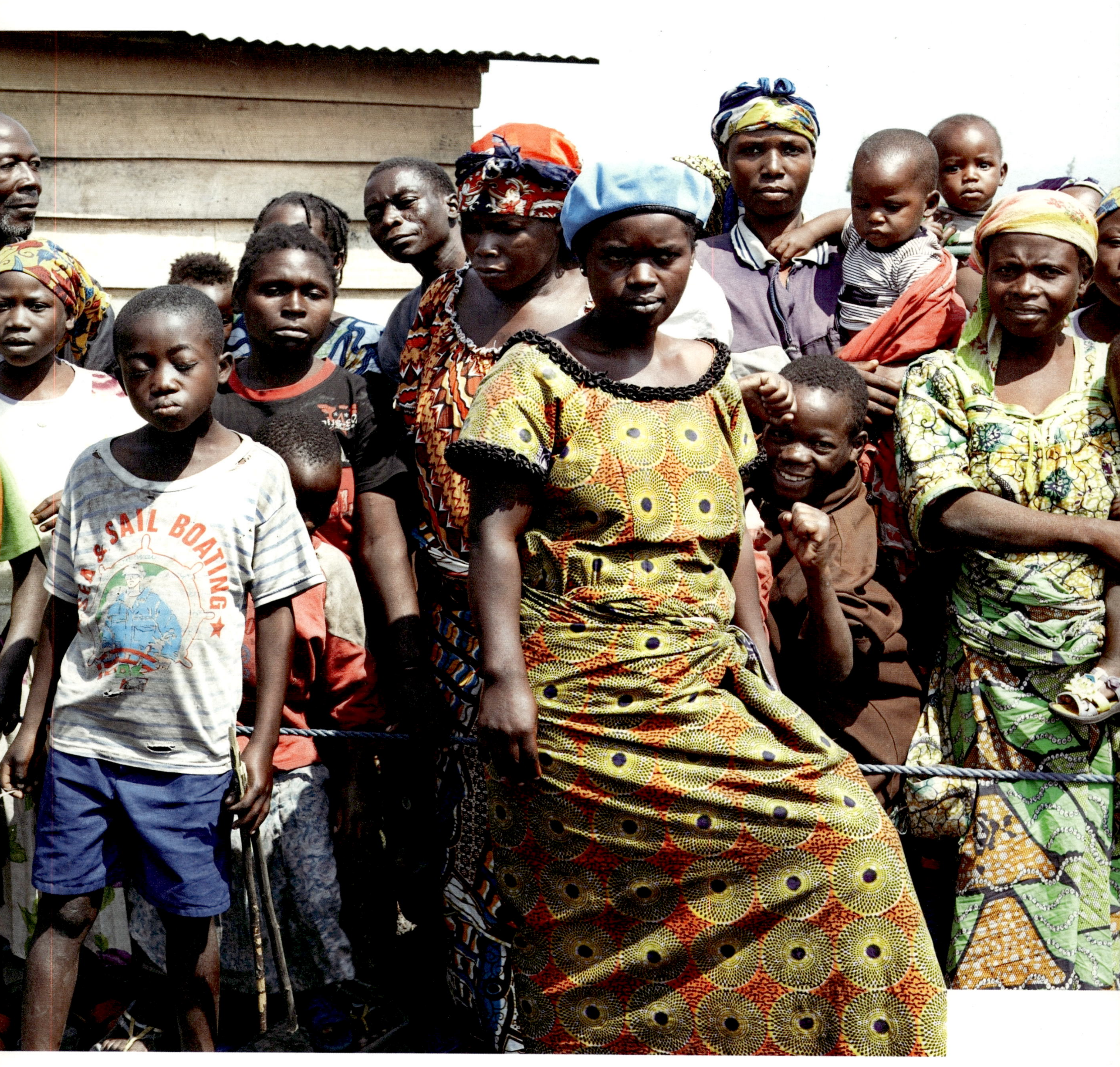

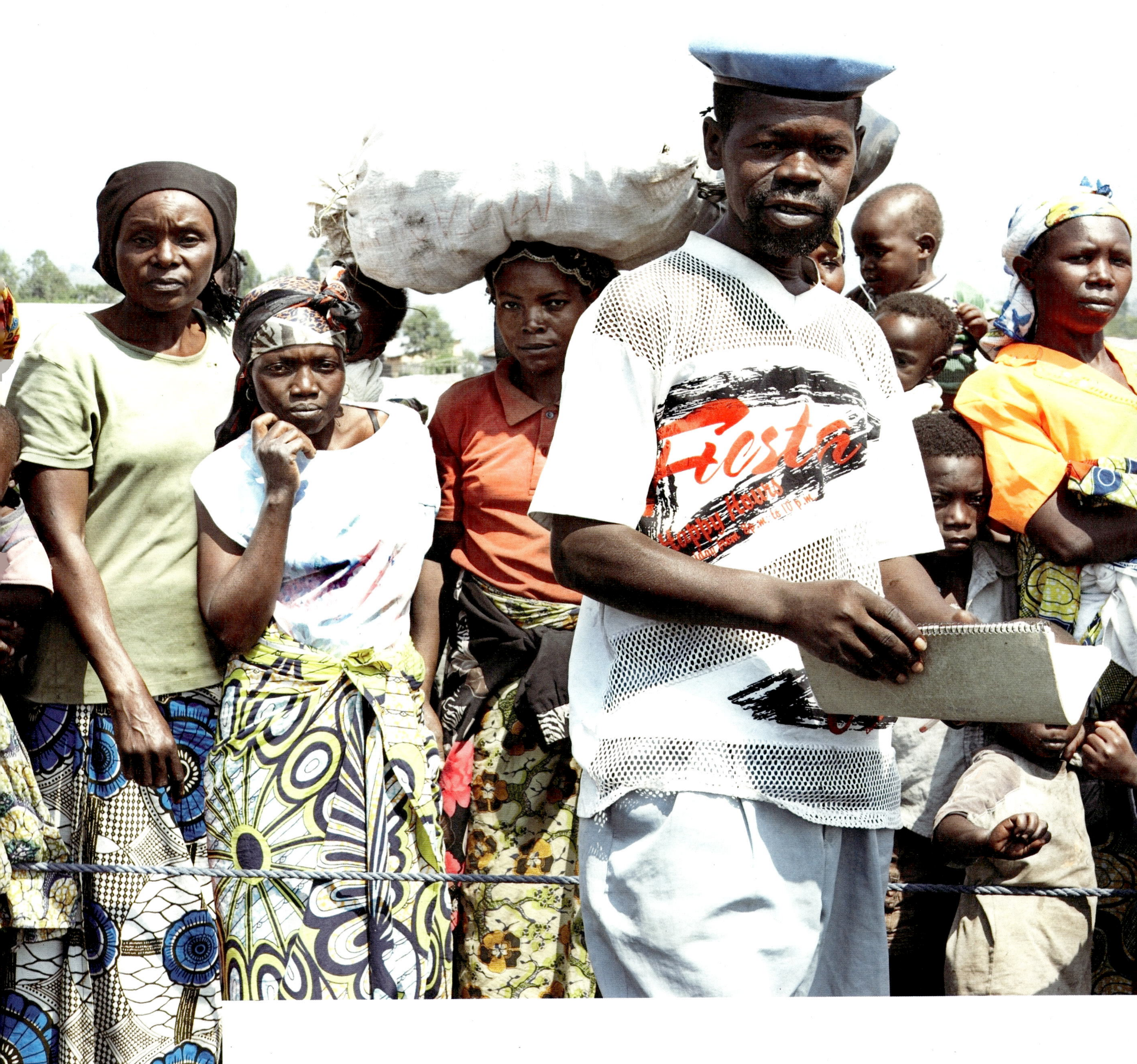

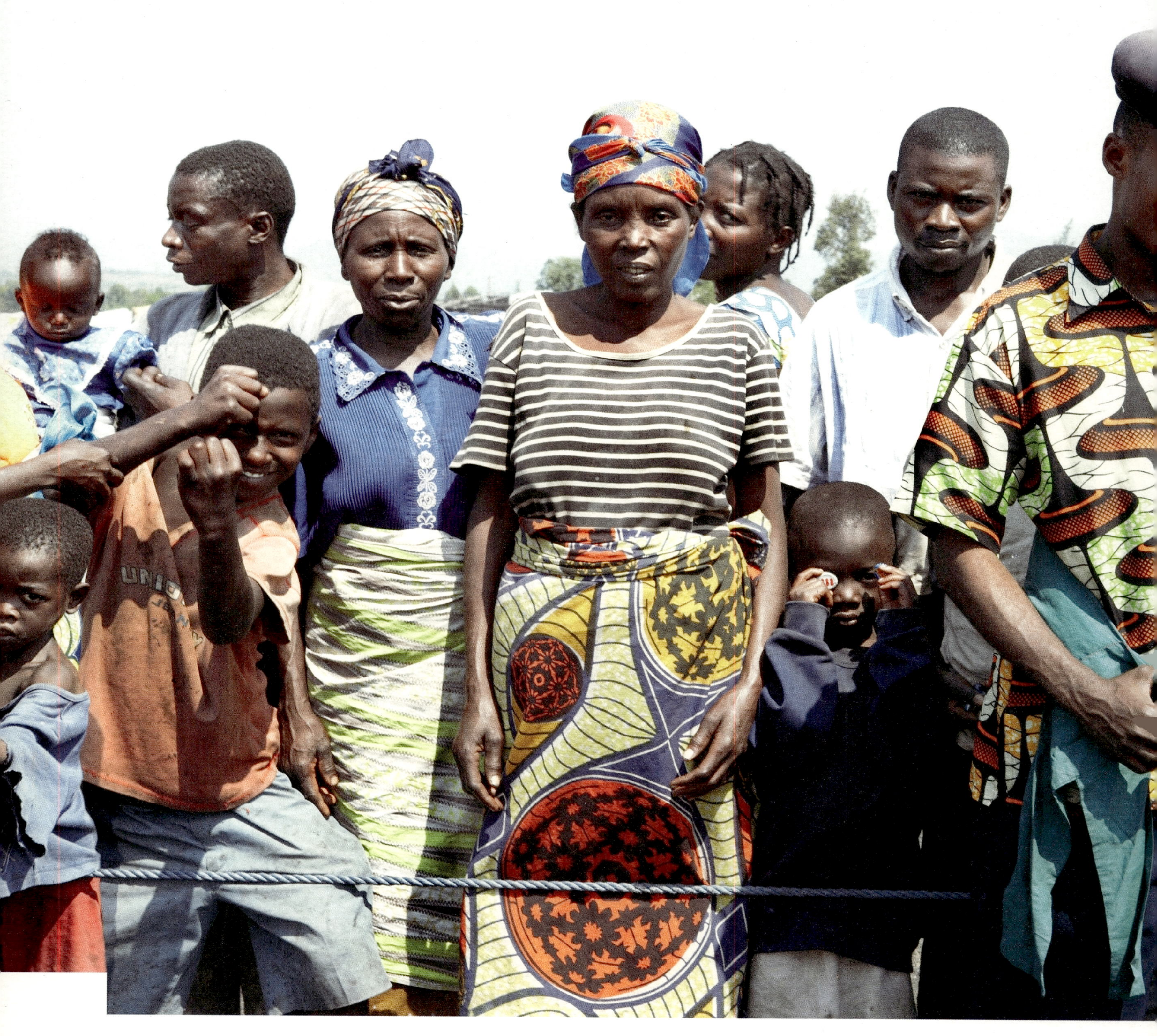

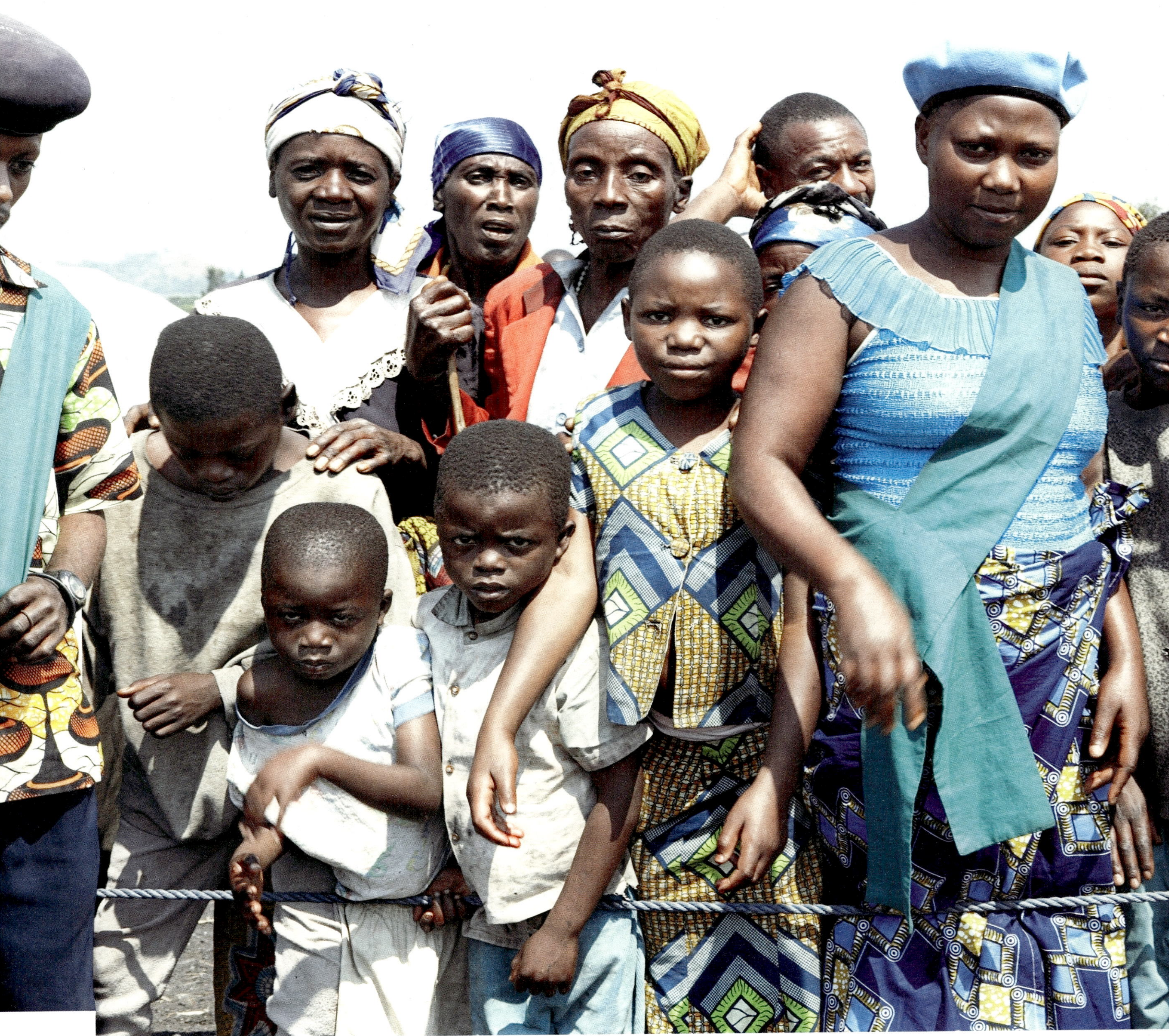

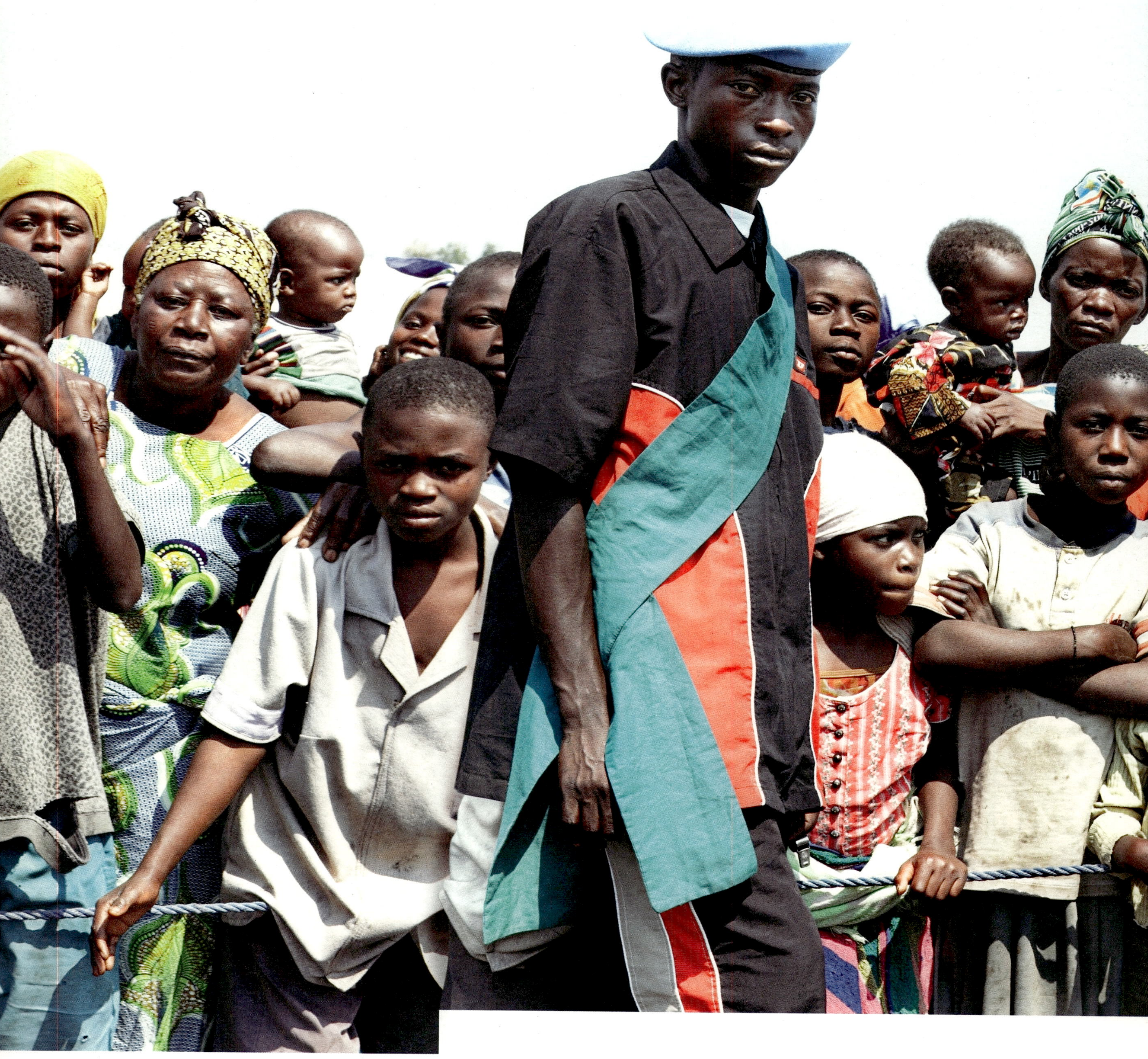

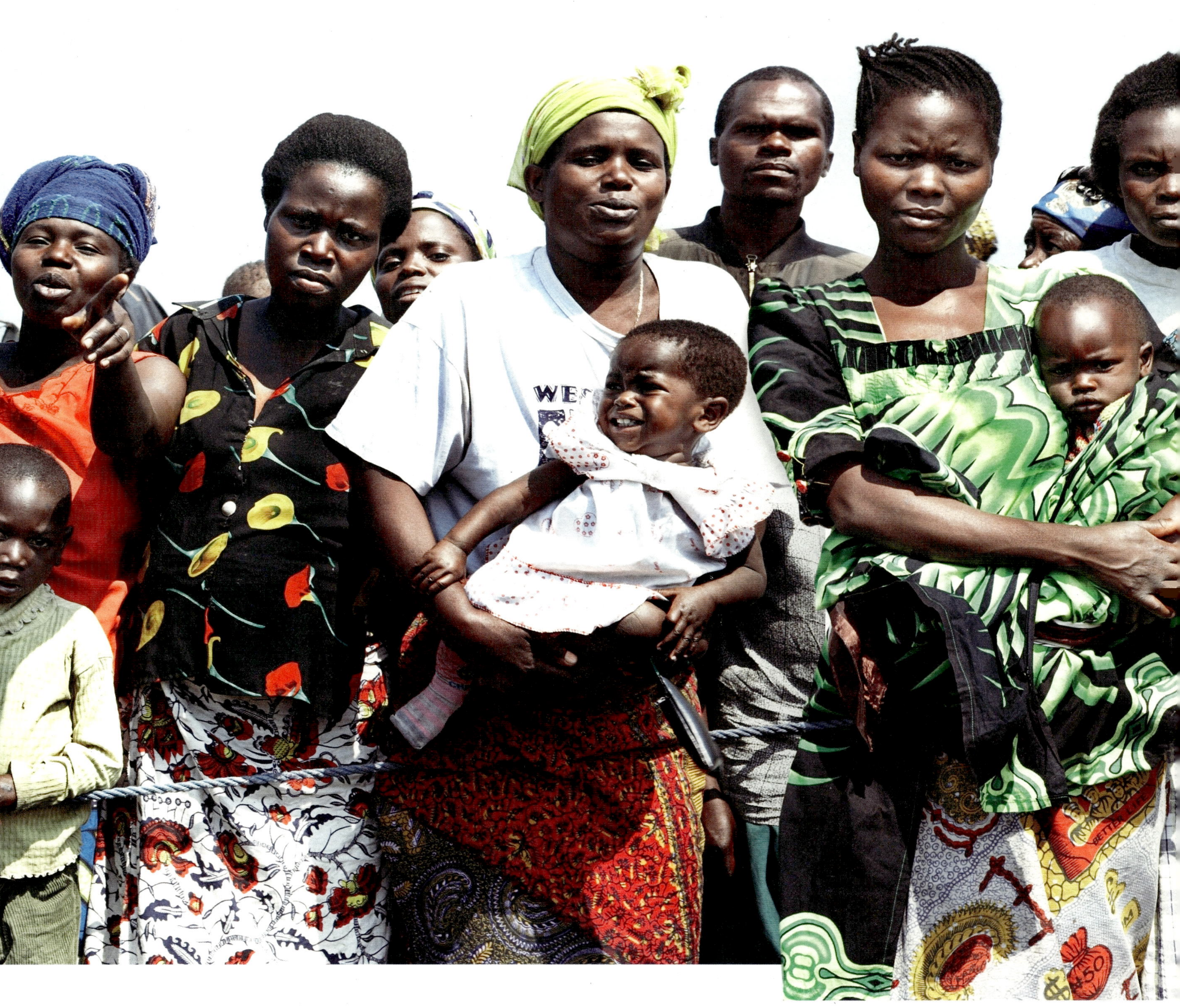

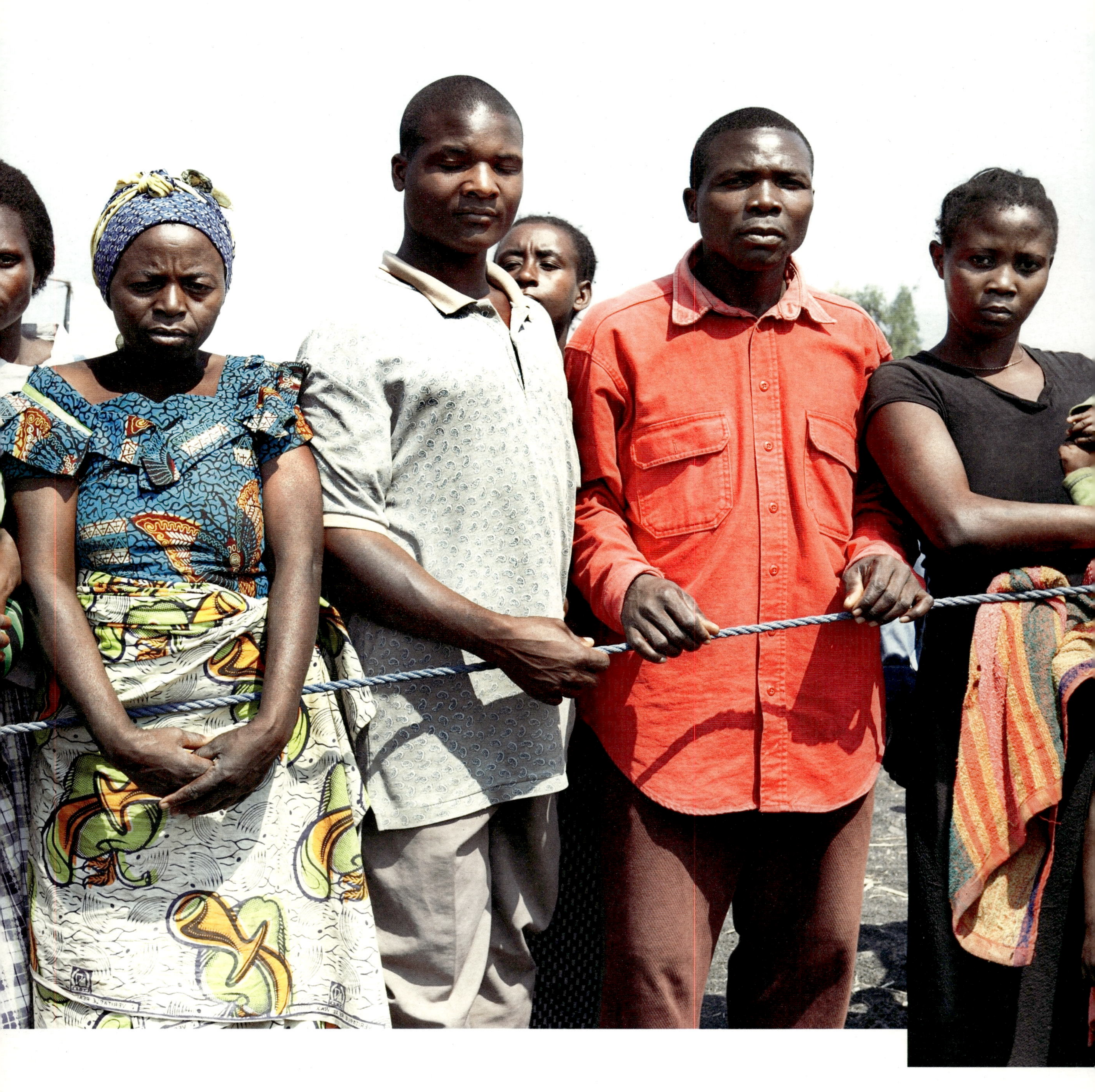

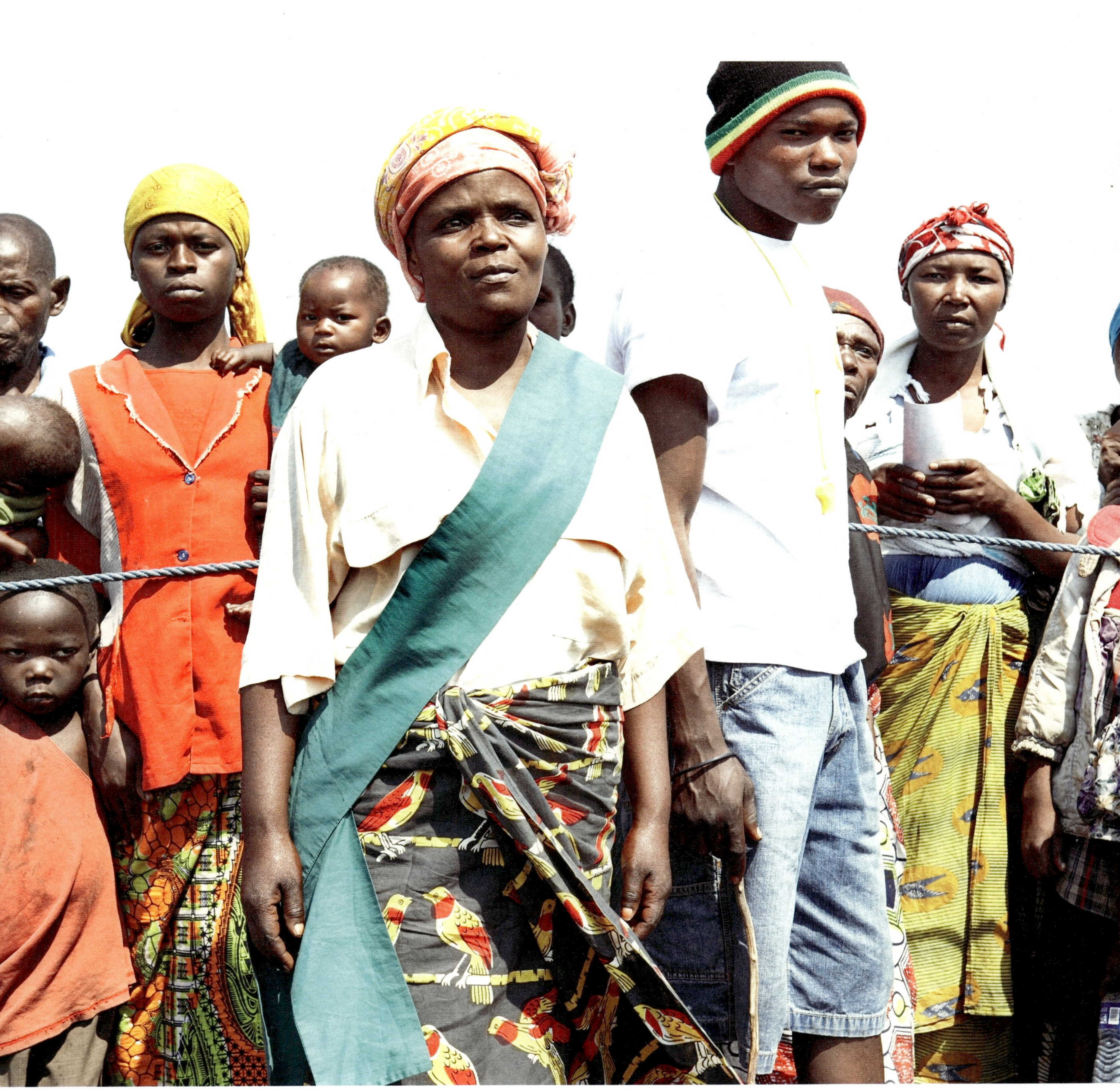

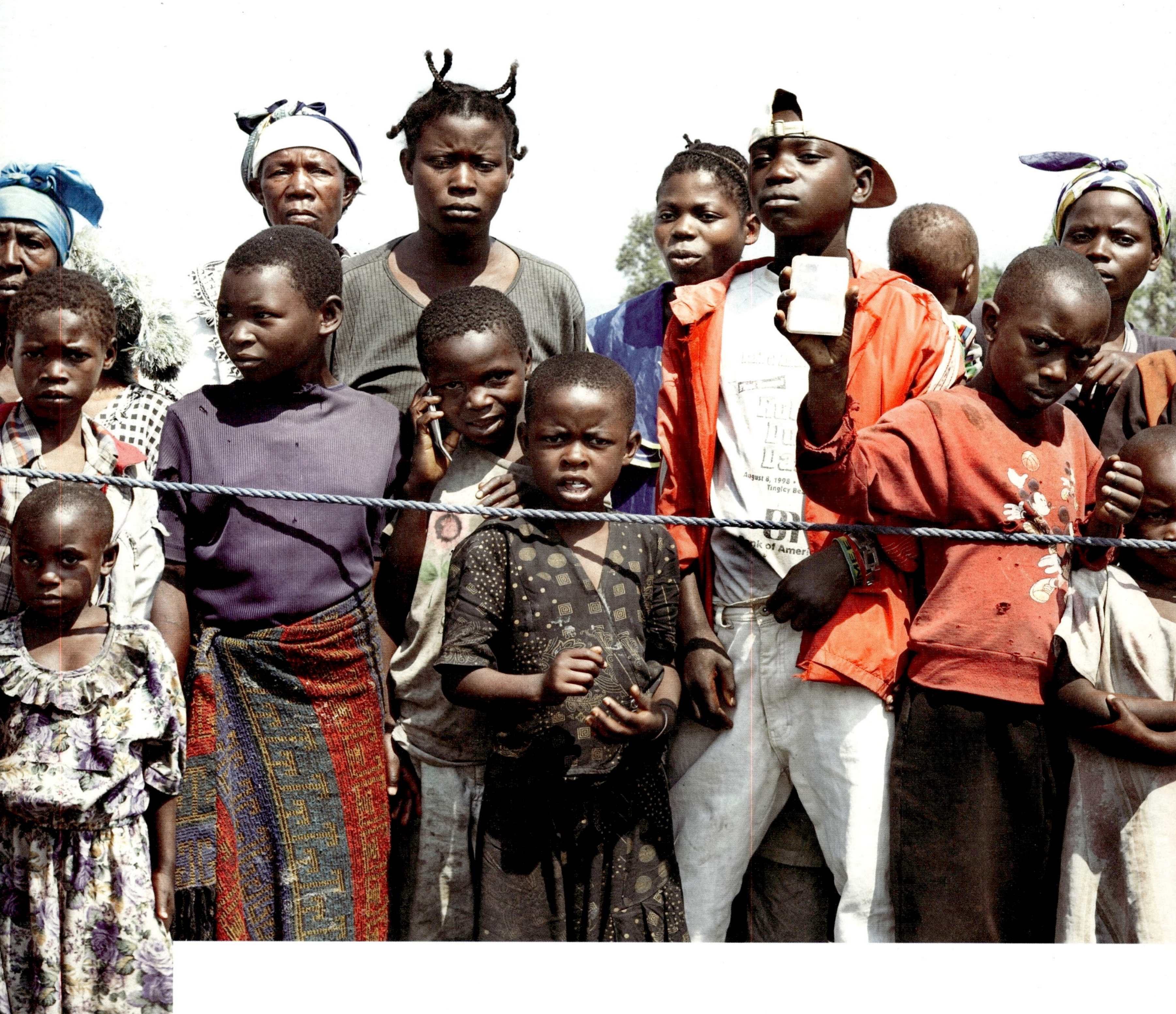

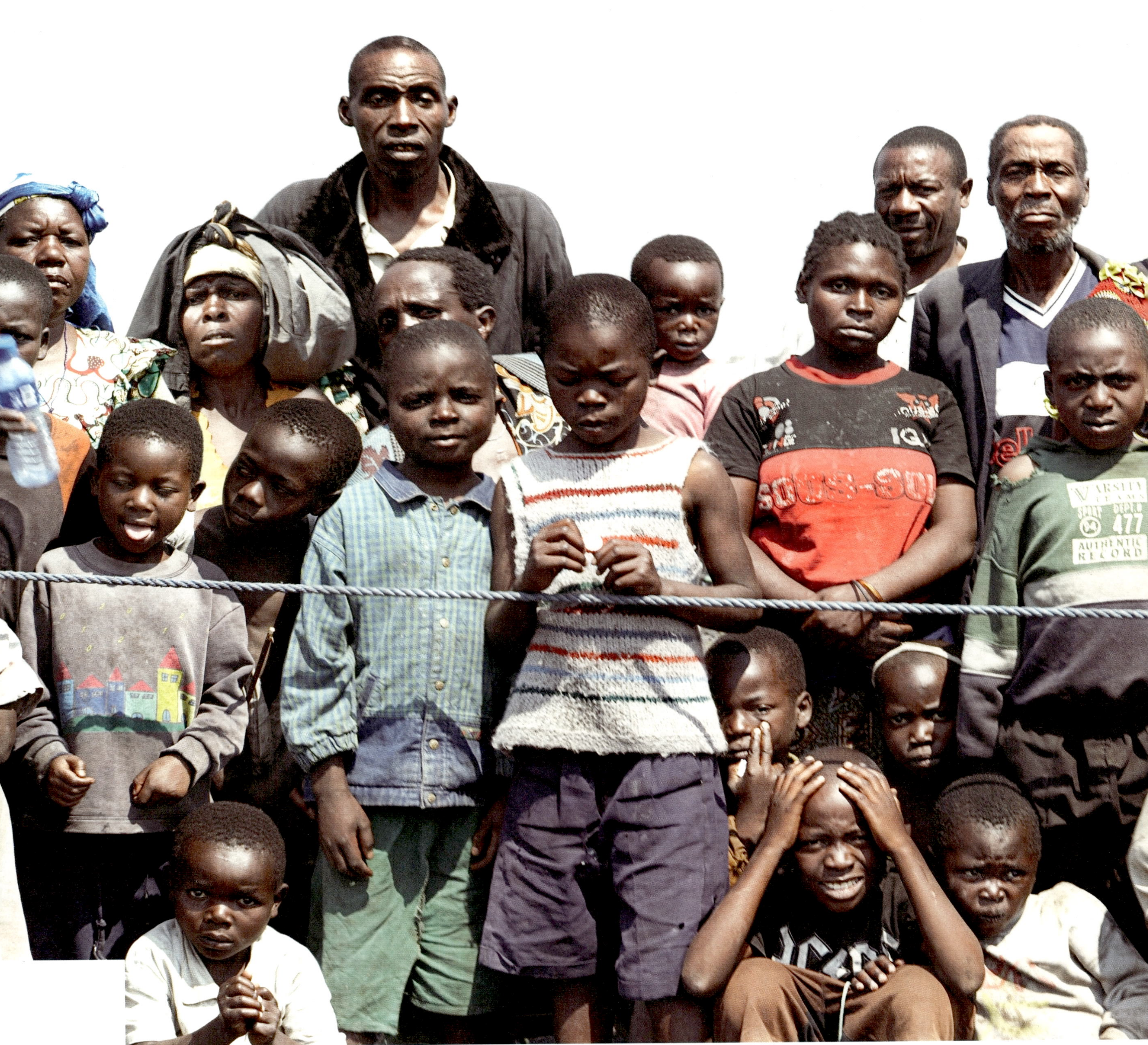

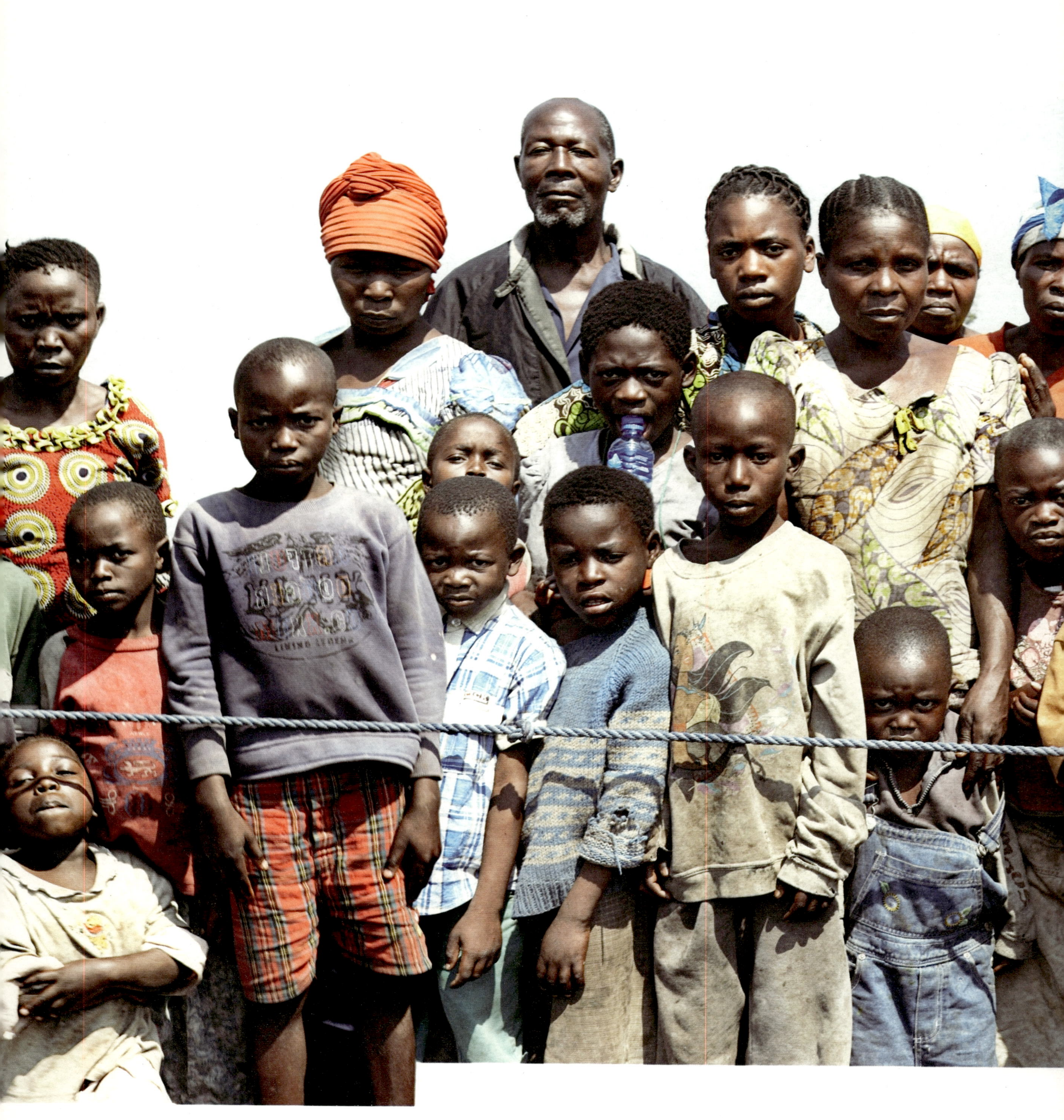

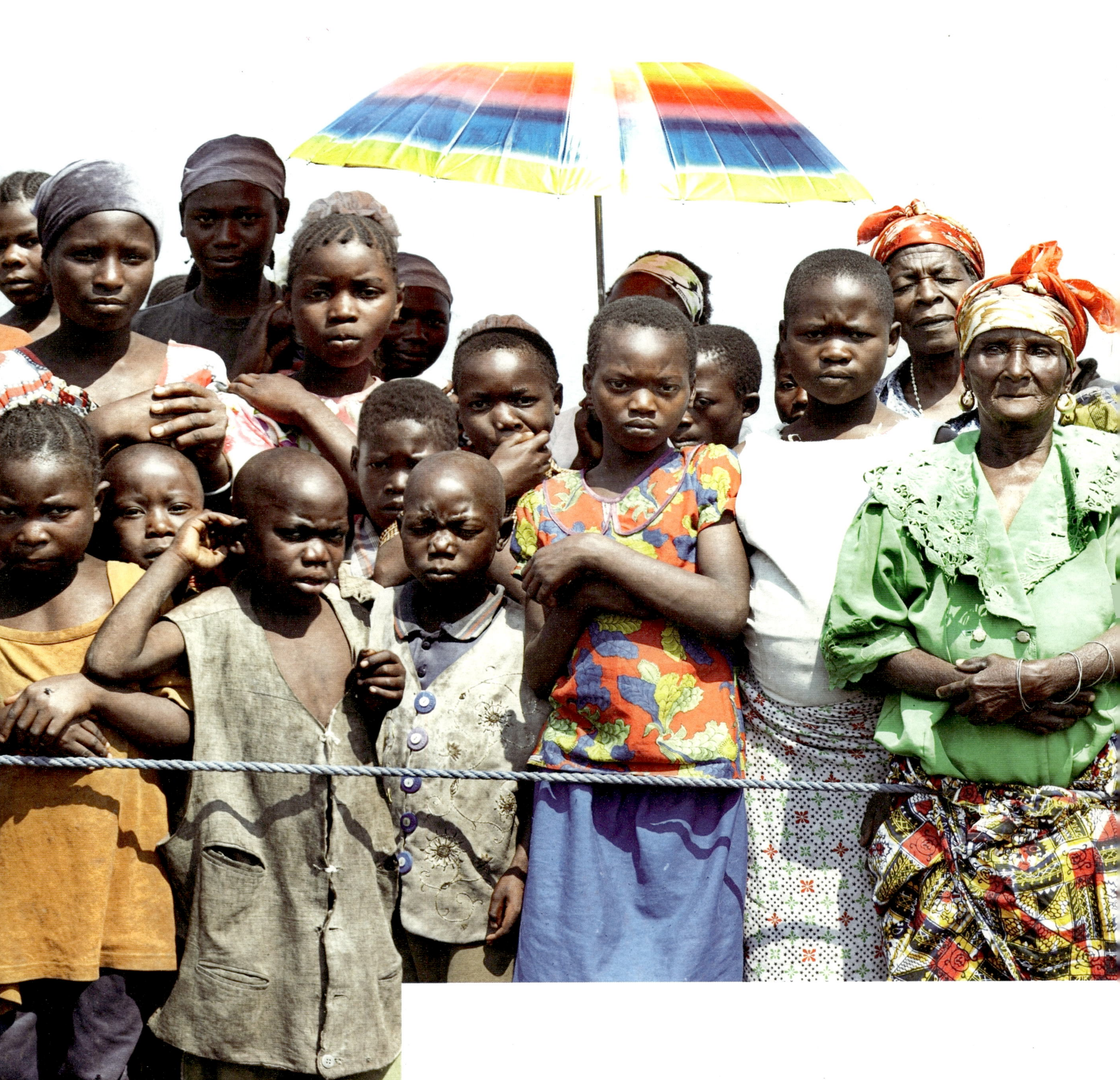

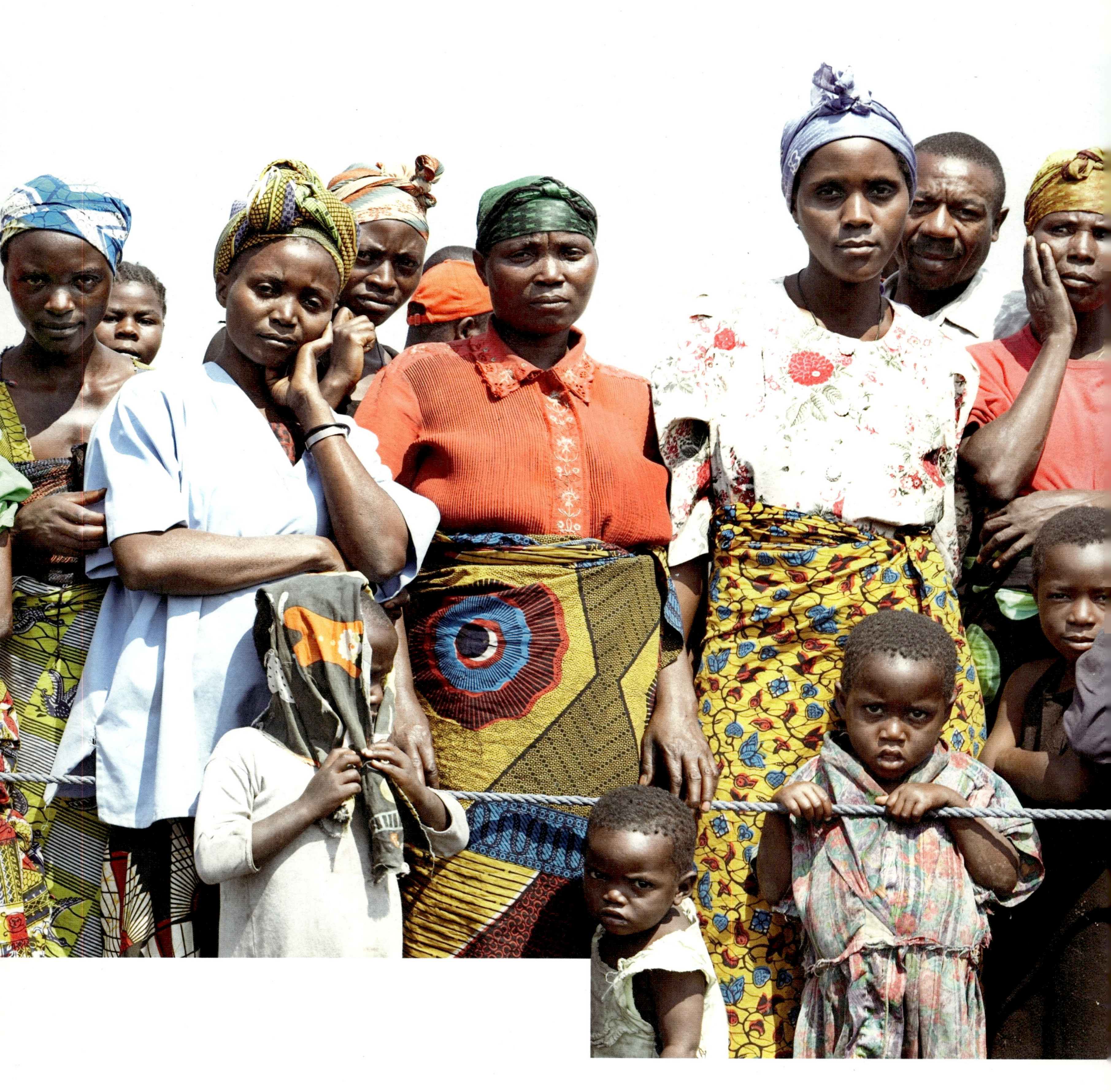

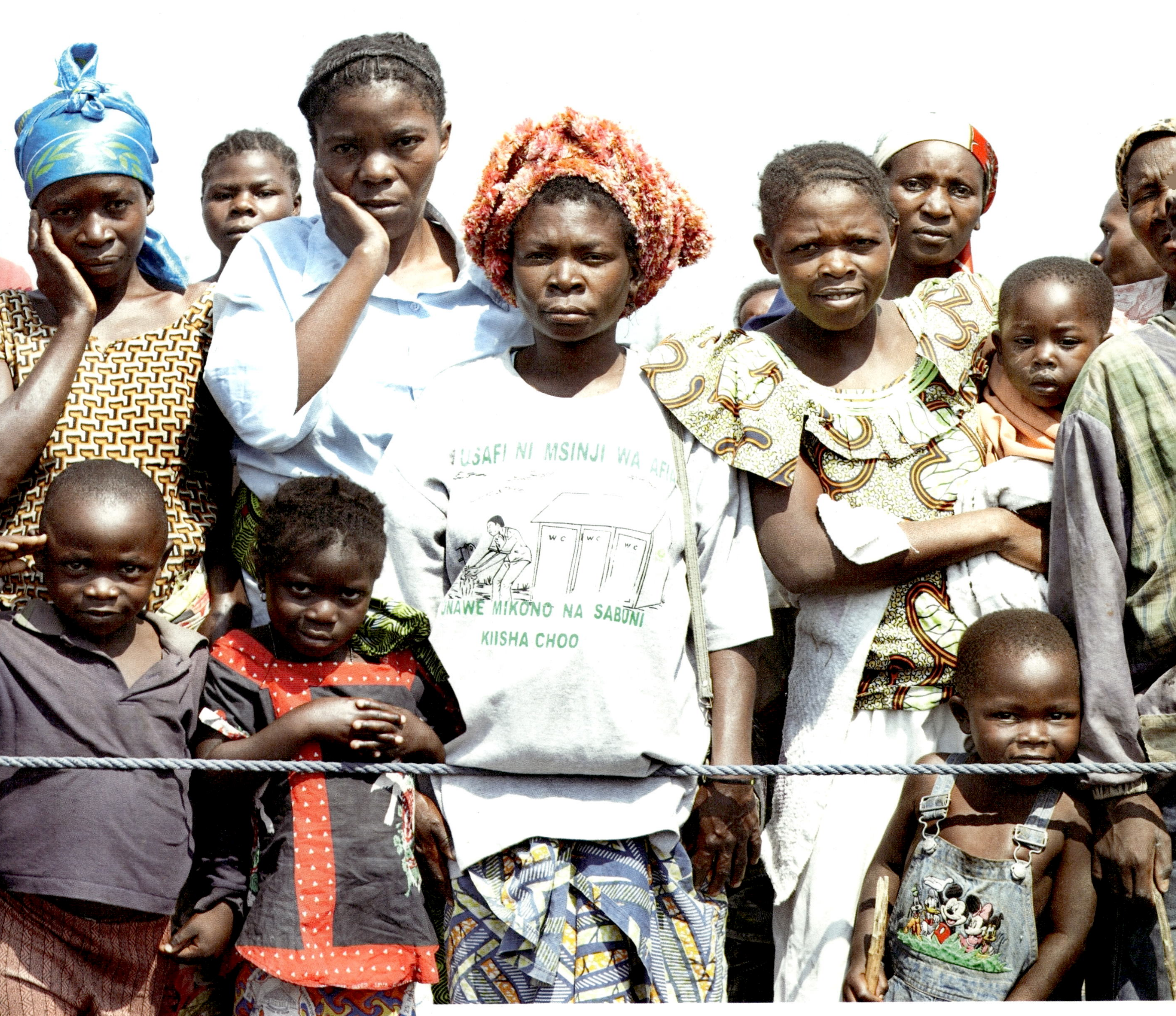

USAFI NI MSINJI WA AFI
UNAWE MIKONO NA SABUNI
KIISHA CHOO
WC WC WC

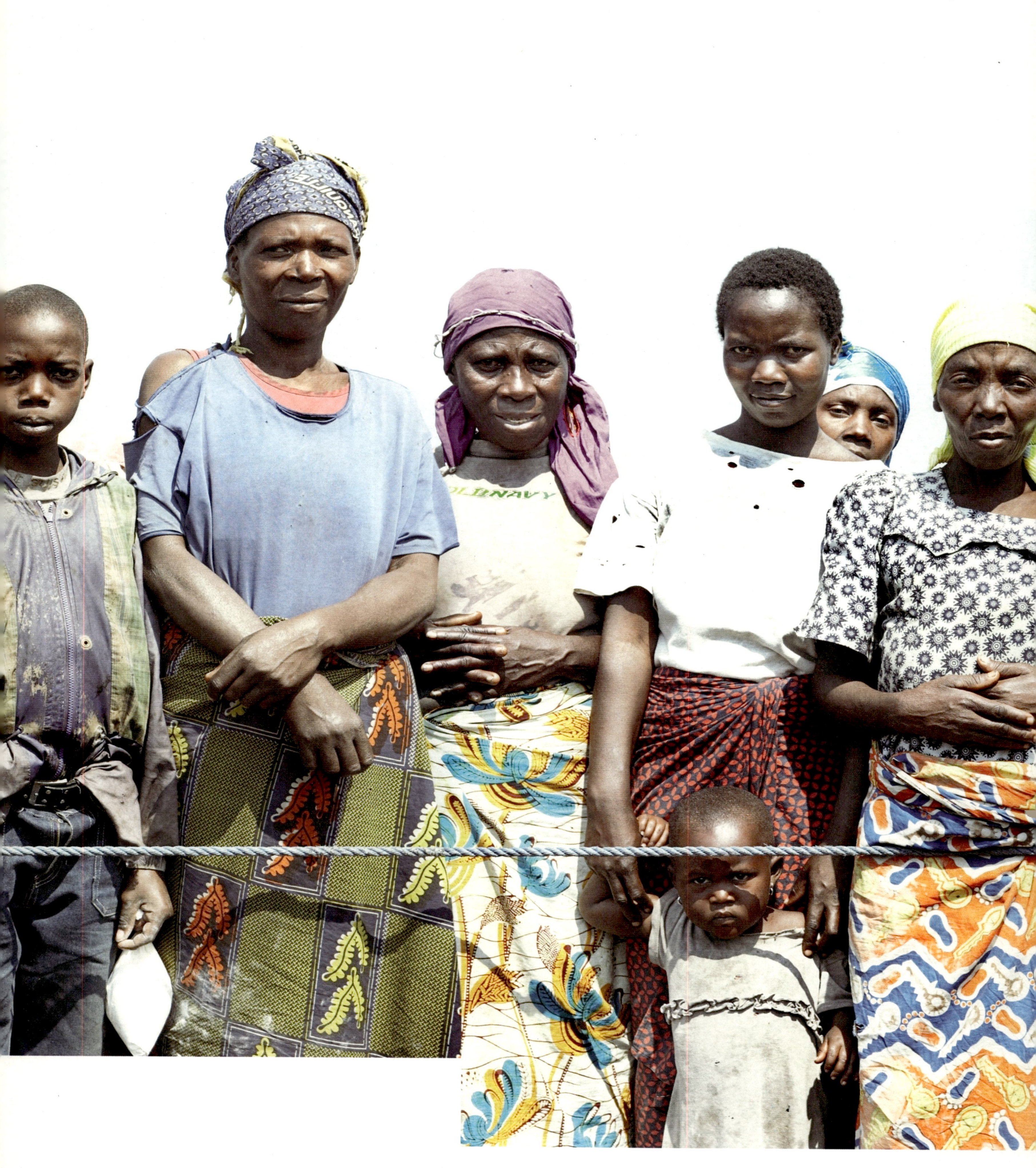

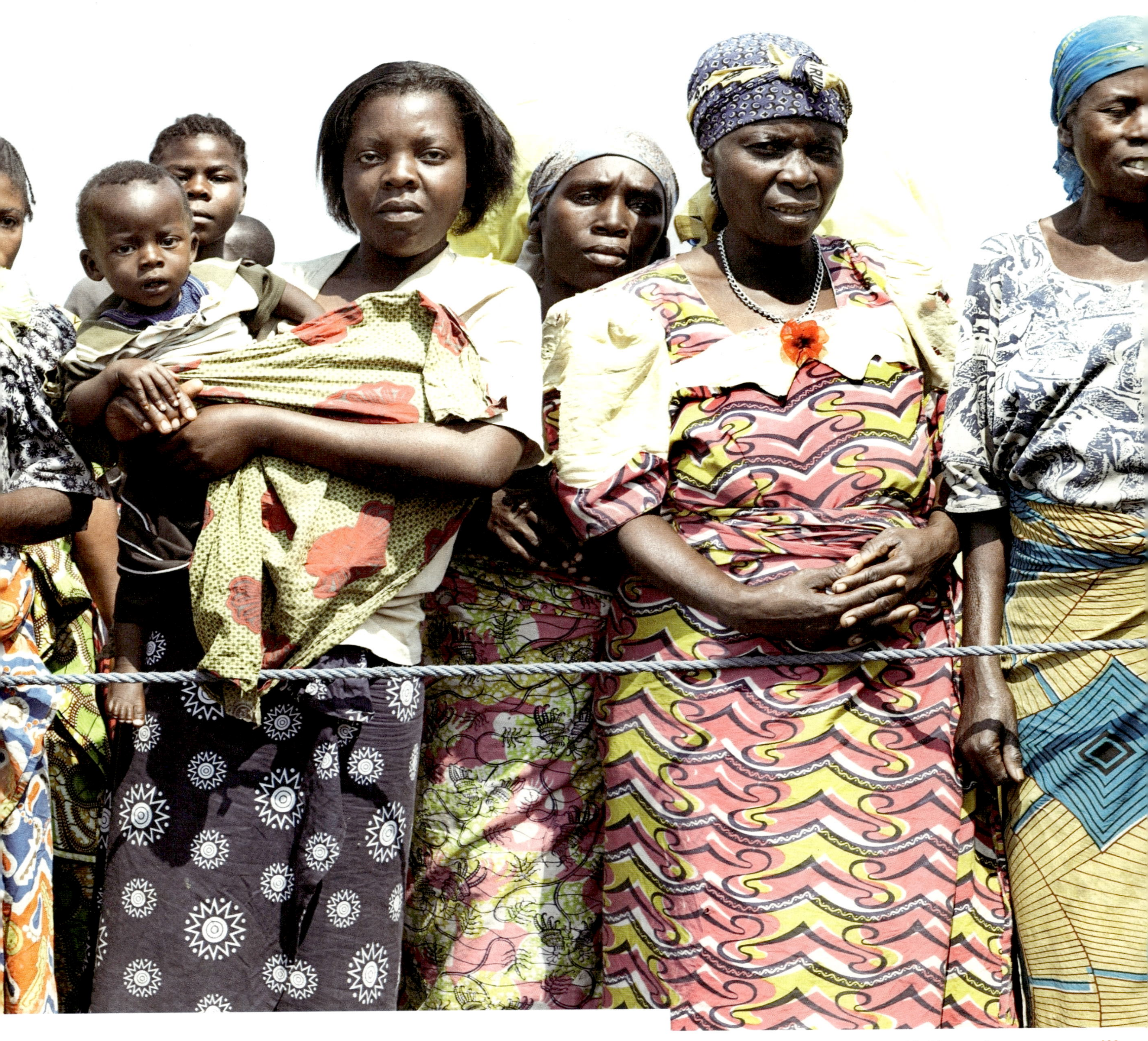

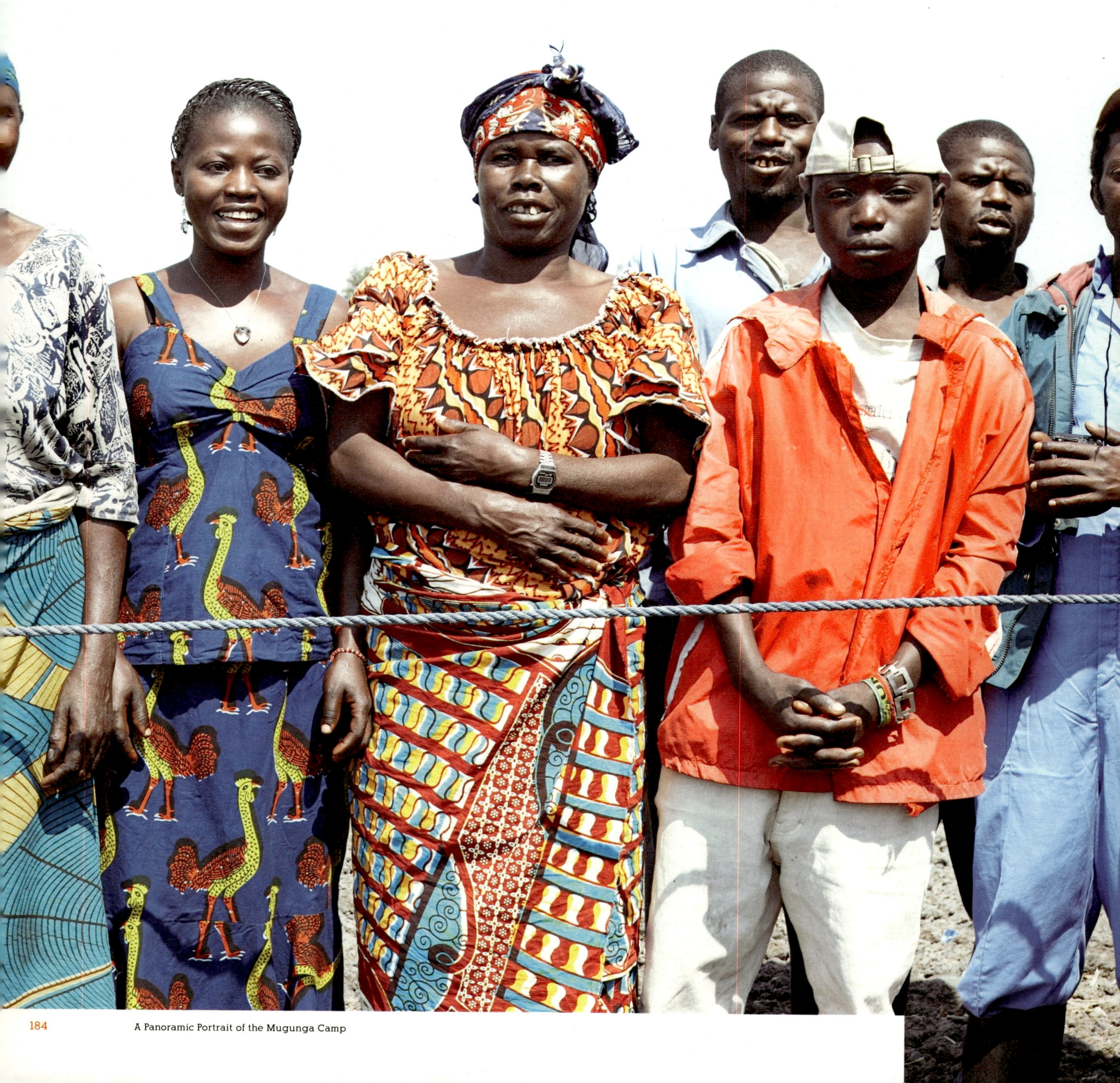

     A Panoramic Portrait of the Mugunga Camp

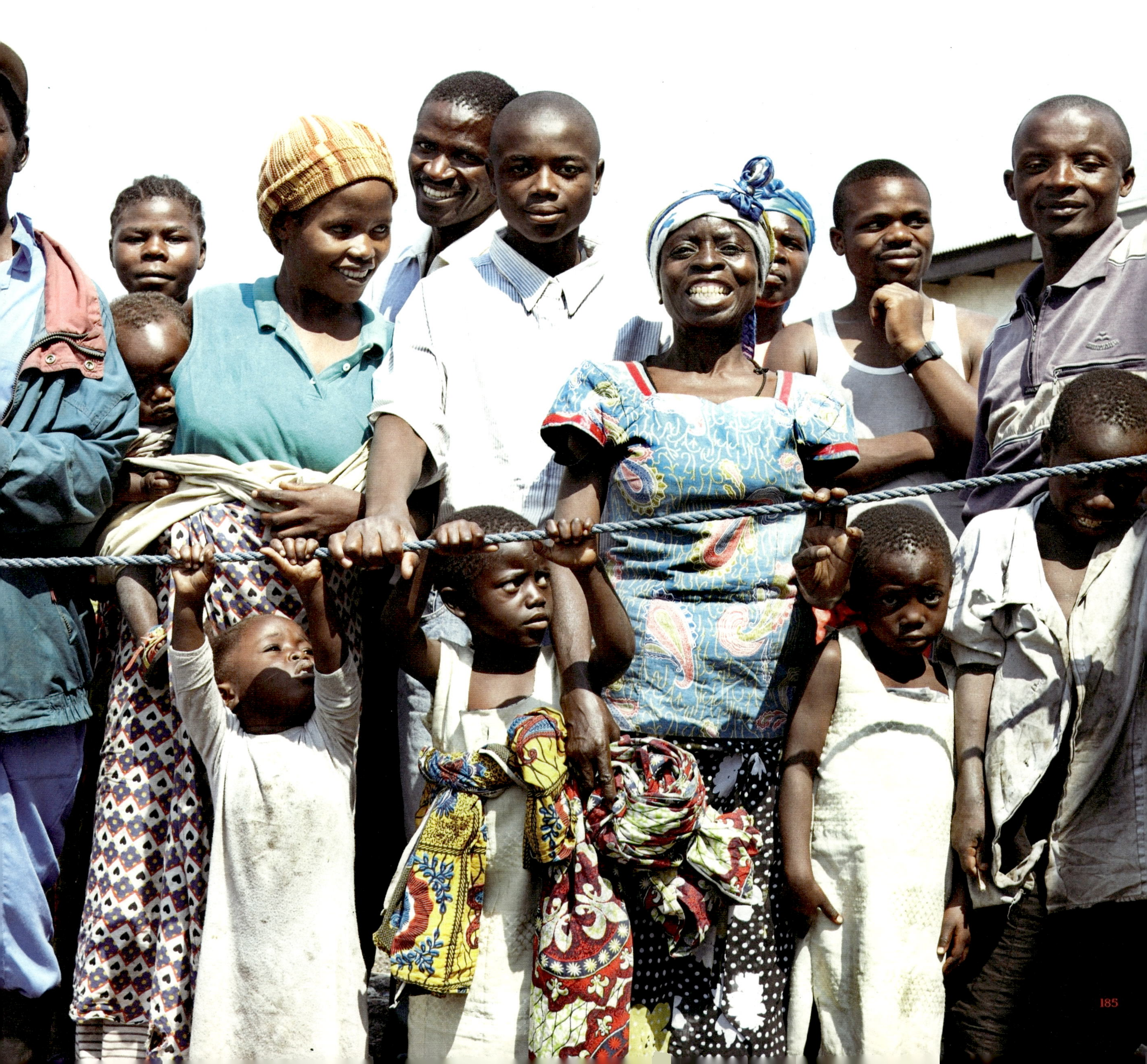

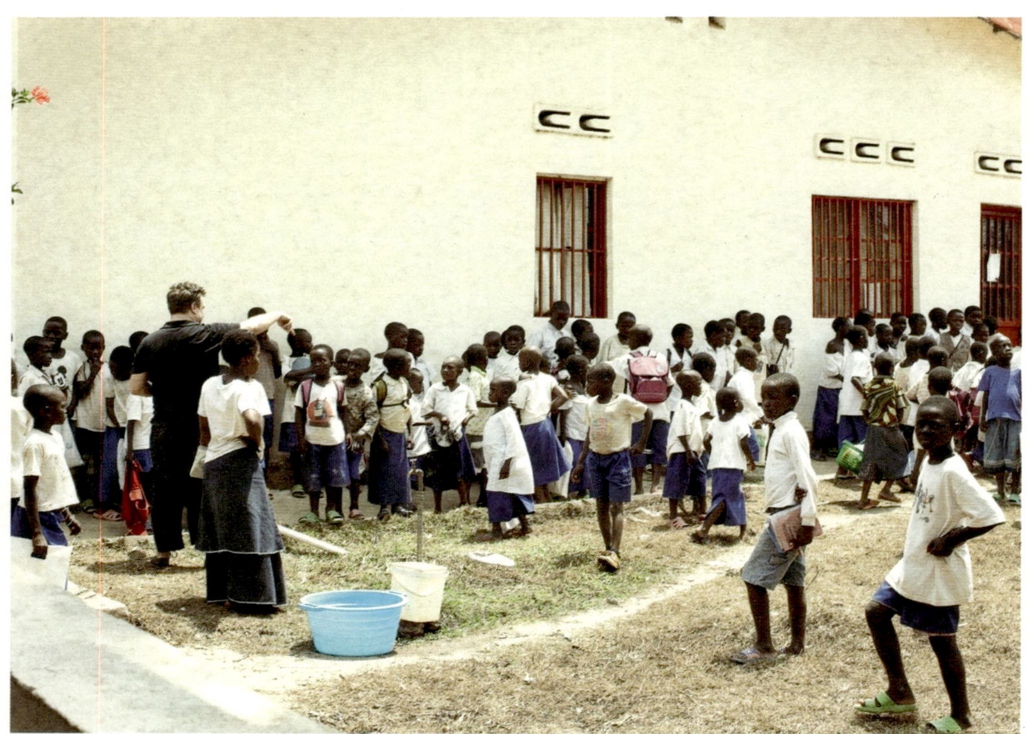

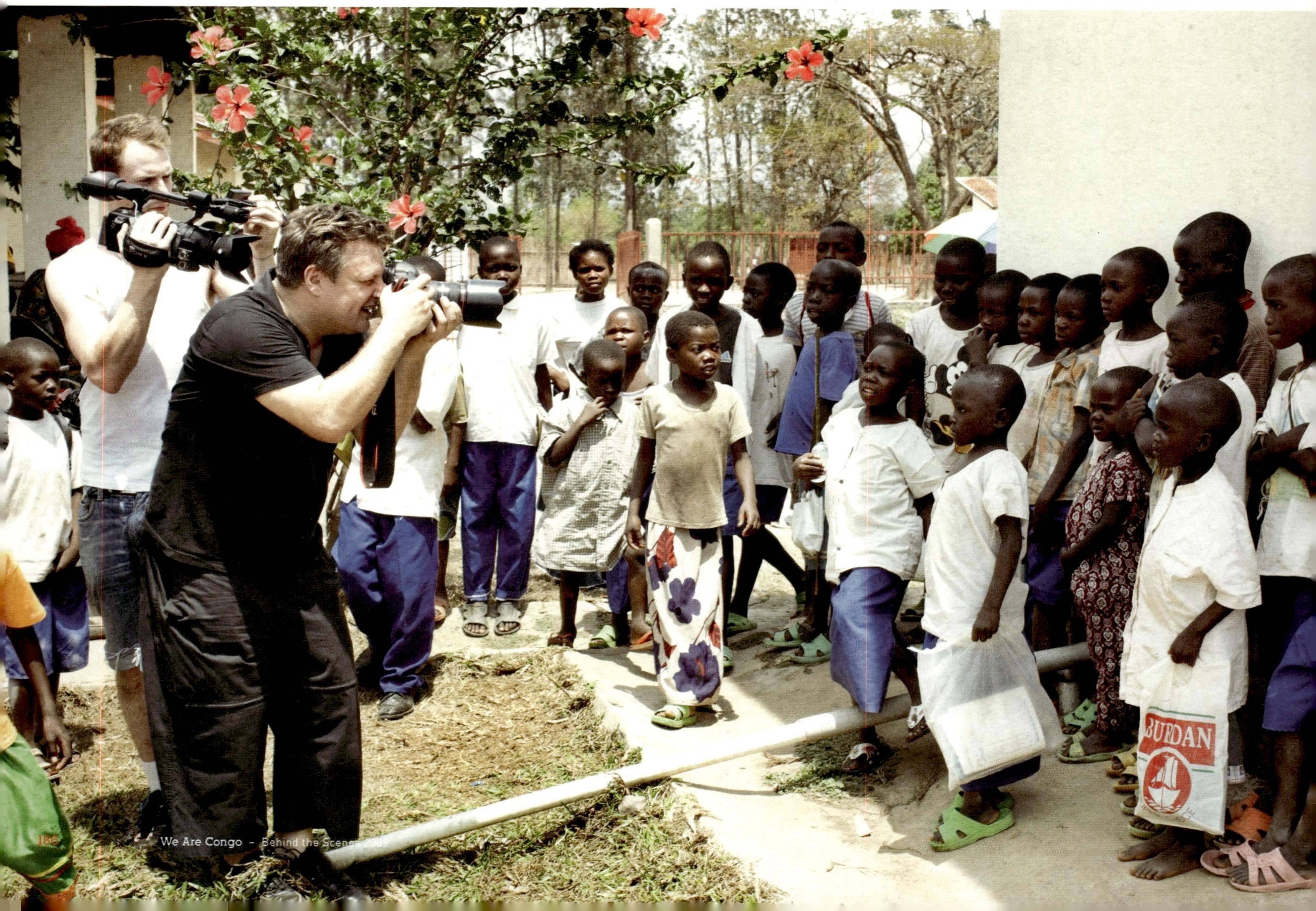

BEHIND THE SCENES
2009/2008

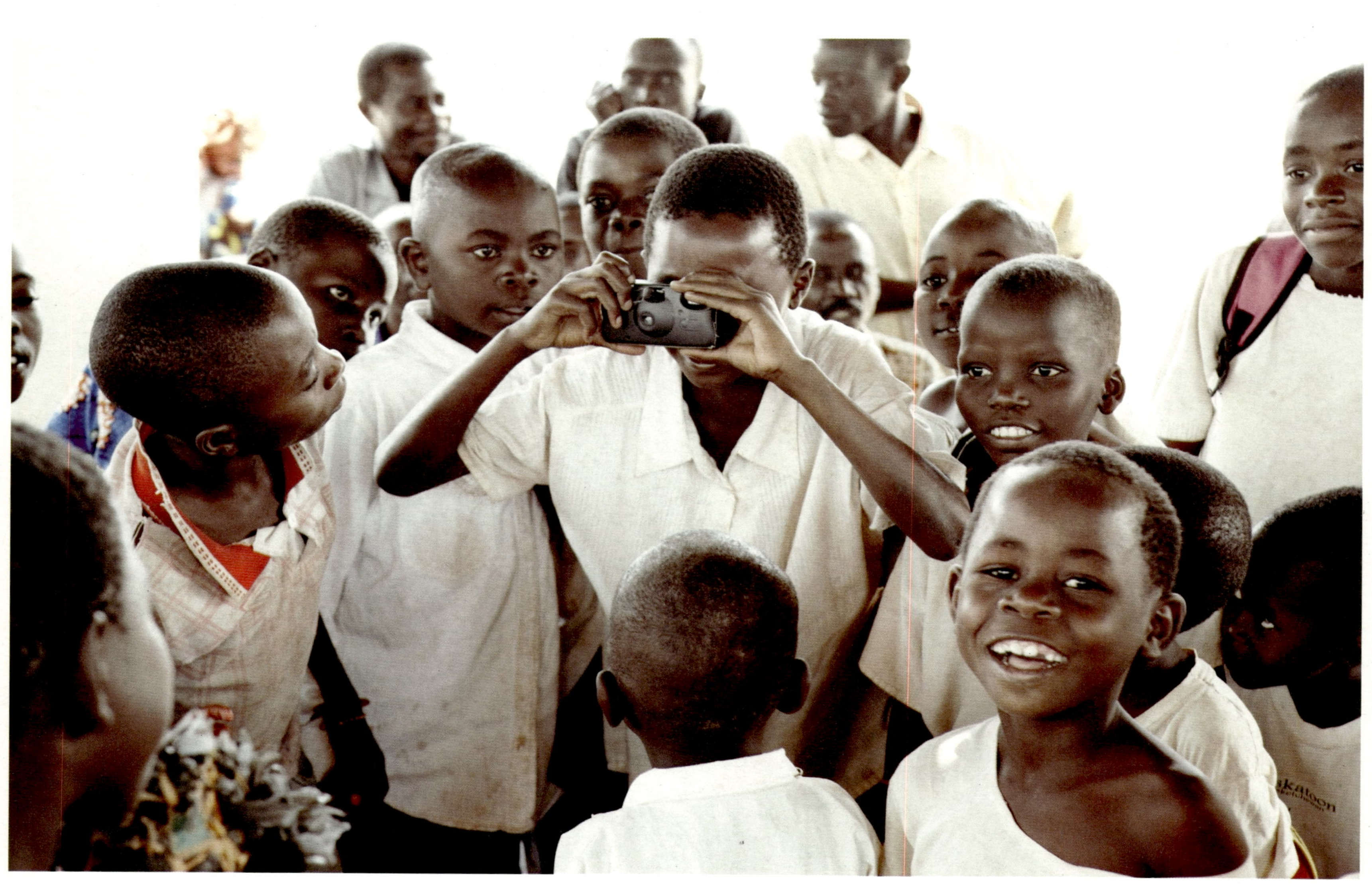

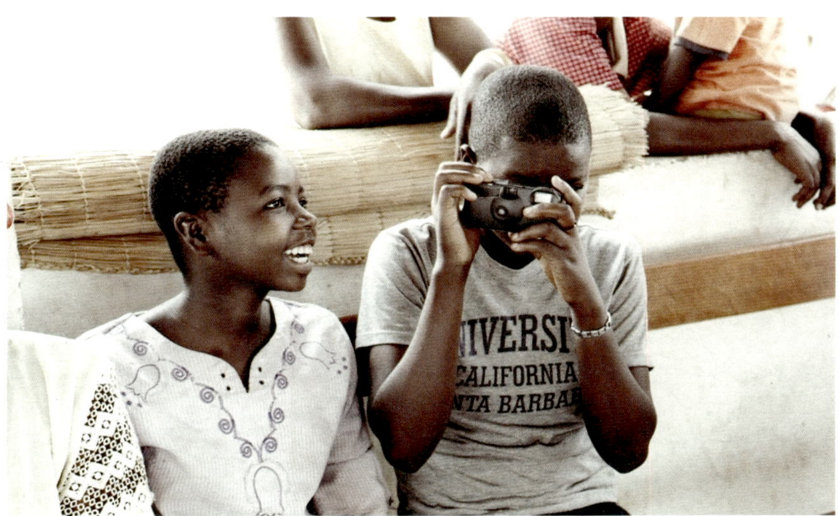

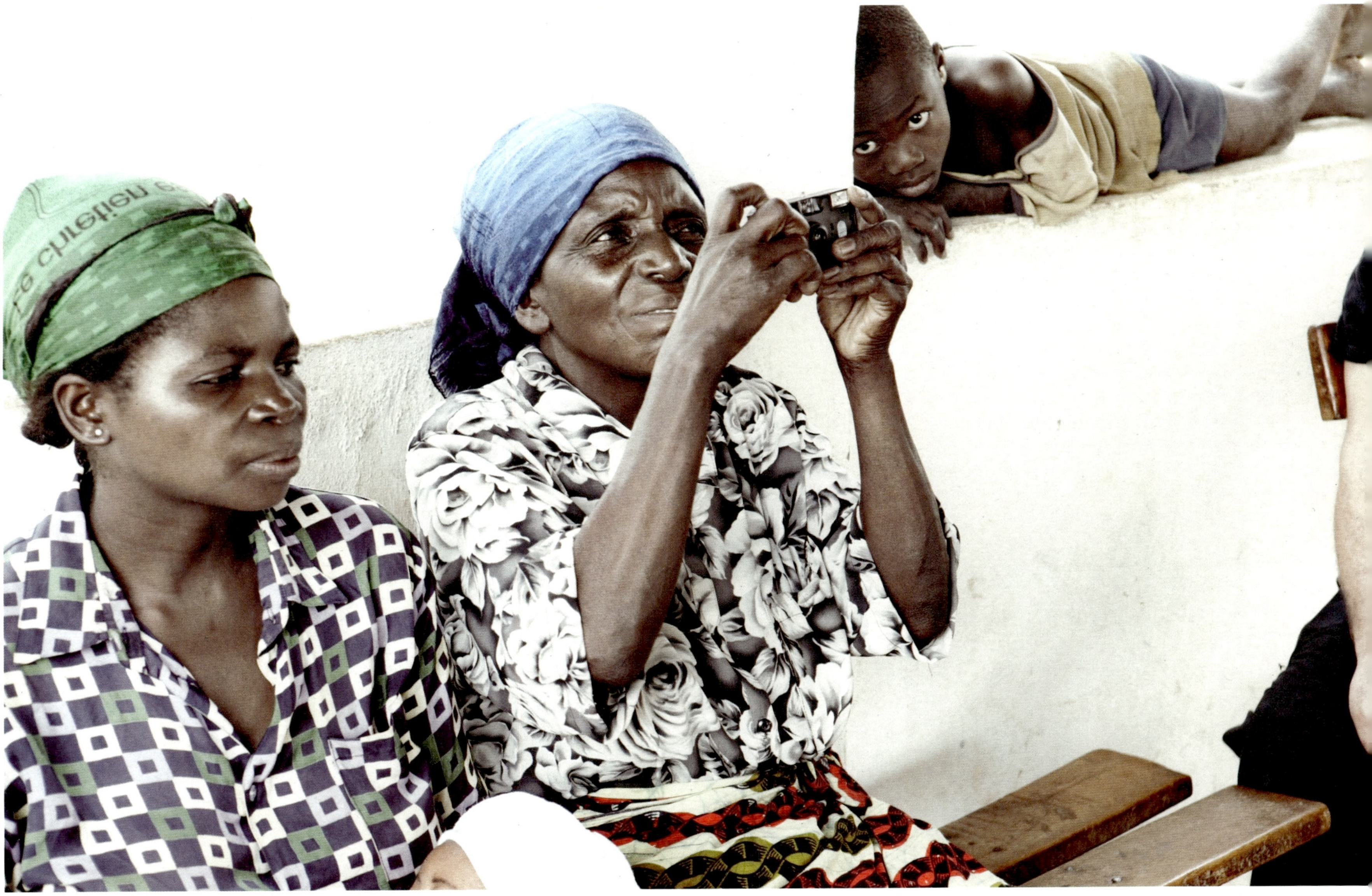

The workshops in Sange. Alfredo **(Top)**, Chantelle and Muvida **(Above)** learn how to use a camera for the first time.

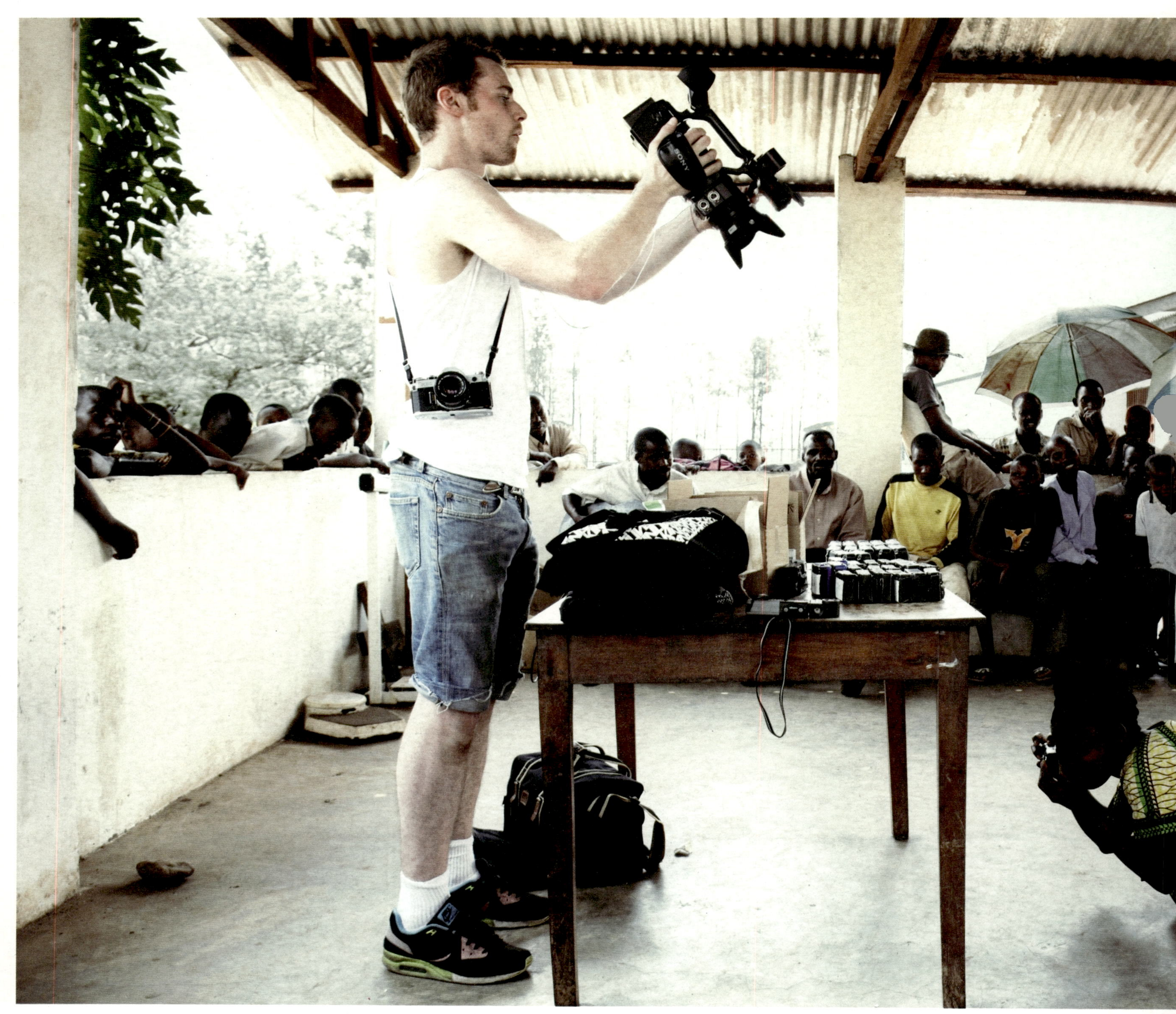

(Above) Zafarini practices the 'interesting angle' shot while Dom documents.
(Top Right) Rankin shows Muvida how to frame a shot.
(Bottom Right) Howie B gets ready to record.

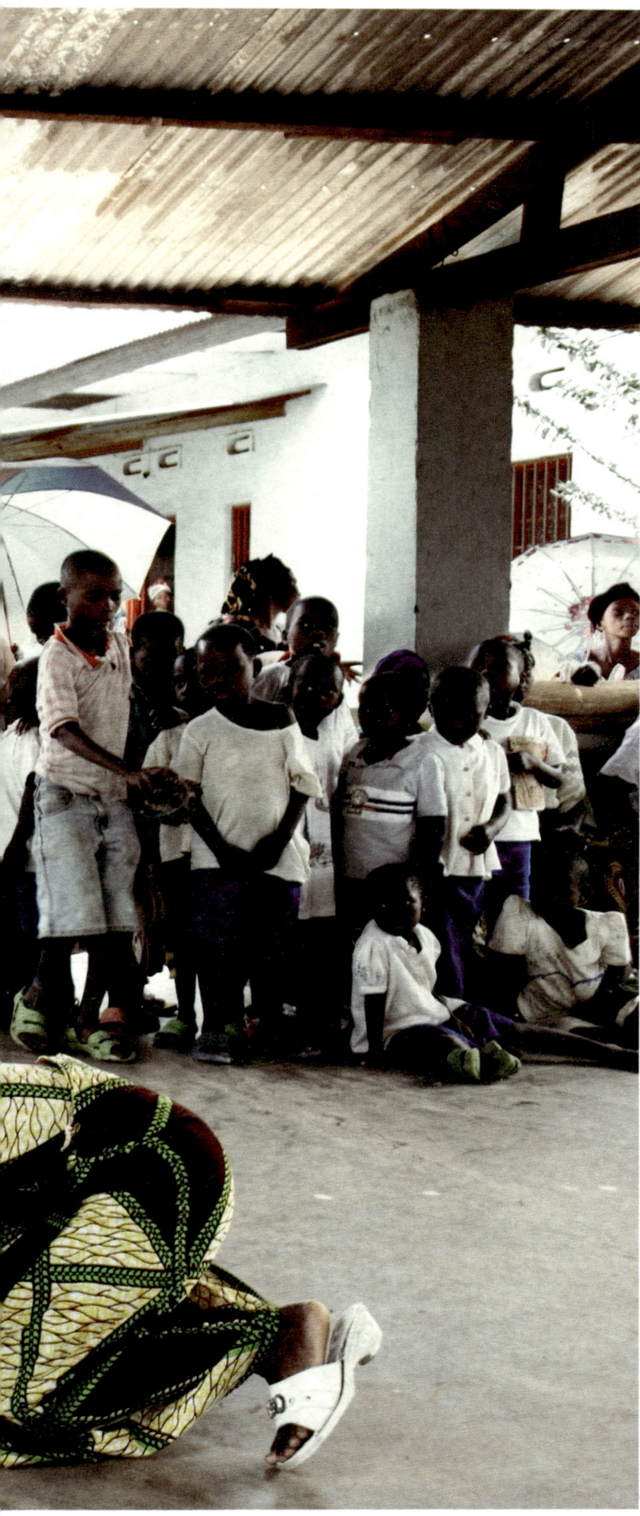

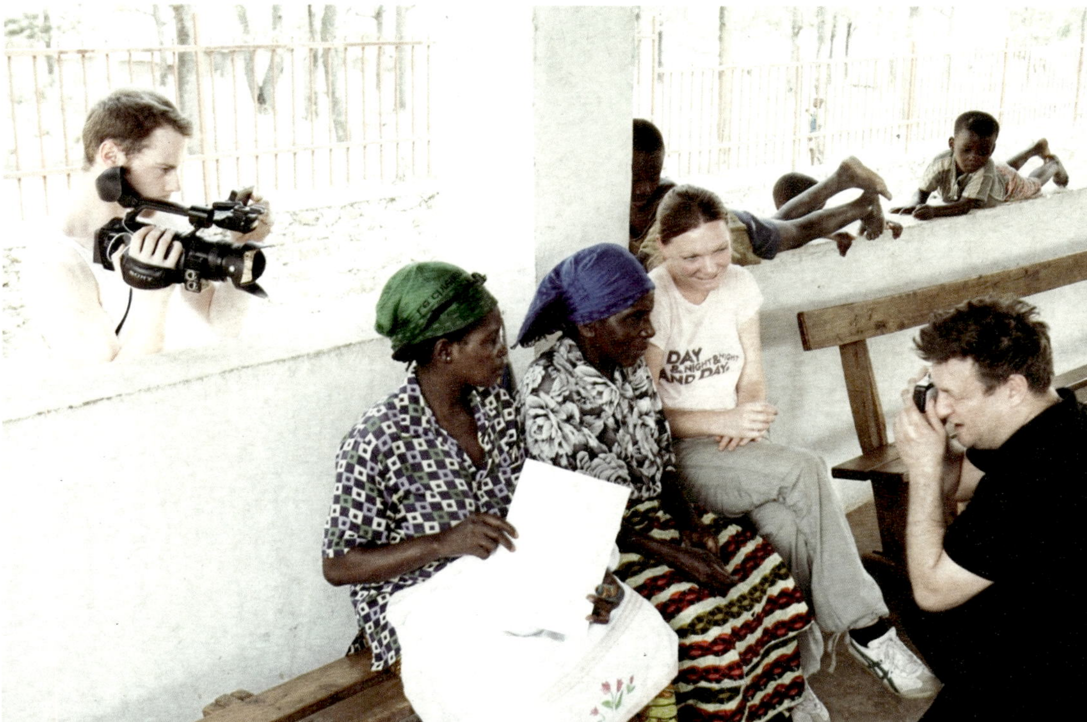

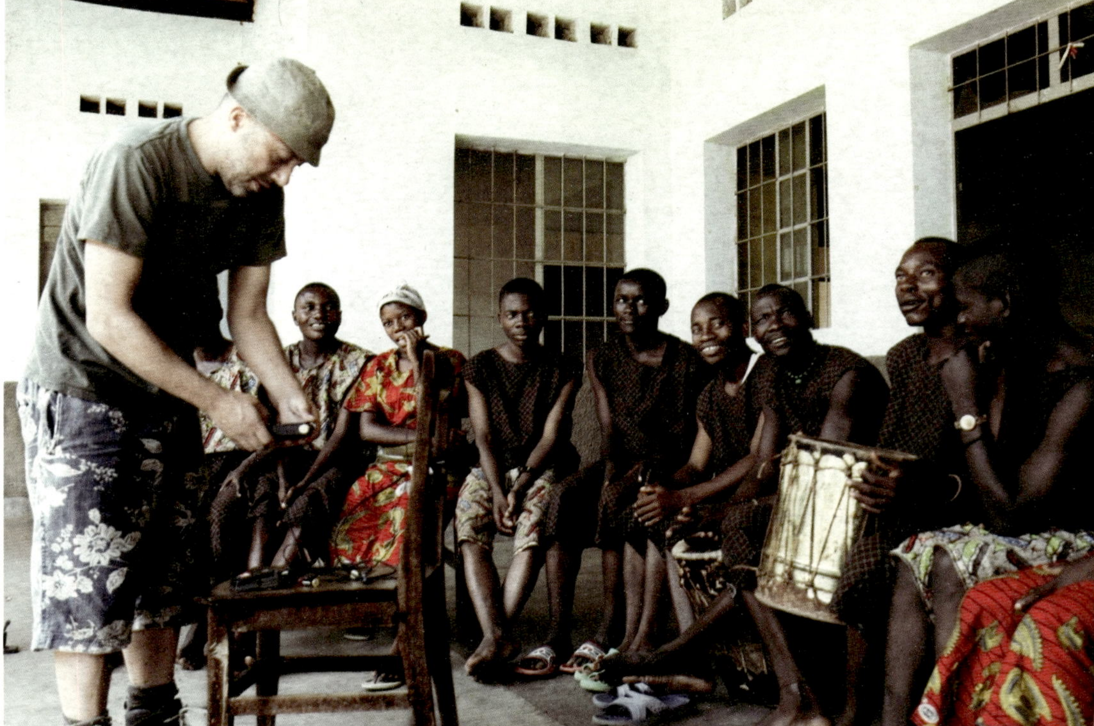

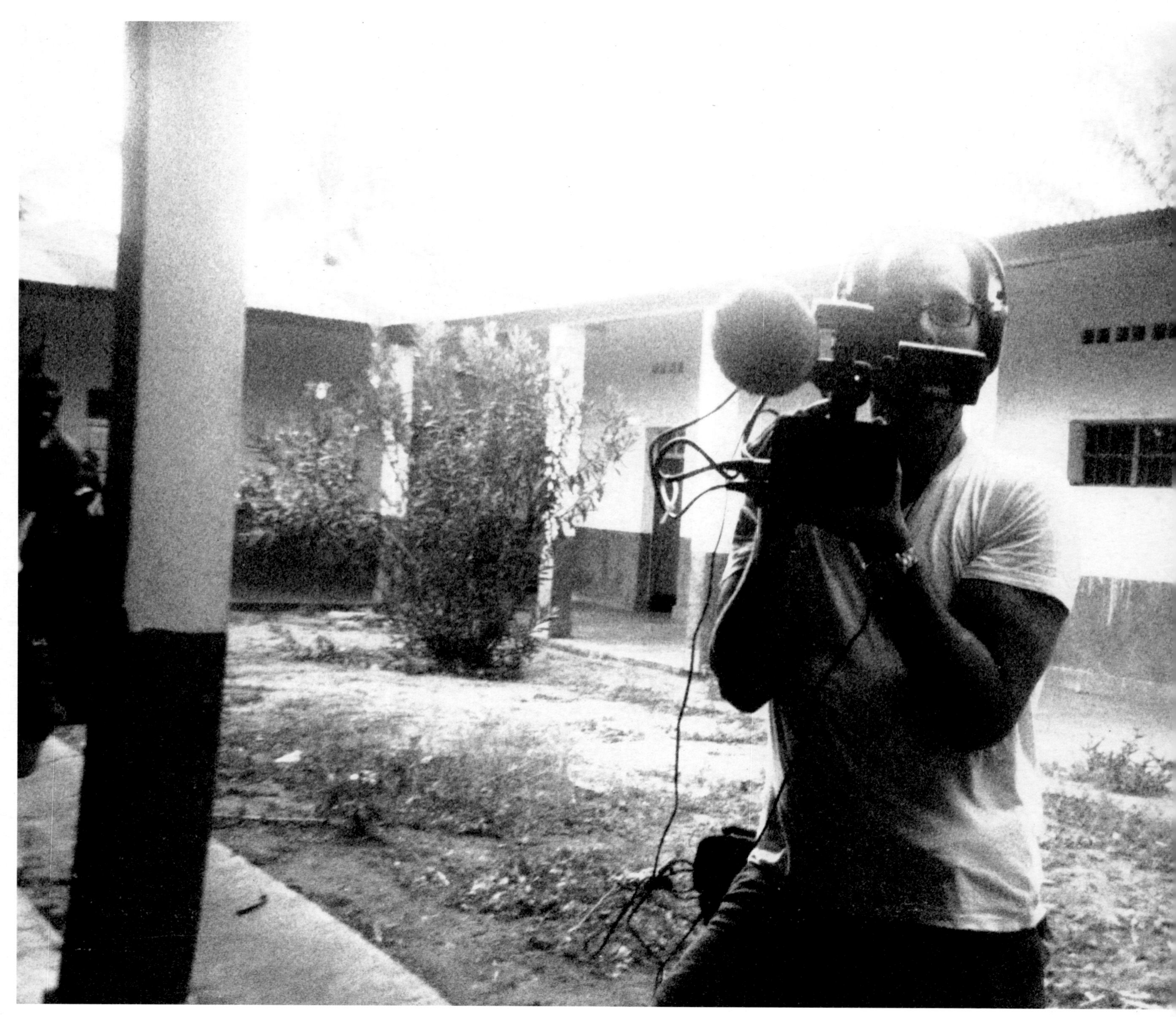

  We Are Congo – Behind the Scenes 2009

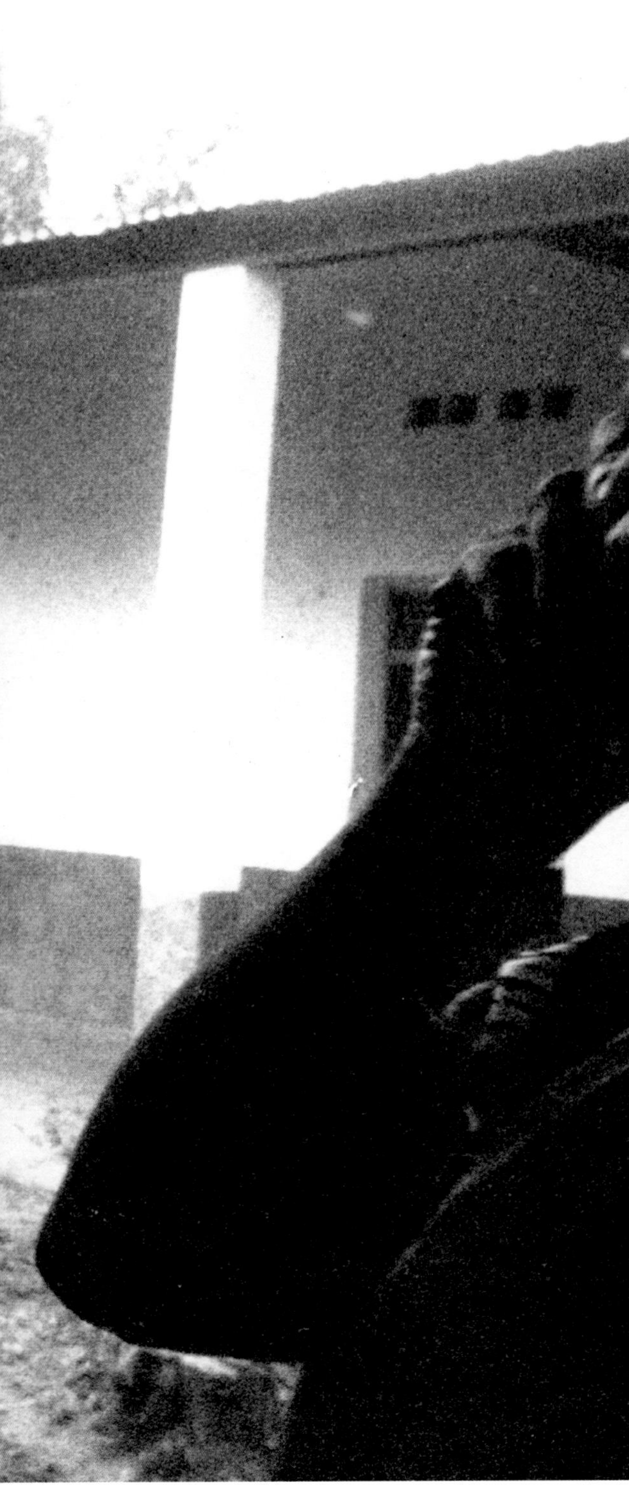
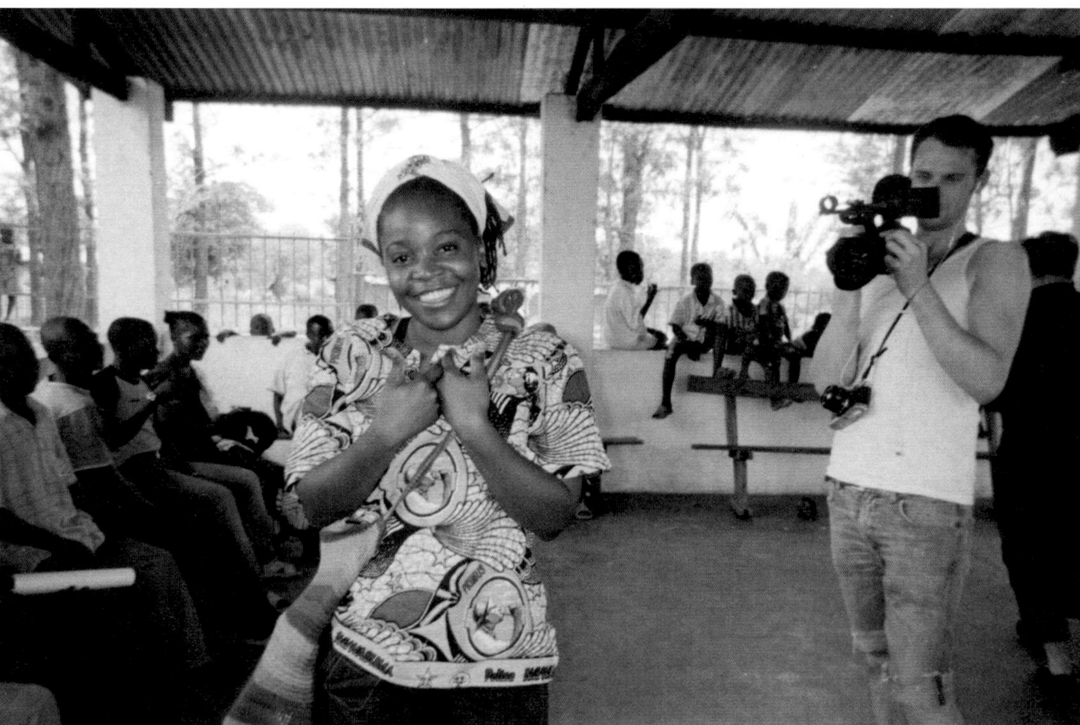
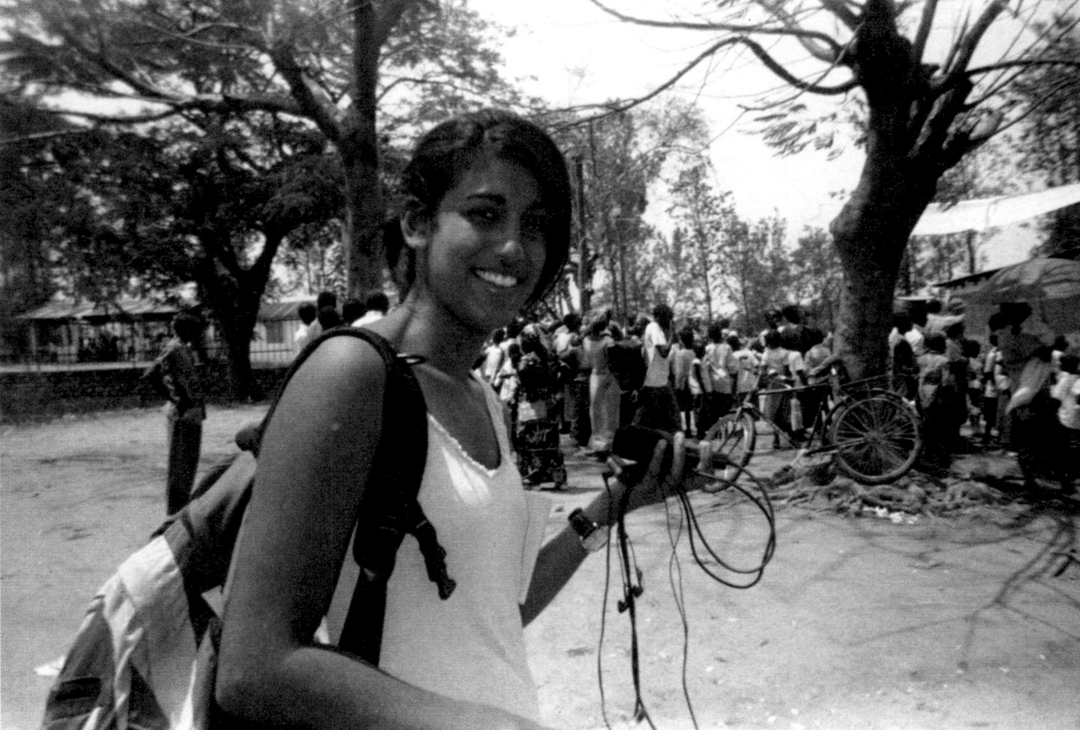

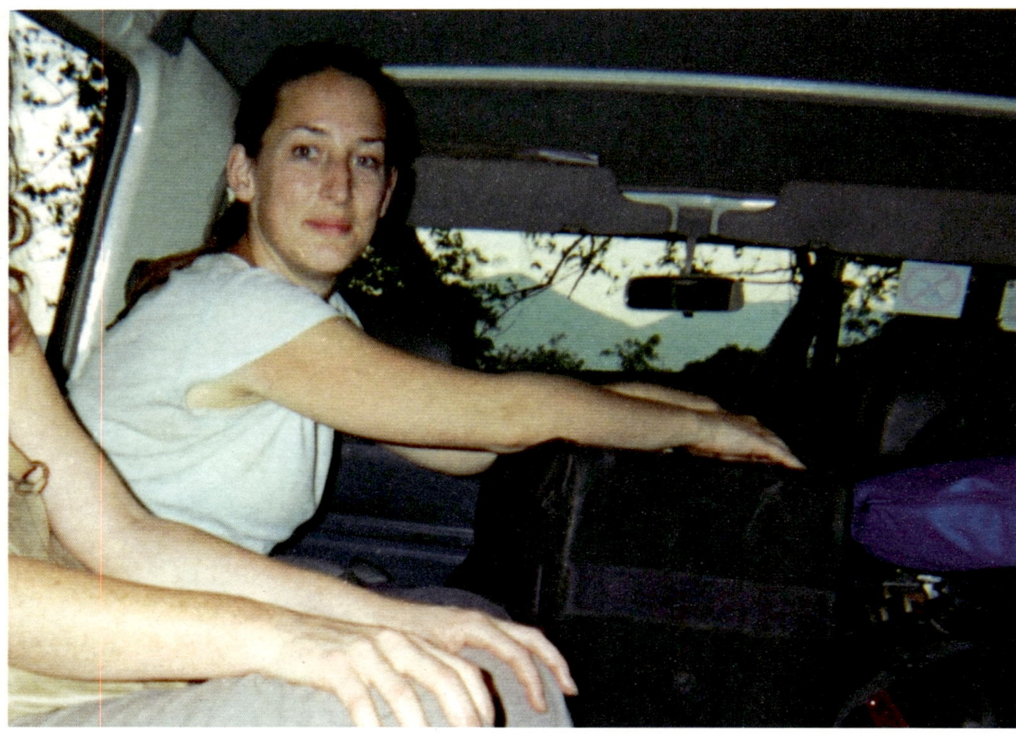

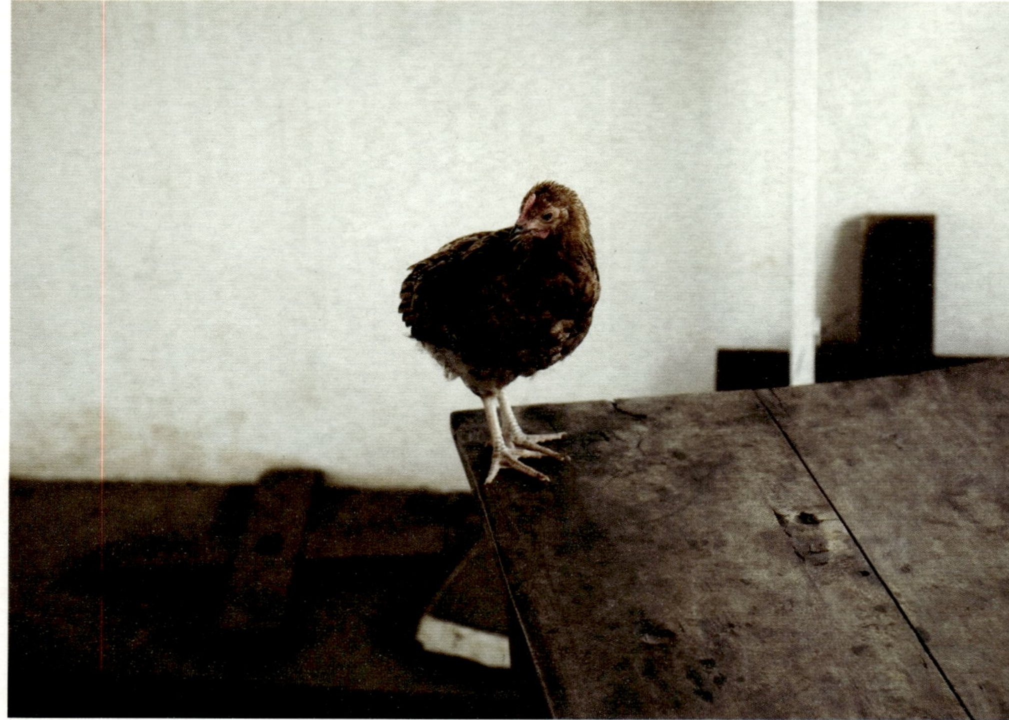

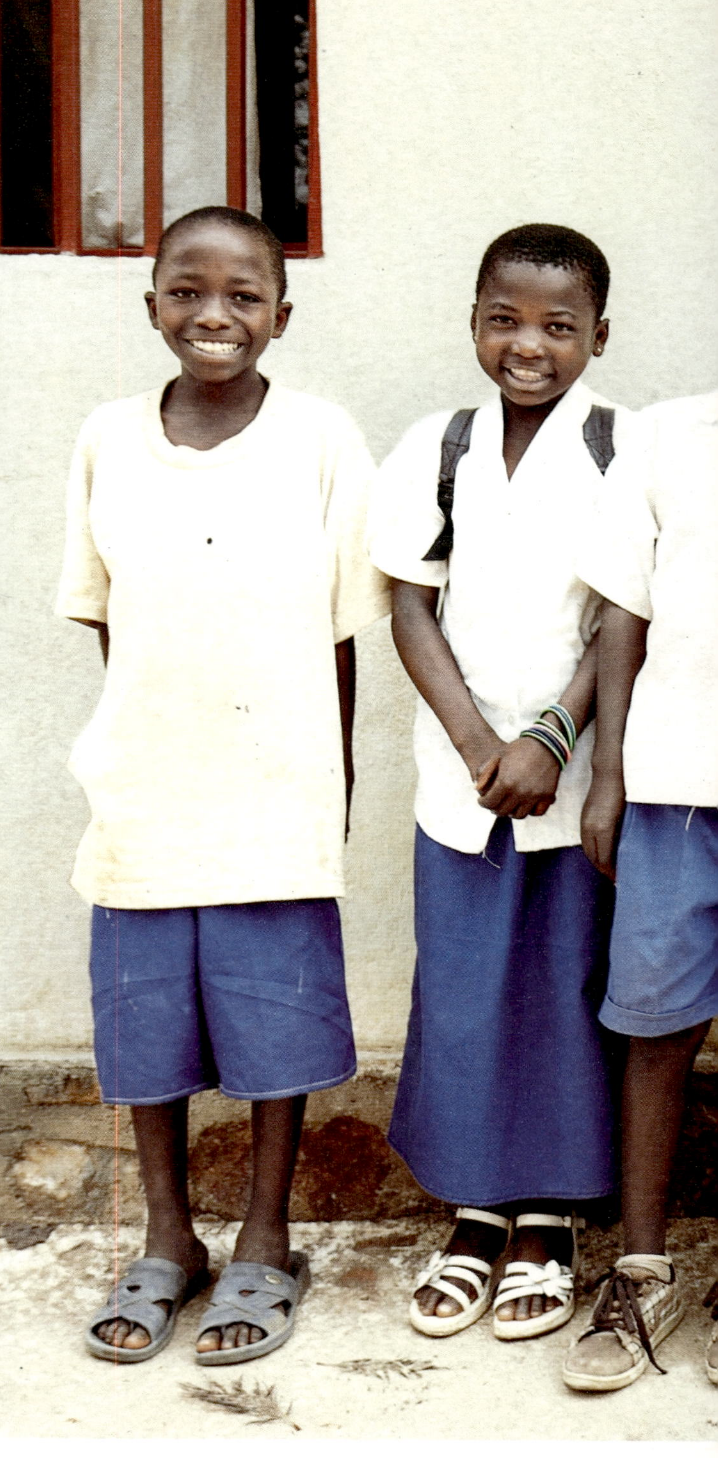

(Top Left) Suzi O'Keefe
(Right) The class of Sange 2009
(Bottom Left) A chick

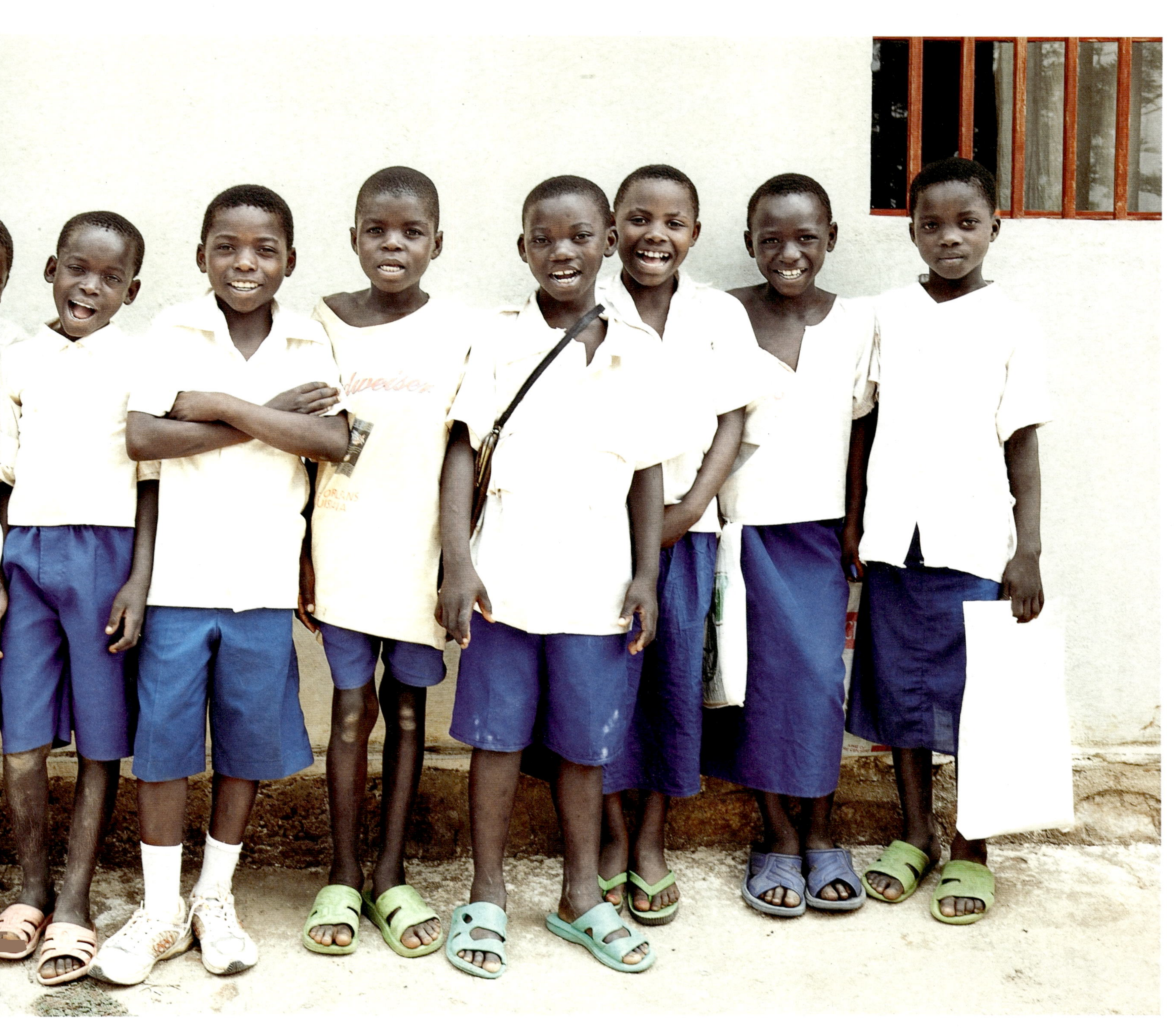

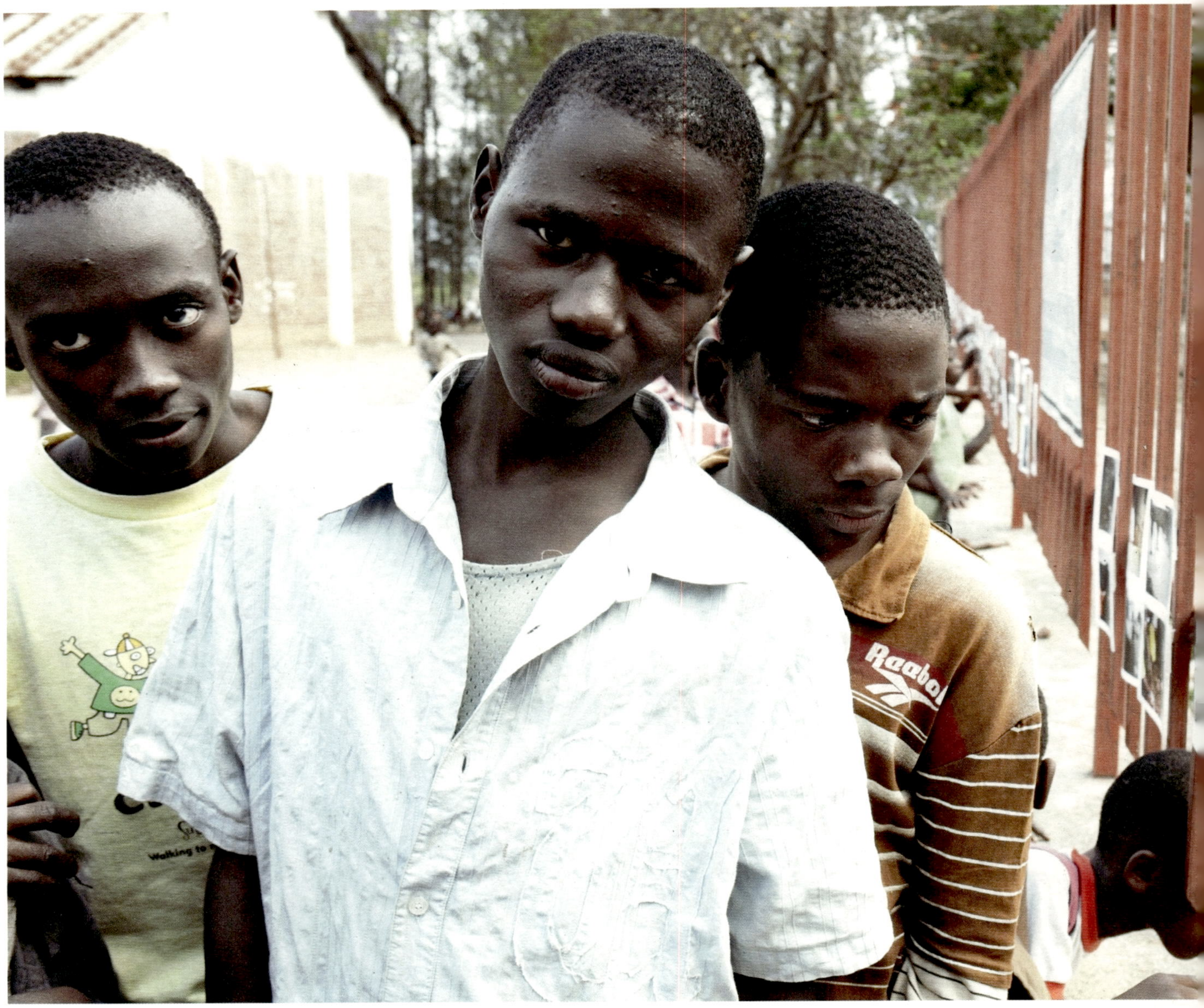

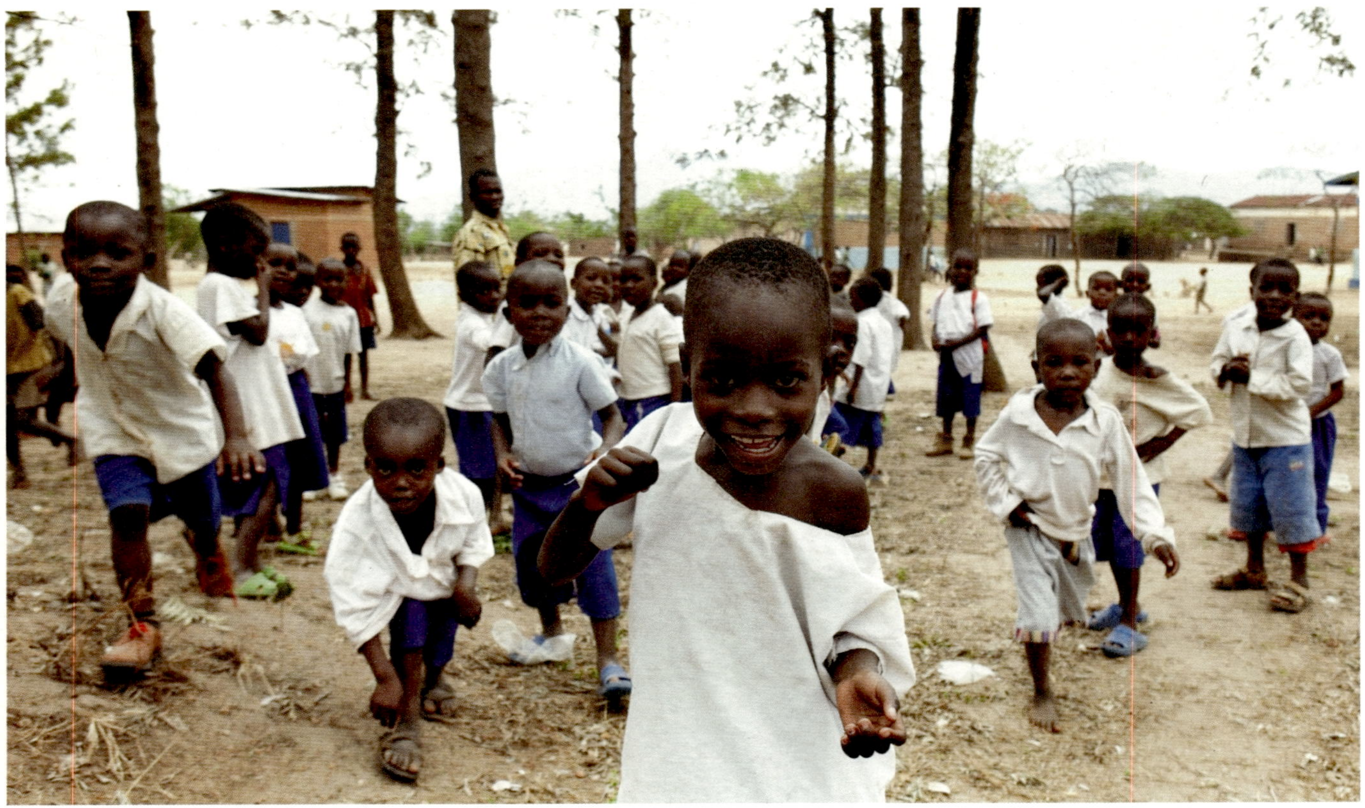

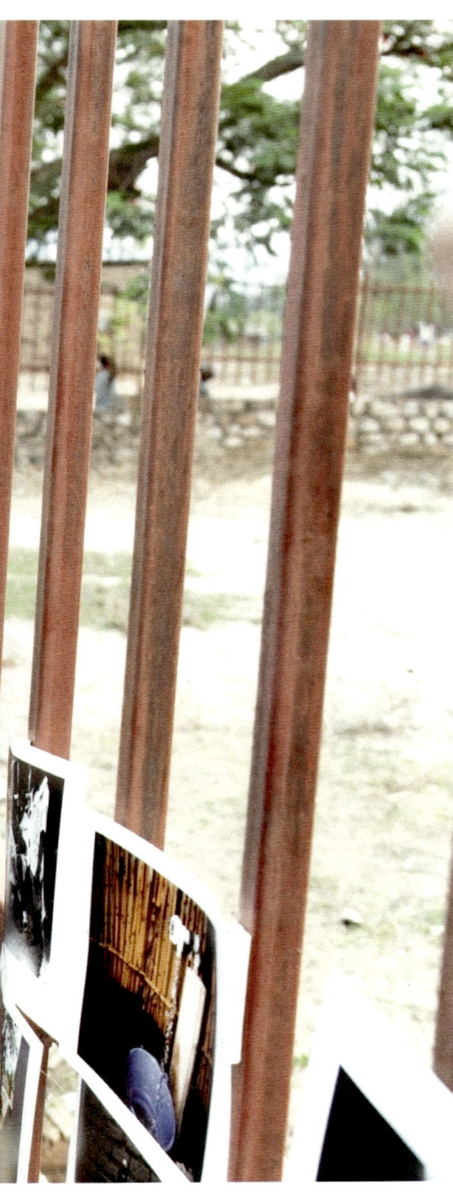

(Top) A job well done. Aciri stands proudly in front of his photos. Come on then?
(Bottom Right) People start to gather to look at the exhibition in Sange.

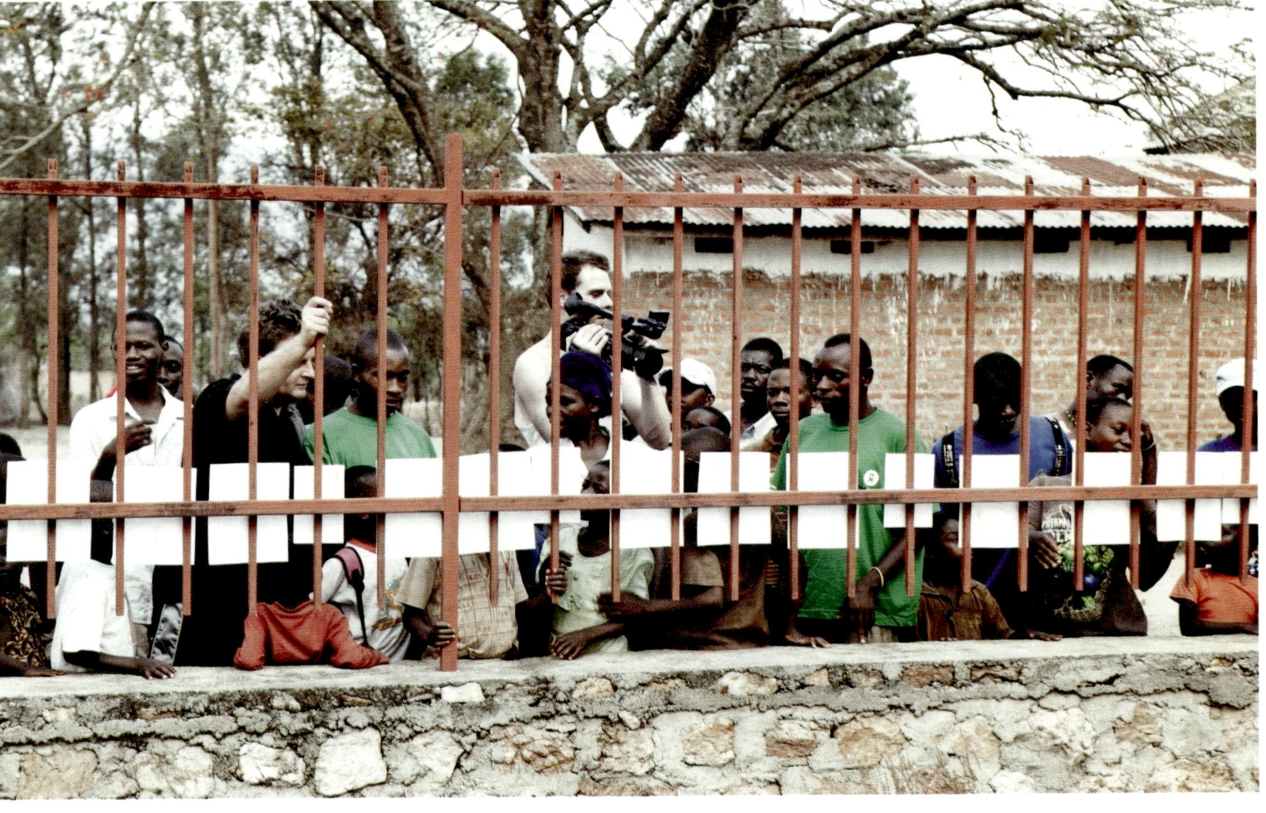

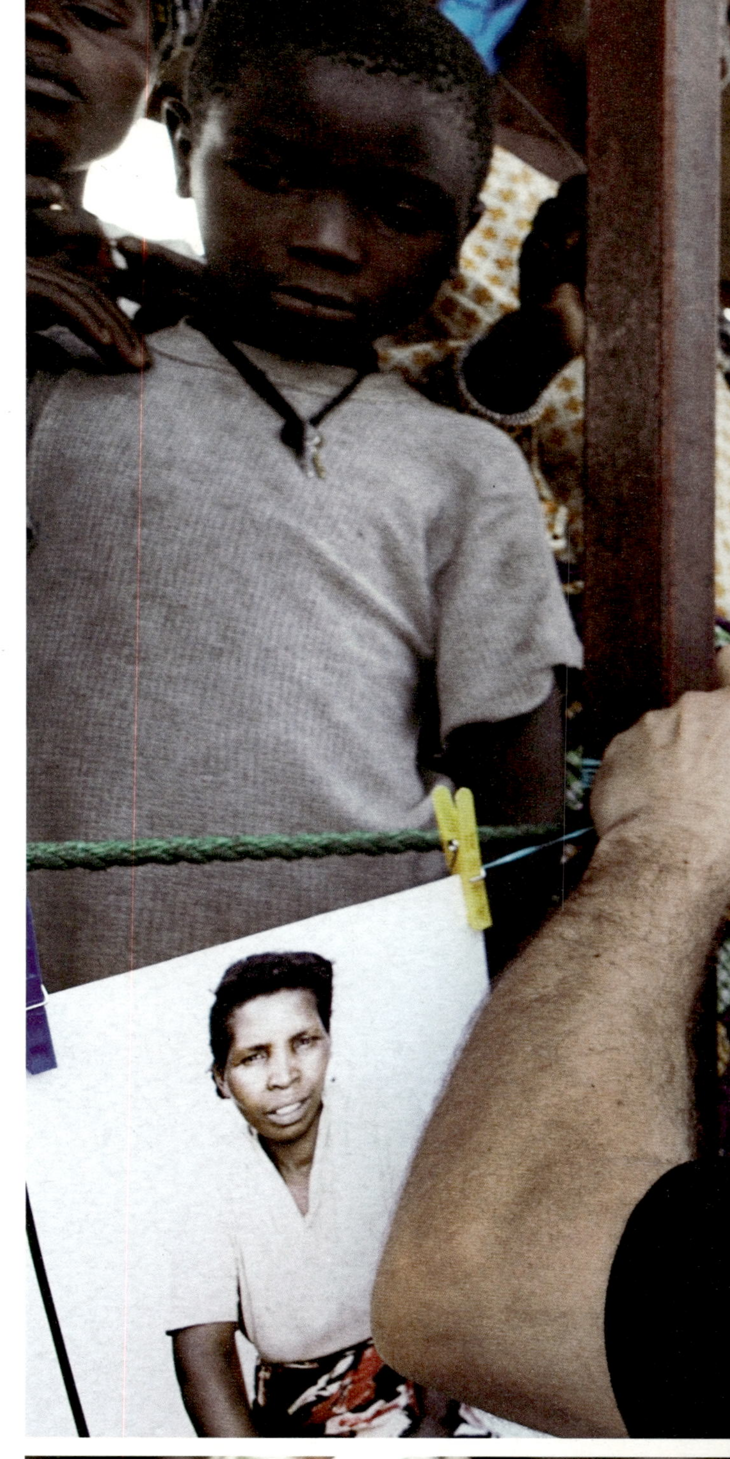

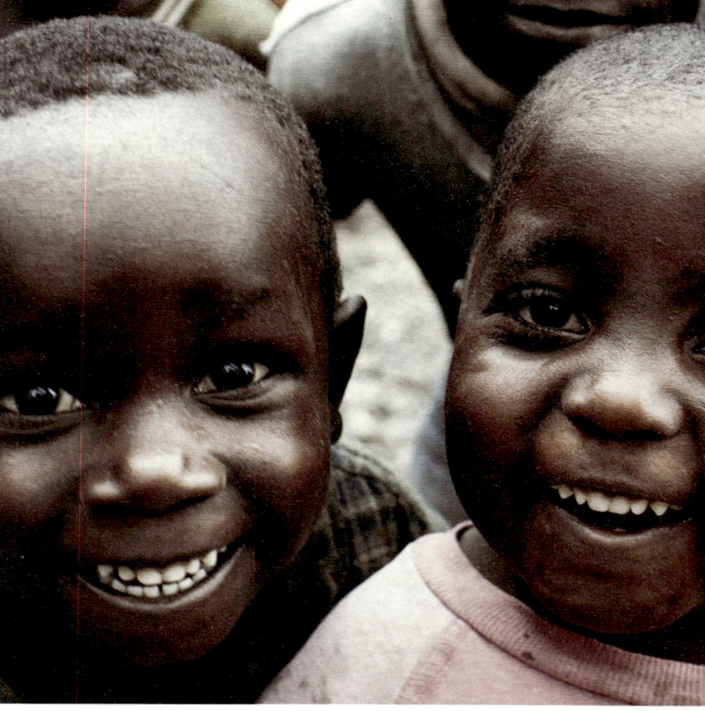

(Top) Rankin pegs out his portraits in the middle of Mugunga camp.
(Bottom) Aime and King Fidel

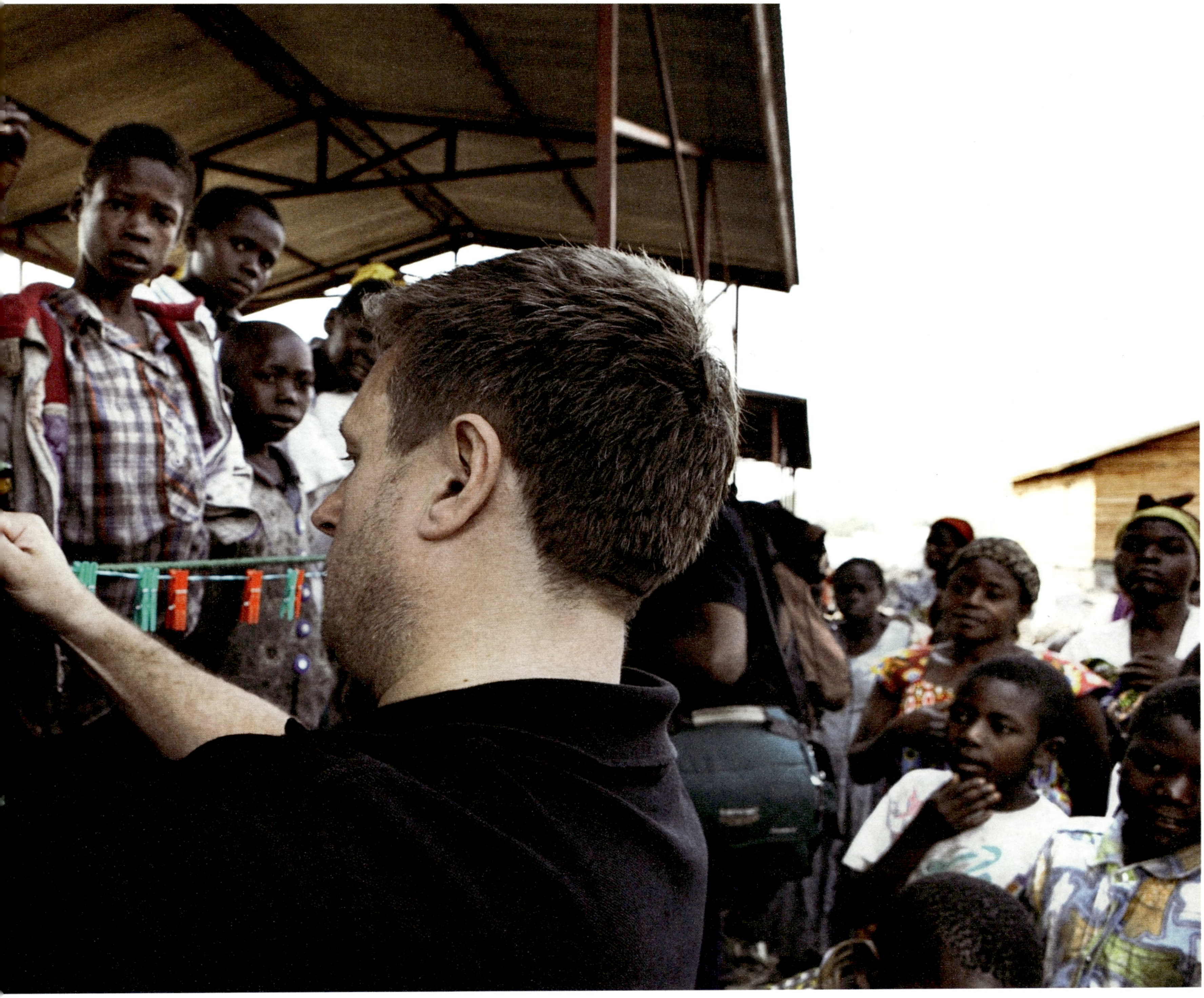

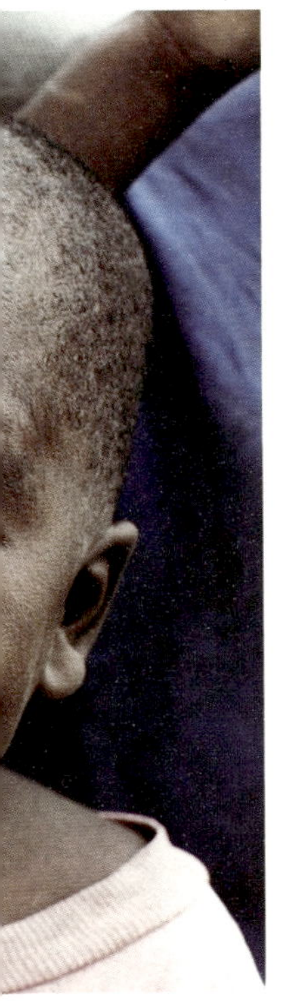

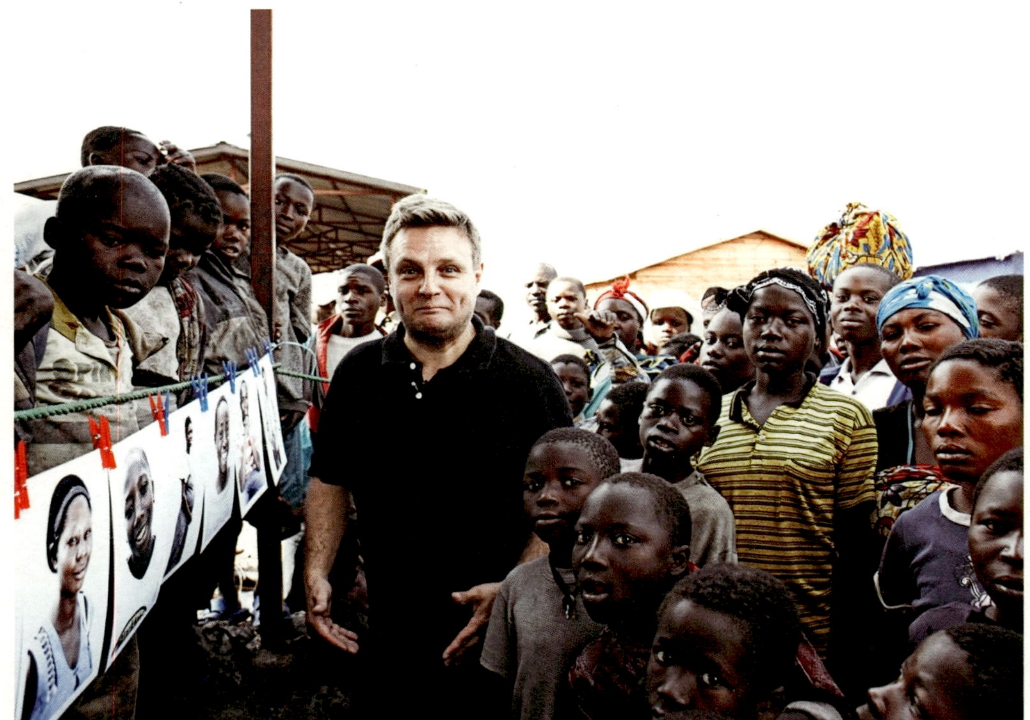

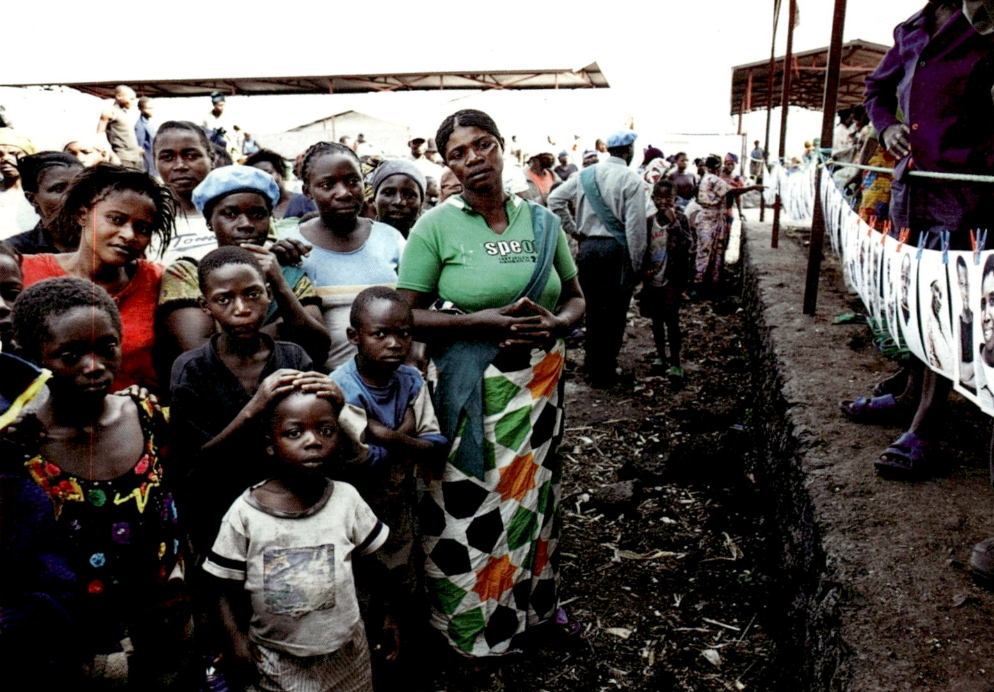

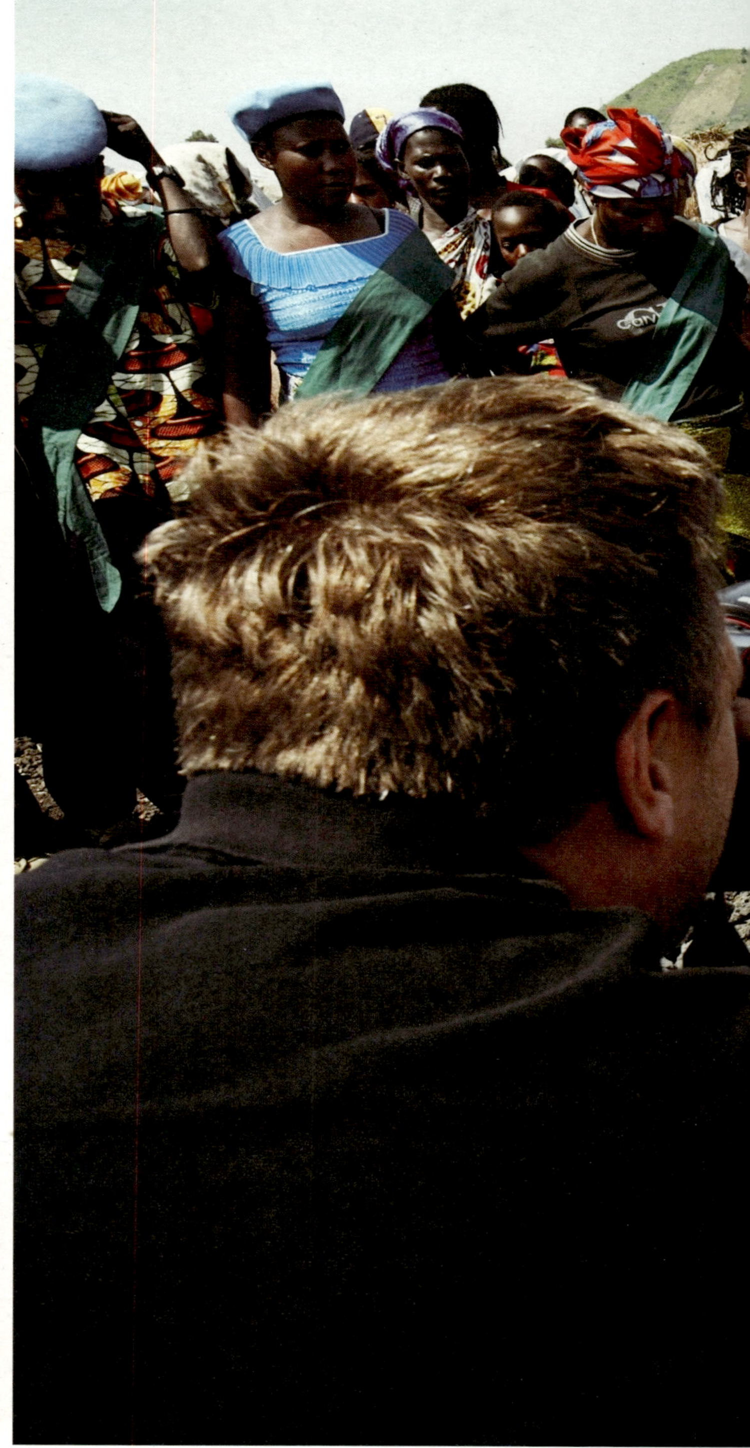

(Top Left) Help! A slightly nervous Rankin waits to
see the reaction as hundreds of people gather at
the exhibition in the middle of the Mugunga camp.
(Top Right) Rankin shooting the 100-metre panoramic portrait, frame by frame.
(Bottom Right) Rankin running from crowds of kids.
(Bottom Left) People take time to study each photo.

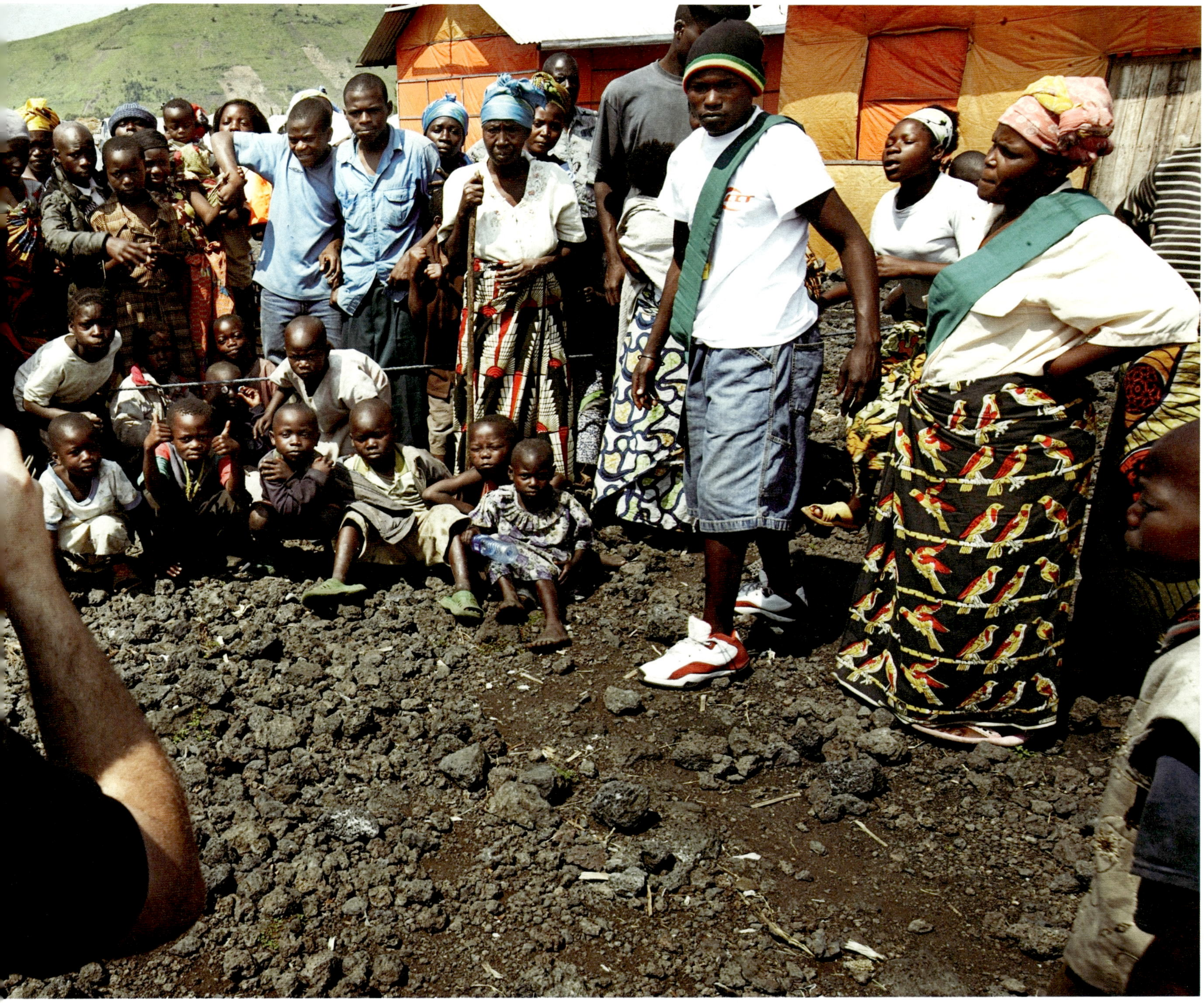

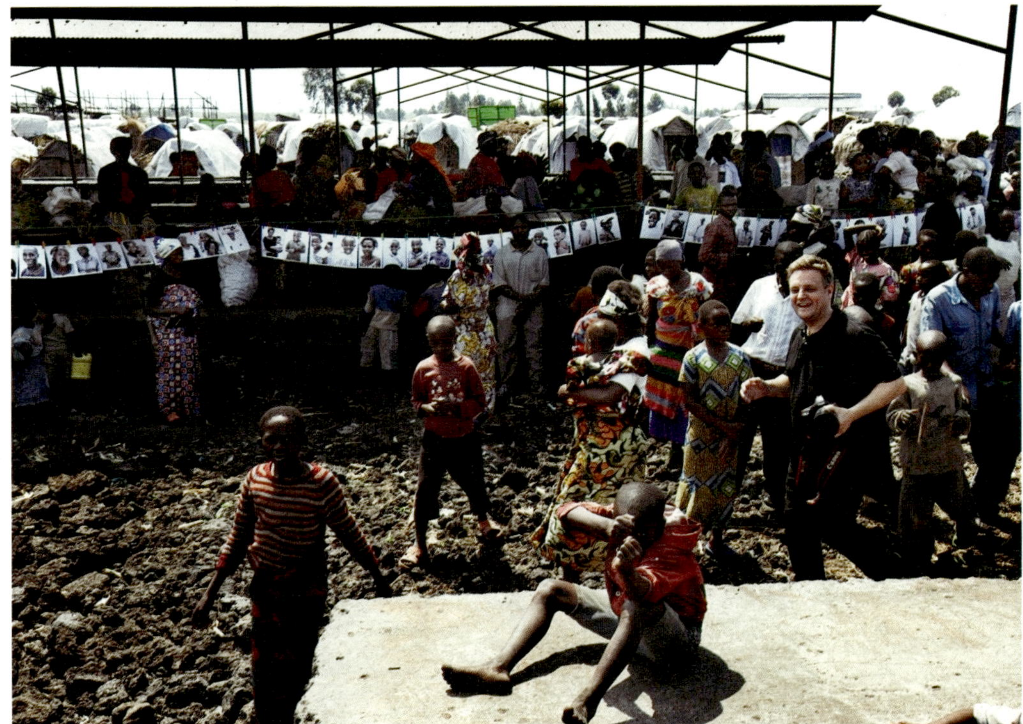

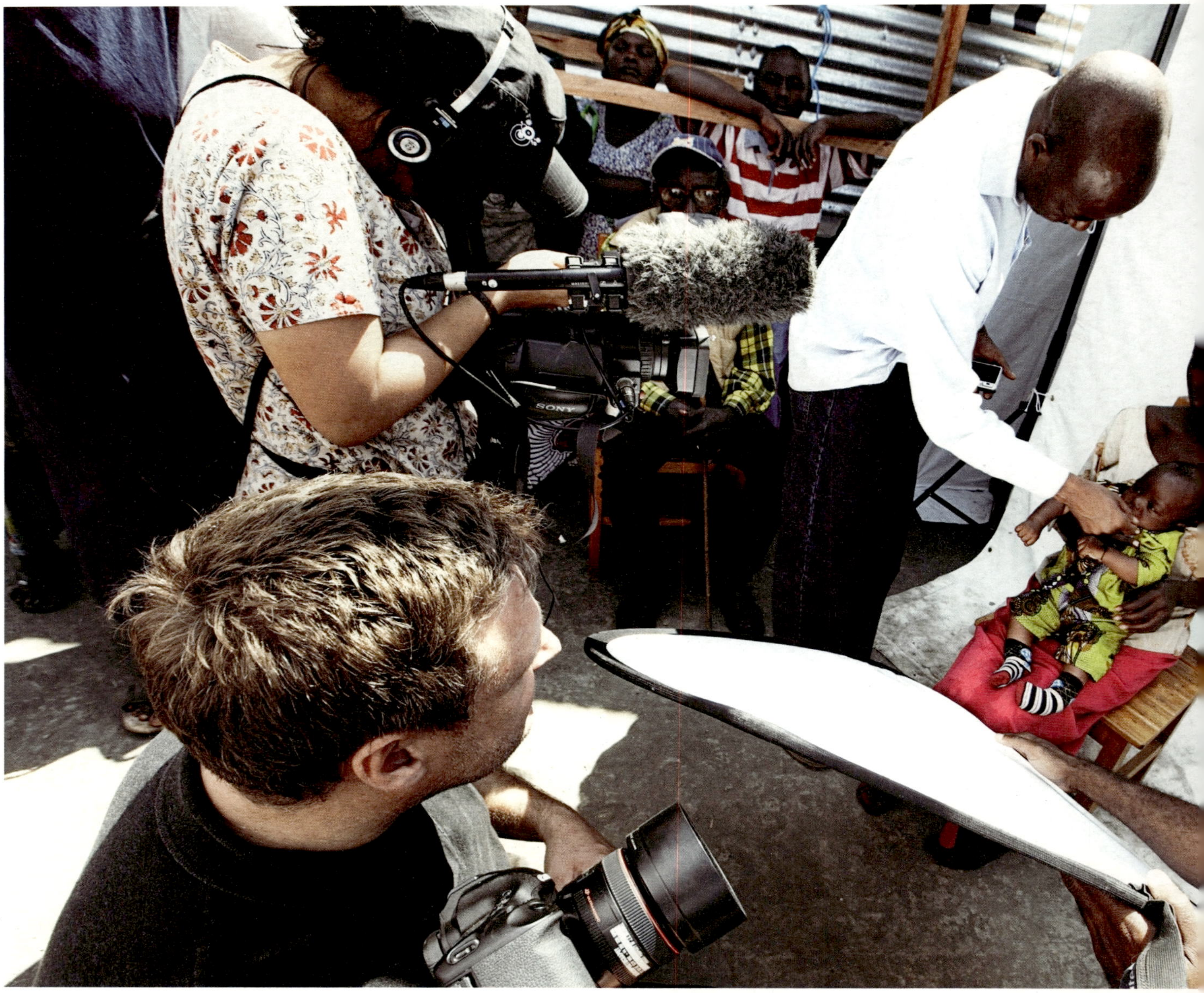

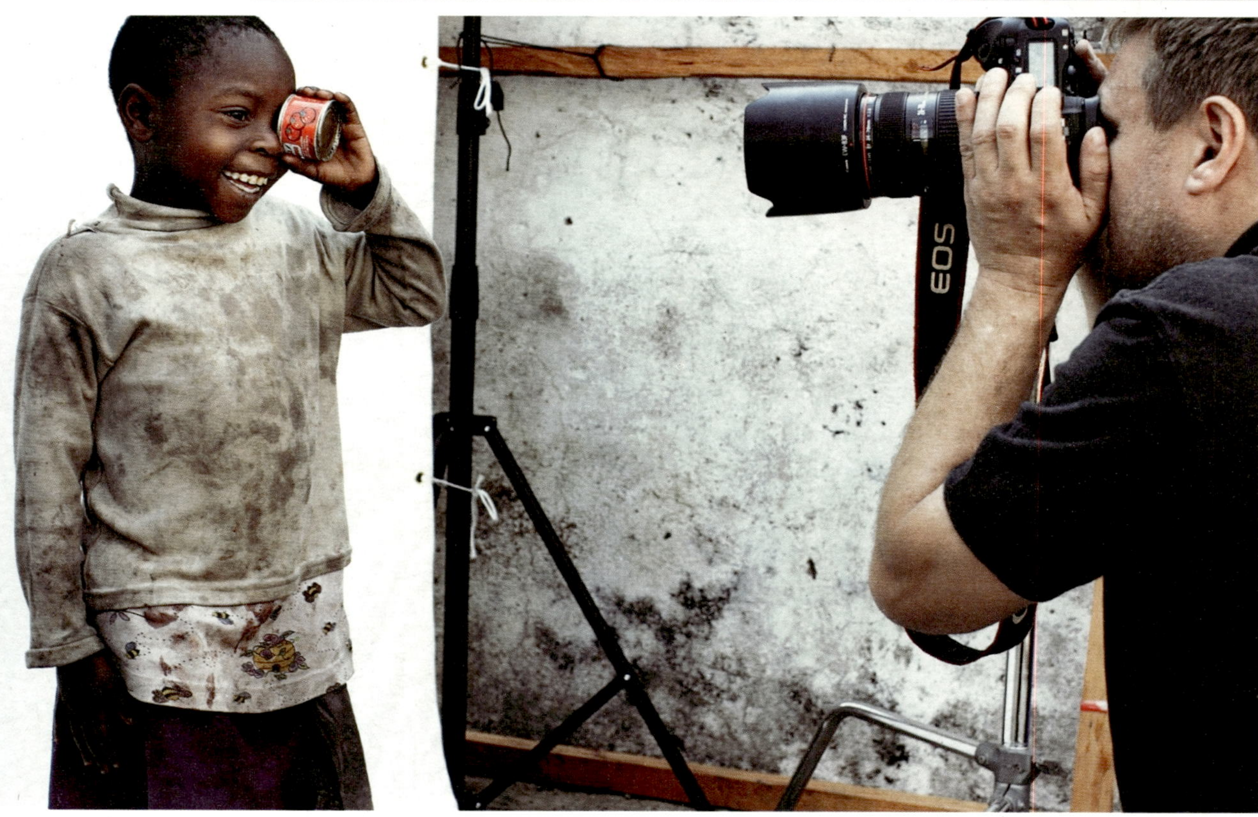

(Top Right) Rankin shoots Tumani the tailor.
(Bottom Right) Messing about.
(Bottom Left) Rankin shooting Jasmine shooting Rankin.
(Top Left) The Lovely Charles making sure that baby
Happiness lives up to his name.

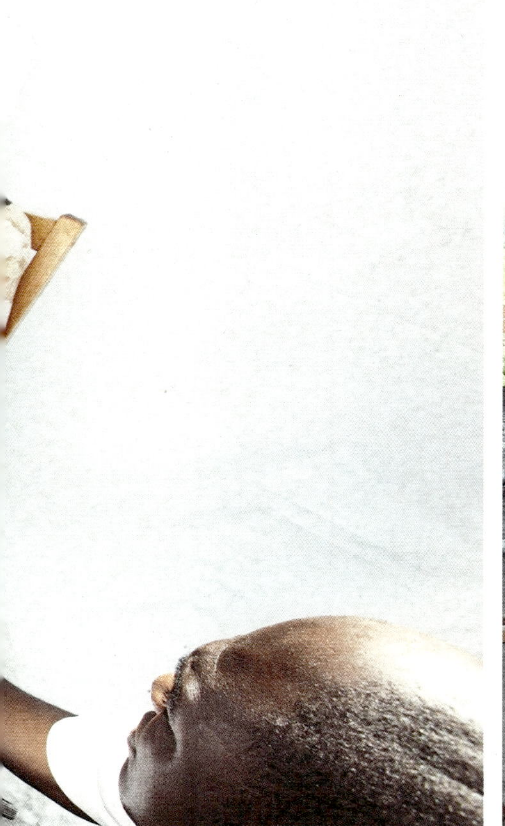

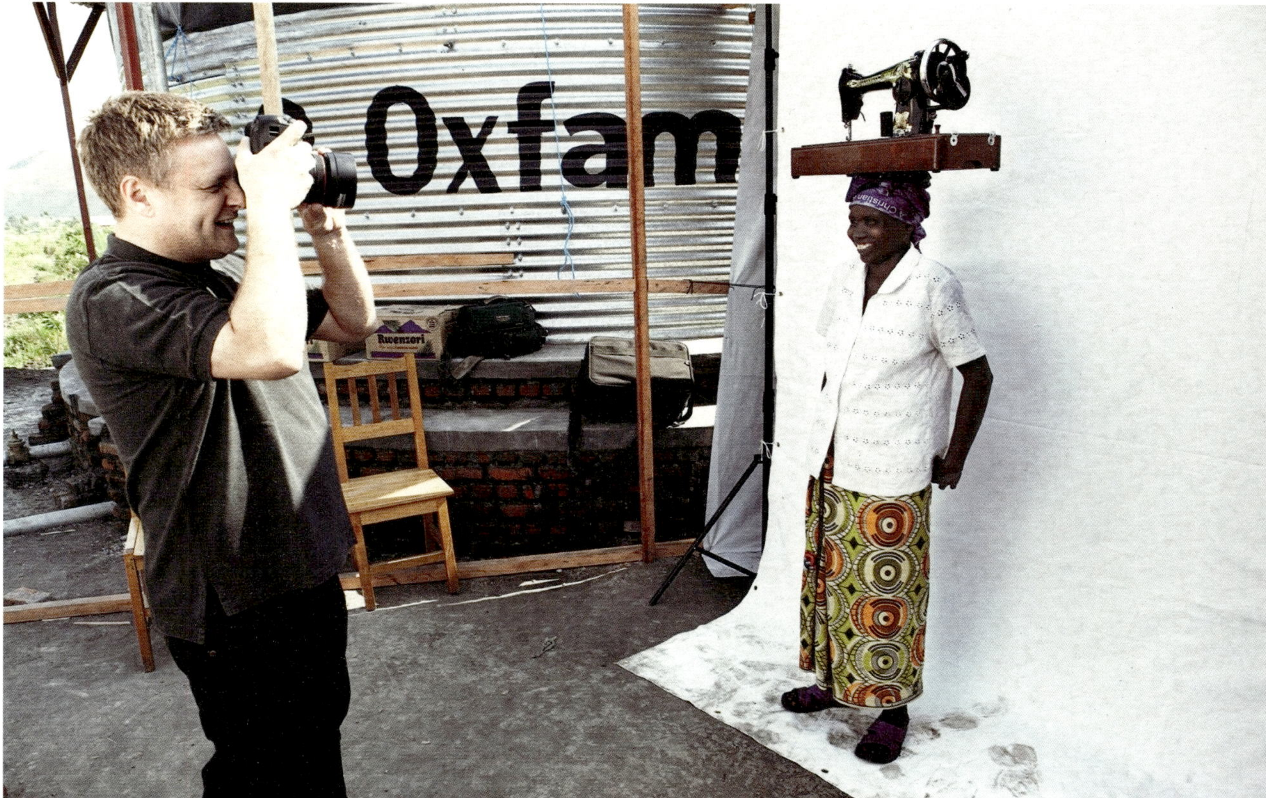

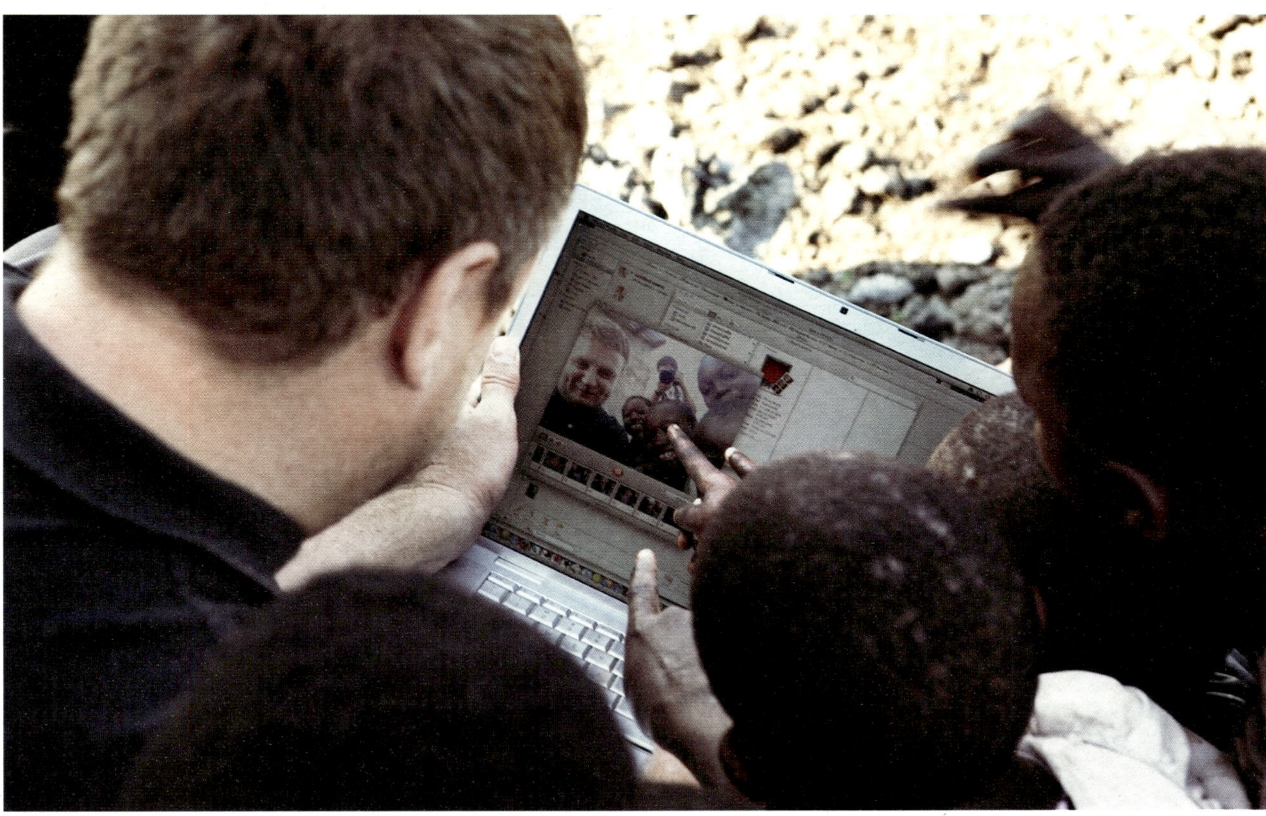

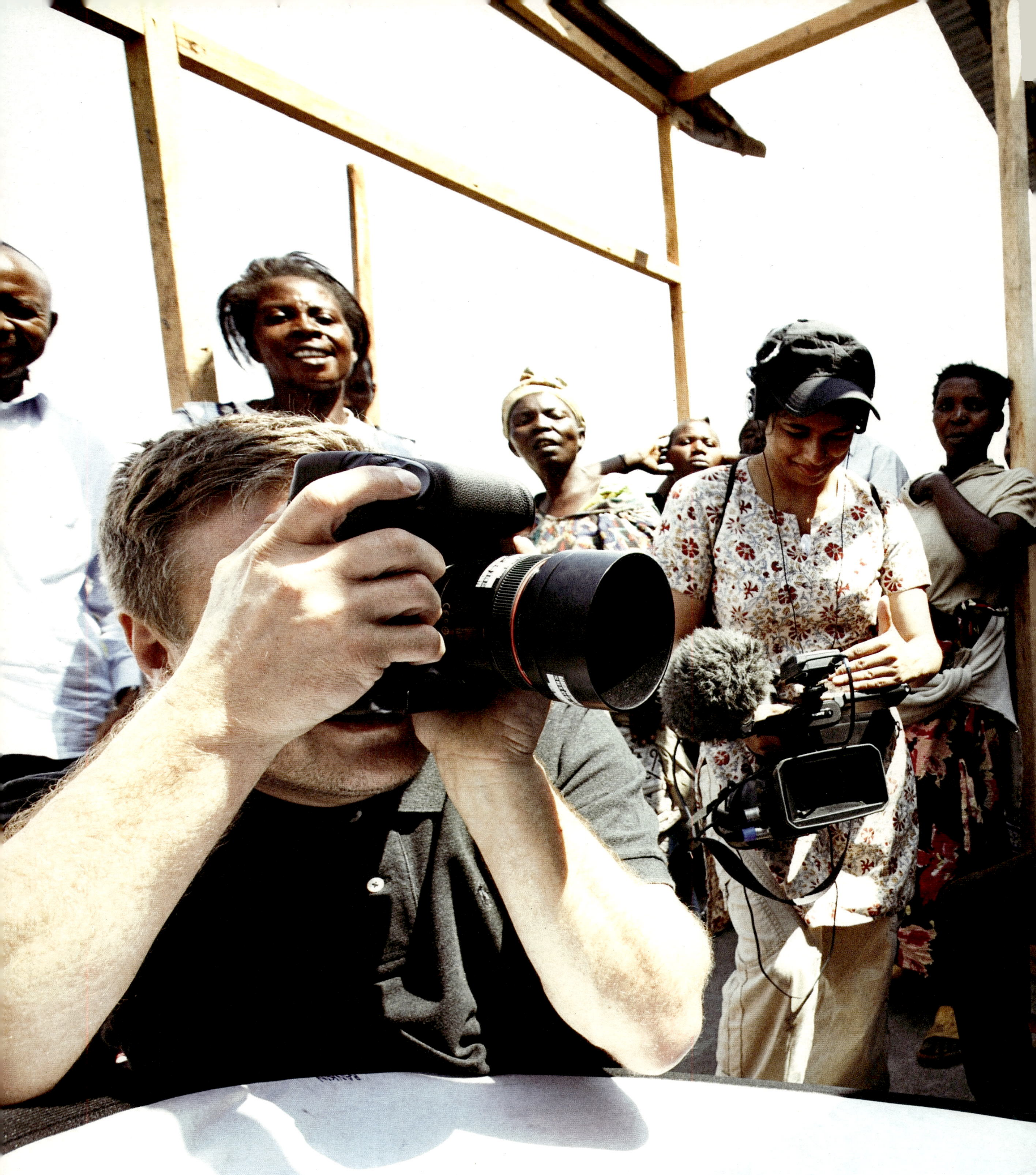

(Above) Rankin shoots Karo and baby Happiness
while crowds of eager onlookers shoot 'Cheka
Kidogo' (meaning "laugh a little" in Swahili)

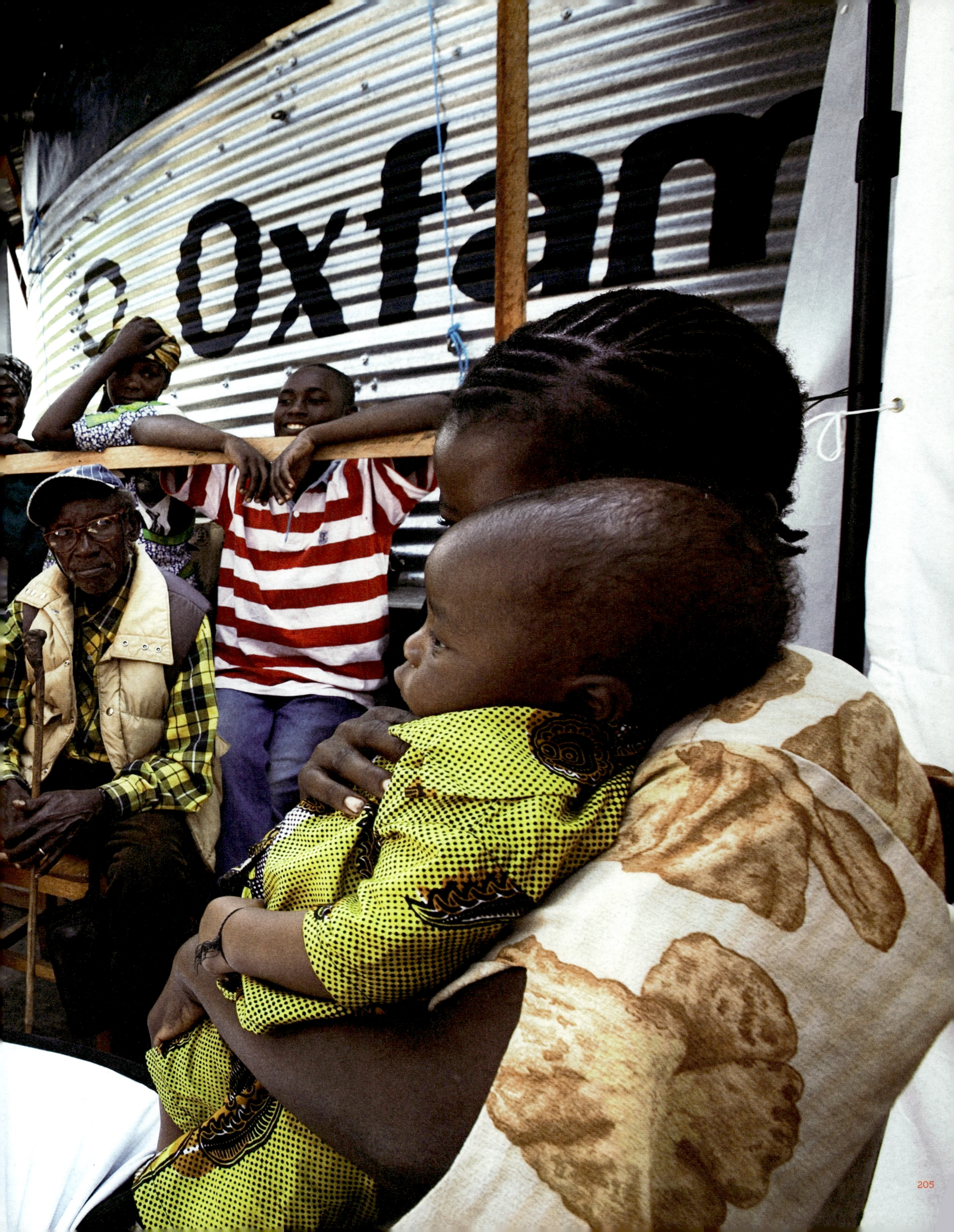

Oxfam

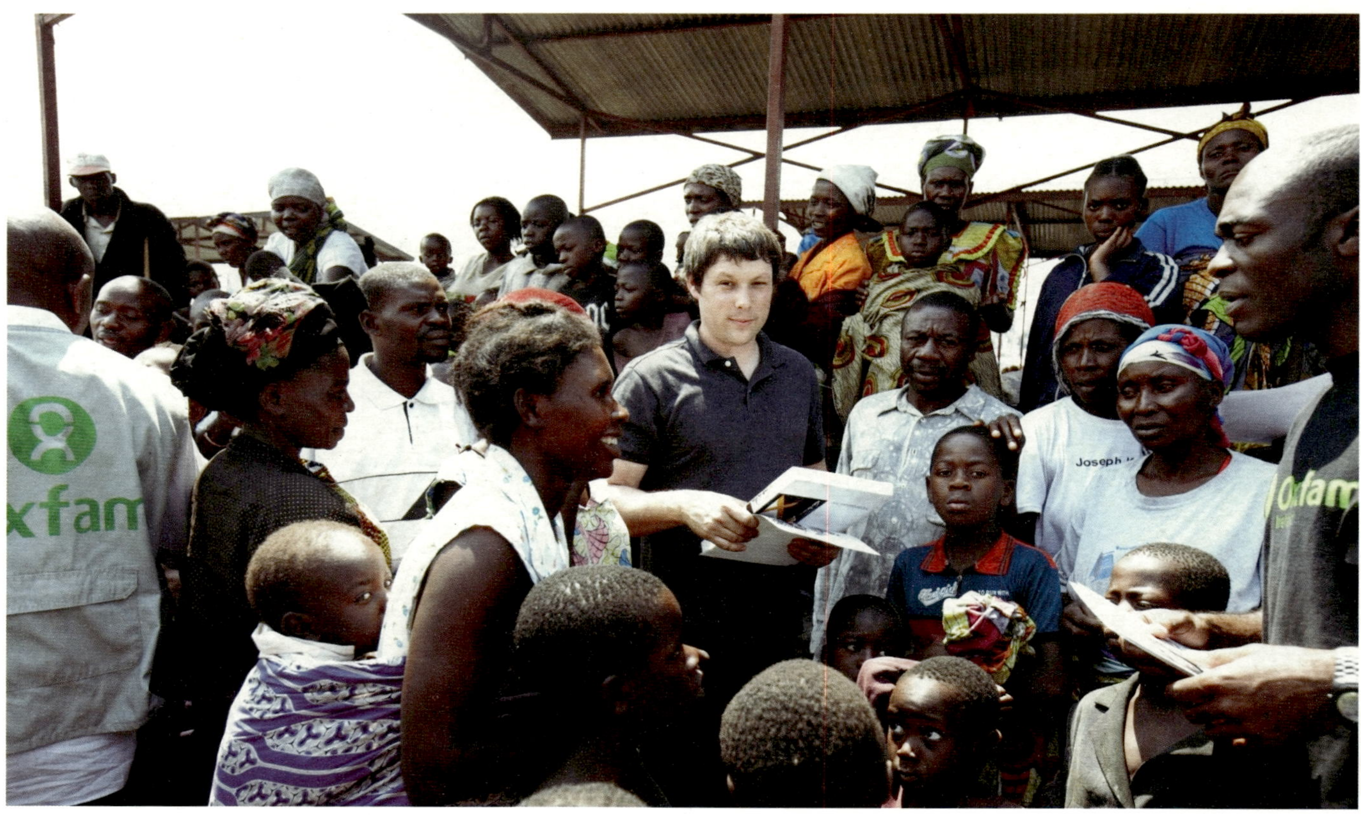

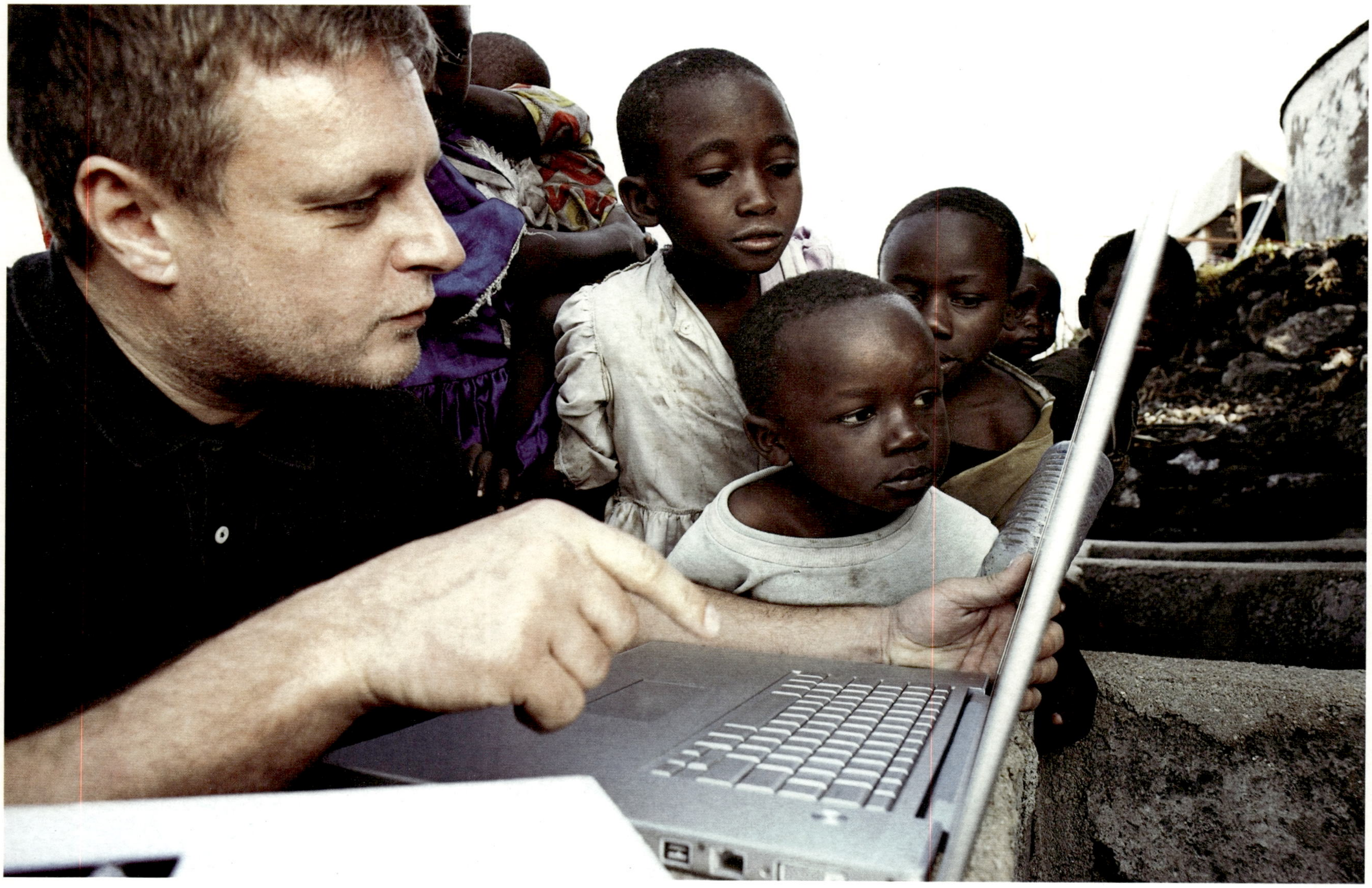

(Top) Andrew hands out the portraits in Mugunga camp.
(Bottom) Rankin seeks the advice of experts.

WHAT'S NEXT?

Music can be heard wherever you go in Congo. Vibrant, passionate and full of energy, it is hard to miss. So, musician and music producer Howie B travelled with Rankin to meet the musicians of Sange. He found people using the power of music to bring the community together, and tell their stories of conflict and hopes for peace. In some cases, they used music simply as a way to forget.
Howie met and recorded the music of three groups in particular: an elderly dance group called Authenticity who danced non-stop for hours; the Sange drum group with their matching outfits and crazy facial expressions; and Shukuru and Basimise, two teenage boys singing about the suffering in Africa. Howie will be releasing a single of the music with an accompanying documentary, directed by Chris Cottam.

Oxfam's work in Eastern Congo continues, focusing on water and sanitation, hygiene promotion, and the distribution of essential items. In major towns in North Kivu, it is working with partners to truck 200,000 litres of clean drinking water every day. These towns are currently the safe havens for many displaced people, and the needs are enormous. In South Kivu, water and sanitation will be supplied to more than 80,000 people, as well as items essential for maintaining good health and hygiene, such as soap and buckets. Oxfam is also working with Congolese partners to help communities prevent and respond to violence and human rights abuses, through supporting community education and advocacy with local civilian and military authorities.
Oxfam is committed to the people of Democratic Republic of Congo. So is Rankin, and he plans to return in the near future. For him, this isn't about charity, and the people of Congo aren't victims. They are the same as us, with dreams and desires just like ours. They want to eat well, be safe and healthy, and live a loving and fruitful life. Yet they can't. And we can. So, in Rankin's words: "We owe it to them to respect their humanity."

CREDITS/ACKNOWLEDGEMENTS

The first and biggest thank you to Kate and Raakhi and all of the people from Oxfam for making this project happen. Thank you too to Howie B and Chris Cottam for believing that people like us could help make a difference.

Thanks to Andrew and Dom for being great assistants and working their arses off to get the exhibitions in the Congo processed, printed and hung. Thanks to all of the people that took part in Rankin Live. And thank you to all the inspirational Congolese people who we met during our two trips.

A special thanks goes to Charles, for being a vital calming influence throughout our trips!

This book has been donated by Rankin Photography. All proceeds will be spent on Oxfam's emergency work in the DRC.
Names have been changed throughout to protect people's identity.

If you are reading this final credit you must really care. Please show how much by donating some of your hard-earned cash to the Oxfam/Congo appeal. Go on, you know you want to!

Photography
 – Rankin and the villagers of Sange

Producer
 – Nina Rassaby-Lewis

Photographic Assistants
 – Andrew Davies, Dom Storer

Book Coordinator
 – Liza Barber

Art Director
 – Ricci Williams

Production Manager
 – Steve Savigear

Words
 – Kate Pattison, Rebecca Wynn (Oxfam)

Researcher
 – Suzi O'Keefe

Distribution
 – Raakhi Shah

Reprographics
 – Mullis Morgan

Printing and Binding
 – Jimenez Godoy, S.A., Spain

Additional Photography
 – Andrew Davies, Dom Storer, Suzi O'Keefe

Documentaries
 – Sandhya Suri and Chris Cottam

Positivity
 – Howie B

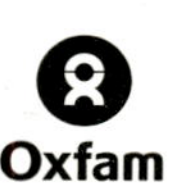
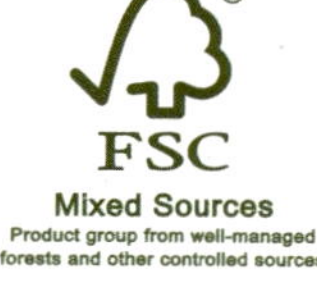